African Penguins at sunset, near Cape Town

South Africa is one of the most diverse and enchanting countries in the world, and for me, its greatest appeal are the beautiful landscapes. Few visitors will fail to be impressed by the sight of iconic Table Mountain with its pretty 'tablecloth' of swirling white clouds, the acacia-studded plains stalked by thousands of animals in Kruger, the sweeping golden beaches of tropical KwaZulu Natal, or the pretty valleys of vineyards, orchards and wild flowers in the Winelands.

This immensely varied terrain supports a rich diversity of flora and fauna and there's an incomparable range of experiences available to enjoy the natural beauty. South Africa is a top-rate safari destination and the choice of excellent parks and reserves across the country virtually guarantee sightings. Being outdoors is very much a way of life and you can try hiking, surfing, scuba-diving or one of the many booming adventure activities, such as bungee-jumping or elephant-riding.

The country's vibrant cities also offer travellers a unique experience and are home to fascinating and exotic combinations of people and culture. There's the fast-paced sophistication of Johannesburg, the steamy humidity and spicy Indian influence of Durban, or the spectacular setting and quirky beach-side hedonism of Cape Town. These have numerous exciting urban attractions as well as the best eating and shopping opportunities on the African continent.

South Africa has a compelling history too, from the early hunter-gatherers to the arrival of the Europeans, the Boer War and the more recent breakdown of Apartheid. This has been well preserved and carefully documented, and the cave paintings, colonial architecture, lively townships, moving battlefields and contemporary museums are another aspect of South Africa to explore.

In short, where you go depends on your time and budget and how you choose to get around. The choice of destinations, activities and itineraries is virtually inexhaustible, so careful planning is needed to make best use of your time.

Lizzie Williams

FIRST STEPS
PUTTING IT ALL TOGETHER

South Africa is a vast country that offers a bewildering choice of destinations and experiences.

South Africa is a vast country that offers a bewildering choice of destinations and experiences. As arrival in the country will probably be either via Cape Town, Durban or Johannesburg, it's best to organize an itinerary accessible from these cities if you are on a shorter holiday. But if you have more time, venture further afield into the other provinces and use these cities as gateways for the beginning and end of a longer tour. Or you could even travel to other countries: South Africa completely surrounds Lesotho and most of Swaziland and these allow cars hired in South Africa to cross their borders.

South Africa has an efficient transport network linking its towns and cities. The road systems and flight networks are the best in Africa, making travelling the considerable distances a straightforward experience. Affordable domestic flights link the cities, a sophisticated army of private coaches criss-crosses the country, and the (albeit slow) train system, offers another way of getting from A to B. Hiring a car for part, or all, of your journey is undoubtedly the best way to see South Africa; you get to travel at your own leisurely pace and explore more out-of-the-way regions without being tied to a tour or a timetable.

These suggested itineraries each cover the highlights of South Africa in about a maximum of three weeks. But none are written in stone and they are far from exhaustible. Rather they are regional suggestions for travellers wishing to explore a certain part of the country, or for returning visitors to travel somewhere new.

If arriving in Johannesburg, an itinerary that starts and finishes there will take in the best of Gauteng, the Northwest Province and Mpumalanga. From Cape Town another itinerary covers the city and surrounds and includes a holiday up the famed Garden Route.

→ DOING IT ALL

Johannesburg → Tshwane (Pretoria) → Sun City → Pilanesberg Game Reserve → Kruger National Park → Panorama Region → Swaziland → Hluhluwe-Imfolozi Game Reserve → iSimangaliso Wetland Park → Dolphin Coast → Durban → Battlefields → uKhahlamba-Drakensberg Park → Wild Coast → Nelson Mandela Bay (Port Elizabeth) → Addo Elephant National Park → Garden Route → Whale Coast → Cape Town → Cape Peninsula → Cape Winelands

1 Hippopotamus, Kruger National Park **2** Victoria and Alfred Waterfront, Cape Town **3** Rugged Cape Peninsula

From Durban, you can combine the highlights of KwaZulu Natal and the Eastern Cape before perhaps continuing the journey to include the Garden Route and Cape Town.

Alternatively, and if you have the time (more than four weeks), combine these four itineraries for a grand tour of South Africa. You could start in Johannesburg and finish in Cape Town (or the other way – both are major air hubs for arrival and departure into South Africa). By covering everything, you'll get a fantastic insight into the diverse and beautiful environments that South Africa has to offer from beaches and mountains, to game reserves and historical sights.

For those who have less time or don't want to spend so much time behind the wheel of a hire car, this can be speeded up by picking out what interests you from each of the four itineraries and linking the major airports of Johannesburg, Durban, Nelson Mandela Bay (Port Elizabeth) by affordable domestic flights and hiring a car from each of these for excursions.

Depending on whether you are a beach lover, an outdoor adventure enthusiast, a safari-goer, or a city-slicker will determine how long you stay and explore each destination, but these four itineraries will point you in the right direction for a Dream Trip of South Africa.

Depending on whether you are a beach lover, an outdoor adventure enthusiast, a safari-goer, or a city-slicker will determine how long you stay and explore each destination.

4 Leopard, Kruger National Park **5** Drakensberg Mountains

DREAM TRIP 1
CAPE TOWN → GARDEN ROUTE → CAPE TOWN

Best time to visit
The Western Cape generally features warm, dry summers with temperatures rising to a beach-friendly 30°C, and mild, moist winters with temperatures averaging a pleasant 18°C. December to January is the peak period, with long hours of sunshine, and the domestic holiday season when people are off work and school, while Cape Town is abuzz with events and activities; reservations need to be made well in advance and hotels add on seasonal supplements. June to September are the coolest and wettest months but they have their own advantages such as whale watching or the mass of wild flowers in the nature reserves.

Allow three weeks to fully explore the beauty and diversity of Cape Town (page 35) and the Western Cape. The 'mother city', as it's affectionately called, is home to historic buildings, museums, the botanical gardens of Kirstenbosch and the famous Constantia wine estates. Climbing or riding the cable car to the top of Table Mountain should definitely be on the agenda, while organized and thought-provoking tours to Robben Island and the townships on the Cape Flats offer a glimpse of South Africa's fragile past.

Allow at least a day for a tour to Cape Point via the spectacular Cape Peninsula (page 62) with its spine of mountains, fishing villages, golden beaches and beautiful bays. On the way include visits to the seal colony offshore from Hout Bay and the African penguin colony at Boulders Beach, while there are numerous opportunities to eat at a seafood restaurant or shop in the craft markets.

After sightseeing, Cape Town offers a number of relaxing social endeavours from sipping sundowners on the impossibly trendy Camps Bay strip of bars, to a fine gourmet meal at the V&A Waterfront (page 52) overlooking the working harbour, or a night at the theatre, ballet or opera. Cape Town also has an exciting and vibrant calendar of events throughout the year, which includes

1 Cape Town aerial view 2 Cape Town beach huts 3 Kirstenbosch National Botanical Garden

Allow at least a day for a tour to Cape Point via the spectacular Cape Peninsula with its spine of mountains, fishing villages, golden beaches and beautiful bays.

4 Hout Bay from Chapman's Peak **5** Seal colony, Hout Bay **6** Western Cape winery

DREAM TRIP 1
CAPE TOWN → GARDEN ROUTE → CAPE TOWN

An additional seasonal activity is spotting southern right whales along the Whale Coast from July to November.

food, wine and film festivals, the Cape Town International Jazz Festival, the Kirstenbosch Summer Concerts, the Cape Town Carnival, the Two Oceans Marathon and the Cape Argus Pick 'n' Pay Cycle Tour (the largest timed cycle race in the world).

An additional seasonal activity is spotting southern right whales along the Whale Coast (page 72) from July to November. An easy day's drive from Cape Town, the cliff tops at Hermanus, overlooking Walker Bay, are considered to be one of the best places in the world for land-based whale watching.

Head further east to join the Garden Route (page 82) at Mossel Bay, stopping off along the way at pretty Swellendam, the third oldest town in South Africa, and also one of its most picturesque. With its appealing, quiet atmosphere, you can visit the museums and historical buildings and sample traditional South African cuisine in one of the many fine restaurants.

Well geared up for local tourism, the Garden Route is the most celebrated region of South Africa, featuring numerous wildlife attractions and outdoor activities, from bungee-jumping and mountain-biking to surfing and sunbathing. There's an excellent choice of accommodation, restaurants and shopping in the tourist-friendly towns like Knysna (page 87) or Plettenberg Bay (page 90), while the beautiful Wilderness and Tsitsikamma sections of the Garden Route National Park (pages 85 and 95) are worth spending time in for hiking through the coastal forests.

→ GOING FURTHER

Drive north to picturesque Tulbagh via the magnificent Bain's Kloof Pass. → p111

Return to Cape Town via the tranquil back-country roads through the Western Cape interior, known locally as Route 62 (page 100), and modelled on the iconic US Route 66. Meandering between Oudtshoorn and Cape Town, this is the scenic alternative to the N2 highway, and is an area of magnificent mountains, picturesque passes, rivers, vineyards and orchards. Little villages and hamlets make intermittent appearances and offer a glimpse into South African rural life.

A final day is warranted to explore the beautiful historic estates in the Cape Winelands (page 113), where the scenic valleys linking the historical towns of Stellenbosch, Paarl and Franschhoek are dotted with vineyards. These are open to the public for wine-tasting alfresco under oak trees or underground in the cool cellars, and many offer superb country restaurants or the chance to stay overnight in a Cape Dutch manor house. The Winelands also make a good day trip from Cape Town.

1 Storms River suspension bridge, Garden Route National Park (Tsitsikamma Section) 2 Southern right whale, Hermanus
3 Garden Route National Park 4 Groot Constantia 5 Cango Caves 6 Garden Route landscape

WESTERN CAPE

Tulbagh

Worcester

1 2 3
Paarl **10** Route 62
4 5 Robben Island
Cape Town *Franschhoek Valley*
6 Stellenbosch
Gordon's Bay
Cape Peninsula Table Mountain National Park
False Bay
Hermanus
7

Swellendam

N

100 km
100 miles

1 Afrikaans Language Monument, Paarl **2** Knysna coastline, Garden Route **3** Stellenbosch scenery

EASTERN CAPE

Cango Caves
9
Oudtshoorn

Route 62

Plettenberg
Wilderness **8** Bay

Sedgefield Knysna Garden Route
National Park
Mossel Bay (Tsitsikamma
Section)

Indian Ocean

2

1 Do the challenging hike or take the dizzying ride on the aerial cableway to the top of Table Mountain for a bird's eye view of Cape Town, Table Bay and the beautiful Atlantic coastline. 2 Enjoy the top-class shopping, eating and entertainment facilities at the world-renowned historic V&A Waterfront, all with a backdrop of Table Mountain and a working harbour. 3 Discover the underwater realms of the Atlantic and Indian oceans at the acclaimed Two Oceans Aquarium, where highlights are the giant kelp forest and predator tanks. 4 Take the ferry to Robben Island for the emotive tour of the prison where Nelson Mandela was held. Combine this trip with a township tour for an enlightening education about Apartheid. 5 Stroll through the beautiful and peaceful Kirstenbosch National Botanical Garden and grab a picnic to eat on the rolling lawns next to the duck ponds. 6 Spend an eventful day on a tour or drive around the Cape Peninsula to admire the dramatic coastlines, nature reserves, pretty seaside towns and marine life, including whales, seals and penguins. 7 Watch southern right whales along the dramatic Whale Coast where Hermanus overlooking Walker Bay is the ideal cliff-top vantage point to witness them breaching and blowing. 8 Take a few days to explore the much-heralded Garden Route: a 200-km stretch of rugged coast backed by mountains, long sandy beaches, leafy forests and friendly holiday resorts. 9 Venture into the Little Karoo around Oudtshoorn to visit an ostrich farm and the eerie Cango Caves, considered one of the world's finest examples of dripstone caverns.
10 Sip wine beneath oak trees on the gorgeous Cape Winelands estates, where many of the 17th-century manor houses are now gourmet restaurants and boutique hotels.

3

DREAM TRIP 2
DURBAN → BATTLEFIELDS → DRAKENSBERG → NELSON MANDELA BAY

Best time to visit
KwaZulu Natal's subtropical climate is generally holiday-friendly throughout the year with hot summer temperatures of 23-33°C, and mild winters of 16-25°C with some humidity June to August. Like Cape Town and the Garden Route, there are seasonal hikes in accommodation rates during the popular domestic holiday season of December to January. Inland, the Drakensberg rise to over 3000 m so the climate is cool throughout the year; the drier winter months are generally best for hiking but it can get chilly at night. The Eastern Cape lies between the subtropical conditions of KwaZulu Natal and the more Mediterranean climate of the Western Cape.

A trip of three weeks between Durban and Nelson Mandela Bay takes you down a length of the South African coast, which changes in character from the more accessible balmy, subtropical golden beaches in KwaZulu Natal to the rugged semi-deserted Wild Coast in the Eastern Cape. It is an ideal route for those who enjoy the outdoors, such as long coastal hikes and marine-based activities like diving, surfing, or whale and dolphin watching. Also on this itinerary, the interior of KwaZulu Natal is worth a detour to see the moving Battlefields sites and the spectacular uKhahlamba-Drakensberg Park, where the lofty peaks are ideal hiking territory and shelter some of the best examples of San rock art to be found in southern Africa.

In Durban (page 131) you can explore the beachfront's Golden Mile, where swimming and surfing is good all year round due to the warm, subtropical climate, visit the Indian district, or perhaps go shopping at the massive Gateway Mall. The leafy northern suburbs of the city open up to the Valley of 1000 Hills (page 144). Once a stronghold of the Zulu people, it was named after the thousands of hills that tumble down to the Umgeni River and the Indian Ocean, and is now marketed as a friendly tourist route through the lush landscape.

A day's drive takes you through the pretty KwaZulu Natal Midlands to the Battlefields (page 144) region around Ladysmith and Dundee, where knowledgeable guides at the most significant

1 Durban 2 San rock art 3 Drakensberg Mountains

The interior of KwaZulu Natal is worth a detour to see the moving Battlefields sites and the spectacular uKhahlamba-Drakensberg Park.

sites talk you through each battle, debating the strategies used, the numbers who perished and the medals and rewards won by the brave. To the west, the spectacular uKhahlamba-Drakensberg Park (page 152) lies along the Lesotho border between the Free State and KwaZulu Natal, and is an area of lofty mountains and deep forests harboured in a number of parks and reserves. Here, visitors can hike in the crisp mountain air, visit a number of San rock art sites, or simply relax in the scenic resorts and campsites.

South of Durban (page 165) is one long line of domestic holiday resorts intercepted by large sugarcane and banana plantations and nature reserves. These are ideal for families on beach holidays and for divers (particularly the offshore Aliwal Shoal, which is famous as a haunt for ragged-tooth sharks).

4 Ragged-tooth shark, Aliwal Shoal 5 Siege of Ladysmith memorial, Battlefields region

1 Xhosa village **2** Drakensberg scenery **3** Port St Johns **4** Addo Elephant National Park

→ **GOING FURTHER**

Head north along KwaZulu Natal's Dolphin Coast for good beaches and snorkelling.
→ p140

5

Further south, the Wild Coast (page 166) is rugged and dramatic, with thick dune forests and windswept open beaches stretching to wild waves. It will appeal for a couple of days for those wanting to explore the caves, cliffs and shipwrecks and get a taste for traditional Xhosa life. A number of roads lead from the N2 Highway as it bisects the Eastern Cape to the isolated and peaceful seaside accommodation between Port St Johns and East London.

Still in the Eastern Cape, historical Grahamstown (page 179) is worth a stop, especially for the National Festival of Arts (the country's biggest festival), held every June or July, while at least one night is warranted in the wonderful Addo Elephant National Park (page 184) to see a good cross section of wildlife. But it is the elephants the park is most famous for, and they can easily be seen in herds more than 100-strong, drinking their fill at the waterholes. Also in this region are a number of fairly new private game reserves that have played an important role in restocking the Eastern Cape with large species of game. Their luxury lodges offer a similar safari experience to the private game reserves bordering the Kruger National Park in Mpumalanga.

The city of Nelson Mandela Bay (formerly Port Elizabeth) (page 191) marks the end of this itinerary and warrants a day to enjoy the holiday atmosphere in the resorts of Summerstrand and Humewood or to visit the Donkin Reserve for the good views over Algoa Bay. From Nelson Mandela Bay frequent flights can take you to Johannesburg or Cape Town or, to extend this itinerary and in keeping with the coastal theme, you could explore more of South Africa's celebrated coastline and combine it with Dream Trip 1, by heading along the Garden Route to Cape Town.

7

5 Lighthouse at Cape Recife, Nelson Mandela Bay **6** Grahamstown **7** Hole in the Wall, Transkei

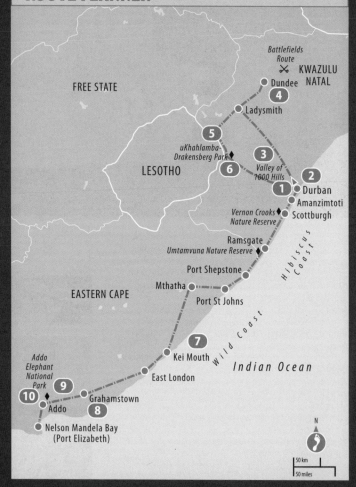

FREE STATE

Battlefields
Route
✕ KWAZULU
NATAL

● Dundee

4

● Ladysmith

5

uKhahlamba-
Drakensberg Park ◆

3

Valley of
1000 Hills

LESOTHO

6

2

1

● Durban

● Amanzimtoti

Vernon Crooks ◆
Nature Reserve

● Scottburgh

Ramsgate ●
Umtamvuna Nature Reserve ◆

Hibiscus Coast

● Port Shepstone

EASTERN CAPE

● Mthatha

● Port St Johns

Wild Coast

7

● Kei Mouth

Addo
Elephant
National
Park

9

● East London

Indian Ocean

10

◆

● Addo

● Grahamstown

8

● Nelson Mandela Bay
(Port Elizabeth)

N

50 km
50 miles

3 Dune beach, KwaZulu Natal coast

→ WISH LIST

1 Stroll along the broad sandy beach and soak up the holiday atmosphere in spicy Indian-influenced Durban and perhaps take a rickshaw ride or visit uShaka Marine World to see the vast aquarium and play on the waterslides. 2 Try outdoor sports like surfing or scuba-diving on KwaZulu Natal's subtropical coast, where the warm and clear Indian Ocean provides perfect conditions and an array of interesting marine life. 3 Follow the route through the Valley of 1000 Hills to the north of Durban, which is dotted with craft shops, tea gardens and Zulu cultural villages. 4 Learn about South Africa's sombre Anglo and Boer wars history on a tour of the evocative and moving Battlefields sites and engage a good guide to bring the stories to life. 5 Hike through the dramatic peaks and flowering meadows of the uKhahlamba-Drakensberg Park, while staying at comfortable mountain resorts in the scenic foothills. 6 Take a guided walk to the fascinating San rock art sites in the Drakensberg's mountain caves and overhangs and learn the history of this ancient hunter-gatherer community. 7 Find solitude along the breathtaking Wild Coast, which features craggy cliff faces, desolate beaches littered with shipwrecks, secluded bays and green rolling hills dotted with Xhosa villages. 8 Visit the museums, churches and monuments in the Eastern Cape settlers town of Grahamstown, home of South Africa's most prestigious university. 9 Enjoy a luxury safari lodge experience away from the crowds in the Eastern Cape's private game reserves, which have been restocked with animals not been seen in the region for more than 150 years. 10 Be guaranteed to see large herds of game in the recently extended Addo Elephant National Park, which is now the only place in South Africa where you can see the Big Seven – elephant, lion, rhino, buffalo, leopard, whale and shark.

DREAM TRIP 3
JOHANNESBURG → SUN CITY → KRUGER → JOHANNESBURG

Best time to visit
Gauteng's high altitude ensures favourable weather throughout the year, with pleasant summer temperatures of 17-28°C accompanied by brief thundershowers, and mild winter days of 19°C, though these can drop at night to 5°C and there can be frosts. The best time to go on safari in Kruger is during the dry season of May to October when wildlife congregates around waterholes and the grass is shorter, though temperatures can get chilly in the middle of winter. The warmer wetter months also have advantages and many young animals are born around November and December, when the bush is lush and there's plenty to eat.

Loud, brash and rich, and built on a high plateau surrounded by the world's richest gold mines, Johannesburg (page 201) is the most likely arrival point for most visitors to South Africa, and OR Tambo International Airport is one of the most important hubs for air travel in the southern hemisphere. There are numerous historical and cultural attractions to keep visitors occupied for a couple of days including some of the country's finest cutting-edge museums, such as the celebrated Apartheid Museum, Constitution Hill and Cradle of Humankind.

Soweto (page 212), once South Africa's largest township and a hotbed for anti-Apartheid activism, has now mushroomed into a city in its own right, and a day tour takes in its fascinating struggle sites. These include the Hector Pieterson Museum, which documents the importance that the activism of school children had in the demise of Apartheid, and Mandela House, the former home of the country's most famous political prisoner.

Loud, brash and rich, and built on a high plateau surrounded by the world's richest gold mines, Johannesburg is the most likely arrival point for most visitors to South Africa.

1 Johannesburg skyline **2** Apartheid Museum, Johannesburg

As a world-class modern city, Johannesburg's other urban draw cards include mega-shopping malls, excellent restaurants and sophisticated nightlife. Many of these are found in the attractive and leafy northern suburbs, where you'll find the best choice of accommodation. Downtown Johannesburg is also worth exploring (but preferably on an organized tour) to ascend its tallest building, the Top of Africa, for wide-spreading views of the City of Gold, and to the Newtown Precinct, for its museums and theatres.

Some 50 km to the north, and connected by an almost unbroken ribbon of development, is South Africa's recently renamed capital, Tshwane (Pretoria) (page 219), with its wide streets lined with jacaranda trees, which bloom a ladylike purple in spring. While Johannesburg was built on gold and industry, Pretoria was founded during the Voortrekker period of South Africa's turbulent past and

3 Jacaranda trees, Tshwane (Pretoria) 4 Piet Retief statue, Voortrekker Monument, Tshwane (Pretoria)

*Another trip from
Johannesburg is to
head west to visit the
outlandish over-the-
top entertainment
resort of Sun City,
accompanied by
a game drive in
the neighbouring
Pilanesberg Game
Reserve.*

it retains rather a stern, bureaucratic atmosphere – albeit softened
by a large student population and a multilingual diplomatic
community. The sights that reflect its history, such as the Voortrekker
Monument and the imposing Union Buildings, can be visited on a
day trip from Johannesburg.

Another trip from Johannesburg is to head west to visit the
outlandish over-the-top entertainment resort of Sun City (page 226),
accompanied by a game drive in the neighbouring Pilanesberg
Game Reserve (page 228) – the closest Big Five destination to
Johannesburg. At least two days are warranted, and most visitors
stay overnight at one of Sun City's glitzy hotels or opt for a more
peaceful safari lodge in Pilanesberg.

Heading east, Kruger National Park (page 231) is half a day's drive
from Gauteng and is South Africa's premier wildlife destination,
deserving at least three or four days. There are numerous ways to
explore and the most popular and most cost-effective is to join a
tour from Johannesburg or to leisurely self-drive on the park's well-
maintained roads, staying in the excellent rest camps. There's also
the option of flying to a luxury safari lodge on the private reserves
bordering the western fringe of Kruger. Although pricier, here you
have the chance to see the Big Five from the comfort of a private

1 Pied kingfisher, Pilanesberg Game Reserve 2 Kudu antelope, Pilanesberg Game Reserve 3 Leopard and cub, Kruger National Park

→ **GOING FURTHER**

Continue south to the wildlife sanctuaries of Swaziland and the game reserves, wetland parks and marine reserves of Maputaland and Zululand.

→ p259 and p263

4

4WD with the promise of excellent accommodation and gourmet food and wine at the end of your game drive.

A visit to Kruger can easily be combined with the Panorama Region (page 251) along the Eastern Drakensberg Escarpment, with its rural landscapes, waterfalls, pretty country towns and Blyde River Canyon (page 252), one of the deepest canyons in the world. A day is needed to drive along the main road, stopping at the viewpoints along the way, and perhaps for lunch at a country restaurant, while activities include mountain biking through the Sabie forests, elephant riding in Hazyview or panning for gold at the historic mining town of Pilgrim's Rest.

From the Panorama Region it's an easy half day's drive back to Johannesburg but, if you have time, this route can be extended further by heading south to the tiny kingdom of Swaziland (page 259). With magnificent mountain scenery of rivers, waterfalls and lush gorges, there are numerous attractions such as well-stocked game parks, fine hotels, craft centres and the opportunity to learn about traditional ways of Swazi rural life in the cultural villages. South of Swaziland and in the northeastern corner of KwaZulu Natal, the Maputaland and Zululand (page 263) regions are beautiful, untouched and sparsely populated parts of South Africa that stretch from the Mozambique border all the way down to Durban. This area features several pristine game reserves, wetland parks, marine reserves and uncrowded beaches. From Durban, there is easy access back to Johannesburg along the N3 highway or with a short flight.

5

6

4 Blyde River Canyon **5** Sabie river **6** Chacma baboons, Hluhluwe-Imfolozi Game Reserve

LIMPOPO

Kruger
National
Park

Letaba

Olifants

Hoedspruit

10

*Blyde
River Canyon*

Orpen

*Kruger
National
Park*

Pilgrim's Rest

9

8

Graskop

Skukuza

Hazyview

Lower Sabie

7 *Pilanesberg
Game Reserve*

Pretoriuskop

Sun City

Berg-En-Dal

6 TSHWANE
(PRETORIA)

Crocodile
Bridge

*Magaliesberg
Mountains*

4

1 **2** **5**

MPUMALANGA

MBABANE

Hlane Royal
National Park

3 Johannesburg

*Mantenga
Nature Reserve*

Ezulwini

Manzini

GAUTENG

*Mlilwane
Wildlife
Sanctuary*

SWAZILAND

N

50 km

50 miles

*Mkhuze
Game Reserve*

KWAZULU NATAL

*iSimangaliso
Wetland*

St Lucia

*Hluhluwe-Imfolozi
Game Reserve*

1 KwaZulu Natal valley 2 Kudu, Kruger National Park

→ WISH LIST

1 Contemplate and reflect for a few hours at the celebrated Apartheid Museum for a fascinating insight into the extreme regime that consumed South Africa for almost 50 years. 2 Spend half a day at Gold Reef City on the site of a historic underground gold mine, which offers a vivid account of the guts, grit and glory that gave birth to Johannesburg. 3 Take a guided tour of Soweto, South Africa's most famous township and a hotbed for anti-Apartheid activism. Visit the freedom struggle sites and eat at a shebeen or township restaurant. 4 Understand the creation of our species at the cutting-edge museum of Maropeng and the archaeological site of Sterkfontein Caves in the Cradle of Humankind World Heritage Site. 5 Shop 'til you drop at Sandton City, Johannesburg's most prestigious mall. Eat alfresco under twinkly lights and a giant statue of Madiba in adjoining Nelson Mandela Square. 6 Take a day or two to visit Tshwane (formerly Pretoria), to admire the Union Buildings, South Africa's seat of government, and the imposing Voortrekker Monument. 7 Take an overnight trip to the hedonist resort of Sun City with its glitzy hotels, casinos and entertainment facilities. Add in an afternoon game drive in neighbouring Pilanesberg Game Reserve. 8 Snuggle up in a blanket and witness nocturnal animal behaviour under spotlight on a guided night drive with a game ranger from the rest camps in Kruger National Park. 9 Splash out on a night in a luxury safari camp on the private reserves adjoining Kruger. The sumptuous accommodation, good food and wine, and personal guides will enrich the safari experience. 10 Spend a day driving through the Panorama Region and pull over at the many viewpoints to see cascading waterfalls and the vistas across Blyde River Canyon and the Lowveld below.

2

DREAM TRIP 4
JOHANNESBURG → SWAZILAND → CAPE TOWN

Best time to visit
South Africa has a
moderate climate and
long sunny days for
most of the year. During
summer it rarely gets
hotter than 30°C, though
Gauteng and KwaZulu
Natal get very humid.
The coast around Cape
Town and the Garden
Route is at its best during
the spring and summer
months, though the
best time for whale
watching is in winter.
During July and August,
in the middle of winter,
it can get cold at night
in Cape Town and the
interior mountains in the
Drakensberg and Eastern
Cape, with frosts and
snowfalls. Most of the
rain falls in the summer
months when there are
often very heavy storms.

By combining the three outlined Dream Trips, travelling between Johannesburg and Cape Town (or visa versa) is perhaps the best itinerary for showcasing the highlights of South Africa, and providing an excellent cross section of its varied environments. But you'll need plenty of time; it takes at least three weeks by road to complete each of the outlined routes. But these itineraries can be reduced as international open-jaw tickets are available in and out of South Africa's main cities, or you can go back to where you started from on a domestic flight. But if you do that, make sure you allocate days for trips to explore some nature- and landscape-based attractions beyond the city limits.

A number of interesting half-day trips are on offer in Johannesburg (page 201) if you don't want to drive yourself, including the Apartheid Museum, Gold Reef City, the Lion Park, Lesedi Cultural Village and a tour of the city centre. A day trip to Tshwane (Pretoria) (page 219) could be added for those with a penchant for South African history, while an overnight trip is recommended to the over-the-top resort of Sun City (page 226) in the North West Province for its glitzy entertainment and a game drive in adjoining Pilanesberg Game Reserve (page 228).

Kruger (page 231) needs at least four days and, given that the main rest camps and private game reserves in southern Kruger are less than five hours' drive from Johannesburg, it's obligatory to add a safari experience in the country's largest and most diverse wildlife destination. A day to explore the pretty Panorama Region (page 251) on the escarpment above Kruger is a nice additive to wildlife watching.

From southern Kruger, it's a day's drive to the tiny independent monarchy of Swaziland (page 259), where a good road bisects the

1 Tshwane (Pretoria) 2 View across Johannesburg

Entering KwaZulu Natal takes you into the Zululand region, an attractive area of long unspoilt beaches, excellent reserves like Hluhluwe-Imfolozi and the iSimangaliso Wetland Park.

entire country and offers easy access to wildlife sanctuaries, nature reserves, cultural villages and craft centres.

Entering KwaZulu Natal takes you into the Zululand region, an attractive area of long unspoilt beaches, excellent reserves such as Hluhluwe-Imfolozi (page 264) and the iSimangaliso Wetland Park (page 266), and the chance to experience traditional Zulu culture. How long you stay here depends on your preferences for game viewing and/or beach time at resorts along the Dolphin Coast (page 140), such as Ballito or Umhlanga.

Durban (page 131) can be explored for a day to visit the Indian-influenced city centre or Golden Mile beachfront, before heading inland via the KwaZulu Natal Midlands to the Battlefields (page 144) sites around Ladysmith and Dundee for those with an interest in the Anglo and Boer wars. To the west, the uKhahlamba-Drakensberg Park (page 152) offers hiking, San rock art sites and comfortable resorts to relax for a couple of days in the beautiful surroundings and crisp mountain air.

From the Drakensberg, a day's drive takes you back to Durban to fly on to Nelson Mandela Bay (Port Elizabeth) (page 191). Alternatively you could continue driving southwest to the Eastern Cape where the resorts along the quiet and scenic Wild Coast make for a couple of days' relaxation. Around Nelson Mandela Bay (Port Elizabeth) another couple of days are warranted to see the Addo Elephant National Park (page 184) and/or one of the neighbouring Big Five private game reserves, before spending three to five days heading west along the Garden Route (page 82). This can be as active or as relaxing as you choose, thanks to the numerous attractions, from beaches, wildlife sanctuaries and nature reserves, to shopping, museums and outdoor activities such as hiking, boat rides and golf.

With its stunning scenery, sightseeing attractions, fantastic hotels and restaurants, Cape Town (page 35) is a holiday in itself, so plan to spend a bare minimum of four days before or after your grand tour of South Africa.

1 Swaziland 2 Rhinoceros in Royal Hlane National Park, Swaziland 3 Blue wildebeest, Hluhluwe-Imfolozi Game Reserve
4 Umhlanga Lighthouse 5 Hippo, iSimangaliso Wetland Park 6 Lion, Kruger National Park 7 Cape Town

→ ROUTE PLANNER

1 Valley of 1000 Hills **2** Table Mountain, Cape Town **3** (next page) Giraffe

→ WISH LIST

1 Put aside a couple of days to take in Johannesburg's varied attractions from contemporary museums and wildlife sanctuaries, to modern shopping malls and vibrant restaurant districts. **2** Spend a few days on safari in the renowned Kruger National Park to spot the Big Five and witness incredible wildlife drama on the grassy plains, meandering rivers and acacia forests. **3** Take a leisurely drive past pretty historical towns, leafy forests, cascading waterfalls and the impressively deep and stunning Blyde River Canyon in the Panorama Region. **4** Cross into Swaziland to experience a little country of scenic bush and mountains, well-stocked game reserves, and a culture well known for its friendliness and craftsmanship. **5** Head to northern KwaZulu Natal for the intriguing Zulu culture, wetlands, nature and wildlife reserves, untrammelled beaches and the inviting warm Indian Ocean in Zululand and Maputaland. **6** Soak up the beachside holiday atmosphere in spicy Indian-influenced Durban or on KwaZulu Natal's north and south coasts, and try outdoor sports such as surfing or scuba-diving. **7** Learn about South Africa's sombre Anglo and Boer wars history on a tour of the evocative and moving Battlefields sites and engage a good guide to bring the stories to life. **8** Hike through the dramatic peaks of the uKhahlamba-Drakensberg Park and visit fascinating San rock paintings, while staying at comfortable mountain resorts in the scenic foothills. **9** Follow the celebrated Garden Route, one of South Africa's most popular attractions for its beautiful coastal and mountain scenery, golden beaches, and tourist-friendly facilities and entertainment. **10** Revel in Cape Town's variety of things to see and do, from climbing Table Mountain and circumnavigating the beautiful Cape Peninsula, to enjoying the superb shopping, eating and nightlife.

2

DREAM TRIP 1:
Cape Town→Garden Route→Cape Town 21 days

GOING FURTHER

DREAM TRIP 1
Cape Town→Garden Route→Cape Town

South Africa's 'Mother City', dominated by Table Mountain and surrounded by the wild Atlantic, has unquestionably one of the most beautiful city backdrops in the world. Despite being a considerable urban hub, its surroundings are surprisingly untamed, characterized by a mountainous spine stretching between two seaboards along the Cape Peninsula edged by rugged coast and dramatic beaches. Central Cape Town with its grandiose colonial buildings, Victorian suburbs, beautiful public gardens and clutch of modern skyscrapers, lies in the steep-sided bowl created by Table Mountain, while the Atlantic Seaboard with its promenade and dense crop of holiday flats and the popular V&A Waterfront development hug the coast.

The southern coast begins with Walker Bay, which claims to have the best land-based whale watching in the world; in season, sightings are almost guaranteed from the clifftops in Hermanus. Further south the waters around Gansbaai are home to seals, penguins and great white sharks, while the lighthouse at Cape Agulhas marks the most southerly point of Africa.

To the east, the undeniably beautiful Garden Route is a 200-km stretch of rugged coast backed by mountains, with long stretches of sand, nature reserves, leafy forests and seaside towns.

The itinerary returns to Cape Town along Route 62 via the Little Karoo, which offers good hiking, Oudtshoorn, where ostriches peer over every fence, and the popular Cango Caves. Then comes the Breede River Valley, best known for its farming.

Finally, and within easy reach of Cape Town, is the beautiful Winelands region, where the old towns of Paarl, Franschhoek and Stellenbosch nestle in a range of low mountains and scenic valleys covered by the historic wine estates which have been cultivating grapes for some 300 years.

CAPE TOWN

To get the best idea of Cape Town's layout, head to the top of Table Mountain. From its summit, the city stretches below in a horseshoe formed by the mountains: Table Mountain is in the centre, with Devil's Peak to the east and Lion's Head and Signal Hill to the west. Straight ahead lies the City Bowl, the central business district backed by leafy suburbs. This is also the site of Cape Town's historical heart and where all the major museums, historical buildings and sights are. Further down is the V&A Waterfront, a slick development of shopping malls and restaurants. Following the coast around to the west, you come to the modern residential districts of Green Point and Sea Point which are dominated by the enormous Cape Town Stadium, which was built for the 2010 FIFA World Cup™. In the opposite direction the southern suburbs stretch west and south, dipping from the mountain's slopes, and here, under a blanket of trees, are Cape Town's largest mansions as well as the beautiful Kirstenbosch National Botanical Garden.

→ ARRIVING IN CAPE TOWN

GETTING THERE
Cape Town International Airport ① *airport enquiries, T021-937 1200, flight information T0867-277888, www.acsa.co.za*, is 22 km east of the city centre on the N2, or, out of rush hour a 20-minute drive.

The airport has a full range of facilities, and domestic and international arrivals and departures are linked by one long terminal and a retail mall. Wi-Fi is available in all public areas. Within international arrivals, **Cape Town Tourism** ① *daily 0700-1700*, can arrange accommodation and has a number of maps and leaflets to give out. The **Master Currency** exchange counters remain open for international arrivals and there are ATMs throughout the airport. You can hire mobile phones and buy local SIM cards at **Vodacom's Rentaphone** ① *www.vodacom.co.za*, at international and domestic arrivals, or from **MTN's Mobile Phone Rental** ① *www.mtnsp.co.za*, at domestic arrivals. Both are open 0500-2400.

All the car hire outlets can be found across the concourse outside the terminal building. Several shuttle services run from kiosks in the international and domestic arrivals halls and drop off at hotels and guesthouses in central Cape Town. They cost around R120 per person plus R30 for each additional person from the same group. Alternatively you can pre-book one through your hotel, guesthouse or backpacker hostel, or directly through **Citi Hopper** ① *T021-386 0077, www.citihopper.co.za*, **Magic Bus** ① *T021-505 6300, www.magicbus.co.za*, or **The Backpacker Bus** ① *T021-439 7600, www.backpackerbus.co.za*. Taxis running between the airport and city centre should have a special airport licence and they must use their meter by law. **Touch Down Taxis** ① *T021-919 4659*, is the authorized airport taxi company and again kiosks are in the arrivals halls; expect to pay around R280-350 to the city centre, depending on traffic.

MyCiTi Bus ① *T0800-65 64 63*, is the relatively new public transport alternative. Buses run between the airport bus station, which is located on the concourse outside the arrivals halls, and the Civic Centre on Hertzog Boulevard near the railway and other bus stations in central Cape Town where there are regular taxis for onward journeys and a drop-and-go facility for private vehicles. The buses depart every 20 minutes between

0510 and 2150 from the airport, and 0420 and 2100 from the Civic Centre, and outside peak traffic hours take around 30 minutes (45-55 minutes in morning and evening rush hours). Tickets are available at kiosks in the stations; R50, children (4-11) R25, under 3s free. The main **railway station** is in the centre of town and is also the terminus for the mainline long-distance bus companies; Greyhound, Intercape and Translux.

MOVING ON

The Cape Peninsula can be visited on a day tour, by bus or by rented car. With stops, it takes three to four hours to drive the 70 km to the Cape of Good Hope.

The easiest way to travel south along the Whale Coast (see page 72) and then east along the Garden Route (see page 82) is to rent a car and drive yourself. If you don't have a car, most of the route can be don on the Baz Bus, www.bazbus.com (see page 276).

GETTING AROUND

Most of Cape Town's oldest buildings, museums, galleries and the commercial centre are concentrated in a relatively small area and are easily explored on foot. However, to explore more of the city, and to visit Table Mountain, the suburbs or the beaches, there are several public transport options, and taxis are affordable, particularly if you use **Rikki**'s shared taxis. There are also a number of day tours to join and, for the greatest flexibility, it's always a good idea to rent a car.

Alternatively, **Sightseeing Cape Town** ① *T021-511 6000, www.citysightseeing.co.za, daily from 0830*, is a red, double-decker, open-top, hop-on hop-off bus that follows a 2¼-hour route around the city. There are two routes; the Red Route has 13 stops and a bus comes by every 15 minutes, while the Blue Route has 13 stops and buses come by every 35 minutes. Audio-commentary is available in eight languages and there's a special kids channel. The main ticket kiosk is outside the Two Oceans Aquarium at the V&A Waterfront, however you can buy tickets on the bus or online and join anywhere on the routes. It's ideal if you don't want to drive, and stops include the Lower Cableway Station, Camps Bay, Kirstenbosch, all the city centre museums, and as far south as Hout Bay on the peninsula. A one-day ticket costs R140, children (5-15) R70, under 5s free, and a two-day ticket is R220/R140. The buses are wheelchair friendly.

TOURIST INFORMATION

Cape Town Tourism ① *The Pinnacle, corner of Burg and Castle streets, T021-487 6800, www. tourismcapetown.co.za, Oct-Mar Mon-Fri 0800-1900, Sat 0830-1400, Sun 0900-1300, closes 1 hr earlier in winter (Apr-Sep)*, the official city tourist office, can help with bookings and tours throughout the Western Cape. It is an excellent source of information and a good first stop in the city. In addition to providing practical information about Cape Town, it can help with accommodation bookings and has plenty of information on nightlife and events. It is also home to **Western Cape Tourism** (same contact details) and there is a **South Africa National Parks** (SANParks) desk ① *www.sanparks.org*, where you can make reservations for the parks. There's also a café, gift shop and internet access.

FIRST PEOPLE

The first evidence of human inhabitants in the Cape has been dated back to nearly 30,000 years ago. Rock art found in the area was created by nomadic San people (also known as Bushmen), a hunter-gatherer group which roamed across much of southern Africa. Some San groups survive today, mostly in Namibia and Botswana, despite continuing persecution. The original San were replaced about two thousand years ago by Khoi groups, a semi-nomadic people who settled in the Cape with herds of sheep and cattle.

FIRST LANDING

António de Saldanha, a Portuguese admiral who lost his way going east, landed in Table Bay in 1503. They called the bay Aguada da Saldanha (it was renamed Table Bay in 1601 by **Joris van Spilbergen**). Saldanha and a party of the crew went ashore in search of drinking water. They followed a stream to the base of Table Mountain and then proceeded to climb to the top. From here Saldanha was able to get a clear view of the surrounding coastline and the confusion caused by the peninsula. On their return they found the crew unsuccessfully trying to barter with local indigenous Khoi for livestock. The trade quickly developed into a row which ended in bloodshed. There was another battle between the Portuguese and the Khoi in March 1510. On this occasion the Khoi had struck back after children and cattle were stolen by the sailors. Seventy-five Portuguese were killed, including **Dom Francisco de Almeida**, who had just finished five years as the first Portuguese Viceroy to India. Few Portuguese ships landed in Table Bay after this.

THE DUTCH AND THE VOC

By the end of the 16th century British and Dutch mariners had caught up with the Portuguese and they quickly came to appreciate the importance of the Cape as a base for restocking ships with drinking water and fresh supplies as they made their long journeys to the East. Indeed, seafarers found that they were able to exchange scraps of metal for provisions to supply a whole fleet.

The first moves to settle in the Cape were made by the Dutch, and on 6 April 1652 **Jan Van Riebeeck** landed in Table Bay. His ships carried wood for building and some small cannons, the first building to be erected being a small fort at the mouth of the Fresh River. The site of the original fort is where Grand Parade in the centre of Cape Town is today. Van Riebeeck was in charge of the supply station that belonged to the Dutch East India Company (Vereenigde Oost-Indische Compagnie or VOC). After the fort was built, gardens for fruit and vegetables were laid out and pastures for cattle acquired. As the settlement slowly grew, the Khoi people were driven back into the interior. Surprisingly, the early settlers were forbidden from enslaving the Khoi; instead, slaves were imported by the VOC from Indonesia and West Africa. Although many died, these slaves were the origin of the Cape Malay community.

In 1662 Jan van Riebeeck was transferred to India. Because of rivalries in Europe, the VOC was worried about enemy ships visiting the Cape, so work started on a new stone fort in 1666. Over the next 13 years several governors came and went. During this time the French and British went to war with Holland, but the British and the Dutch East India companies joined in a treaty of friendship in March 1674, and then in July of the same year a ship arrived with the news that the British and Dutch had made peace. In October 1679 one of the most energetic governors arrived in the Cape, **Simon van der Stel**. For the next

20 years van der Stel devoted his energies to creating a new Holland in southern Africa. During his period as Governor, van der Stel paid particular attention to the growth and development of Cape Town and the surrounding farmlands. The company garden was replanted, nursery plots were created and new experimental plants were collected from around the world. North of the gardens he built a large hospital and a lodge to house VOC slaves. New streets were laid out which were straight and wide with plenty of shade. New buildings in the town were covered in white limewash, producing a smart and prosperous appearance. In 1685, in appreciation for his work, he was granted an estate by the VOC, which he named **Constantia**. During his life he used the estate as an experimental agricultural farm and to grow oak trees which were then planted throughout the Cape.

One of his more significant contributions was the founding of the settlement at Stellenbosch. He directed the design and construction of many of the town's public buildings, and then introduced a number of the crops to be grown on the new farms. For many years he experimented with vines in an effort to produce wines as good as those in Europe. He was particularly pleased when in 1688 French Protestant Huguenot refugees arrived in the Cape. He saw to it that they were all settled on excellent farmlands in what became to be known as **Franschhoek** (French glen), the upper valley of the Berg River. In 1693 he had the foresight to appoint the town's first engineer to tackle problems of a clean water supply and the removal of rubbish. Van der Stel died in June 1712 at Constantia.

UNDER THE BRITISH

The next period of Cape Town's history was closely related to events in Europe, particularly the French Revolution. The ideas put forward by the Revolution of Liberty, Fraternity and Equality were not welcome in colonies such as the Cape. The Dutch East India Company was seen to be a corrupt organization and a supporter of the aristocracy. When the French invaded Holland, the British decided to seize the Cape to stop it from falling into French hands. After the Battle of Muizenberg in 1795, Britain took over the Cape from the representatives of the Dutch East India Company, which was bankrupt. In the Treaty of Amiens (1803) the Cape was restored to the Batavian Republic of the Netherlands. In 1806 the British took control again at the resumption of the Anglo-French wars.

When the British took over power it was inevitable that they inherited many of the problems associated with the colony. The principal issue was how to manage European settlement. The Dutch East India Company had only encouraged settlement as a cheap and efficient means of supplying their base in Cape Town. Thereafter they were only interested in controlling the Indian Ocean and supplying ships. By the time the British arrived, the Dutch settler farmers (the Boer) had become so successful that they were producing a surplus. The only problem was high production costs due to a shortage of labour. To alleviate the situation, a policy of importing slaves was implemented. This in turn led to decreased work opportunities for the settler families. Gradually the mood changed and the Boer looked to the interior for land and work. They were not impressed by the British administration and in 1836 the Great Trek was under way.

THE GROWTH OF THE CITY AND THE PORT

Industrialization in Europe brought great change, especially when the first steamship, the *Enterprise*, arrived in Table Bay in October 1825. After considerable delay and continual loss of life and cargoes, work began on two basins and breakwater piers. The first truckload of construction rocks was tipped by Prince Alfred, the 16-year-old son of

Queen Victoria, on 17 September 1860. The Alfred Basin was completed in 1870 and a dry dock was added in 1881.

No sooner had the first basin been completed than diamonds and gold were discovered in South Africa. Over the next 40 years Cape Town and the docks were to change beyond recognition. In 1900 work began on a new breakwater which would protect an area of 27 km. After five years' work the **Victoria Basin** was opened. This new basin was able to shelter the new generation of ships using Table Bay but was unable to cope with the increase in numbers during the **Anglo-Boer War**. A third basin was created to the east of Victoria Basin in 1932 and for a while this seemed to have solved the problem, but fate was against Cape Town. In January 1936 the largest ship to visit South Africa docked with ease at B berth in the new basin. The boat, which was being used to help promote tourism in South Africa, was filled with wealthy and famous visitors. The morning on which she was due to sail, a strong southeasterly wind blew up and pressed the liner so firmly against the quay that she couldn't sail. In one morning all of the new basin's weaknesses had been exposed.

The next phase of growth was an ambitious one, and it was only completed in 1945. The project involved the dredging of Table Bay and the reclaiming of land. The spoil from the dredging provided 140 sq km of landfill, known as Foreshore. This new land extends from the present-day railway station to **Duncan Dock**. As you walk or drive around Cape Town today, remember that just over 50 years ago the sea came up to the main railway station.
▸▸ *For the best record of the vibrant community that once thrived here, visit the excellent District Six Museum, see page 48.*

IMPACT OF THE APARTHEID YEARS

The descendants of the large and diverse slave population have given Cape Town a particularly cosmopolitan atmosphere. Unfortunately, Apartheid urban planning meant that many of the more vibrant areas of the city in the earlier part of this century were destroyed. The most notorious case is that of District Six, a racially mixed, low income housing area on the edge of the City Bowl. The Apartheid government could not tolerate such an area, especially so close to the centre of the city, and the residents, most of whom were classified as 'Coloured', were moved out to the soulless townships of the Cape Flats, such as Mitchell's Plain. The area was bulldozed but few new developments have taken place on the site: this accounts for the large areas of open ground in the area between the City Bowl and the suburb of Woodstock. Happily, the government recently handed over the first pocket of re-developed land to a small group of ex-residents of District Six and their descendants. What the area will become remains to be seen – the issue remains controversial as many ex-residents feel the open, barren land should remain as a poignant testimony to the forced removals.

Other reminders of the cosmopolitan history of Cape Town can be experienced in the area to the west of Buitengracht Street. This district, known as **Bo-Kaap**, is still home to a small Islamic (Cape Malay) community that somehow managed to survive the onslaught of Apartheid urban planning. The coloured population of Cape Town has historically outweighed both the white and African populations, hence the widespread use of Afrikaans in the city. This balance was maintained by Apartheid policies that prevented Africans from migrating into the Western Cape from the Eastern Cape and elsewhere. This policy was not, however, able to withstand the pressure of the poor rural Africans' desire to find opportunities in the urban economy. Over the past couple of decades there has been an enormous growth in the African population of Cape Town. Many of these new migrants

ON THE ROAD
Desmond Tutu

Desmond Tutu was a stalwart opponent of Apartheid and, like Nelson Mandela, became an influential and respected figure far beyond the borders of South Africa. His powerful oration and his simple but brave defiance of the Apartheid state impressed the world, and won him the Nobel Peace Prize in 1984. He was born in Klerksdorp in 1931 and, after being educated in church schools in Johannesburg and at university in England, he rose through the ranks to become secretary general of the South African Council of Churches from the 1970s. He first caught the international headlines with his call for the international community to stop buying South African goods, which lead to economic sanctions from 1985 to pressurize the government towards reform.

Tutu's opposition to Apartheid was vigorous and unequivocal, and he was outspoken both in South Africa and abroad. As a result, the government twice revoked his passport and he was jailed briefly in 1980 after a protest march. However, it was thought by many that Tutu's increasing international reputation and his rigorous advocacy of non-violence protected him from harsher penalties. He became the first black Anglican Archbishop of Cape Town from 1986 until 1996, and it was from this position that he consistently advocated reconciliation between the parties as Apartheid began to be dismantled.

After Apartheid, Tutu chaired the hearings of the Truth and Reconciliation Commission in 1996, and argued forcibly that the policy of granting amnesty to all who admitted their crimes was an important step in healing the nation's scars. Since then, Tutu has used his voice in the fight against AIDS, poverty and racism in South Africa, and in international conflict resolution. Nelson Mandela once said of him, "sometimes strident, often tender, never afraid and seldom without humour, Desmond Tutu's voice will always be the voice of the voiceless".

have been forced to settle in squatter areas, such as the notorious Crossroads Camp next to the N2 highway. During the Apartheid era these squatter camps were frequently bulldozed and the residents evicted but as soon as they were cleared they sprang up again. Crossroads was a hotbed of resistance to the Apartheid state and much of the Cape Flats area existed in a state of near civil war throughout much of the 1980s.

Today, Cape Town remains the most cosmopolitan city in South Africa. The official colour barriers have long since disappeared and residential boundaries are shifting. The economic balance, too, is beginning to change, and the black and coloured middle class has strengthened considerably. There are still pockets of low-income housing, notably the sprawling townships on the Cape Flats, but large areas in the northern suburbs have expanded into middle-income districts, and the Atlantic seaboard and southern suburbs continue to boast some of the most exclusive and expensive real estate on the African continent.

→ TABLE MOUNTAIN NATIONAL PARK

ⓘ *www.sanparks.org. The most popular ascent of the mountain directly above the City Bowl is described below; other parts of the park are covered later in the chapter.*

Cape Town is defined, first and foremost, by Table Mountain. Rising a sheer 1073 m from the coastal plain, it dominates almost every view of the city, its sharp slopes and level top making it one of the world's best-known city backdrops. For centuries, it was the first sight of Cape Town afforded to seafarers, its looming presence visible for hundreds of kilometres. Certainly, its size continues to astonish visitors today, but it is the mountain's wilderness, bang in the middle of a bustling conurbation, that makes the biggest impression. Table Mountain sustains over 1400 species of flora, as well as baboons, dassies (large rodents) and countless birds. The Table Mountain National Park encompasses the entire peninsula stretching from here to Cape Point. Between September and March you have the additional pleasure of seeing the mountain covered in wild flowers. The most common vegetation is fynbos, of which there is an extraordinary variety, but you'll also see proteas plus the rare silver tree, *Leucadendron argenteum*.

AERIAL CABLEWAY

ⓘ *Tafelberg Rd, information line T021-424 8181, www.tablemountain.net; the first car up is at 0800, the last car down varies from 1800 to 2130 depending on the time of year, both the information line and the website has up-to-the-minute details of times and, given Cape Town's unpredictable weather, will tell you if the cableway is open or not (always check before going up to the Lower Cableway Station). Return ticket R195, children (4-18) R95, one-way ticket R100, children (4-18) R50, under 4s free. Also check the website for special offers; 2 for the price of 1 on summer evenings to watch the sunset for example. Tickets bought online or at the Cape Town Tourism offices (not a bad idea to avoid lengthy queues at the ticket office at the lower cableway station in summer) are valid for 14 days. The cableway is closed for annual maintenance for 2 weeks end Jul/beginning Aug (check the website for exact dates). There are a number of options of getting to the lower cableway station; you can drive and parking is along Tafelberg Rd on either side of the station, go by taxi and once you come back down there is a taxi rank at the station, by Rikki Taxi and there is a free Rikki phone at the station, by the Cape Town City Sightseeing bus, or by regular Golden Arrow bus from the city centre to Camps Bay and get off at Kloof Nek, from where it is a 1.5-km walk up Tafelberg Rd to the station.*

The dizzying trip to the top in the Aerial Cableway is one of Cape Town's highlights. The first cableway was built in 1929, and since then has had three upgrades, the latest being in 1997. It's estimated to have carried up some 20 million people to date. There are two cars, each carrying up to 65 passengers, and as you ride up the floor rotates, allowing a full 360° view. Journey time is just under five minutes. In the base of each car is a water tank that can carry up to 4000 litres of fresh water to the top. There is the Table Mountain Café at the top station, which also has a deli for takeaway sandwiches, cheese and sushi platters and other light meals. To conserve water, they've recently introduced compostable plates and containers. An extensive network of paths has been laid out from the top station, allowing walks of various lengths, leading to different lookout points with stunning views of the City Bowl, Cape Flats, Robben Island and back along the peninsula. There are also free guided walks daily at 1000 and 1200.

HIKING

ⓘ *Mountain Rescue: T10177.*

The entire area is a nature reserve, and the mountain is protected as a national monument. There are numerous paths climbing to the top. The most popular route starts 1.5 km beyond the Lower Cableway Station and follows a course up Platteklip Gorge; there's another path from Kirstenbosch National Botanical Garden. Both take about two to three hours to the top, although they are both fairly tough and should not be taken lightly. Given Table Mountain's size and location, conditions can change alarmingly quickly. The weather may seem clear and calm when you set out, but fog (the famous 'Table Cloth' which flows from the top) and rain can descend without warning. Numerous people have been caught out and the mountain has claimed its fair share of lives. There have also been recent muggings in Platteklip Gorge, though authorities are presently doing their best to address the problem.

Before venturing out, make sure you have suitable clothing, food and water. Take warm clothes, a windbreaker, a waterproof jacket, a hat, sunscreen, sunglasses, plenty of water (2 litres per person) and energy foods. Never climb alone and inform someone of which route you're taking and what time you should be back. Also be aware that if the weather is too unfavourable for the cableway to be open, don't rely on it being open to take you back down, so allow enough daylight hours to make the descent on foot. For those wanting to spend more time on the mountain, there is the 75-km overnight – **Hoerikwaggo Trail** (meaning 'sea mountain' in Khoi). The five-day trek involves sleeping in tented camps dotted along the top of the mountain. It starts at Cape Point and then follows the spine of the peninsula to finish at the lower cableway station after descending Platteklip Gorge. For full details, contact SANParks (see Tourist information, page 36).

SIGNAL HILL

Signal Hill's summit offers spectacular views of the city, the Twelve Apostles (the mountainous spine stretching south from Table Mountain) and the ocean. It is possible to drive to the 350-m summit, which means that it can get pretty busy with tour groups around sunset. Nevertheless, watching the sun dip into the Atlantic from this viewpoint with a cold sundowner in hand is a highlight of a visit to Cape Town. Avoid being there after dark, as there have been reports of muggings, although the presence of security officers has now reduced this considerably. From the town centre, follow signs for the Lower Cableway station and take a right at Kloof Nek opposite the turning for the cableway station. On the lower slopes of Signal Hill, above and accessed from Wale Street in Bo-Kaap, is the Noon Day Gun which is fired electronically at noon every day, except Sunday. Originally at the castle and fired to announce the arrival of ships, the two cannon were moved to Signal Hill in 1902 as time-keeping instruments. The view from here takes in the high-rises in the commercial area of the City Bowl, and the harbour and V&A Waterfront. There's a small café.

LION'S HEAD

Halfway along the road up Signal Hill you pass Lion's Head, a popular hiking spot. The climb to the peak is fairly easy going, takes about two hours and is signposted; the 360° views from the top are incredible. In the 17th century the peak was known as Leeuwen Kop (Lion's Head) by the Dutch, and Signal Hill was known as Leeuwen Staart (Lion's Tail), as the shape resembles a crouching lion.

→ CITY BOWL

From the Table Mountain Lower Cableway Station, you look out over the central residential suburbs of Tamboerskloof (Drummers' Ravine), Gardens, Oranjezicht (Orange View) and Vredehoek (Peaceful Corner), and beyond here lie the high-rise blocks of the business district. Together these form the City Bowl, a term inspired by the surrounding mountains. Closest to the mountain is **Oranjezicht**, a quiet district that was, up until 1900 the area was a farm of the same name. On the boundary with Gardens are the **De Waal Park** and

Molteno Reservoir, originally built as a main storage facility for the city in 1881, which now provides a peaceful wooded spot from where you can enjoy a view of the city.

There is nothing peaceful about **Vredehoek** today, as the De Waal Drive (M3) brings rush hour traffic into the top end of town from the southern suburbs and beyond. Most of the area has been given over to ugly high-rise apartments, though the residents benefit from some excellent views. This was the area in which many Jewish immigrants from Eastern Europe settled, and have to a large part remained.

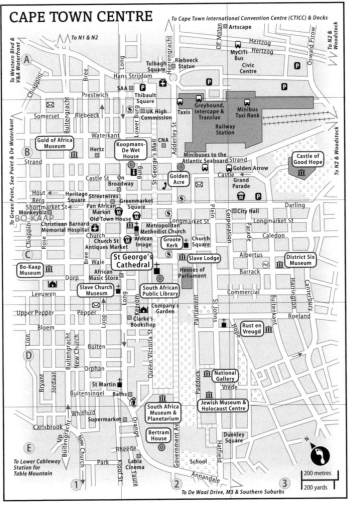

CAPE TOWN CENTRE

Gardens is a lively neighbourhood with a choice of quality restaurants and comfortable guesthouses. Cape Town's best-known hotel, the **Mount Nelson**, is situated here in its own landscaped gardens. The grand gateway to the hotel was built in 1924 to welcome the Prince of Wales.

From here the land slopes gently towards the harbour and the V&A Waterfront, with the commercial heart of the city laid out in between. This was the area where the Dutch East India Company first created fruit and vegetable gardens to supply the ships' crews who suffered greatly from scurvy. Across Orange Street from the entrance to the Mount Nelson Hotel is the top end of **Government Avenue**, a delightful pedestrian route past Company's Garden and many of the city's main museums. Originally sheltered by lemon trees, it is now lined with oaks and myrtle hedges, and is one of Cape Town's most popular walks.

SOUTH AFRICA MUSEUM AND PLANETARIUM

ⓘ *25 Queen Victoria St, at the top end of Company's Garden, T021-481 3800, www.iziko.org. za, 1000-1700, R25, under 18s free.*

This, the city's most established museum, specializes in natural history, ethnography and archaeology, and is a good place to take children. There are extensive displays of the flora and fauna of southern Africa, including the popular Whale Well and interactive Shark World area, but the highlight is the 'IQe – the Power of Rock Art' exhibition. The displays of ancient San rock art have been in the museum for almost 100 years but, following a process of consultation and dialogue with Khoi-San communities, they have been re-interpreted in a far more sensitive and illuminating manner. The exhibits focus on the significance and symbolism of San rock art, with some fascinating examples including the beautifully preserved Linton panel, which depicts the trance experiences of shamans. Other themes explored include rainmaking and the significance of animal imagery; the eland, for example, appears more often than any other animal in San rock art, and it holds a central role in all major rituals, from teenage initiation to marriage and rainmaking. The whole exhibition, although short, is beautifully arranged and accompanied by the sound of San singing, a disjointed and haunting sound.

Nearby are the ethnographic galleries, offering interesting displays on the San, Khoi and Xhosa, among others, as well as the original Lydenburg Heads. There is also a small display of pieces recovered from Great Zimbabwe that illustrate its importance as a trade centre – there are beads from Cambay, India, Chinese Celadon ware, 13th-century Persian pottery and Syrian glass from the 14th century. The Stone Bones is an exhibition about the fossilized skeletons found in the Karoo, which date back 250 million years – predating dinosaurs. There are life-sized reproductions of the reptile-like creatures, including walk-around dioramas and examples of the actual fossils. Every year in spring the museum hosts the excellent BBC Wildlife Photographer of the Year exhibition. Contact the museum for exact dates.

Next door, at the **Planetarium** ⓘ *T021-481 3900, www.iziko.org.za, 1000-1700, show times vary depending on what's on; check the website, R25, children (5-18) R10, under 5s free*, presentations change every few months, but usually a view of the current night sky is shown and visitors receive a star map to find the constellations and planets that are visible each month. Shows last an hour and are fascinating. Children (aged 5-10) will enjoy the Davy the Dragon show, which sends Davy off into space to learn how to the best flying dragon ever.

BERTRAM HOUSE

ⓘ *Corner of Government Av and Orange St, T021-424 9381, www.iziko.org.za, Mon-Fri 1000-1700, R10, under 18s free.*

This early 19th-century red-brick Georgian House has a distinctly English feel to it. The building houses a collection of porcelain, jewellery, silver and English furniture, the majority of which was bequeathed by Ann Lidderdale. Winifred Ann Lidderdale was an important civic figure in Cape Town in the 1950s. After her marriage to Henry Maxwell Lidderdale, she lived in England and the USA, but in 1951 the couple returned to Cape Town for their retirement. It was her desire to establish a house museum to commemorate the British contribution to life at the Cape. Downstairs the two drawing rooms contain all the trappings of a bygone elegant age – card tables, a Hepplewhite settee, a square piano and a fine harp. Three rooms have wallpaper from London, a very expensive luxury for the period.

JEWISH MUSEUM

ⓘ *88 Hatfield St, T021-465 1546, www.sajewishmuseum.co.za, Sun-Thu 1000-1700, Fri 1000-1400, closed on Jewish and public holidays, R50, children R20.*

Inside this excellent, contemporary museum is a rich and rare collection of items depicting the history of the Cape Town Hebrew Congregation and other congregations in the Cape Province. The history of the community is interesting in itself: in 1841 a congregation of 17 men assembled for the first time in Cape Town to celebrate Yom Kippur. At the meeting they set about the task of raising funds to build a synagogue, and in 1862 the foundation stone was laid for the first synagogue in southern Africa. The following year the building was completed and furnished – quite a feat for such a small community at the time. On display upstairs are bronze Sabbath oil lamps, *Chanukkah* lamps, *Bessamin* spice containers, *Torah* scrolls, *Kiddush* cups and candlesticks. There is a beautiful stained-glass window depicting the Ten Commandments in Hebrew. From here a glass corridor leads you to a newer section of the museum that is devoted to the history of Jewish immigration to the Cape, mainly from Lithuania. A lot of thought has been put into the displays, which include photographs, immigration certificates, videos and a full reconstruction of a Lithuanian *shtetl*, or village. There are special displays outlining the stories of famous Jewish South Africans, including Helen Suzman and Isie Maisels. The museum complex also houses a library, café and bookshop.

HOLOCAUST CENTRE

ⓘ *88 Hatfield St, T021-462 5553, www.ctholocaust.co.za, Sun-Thu 1000-1700, Fri 1000-1400, entry by donation.*

An intelligent and shocking examination of the Holocaust can be found next door at this modern museum. Exhibits follow a historical route, starting with a look at anti-Semitism in Europe in previous centuries, and then leading to the rise of Nazism in Germany, the creation of ghettos, death camps and the Final Solution, and liberation at the end of the war. Video footage, photography, examples of Nazi propaganda and personal accounts of the Holocaust produce a vividly haunting and shocking display. The exhibits cleverly acknowledge South Africa's emergence from Apartheid and draw parallels between both injustices, as well as looking at the link between South Africa's Greyshirts (who were later assimilated into the National Party) and the Nazis. The local context is highlighted further at the end of the exhibition, with video accounts of Jews who survived the Holocaust and moved to Cape Town.

NATIONAL GALLERY

ⓘ *Government Av, T021-467 4660, www.iziko.org.za, 1000-1700, R20, under 18s free.*

The National Gallery houses a permanent collection but also hosts some excellent temporary exhibitions that include the best of the country's contemporary art. The original collection was bequeathed to the nation in 1871 by Thomas Butterworth Bailey, and features a collection of 18th- and 19th-century British sporting scenes, portraits and Dutch paintings. Far more interesting are the changing exhibitions of contemporary South African art and photography. Check the website to see what's on. There's a good souvenir shop on site.

RUST EN VREUGD

ⓘ *78 Buitenkant St, T021-481 3800, www.iziko.org.za, Mon-Fri 1000-1700, entry by donation.*

A few hundred metres east of the National Gallery, hidden behind a high whitewashed wall, is this 18th-century mansion. Today it houses six galleries displaying a collection of watercolours, engravings and lithographs depicting the history of the Cape. Of particular note are Schouten's watercolour of Van Riebeeck's earth fort (1658), watercolours by Thomas Baines (a British artist who travelled extensively in South Africa and Australia) of climbing Table Mountain, lithographs by Angas of Khoi and Zulus, and a collection of cartoons by Cruikshank depicting the first British settlers arriving in the Cape.

COMPANY'S GARDEN

ⓘ *Daily 0700-1900, closes 1800 Jun-Aug, café, 0900-1700.*

Running alongside Government Avenue are the peaceful Company's Garden, situated on the site of Jan van Riebeeck's original vegetable garden, which was created in 1652 to grow produce for settlers and ships bound for the East. Cape Town's earliest records show that the Garden was originally divided into rectangular fields protected by high trimmed myrtle windbreaks, and watered via a system of open irrigation furrows fed by mountain streams. The design was typical Dutch agricultural practice of the time, apart from the furrows, which had been adapted to suit the region's weather. It is now a small botanical garden, with lawns, a variety of labelled trees, ponds filled with Japanese koi and a small aviary. It's a popular spot with office workers at lunchtime. The grey squirrels living amongst the oak trees were introduced by Cecil Rhodes from America. There are also a couple of statues here: opposite the South African Public Library at the lower end of the garden, is the oldest statue in Cape Town, that of Sir George Grey, governor of the Cape from 1854 to 1862. Close by is a statue of Cecil Rhodes, pointing northwards in a rather unfortunate flat-handed gesture, with an inscription reading, "Your hinterland is there", a reminder of his ambition to paint the map pink from the Cape to Cairo. There is a café in the garden, serving drinks and snacks beneath the trees; best known for its scones, jam and cream.

SOUTH AFRICAN PUBLIC LIBRARY

ⓘ *5 Queen Victoria St, behind St George's Cathedral, T021-424 6320, www.nlsa.ac.za, Mon-Fri 0900-1700, free.*

Adjoining the garden is the South African Public Library, which opened in 1818. It is the country's oldest national reference library and was one of the first free libraries in the world. Today it houses an important collection of books covering South Africa's history. The building also has a bookshop and an internet café.

HOUSES OF PARLIAMENT

ⓘ *Entry via Parliament St gate, T021-403 2266, www.parliament.gov.za, public gallery tickets available during parliamentary sessions Jan-Jun, overseas visitors must present their passports, phone ahead for tours of the chambers and Constitutional Assembly.*

On the other side of the avenue are the Houses of Parliament. The building was completed in 1885, and when the Union was formed in 1910 it became the seat for the national parliament. In front of the building is a marble statue of Queen Victoria, erected by public subscription in honour of her Golden Jubilee. It was unveiled in 1890.

ST GEORGE'S CATHEDRAL

ⓘ *5 Wale St, T021-424 7360, Mon-Fri 0800-1600 and during services in the evenings and at weekends.*

The last building on Government Avenue and on the corner of Wale Street is St George's Cathedral, best known for being Archbishop Desmond Tutu's territory from 1986 until 1996 (see box, page 40). It is from here that he led over 30,000 people to City Hall to mark the end of Apartheid, and where he coined the now universal phrase 'Rainbow Nation'. The building was designed by Sir Herbert Baker in the early 20th century. Inside, some of the early memorial tablets have been preserved, while over the top of the stairs leading to the crypt is a memorial to Lady D'Urban, wife of Sir Benjamin D'Urban, the Governor of the Cape from 1834 to 1838. Under the archway between the choir and St John's Chapel is a bronze recumbent statue of Archbishop West Jones, the second Archbishop of Cape Town (1874-1908). The Great North window is a fine piece of stained glass depicting the pioneers of the Anglican church. There is a small café, The Crypt, open during the day for light snacks and breakfasts. The Cathedral's choir is superb and they regularly perform at evensong.

SLAVE LODGE

ⓘ *T021-460 8242, www.iziko.org.za, Mon-Sat 1000-1700, R20, under 18s free.*

On the corner of Adderley and Wale streets is Slave Lodge, the second oldest building in Cape Town. The building has had a varied history, but its most significant role was as a slave lodge for the VOC (see page 37) – between 1679 and 1811 the building housed up to 1000 slaves. Local indigenous groups were protected by the VOC from being enslaved; most slaves were consequently imported from Madagascar, India and Indonesia, creating the most culturally varied slave society in the world. Conditions at the lodge were appalling and up to 20% of the slaves died every year.

It has now been developed into a museum chartering the history of the building and slavery in South Africa. At the entrance to the exhibition is a slick cinema room, with two flat-screen TVs showing a 15-minute film on the history of slavery in the Cape, highlighting the rules under which slaves lived, the conditions in which they were imported and sold, and the fundamental role slavery played in the success of Cape Town. Beyond here, the museum has a series of displays, including a model of a slave ship and images and sounds of what life was like in the lodge. The top floor houses a muddle of British and VOC weapons, household goods, furniture and money, as well as relics from Japan and ancient Rome, Greece and Egypt.

GROOTE KERK

ⓘ T021-422 0569, www.grootekerk.org.za, 1000-1900, free guided tours available.

Nearby is one of Cape Town's older corners, **Church Square**, site of the Groote Kerk. Up until 1834 the square was used as a venue for the auctioning of slaves from the Slave Lodge, which faced onto the square. All transactions took place under a tree – a concrete plaque marks the old tree's position.

The Groote Kerk was the first church of the Dutch Reformed faith to be built in South Africa (building started in 1678 and it was consecrated in 1704). The present church, built between 1836 and 1841, is a somewhat dull, grey building designed and constructed by Hermann Schutte after a fire had destroyed most of the original. Many of the old gravestones were built into the base of the church walls, the most elaborate of which is the tombstone of Baron van Rheede van Oudtshoorn. Inside, more early tombstones and family vaults are set into the floor, while on the walls are the coats of arms of early Cape families. Note the locked pews, which were rented out to wealthy families in the 19th century. Two of the Cape's early governors are buried here – Simon van der Stel (1679-1699) and Ryk Tulbagh (1751-1771).

DISTRICT SIX MUSEUM

ⓘ 25A Buitenkant St, T021-466 7200, www.districtsix.co.za, Mon 0900-1400, Tue-Sat 0900-1600, entry by donation, café and bookshop.

Housed in an old Methodist Church, this is one of Cape Town's most powerful museums and gives a fascinating glimpse of the inanity of Apartheid. District Six was once the vibrant, cosmopolitan heart of Cape Town, a largely coloured inner city suburb renowned for its jazz scene. In February 1966, PW Botha, then Minister of Community Development, formally proclaimed District Six a 'white' group area. Over the next 15 years, an estimated 60,000 people were given notice to leave their homes and were moved to the new townships on the Cape Flats. The area was razed, and to this day remains largely undeveloped. Over the years there has been much talk about relocating some of those who were originally displaced to new housing in the area, but as yet there has been no progress.

The museum contains a lively collection of photographs, articles and personal accounts depicting life before and after the removals. There are usually a couple of musicians at the back, tinkering away at their guitars and tin pipes and adding immeasurably to the atmosphere of the place. Highlights include a large map covering most of the ground floor on which ex-residents have been encouraged to mark their homes and local sights. The **Namecloth** is particularly poignant: a 1.5-m-wide length of cloth has been provided for ex-residents to write down their comments, part of which hangs by the entrance. It has grown to over 1 km, and features some moving thoughts. A display in the back room looks at the forced removals from the Kirstenbosch area.

CASTLE OF GOOD HOPE

ⓘ Buitenkant St, entry from the Grand Parade side, T021-481 7223, www.castleofgoodhope.co.za, www.iziko.org.za, 0900-1600, R28, children (5-16) R12, under 5s free, reduced rates on Sun. Free guided tours Mon-Sat 1100, 1200 and 1400. Expect to have any bags checked since the castle is still used as the regional offices for the National Defence Force.

Beyond the Grand Parade, on Darling Street, is the main entrance of South Africa's oldest colonial building, the Castle of Good Hope. Work was started in 1666 by Commander Zacharias Wagenaer and completed in 1679. Its original purpose was for the Dutch East India Company to defend the Cape from rival European powers, and today it is an imposing sight, albeit a rather gloomy one. Under the British, the castle served as government headquarters and since 1917 it has been the headquarters of the South African Defence Force, Western Cape.

Today the castle is home to three museums. The **William Fehr Collection** is one of South Africa's finest displays of furnishings reflecting the social and political history of the Cape. There are landscapes by John Thomas Baines and William Huggins, 17th-century Japanese porcelain and 18th-century Indonesian furniture. Upstairs is an absurdly huge dining table which seats 104, in a room still used for state dinners.

To the left of the William Fehr Collection is the **Secunde's House**. The Secunde was second in charge of the settlement at the Cape, responsible for administrative duties for the Dutch East India Company. None of the three rooms contain original furniture from the castle, but they do recreate the conditions under which an official for the Dutch East India Company would have lived in the 17th, 18th and early 19th centuries. The third museum is the **Military Museum**, a rather indifferent collection depicting the conflicts of early settlers. More absorbing are the regimental displays of uniforms and medals.

The free guided tours are informative and fun, although a little short. Tour highlights include the torture chambers, cells, views from the battlements and Dolphin Court, where Lady Anne Barnard was supposedly seen bathing in the nude by the sentries. While waiting for a tour you can enjoy coffee and cakes at a small café, or explore van der Stel's restored wine cellars, where you can taste and buy wines. There is full ceremonial changing of the guard at noon, which coincides with the firing of the Noon Gun from Signal Hill.

ADDERLEY STREET AND HEERENGRACHT

Adderley Street is one of the city's busiest shopping areas, and is sadly marred by a number of 1960s and 1970s eyesores, but it does still boast some impressive bank buildings. On the corner of Darling Street is the **Standard Bank Building** (1880), a grand structure built shortly after the diamond wealth from Kimberley began to reach Cape Town. Diagonally across is the equally impressive **Barclays Bank Building** (1933), a fine Ceres sandstone building which was the last major work by Sir Herbert Baker in South Africa. At the corner of Adderley Street and Strand Street stands a modern shopping mall complex, the **Golden Acre**. On the lower level of the complex the remains of an aqueduct and a reservoir dating from 1663 can be viewed.

Continuing down towards the docks, Adderley Street passes Cape Town Railway Station and becomes Heerengracht. At the junction with Hans Strijdom Street is a large roundabout with a central fountain and a bronze statue of Jan van Riebeeck, given to the city by Cecil Rhodes in 1899. At the bottom end of Heerengracht on the foreshore are statues of Bartholomew Dias and Maria van Riebeeck, donated respectively by the Portuguese and Dutch governments in 1952 for Cape Town's tercentenary celebrations. The palm trees here once graced a marine promenade in this area, a further indication of how much additional land has been reclaimed from Table Bay over the years. At the end of Heerengracht, on the corner of Coen Steytler Street, is the Cape Town International Convention Centre (CTICC). This is a much-used venue with several exhibition spaces, that regularly holds events for the public such as the Design Indaba, Cape Town Book Fair, Decorex and the Cape Town International Jazz Festival. Check press for details or visit www.cticc.co.za.

GREENMARKET SQUARE

A couple of blocks south of the junction of Strand Street and St George's Mall, a pedestrianized road lined with shops and cafés, is Greenmarket Square, the old heart of Cape Town and the second oldest square in the city. It has long been a meeting place, and during the 19th century it became a vegetable market. In 1834 it took on the significant role of being the site where the declaration of the freeing of all slaves was made. Today it remains a popular meeting place, with a busy market (Monday to Saturday) selling African crafts and jewellery.

Dominating one side is a **Park Inn** hotel, housed in what was once the headquarters of Shell Oil – note the shell motifs on its exterior. Diagonally opposite is the **Old Town House** ⓘ *T021-481 3933, www.iziko.org.za, Mon-Sat 1000-1700, R10, under 18s free*, (1751) originally built to house the town guard. It became the first town hall in 1840 when Cape Town became a municipality. Much of the exterior remains unchanged, and with its decorative plaster mouldings and fine curved fanlights, it is one of the best preserved Cape baroque exteriors in the city. The first electric light in Cape Town was switched on in the Old House on 13 April 1895. Today the white double-storeyed building houses the Michaelis Collection of Flemish and Dutch paintings. At the entrance to the house is a circle set into the floor which marks the spot from which all distances to and from Cape Town are measured.

KOOPMANS-DE WET HOUSE

ⓘ *Strand St, T021-481 3935, www.iziko.org.za, Mon-Fri 1000-1700, R10, under 18s free.*
Just off St George's Mall, is the delightfully peaceful Koopmans-De Wet House. The house is named in memory of Marie Koopmans-De Wet, a prominent figure in cultured Cape Society who lived here between 1834 and 1906. The inside has been restored to reflect the period of her grandparents who lived here in the late 18th century. All of the pieces are numbered and a small catalogue gives a brief description. Though not too cluttered, there is a fascinating collection of furnishings which gives the house a special tranquil feel. Look out for the early map of the Cape coastline at the head of the stairs, dating from 1730 – Saldanha Bay and Cape Agulhas are clearly visible. At the back of the house is a shaded courtyard and the original stables with the slave quarters above.

GOLD OF AFRICA MUSEUM

ⓘ *96 Strand St, T021-405 1540, www.goldofafrica.com, Mon-Sat 0930-1700, R30, children R20.*
A few blocks west of Koopmans-De Wit House is the **Lutheran Church**, and next door is the **Martin Melck House**, now home to the Gold of Africa Museum. Originally the house served as a clandestine Lutheran church, as in the 18th century the Dutch authorities refused to tolerate any churches other than those belonging to the Dutch Reformed Church. The present museum houses a slick display of the history of gold mining, outlining the first mining by Egyptians in 2400 BC and the subsequent development of trade networks across Africa. There are comprehensive displays of 19th- and 20th-century gold artworks from Mali, Ghana and Senegal, including jewellery, masks, hair ornaments and statuettes. It's an absorbing collection, given the amount of valuable precious metals on display. Downstairs there's a shop and workshop where you can watch goldsmiths at work. In the leafy courtyard is the **Gold Restaurant** ⓘ *T021-421 4653, www.goldrestaurant.co.za, daily 1000-2300, and if you are visiting for dinner, evening guided tours are available of the museum for R50 per person which includes a glass of wine sprinkled with gold leaf.* This is a nice option and the restaurant serves excellent traditional South African cuisine and drummers entertain.

LONG STREET

Stretching for more than 20 blocks in the CBD, Long Street is one of the trendiest and most energetic streets in Cape Town and it gets particularly lively at night. Lined with street cafés, fashionable shops, bars, clubs and backpacker hostels, it has a distinctly youthful feel about it, although a clutch of new boutique hotels, posh apartment complexes and upmarket restaurants are injecting the area with a new sophisticated edge. Long Street is also home to some fine old city buildings. One of Cape Town's late Victorian gems is at No 117, now an antiques shop. On the outside is an unusual cylindrical turret with curved windows; inside is a fine cast-iron spiral staircase leading to a balustraded gallery.

The **Slave Church Museum** ① *No 40, T021-423 6755, Mon-Fri 0900-1600, free*, is the oldest mission church in South Africa, built between 1802 and 1804 as the mother church for missionary work carried out in rural areas by the South African Missionary Society. It was used for religious and literacy instruction of slaves in Cape Town. Inside are displays of missionary work throughout the Cape, and behind the pulpit are displays showing early cash accounts and receipts for transactions such as the transfer of slaves.

HERITAGE SQUARE

Two blocks north of Long Street, the entrance is on Shortmarket Street, is this renovated block of 17th- and 18th-century townhouses, which include one of the city's oldest blacksmiths, but is better known for its excellent restaurants and the **Cape Heritage Hotel**. In the centre is a cobbled courtyard holding the Cape's oldest living grape vine, which was planted in 1781.

BO-KAAP AND THE BO-KAAP MUSEUM

About 600 m west along Wale Street is Bo-Kaap, Cape Town's historical Islamic quarter and one of the city's most interesting residential areas. The area was developed in the 1760s and today feels a world away from the nearby CBD. Here the streets are cobbled and tightly woven across the slopes of Signal Hill, and the closely packed houses are painted in bright hues of lime, pink and blue. The name means 'upper Cape' and it developed as a working-class district for freed slaves, who were mostly imported by the Dutch from Malaysia, Indonesia and other parts of Asia. Today's Cape Malay community in Bo-Kaap are the descendents of these. It was this community who also introduced Islam to South Africa and the Owal Mosque on Dorp Street, built in 1794, is the oldest mosque in the country and there are nine other mosques in the district. The air here rings with muezzin calls before the five daily prayers. Opposite the museum on Wale Street, **Atlas Trading** is a shop worth stopping by to see the shelves stacked with relishes and pickles and at the back the wooden boxes of spices used in Cape Malay cooking. You can do a great half-day tour of Bo-Kaap with **Andulela Experience**, which includes a walkabout, a visit to the museum and a cookery class and lunch in a local family's home. To the west, Bo-Kaap blends into the trendy new shopping and nightlife area of De Waterkant (see below).

The **Bo-Kaap Museum** ① *71 Wale St, T021-481 3900, www.iziko.org.za, Mon-Sat 1000-1700, R10, under 18s free*, housed in an attractive 18th-century house, is dedicated to the Cape's Malay community and contains the furnishings of a wealthy 19th-century Muslim family. There are antique furnishings and Islamic heirlooms such as an old Koran and *tasbeh* beads set in front of the mihrab alcove, while the back room has displays dedicated to the input that slaves had in the economy and development of Cape Town. The photos are the most interesting articles, giving a fascinating glimpse of life in the Bo-Kaap in the early 20th century. At the back is a community centre, with temporary photographic exhibitions. The house itself is one of the oldest buildings in Cape Town surviving in its original form. It was built by Jan de Waal for artisans in 1763 and it was here that Abu Bakr Effendi started the first Arabic school and wrote important articles on Islamic law. He originally came to Cape Town as a guest of the British government to try and settle religious differences amongst the Cape Muslims.

→VICTORIA AND ALFRED WATERFRONT

① *Information desks on Dock Rd next to the Ferryman's Pub and on the lower floor of Victoria Wharf, 0900-2100, information line T021-408 7600, www.waterfront.co.za, shops open 0900-2100, restaurants and other attractions vary; details of all amenities can be found on the website.*

The V&A (Victoria and Alfred) Waterfront, Cape Town's original Victorian harbour, the city's most popular attraction, receives in excess of 10 million visitors a year. The whole area was completely restored in the early 1990s, and today it is a lively district packed with restaurants, bars and shops, and there is a whole host of things to see and do. Original buildings stand shoulder to shoulder with mock-Victorian shopping malls, museums and cinemas, all crowding along a waterside walkway with Table Mountain towering beyond. Despite being geared towards tourists it remains a working harbour, which provides much of the area's real charm. To explore the harbour and beyond, there are boat companies along Quay 5 in front of Victoria Wharf offering all manner of boat cruises, from short half-hour harbour tours to two-hour sails to Camps Bay by schooner.

The choice of shops, restaurants and entertainment is unrivalled. When the main mall **Victoria Wharf** opened, it was similar to any other South African shopping mall and featured the usual chain stores. Over the years and with growing popularity the quality of shops has shifted upmarket. The majority now sell clothes, souvenirs, jewellery and specialist items, with luxury brands such as Gucci, Jimmy Choo and Burberry. There are more than 80 restaurants. However, the location and popularity come at a price, and the cost of a meal here is considerably more than elsewhere in Cape Town.

ARRIVING ON THE V&A WATERFRONT

Getting there To get here there is a MyCiTi bus service that runs from Herzog Boulevard near the railway station in the city centre or there's a Golden Arrow bus service that runs along Beach Road in Sea Point and Green Point to the V&A. **City Sightseeing** has its ticket office outside the aquarium. If you're driving there are several multi-storey car parks. The one underneath Victoria Wharf is the most expensive – put it this way, if you went to see a movie, it would cost more to park than the price of a movie ticket. The other car parks are half the price.

BACKGROUND

The V&A Waterfront derives its name from the two harbour basins around which it is developed. Construction began in 1860, when Prince Alfred, Queen Victoria's second son, tipped the first load of stone to start the building of the breakwater for Cape Town's harbour. Alfred Basin could not handle the increased shipping volumes and subsequently a larger basin, the Victoria Basin, was built. A number of original buildings remain around the basins and are an interesting diversion from the razzmatazz of the shops and restaurants.

CLOCK TOWER

At the narrow entrance to the Alfred Basin, on the Berties Landing side, is the original Clock Tower, built in 1882 to house the port captain's office. This is in the form of a red octagonal Gothic-style tower and stands just in front of the **Clock Tower Centre**, a modern mall with a collection of shops, offices and restaurants. The Clock Tower Centre houses the Nelson Mandela Gateway to Robben Island, from where you catch the main ferry to the island (see page 55). Just next to the Clock Tower Centre, is the small **Chavonnes Battery Museum** ① *T021-416 6230, www.chavonnesmuseum.co.za, Wed-Sat 0900-1600, R25, children (10-18)*

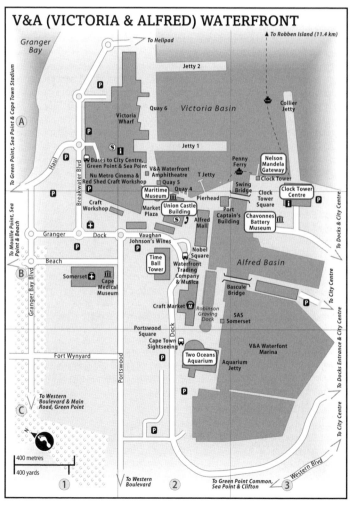

V&A (VICTORIA & ALFRED) WATERFRONT

R10, which lies underneath a modern office building and displays relics of a fortified structure built by the Marquais of Chavonnes of the Dutch East India Company in 1726. Built in an arc shape, it once held a battery of 16 cannons ready to fire out to sea over a 180° angle. It remained in service until 1860 when the construction of Alfred Basin began and some of the demolished walls were used to fortify the new docks. Parts of the remaining walls can be seen, there are exhibits about Cape Town's history as a military outpost, and visitors can help load an 18-pound cannon. This side of the Waterfront is connected the bulk of the area by a swing bridge, which swings open every 10 minutes to allow boats to pass underneath.

UNION CASTLE BUILDING

Walking across the swing bridge (look out for the Cape fur seals on a landing to your right as you cross), you come to the stocky square building known as **Union Castle Building** (1919), designed by the firm of architects owned by Sir Herbert Baker. The Union Steamship Company and the Castle Line both ran monthly mail ships between Britain and South Africa in the late 19th century. In 1900 they amalgamated and from then on mail was delivered every week. The last Union Castle ship to sail to England with the mail was the *Windsor Castle* in 1977. This is now home to the **Maritime Museum** ① *T021-405 2880, www.iziko.org.za, 1000-1700, R10, under 18s free*, a collection of model ships and objects associated with the era of mail ships. It also holds an archive of over 19,000 photographs of ships that visited Cape Town from the 1920s to the 1960s. Nearby is the museum ship, the *SAS Somerset*, a boom defence vessel that is permanently moored for public viewing.

Opposite the Union Castle Building is the **Victoria & Alfred Hotel**. Now a luxury four-star hotel and shopping mall, the building was originally a coal store before being converted into Union Castle's warehouse and customs baggage store.

To the south of the hotel is **Nobel Square** ① *www.nobelsquare.com*, which was opened on 16 December 2006, the Day of Reconciliation, and pays tribute to four of South Africa's Nobel Peace Prize laureates – the late Nkosi Albert Luthuli (1961), Archbishop Desmond Tutu (1984) and FW de Klerk and Nelson Mandela who jointly won it in 1993. Slightly larger than life-size statues of the four formidable men stand next to each other with a backdrop of Table Mountain and, in front of the sculpture, the Laureates' preferred quotations engraved in their chosen language. In the middle of the square, the Peace and Democracy sculpture – a narrative work of a jumble of people and faces on top of each other – represents the contribution made by women and children to the attainment of peace in South Africa.

TIME BALL TOWER

Heading west, on the other side of Dock Road above the car park, is the 1894 Time Ball Tower; its purpose was to act as an accurate reference for ships' navigators who set their clocks as the ball on the roof fell. Correct time was vital for navigators to be able to determine precise longitude.

TWO OCEANS AQUARIUM

① *Entrance is on Dock Rd, by the Waterfront Craft Market, T021-418 3823, www.aquarium. co.za, 0930-1800, R100, children (4-13) R48 (14-17) R75, under 4s free.*

Focusing on the unique Cape marine environment created by the merging of the Atlantic and Indian Ocean, this aquarium is the top attraction on the Waterfront. The display begins with a walk through the Indian Ocean, where you'll follow a route past tanks filled with a multitude of colourful fish, turtles, seahorses and octopuses. Highlights include giant spider crabs and phosphorescent jellyfish floating in a mesmerizing circular current. Then you walk past touch pools, where children can pick up spiky starfish and slimy sea slugs. Free puppet shows and face painting keep children busy at the **Alpha Activity Centre** in the basement. The main wall here looks out into the water of the actual harbour, and you can watch Cape fur seals dart and dive before the glass. The seals are fed at 1100 and 1400. Upstairs is a vast tank holding the Kelp Forest, an extraordinary tangle of giant kelp that sways drunkenly in the artificial tides. The highlight is the Predators exhibit, a circular tank complete with glass tunnel, holding ragged-tooth sharks, eagle rays, turtles and some impressively large hunting fish. There are daily feeds at 1500 and, with an Open Water diving certificate, you can arrange to dive with the sharks for R595.

→ ROBBEN ISLAND

Tours to the island are run by the **Robben Island Museum** ① *T021-413 4220, www.robben-island.org.za*. The Nelson Mandela Gateway at the Clock Tower Centre is the embarkation and disembarkation point for tours. The Gateway also houses a shop, the ticket office and a small museum with photographic and interactive displays on Apartheid and the rise of African nationalism, open 0730-2100. An air-conditioned catamaran completes the half-hour journey to the island. Tickets cost R220, children under 18 R110. Tours begin with a 45-minute drive around the key sites, including Sobukwe's house, the lime quarry where Mandela was forced to work, the leper cemetery and the houses of former warders. Tours around the Maximum Security Prison are conducted by ex-political prisoners whenever possible, who paint a vivid picture of prison life here. Departures are daily at 0900, 1100 and 1300, and the whole excursion lasts 3½ hours. You must remain with your guide throughout the tour. Be sure to book a day ahead (or several days in peak season) as tickets sell out quickly, and always phone ahead to see if the ferry is running in bad weather. Do not drink any tap water on the island.

Lying 12 km off Green Point's shores, Robben Island is best known as the notorious prison that held many of the ANC's most prominent members, including Nelson Mandela and Walter Sisulu. It was originally named by the Dutch, after the term for seals, 'rob' – actually a misnomer as none are found here. The island's history of occupation started in 1806, when John Murray was granted permission by the British to conduct whaling from the island. During this period the authorities started to use the island as a dumping ground for common convicts; these were brought back to the mainland in 1843, and their accommodation was deemed suitable only for lepers and the mentally ill. These were in turn moved to the mainland between 1913 and 1931, and the island entered a new era as a military base during the Second World War. In 1960 the military passed control of the island over to the Department of Prisons, and it remained a prison until 1996. On 1 December 1999 the island was declared a World Heritage Site by UNESCO.

Robben Island's effectiveness as a prison did not rest simply with the fact that escape was virtually impossible. The authorities anticipated that the idea of 'out of sight, out of mind' would be particularly applicable here, and to a certain extent they were correct. Certainly, its isolation did much to break the spirit of political prisoners, not least Robert Sobukwe's. Sobukwe, the leader of the Pan African Congress, was kept in solitary confinement for nine years. Other political prisoners were spared that at least, although in 1971 they were separated from common law prisoners, as they were deemed a 'bad' influence. Conditions were harsh, with forced hard labour and routine beatings. Much of the daily running of the maximum security prison was designed to reinforce racial divisions: all the wardens, and none of the prisoners, were white; black prisoners, unlike those deemed coloured, had to wear short trousers and were given smaller food rations. Contact with the outside world was virtually non-existent – visitors had to apply for permission six months in advance and were allowed to stay for just half an hour. Newspapers were banned and letters were limited to one every six months.

Yet despite these measures, the B-Section, which housed Mandela and other major political prisoners, became the international focus of the fight against Apartheid. The last political prisoners left the island in 1991.

→ SOUTHERN SUBURBS

Primarily encompassing the more affluent residential areas of Cape Town, the suburbs, stretching southeast from the centre, are an interesting diversion to the usual tourist spots. Although a car is the best way to visit them, it's possible to reach all by train – the Metrorail service between the city centre and Simon's Town runs through the suburbs and there is the option of buying a hop-on hop-off ticket on this line as part of the Southern Line initiative (see page 66); but to get to the sights away from the railway line you'll need a car, or the City Sightseeing bus (page 52), which stops at some.

WOODSTOCK AND OBSERVATORY

The first suburb, less than 3 km from the city centre, is **Woodstock**, a mixed commercial and residential area, and historically a working-class coloured district. Today it is somewhat run down, although the back streets are an attractive mesh of Victorian bungalows, some of which have been taken over by fashionable bars and restaurants, and both Main and Albert roads are dotted with junk and decor shops. Woodstock's most popular attraction is the **Old Biscuit Mill** ① *373-375 Albert Rd, T021-447 8194, www.theoldbiscuitmill.co.za, Mon-Sat 1000-1700*, a converted mill and now home to a variety of 'lifestyle' shops – furniture, interior design and art galleries – and restaurants. The overwhelming reason to come to Woodstock is the **Neigbourgoods Market** ① *T021-448 1438, www.neighbourgoodsmarket. co.za, Sat 0900-1400*, held at the Old Biscuit Mill on a Saturday morning. The stalls sell organic veg, home-made bread, pastries, cupcakes, chutneys, jams, goat's cheese, chocolate and many more delicious goodies. You can also get meals like Indian curries, Mexican wraps, Greek kebabs, sushi and pizza, accompanied by a glass of fizz or a bloody Mary, and sit on sociable trestle tables or hay bales to eat.

After Woodstock, **Observatory** is an appealing area of tightly packed houses, narrow streets and, being close to the university, student hangouts The observatory after which the suburb is named is where Station Road intersects Liesbeeck Parkway. Aside from making astronomical observations the observatory is responsible for accurate standard time in South Africa, and has a seismograph which records earthquakes around the world. Observatory is also where you'll find the **Groot Schuur Hospital**, the site of the world's first heart transplant performed by Professor Christiaan Barnard. The **Heart of Cape Town Museum** ① *Groot Schuur Hospital, Main Rd, Observatory, T021-404 1967, www. heartofcapetown.co.za, 2-hr guided tours run daily at 0900, 1100, 1300 and 1500 and must be pre-booked, R200, children (10-16) R100, under 10 free*, explains the story and has a number of rooms including the two adjoining theatres that were used for the transplant, which took place in 1967. The informative tours go a long way to recreate the tension of the night of 2 December, and the eerie waxwork figures of Barnard and his team are brought to life with a soundtrack of clinking scalpels.

MOWBRAY, ROSEBANK AND RONDEBOSCH

The next suburbs of Mowbray, Rosebank and Rondebosch lie just below the **University of Cape Town (UTC)**. Again, they are popular with students and have a good selection of restaurants and shops. **Mowbray** was originally known as Driekoppen, or three heads, after the murder by three slaves of a European foreman and his wife in 1724. On their capture they were beheaded and their heads impaled on stakes at the farm entrance to act as a deterrent. **Rondebosch**, is well known for being associated with education, and aside from the university, several important schools were founded in the district. The area was also important from a practical point of view: in 1656 Van Riebeeck realized that Company's Garden was exposed to a damaging southeast wind. His first choice of a more sheltered spot was Rondebosch. This proved a success and a grain storage barn was built. Early accounts describe the area as wild country, with the farmers frequently losing livestock to hyenas, lions and leopards – an image that is hard to imagine as you sit in the evening rush hour on Rhodes Drive. Also in Rondebosch is the **Groot Schuur Estate**, the President's official residence and the original residence of the Cape Governor over 200 years ago.

IRMA STERN MUSEUM

ⓘ *Cecil Rd, Rosebank, T021-685 5686, www.irmastern.co.za, Tue-Sat 1000-1700, R10, children (under 16) R5.*

Irma Stern was one of South Africa's pioneering artists and her lovely house displays a mixture of her own works, a collection of artefacts from across Africa and some fine pieces of antique furniture from overseas, including 17th-century Spanish chairs, 19th-century German oak furniture and Swiss *mardi gras* masks. Her portraits are particularly poignant and those of her close friends are superb, while her religious art is rather more disturbing. Stern's studio, complete with paint brushes and palettes, has been left as it was when she died.

RHODES MEMORIAL

ⓘ *Cearly signposted off Rhodes Dr (M3), by the Rondesbosch turning, T021-689 9151, www.rhodesmemorial.co.za, Nov-Apr 0700-1900, May-Oct 0800-1800.*

The imposing granite memorial to Cecil John Rhodes (Cape Prime Minister from 1890 to 1896) was designed by Francis Masey and Sir Herbert Baker. Four bronze lions flank a wide flight of steps which lead up to a Greek Temple. The temple houses an immense bronze head of Rhodes, wrought by JM Swan. Above the head are the words "slave to the spirit and life work of Cecil John Rhodes who loved and served South Africa". At the base of the steps (one for each year of his short 49-year life) is an immense bronze mounted figure of *Physical Energy* given to South Africa by GF Watts, a well-regarded sculptor of the time; the original stands in Hyde Park, London. Other than the memorial, the great attraction here is the magnificent view of the Cape Flats and the southern suburbs. Behind the memorial are a number of popular trails leading up the slopes of Devil's Peak. Also tucked away here is an excellent little tea house (0900-1700) set in a garden of blue hydrangeas that serves breakfasts, light meals and excellent cheesecake and cream teas. Bookings (T021-689 9151) are advised for brunch on summer weekends.

SOUTH OF RONDESBOSCH

By this point the southern suburbs have reached right around Devil's Peak and the shadowy mountains now dominating the views represent an unfamiliar view of Table Mountain. The suburb of **Newlands** backs right up to the slopes of the mountain and is probably best known for being the home to Western Province Rugby Union and the beautiful Newlands cricket Test Ground, now known as Sahara Park. There are several good hotels and guesthouses in the area.

Newlands ① *Boundary Rd, a few minutes' walk from Newlands Station, T021-659 6700, www.newlandstours.co.za, pre-booked tours run Mon-Fri 0900-1700, from R44, children (under 16) R28.* The first official rugby match at Newlands was played in 1890 and the stadium was a venue for 1995 World Cup matches. The first recorded cricket match in Africa took place between officers in the British army in Cape Town in 1808, and the Newlands cricket oval opened in 1888. In 2003 it hosted the Cricket World Cup opening match. There are a number of options here run by Newlands Tours. You can visit the rugby stadium and enter through the players' entrance, see the changing rooms and run through the players' tunnel. At the cricket ground you can walk across the pitch and visit the scorer's and third umpire's booths. Both these can be combined with a tour of the **South Africa Rugby Museum**, a somewhat chaotic collection which commemorates the history of the sport in the country and is also home to the Currie Cup, the premier domestic competition trophy. Great South African rugby moments are shown on TV.

Opposite Newlands and also on Boundary Road, **Josephine Mill** ① *T021-686 4939, www.josephinemill.co.za, Mon-Fri 1000-1600, Sat 1000-1400, R10, milling demonstrations Mon-Fri 1100 and 1500, R20,* the only surviving watermill in Cape Town, has been restored as a working flour mill; note the massive iron waterwheel. The building is in the style of a Cornish red-brick mill, built by a Swede, Jacob Letterstedt in 1840, and named in honour of his Crown Princess, Josephine. The mill is tucked away near the rugby stadium and has a shop selling organic stone-milled flour and bread and a peaceful tea garden and deli.

KIRSTENBOSCH NATIONAL BOTANICAL GARDEN

① *Off Rhodes Dr (M3) and clearly signposted, T021-799 8783, www.sanbi.org, Sep-Mar 0800-1900, Apr-Aug 0800-1800, R37, children (6-17) R10, under 6s free. By far the easiest way of getting here is by car. Otherwise there are trains to the nearest station at Mowbray, 10 mins from the city centre. From here there is an erratic bus service or a very long walk. Alternatively, take a Rikki Taxi – they will pick up and drop off at any time other than rush hour. Most of the organized city tours also include the garden on their itinerary and the City Sightseeing bus stops here.*

Kirstenbosch, 13 km south of the city centre is South Africa's oldest, largest and most exquisite botanical garden. The gardens stretch up the eastern slopes of Table Mountain, merging seamlessly with the fynbos of the steep slopes above. Cecil Rhodes bought Kirstenbosch farm in 1895 and promptly presented the site to the people of South Africa with the intention that it become a botanical garden. It was not until 1913 that it was proclaimed a National Botanical Garden – the Anglo-Boer War had caused the delay. The first director of the gardens was Professor Harold Pearson, who died just three years after the garden's creation. A granite Celtic Cross marks his grave in the Cycad garden. There is a fitting epitaph: "If ye seek his monument, look around you." The real development was under Professor RH Compton, who cared for the gardens for 34 years. The herbarium, named after him, houses over 250,000 specimens, including many rare plants.

A great deal of time and effort has been put into making the gardens accessible to the general public, ensuring they provide pleasure for both serious botanists and families enjoying a day out on the slopes of Table Mountain. In the **Fragrance Garden** herbs and flowers are set out so as to make appreciating their scents effortless. On a warm day, when the volatile oils are released by the plants, there are some rather overpowering aromas. The plaques are also in Braille. The **Dell** follows a beautifully shaded path snaking beneath ferns and along a stream. Indigenous South African herbs can be inspected in the **Medicinal Plants Garden**, each one identified and used by the Khoi and San peoples in the treatment of a variety of ailments. The plants' uses are identified on plaques, and it seems that most ailments are covered – kidney trouble, rheumatics, coughs, cancer, piles and bronchitis. For a sense of the past, it is worth visiting what is known as **Van Riebeeck's Hedge**. Back in 1660 a hedge of wild almond trees (*Brabejum stellatifolium*) was planted by Van Riebeeck as part of a physical boundary to try and prevent cattle rustling. Segments still remain today within the garden. The **Skeleton Path** can be followed all the way to the summit of Table Mountain. It starts off as a stepped path, but becomes fairly steep near the top. It involves a climb up a rocky waterfall; take special care in the wet season.

Perhaps the most enjoyable way of experiencing the gardens is at one of the Sunday sunset concerts held throughout summer. Also available for a small fee are eco-adventure tours, and tours by motorized golf cart. Just beyond the entrance is a shop and café on the courtyard terrace. The shop has the usual collection of curios, along with a good choice of books on South Africa and a selection of indigenous plants. The café serves overpriced sandwiches and cakes; better value and with far nicer views is the **Silver Tree and Fynbos Deli** inside the gardens, which serves good meals (until 2200). And, for a reasonable price, you can have a ready-made picnic with wine and join the Capetonians on the lush lawns.

CAPE TOWN LISTINGS

WHERE TO STAY

$$$$ 15 On Orange, 15 Orange St, City Bowl, T021-430 5302, www.africanpride hotels.com/15-on-orange-hotel. Great location near sights and restaurants, new sleek glass-and-steel hotel with 112 large rooms, all mod cons including DVD player and Wi-Fi, and disabled facilities. Vast 7-storey high central atrium with white marble floors and retro furnishings, bar with snooker table and Table Mountain views, restaurant and luxury spa.

$$$$ Cape Grace, West Quay Rd, V&A Waterfront, driving access is from the Clock Tower side of the Waterfront, T021-410 7100, www.capegrace.com. This has become one of the most luxurious hotels in Cape Town, and an iconic feature of the V&A, with 122 enormous rooms with all mod cons and plush decor, balconies have mountain or harbour views. Service and food is excellent, 2 bars and the celebrated **Signal** restaurant, attractive swimming pool and deck, and there's a lovely rooftop spa.

$$$$ Mount Nelson, 76 Orange St, Gardens, T021-483 1000, City Bowl, www.mountnelsonhotel.co.za. Cape Town's famous colonial hotel which opened in 1899 and has always welcomed celebrity guests, with 209 luxurious rooms in 6 wings overlooking Table Mountain, the parkland-type gardens, or 1 of the 2 vast heated swimming pools. Rates vary widely from R3500-11,000 depending on room and season. The celebrated **Planet Restaurant** serves Cape specialities and contemporary fare to live jazz, while the **Oasis Restaurant** is well worth visiting for the daily cream teas on the veranda.

$$$$ Radisson BLU, Beach Rd, Granger Bay, De Waterkant and Green Point, T021-441 3000, www.radissonblu.com/ hotel-capetown. Quality large hotel in an unbeatable location right on the ocean's edge and a short walk from the V&A. All 177 rooms are spacious with sunny decor and have all mod cons including Wi-Fi. **Tobago's** restaurant and bar is very popular for sundowners and outside tables are set around the stunning infinity pool and there's a state-of-the-art spa and fitness centre.

$$$$ Taj Cape Town, Wale St, City Bowl, T021-819 2000, www.tajhotels.com. Impressive new offering from the Taj luxury hotel group opposite St George's Cathedral; the façades of the old South African Reserve Bank have been kept. 177 palatial rooms, extras include iPod docking stations and international plug sockets, the **The Bombay Brasserie** is a superb Indian restaurant, there's a champagne and oyster bar, gym and spa.

$$$ Cape Heritage Hotel, Heritage Sq, 90 Bree St, City Bowl, T021-424 4646, www.capeheritage.co.za. Charming hotel set in a rambling renovated town house dating from the late 17th century. The 17 huge rooms are individually styled, with muted coloured walls and contemporary decor but retain the high teak ceilings and yellowwood floors. Breakfast is served under a historical vine in the courtyard,

$$$ Grand Daddy, 38 Long St, City Bowl, T021-424 7247, www.granddaddy.co.za. Long St's most eccentric boutique hotel, with 45 rooms, is decorated throughout by local artists and the design element is stunning. Talk of the town are the 7 vintage Airstream trailers (**$$**) on the roof; it's a unique way to sleep in Cape Town. **Daddy Cool** is a sexy and stylish cocktail bar and the **Showroom Cafe** offers good food with an organic and low-calorie slant.

$$-$ The Backpack, 74 New Church St, City Bowl, T021-423 4530, www.backpackers.co.za. Cape Town's first hostel and today one of the most comfortable and best run in town. Set across several houses with spotless dorms, doubles and singles.

Polished wood floors, upmarket decor, tiled courtyard and linked gardens with pool, lovely bar with TV, meals and snacks served throughout the day.

RESTAURANTS

$$$ Africa Café, Heritage Sq, 108 Shortmarket St, City Bowl, T021-422 0221, www.africacafe.co.za. 1800-2300. African-themed restaurant geared at tour groups, offering an excellent introduction to the continent's cuisines. The menu is a set 'feast' and includes 13 dishes from around Africa, such as Egyptian-smoked fish, Kenyan maize patties, Cape Malay mango chicken curry and springbok stew. The price includes as many dishes you like, as well as coffee and dessert. A great experience, but it's pricey and very touristy.

$$$ Aubergine, 39 Barnet St, Gardens, T021-465 4909, www.aubergine.co.za. Tue-Fri 1200-1400, Mon-Sat 1900-2230. Sophisticated and award-winning menu, with a modern slant on classical European dishes such as foie gras and quail, excellent wine list. One of the best restaurants in town, with a stylish shaded courtyard, lounge/bar, good service, and the 3- to 5-course degustation menu is an elaborate affair when wine is paired to food.

$$$ Baia, Victoria Wharf, V&A Waterfront, T021-421 0935, www.baiarestaurant.co.za. 1200-1500, 1900-2300. Fine seafood restaurant spread over 4 terraces with moody, stylish decor and lighting and views of Table Mountain. Expensive but delicious seafood dishes follow a Mozambique theme – try the spicy coconut prawns – and some rare wine vintages.

$$$ Savoy Cabbage, Heritage Sq, 101 Hout St, City Bowl, T021-4242626, www.savoycabbage.co.za. Mon-Fri 1200-1430, Mon-Sat 1900-2230. Widely regarded as one of the best restaurants in Cape Town, serving beautifully prepared contemporary South African cuisine. The menu changes daily, and includes dishes such as gemsbok carpaccio, free-range duck breast and a gorgeous soft-centred chocolate pudding. Good wine list too, especially on reds. Bookings essential.

$$$ Top of the Ritz, Ritz Hotel, Sea Point, T021-439 6988, www.ritzrestaurants.co.za. Daily 1800-2230, Sun lunch 1200-1500. Iconic revolving restaurant on the 21st floor with gorgeous views of Table Bay, Robben Island, Cape Town Stadium and the Sea Point high-rises. The menu is a throwback to the 1970s when it opened – prawn cocktail, lobster bisque chateaubriand and crêpes suzettes. Booking essential.

$$ Mama Africa, 178 Long St, City Bowl, T021-424 8634. Tue-Fri 1200-1600, Mon-Sat 1900-late. Popular restaurant and bar serving 'traditional' African dishes with a great atmosphere and often with live music. Looking a little faded around the edges, but remains popular with tourists, and the food is tasty, despite the notoriously slow service. Centrepiece is a bright green carved mamba-shaped bar.

$$ Quay Four, Quay 4, V&A Waterfront, T021-419 2008, www.quay4.co.za. 1100-2400. Hugely popular tavern and bistro with great views over the water from the broad wooden deck. Seafood is the focus, the calamari and fish and chips served in giant frying pans are excellent value, but also has grills and vegetarian options. Draught beer, and there's often live music in the evening.

$$-$ Chef Pon's Asian Kitchen, 12 Mill St, Gardens, T021-465 5846. Mon-Sat 1800-2230. There's a long menu of favourite dishes from across Asia, and everything arrives freshly cooked and sizzling hot but it's the Thai food that wins hands down. Decor is simple and dark, but cosy on a winter's night, and lingering after your meal is discouraged if they need the table (which they frequently do).

CAPE PENINSULA

The most popular day trip from central Cape Town is a leisurely loop around the Cape Peninsula. The stunning coast road winds its way through the city's swanky suburbs on the Atlantic Seaboard on the western side, down to Cape Point and the Cape of Good Hope at the southern tip of the peninsula, and then up again through the quaint fishing settlements on the False Bay coast on the eastern side. This can be done under your own steam and a day's hire car is an ideal way to explore at your own pace; alternatively, all the tour operators offer the excursion – some take mountain bikes too, for a spot of cycling in the Table Mountain National Park. As well as fine ocean and mountain views, there are a number of attractions to stop for including the boat trip from Hout Bay to see the seals on Duiker Island, the spectacularly scenic Chapman's Peak Drive, climbing to the lighthouse at Cape Point, and the penguins at Boulders Beach. There are also ample places to stop for lunch, be it simple fish and chips or a gourmet meal, and there are many tourist shops, art galleries and roadside stalls to grab your attention along the way.

→ATLANTIC SEABOARD

The Atlantic Seaboard refers to Cape Town's wealthy suburbs on the west side of the peninsula. Exclusive Clifton, Camps Bay and Llandudno have some of Cape Town's most sought after properties and whitewashed modern mansions and luxury apartments with their brilliantly blue swimming pools climb up the hillsides, while the pristine beaches are popular with the beautiful people. Further south the road winds its way above the rocky shoreline and below the magnificent Twelve Apostles, the spine of mountains from the back of Table Mountain, before dropping into Hout Bay and the back end of the Constantia Valley, before continuing south towards Cape Point.

ARRIVING ON THE ATLANTIC SEABOARD
The tour operators take the Atlantic Seaboard route on Cape Peninsula day tours, but a car is a logical option if you want to stop and explore the less visited attractions and the beaches. Some minibus taxis from central Cape Town go beyond Green Point and Sea Point as far as the police station on the main seaside strip of Camps Bay. Golden Arrow buses also ply this route and some (roughly one an hour) continue on to Hout Bay. The **Sightseeing Cape Town** bus (see page 36) goes as far as Hout Bay on its Blue Route. On the False Bay side, there is also the option of taking a leisurely day trip on the train, which goes along a spectacularly scenic route, which in parts couldn't be closer to the sea, from the railway station in central Cape Town as far as Simon's Town. There is a tourism initiative known as the Southern Line – a hop-on hop-off ticket designed for tourists visiting the False Bay villages and sights.

CLIFTON BEACH
Cape Town's best-known beaches stretch along Clifton, and are renowned as the playground of the young and wealthy – this is the place to see and be seen. Other than being hotpots of high society, Clifton's four sheltered beaches are stunning, perfect arches of powder-soft white sand sloping gently into turquoise water. The beaches, reached be a series of winding footpaths, are divided by rocky outcrops and are unimaginatively named First, Second, Third and Fourth. Each has a distinct character – if you're bronzed and

beautiful, head to First Beach. More demure visitors may feel more comfortable on Fourth, which is popular with families and has been an award-winning Blue Flag beach for many years now. The sunbathing and swimming are good on all the beaches and lifeguards are on duty, but note that the water is very cold – usually around 12°C. Most of the relatively small-scale, high-luxury development has been behind the beaches (some impressive houses can be glimpsed from the winding steps leading down). Be warned that there is limited parking in high season, so get here early.

CAMPS BAY

Following the coast south, you soon skirt around a hill and come out over Camps Bay, a long arch of sand backed by the Twelve Apostles. This is one of the most beautiful (and most photographed) beaches in the world and it also has Blue Flag status, but the calm cobalt water belies its chilliness. The sand is also less sheltered than at Clifton, and sunbathing here on a windy day can be painful. But there are other distractions; the beachfront is lined with excellent seafood restaurants, and a sundowner followed by a superb meal is quite the perfect ending to a day in Cape Town.

The drive between Camps Bay and Hout Bay runs along the slopes of the Twelve Apostles and is beautiful. Apart from the turning to Llandudno, there is no easy access to the coast until you reach Hout Bay. **Llandudno** itself is a small, exclusive settlement with only one road in and out and no shops, and a fine beach and excellent surf but again parking can be difficult on a sunny day.

HOUT BAY

Hout Bay, a historical fishing harbour with an attractive beach, attracts swarms of South African families during peak season. Most come for the seafood restaurants and boat trips, but the best reason for heading here is for spectacular Chapman's Peak Drive (see below), which begins just outside town. As the sun sets in the summer months every lay-by along the road is filled with spectators, drink in hand.

Hout Bay itself is fairly attractive, with a busy fishing harbour at the western end of the bay; at the other end is a collection of shops and popular restaurants. By the harbour is a commercial complex known as **Mariners Wharf**, a popular attraction, although looking a little wind-worn these days. It is based upon Fisherman's Wharf in San Francisco, with a whole string of fish and chips restaurants, souvenir shops, boats for hire and **Snoekies Fresh Fish Market**, close to the harbour gates. Even if you're not intending to buy anything it is worth a quick look to see the huge variety of fish that are caught off this coast. Boats run from here to see the seals on **Duiker Island**.

Back in the town, next to the **tourist office** ① *T021-791 8380, www.tourismcapetown. co.za, Mon-Fri 0830-1730, Sat-Sun 0900-1300*, is the **Hout Bay Museum** ① *4 Andrews Rd, T021-790 3474, Tue-Sat 1000-1230, 1400-1630, R5*, with displays on the history of the area, aimed at visiting school groups. More popular with families is **The World of Birds** ① *Valley Rd, T021-790 2730, www.worldofbirds.org.za, daily 0900-1700, R70, children R40*, with over 400 species of birds housed in impressive walk-through aviaries. There's also the **Monkey Jungle**, populated with squirrel monkeys.

CHAPMAN'S PEAK DRIVE

① *T021-791 8220, www.chapmanspeakdrive.co.za, R30 per car, though from the Hout Bay side you can get a day pass for free and drive the first 3 km to stop at the viewpoints, but you must go back the same way.*

Chapman's Peak Drive is a breathtaking 9-km route with 114 curves, carved into the cliffs 600 m above the sea. Not surprisingly, it's a favourite spot for filming car commercials. It was the brainchild of Sir Francis de Waal, a former administrator of the Cape Province (De Waal Drive in central Cape Town is named after him), and work began in 1915 and it was opened in 1922. Unfortunately, rock fall caused it to close in 2000, but, following extensive engineering works including the rigging of giant nets to catch falling rocks and an impressive cutaway section of the road right into the mountainside, it was reopened in 2003, and is now a toll road. The best time to drive along here is close to sunset in the summer, but the views of the craggy coastline and thrashing ocean, and the crescent of white sand at Hout Bay on one side, and the vast stretch of Noordhoek on the other, are recommended at any time. The Drive sometimes closes in bad weather; check its up-to-the-minute status on the website.

→TABLE MOUNTAIN NATIONAL PARK

① *T021-701 8692, www.sanparks.org, www.capepoint.co.za, Oct-Mar 0600-1800, Apr-Sep 0700-1700, R90, children (2-11) R40.*

Formerly the Cape of Good Hope Nature Reserve, this is now part of Table Mountain National Park, and was established to protect the unique flora and fauna of this stretch of coast. In 1928 the area came under threat from developers who were looking to build seaside resorts. Those in favour of a reserve persuaded local families to sell their land, and in 1939 the reserve came into existence. Some game animals were introduced and the land has since been left to its own devices. Today, it is a dramatically wild area of towering cliffs, stupendous ocean views, some excellent hiking and, to top it all off, beautiful, deserted beaches.

ARRIVING IN TABLE MOUNTAIN NATIONAL PARK

Getting there Given its location at the southern tip of the peninsula, you can approach the reserve from two directions: along the False Bay shoreline via Muizenberg and Simon's

Town; or by the quieter M65 via Kommetjie and Scarborough. It is about 70 km from Cape Town centre to the reserve gates. There is no public transport to the reserve.

Getting around The reserve is visited as part of day trips from the city or you can self drive. A **funicular railway** ① *0900-1700, R45 return, R35 single, R20/15 children (6-16), under 6s free*, takes visitors up from the main car park to the original lighthouse. The walk is about 500 m, is fairly steep and takes about 20 minutes. Next to the car park is the **Two Oceans Restaurant** ① *T021-780 9200, www.two-oceans.co.za, 0900-1700*, specializing in seafood and there is also a takeaway cafeteria.

AROUND THE RESERVE

The Cape of Good Hope is an integral part of the Cape Floristic Kingdom, the smallest but richest of the world's six floral kingdoms. A frequently quoted statistic is that within the 7750 ha of the reserve there are as many different plant species as there are in the whole of the British Isles. In addition to all this there are several different species of antelope: eland, bontebok, springbok, cape grysbok, red hartebeest and grey rhebok, as well as the elusive cape mountain zebra, snakes, tortoises and pesky baboons.

Although the strong winds and the low-lying vegetation are not ideal for birds, over 250 species have been recorded here. There are plenty of vantage points where you can watch open-sea birds such as the Cape gannet, shy albatross, Sabine's gull and Cory's shearwater.

CAPE POINT

Cape Point Lighthouse is nothing special in itself, but the climb is well worth it for spectacular views of the peninsula. On a clear day the ocean views stretching all around are incredible – as is the wind, so be sure to hold on to hats and sunglasses. You can take the funicular to the top, but the 20-minute walk allows better views of the coast. There are plenty of viewpoints, linked by a jumble of footpaths.

The first lighthouse came into service in May 1860, but it quickly became apparent that the most prominent point on a clear day was far from ideal in poor weather. It was quite often shrouded in cloud while at sea level all was clear. In 1872 the Lighthouse Commission decided on a lower site, but it was only after the Portuguese ship, the *Lusitania*, struck Bellows Rock in April 1911, that work started on a new lighthouse. This was built just 87 m above sea level, close to Diaz Rock and remains the Cape's most important lighthouse today. The current beam can be seen up to 63 km out to sea, and 18 km out there is a red lamp that warns ships that they are in the danger zone.

From the top point of the railway there are still approximately 120 steps to the old lighthouse where you get some of the finest views. If you are reasonably fit and have a good head for heights, there is a spectacular walk to the modern lighthouse at Diaz Point. From the renovated old lighthouse you can see the path running along the left side of the narrow cliff that makes up the point. The round trip takes about 30 minutes, but do not attempt it if it is windy – the winds around the Cape can reach up to 55 knots.

DIAZ BEACH

Apart from visiting Cape Point and the Cape of Good Hope there are a few minor attractions dotted about the reserve as well as three excellent walks, probably the best way of appreciating the splendour of the coastline. You can drive down to the Cape of Good Hope and then walk to beautiful **Diaz Beach** via Maclear's Peak, a very steep walk in parts. You can also approach Diaz Beach via a 253-step staircase. **Diaz Cross**, further inland, is a memorial to the explorer Bartholomew Diaz. Note how it is painted black on one side so that sailors can see it against the horizon.

HIKING AROUND THE CAPE OF GOOD HOPE

Hiking is encouraged within the reserve. There are several marked paths and maps are available from the information centre. One of the most spectacular routes is along the coast from Rooikrans towards Buffels Bay. Look out for the wreck of *Tania* (1972). On the west side close to Olifants Bay there are a couple of walks; one to the inland lake, Sirkels Vlei, the other along the coast where you can see the wrecks of the *Thomas Tucker* (1942) and *Nolloth* (1964). You can light a braai at one of the designated areas at Buffels Bay and Bordjiesrif, but again watch out for the baboons.

→ FALSE BAY

On the eastern side of the peninsula lies False Bay, a popular stretch of coast thanks to the warmer waters – temperatures can be as much as 8°C higher. The area is also more sheltered and well developed for tourism, although some of the landscape seems almost dull after the Atlantic seaboard. Nevertheless, the area has some excellent beaches and gets busy with domestic tourists in summer. In spring, False Bay is the favoured haunt of calving whales, offering excellent opportunities to see southern right, humpback and Bryde whales. There are also some interesting fishing villages. False Bay is also known for its population of white sharks. A shark watch service operates from Muizenberg, signalling alerts when sharks come in proximity of bathers and surfers.

ARRIVING IN FALSE BAY

False Bay is easily accessed from the city centre by the M3, which runs around the mountain and along the coast. There are also two routes across the mountainous spine linking the roads that hug the coast around the peninsula: you can cross from Noordhoek to Fish Hoek via the M65 and Sun Valley or, further south, take the Red Hill road from Scarborough to Simon's Town. Each route is convenient if your time is short, but the most scenic route is to follow the M65 along the coast from the Atlantic seaboard to False Bay. It is impossible to get lost as there is only one road along the shoreline.

Alternatively, **Metrorail** ① *T0800-65 64 63, www.capemetrorail.co.za, for up-to-date times,* has a line running from central Cape Town through the southern suburbs to Simon's Town – the stretch following False Bay is spectacular and this may be the only place in the world where you can spot whales from a train carriage window. Trains go as far as Simon's Town and leave every 30 minutes, and take one hour and 15 minutes without stops, with the last trains leaving Simon's Town at around 2000. The **Southern Line** initiative is a hop-on hop-off rail ticket designed for tourists. Tickets, R30 for a one-day pass and R50 for a two-day pass, allow unlimited travel on the line and can be purchased from any of the stations and are valid 0830-1600 (outside of commuter hours). Many of the attractions for tourists in Observatory, Newlands, Muizenberg, Kalk Bay, Fish Hoek and Simon's Town, are within walking distance (or no more than a short taxi ride) from each of the stations. Brochures can be downloaded from the Metrorail website.

BOULDERS BEACH

About 2 km south of Simon's Town is a lovely series of little sandy coves surrounded by huge boulders (hence the name).

The attraction here is the colony of African penguins that live and nest between the boulders. **Boulders Visitor Centre** ① *T021-786 2329, www.sanparks.org, Apr-Sep 0800-1700, Oct-Nov and Feb-Mar 0800-18300, Dec-Jan 0700-1930, R45, children (12-16) R35, (2-11) R20*, has been created to protect the little creatures, and their numbers have flourished. One of the highlights of a visit to Cape Town is watching them happily go about their business of swimming, waddling and braying (their characteristic braying was the reason they were, until recently, known as Jackass penguins). This is one of two colonies on mainland Africa, the other being in Betty's Bay (see page 73), and is now a protected area as part of Table Mountain National Park. From the visitor centre a (wheelchair accessible) boardwalk leads you down to viewpoints over the beach. Look out for the little concrete half moon huts that have been installed for the penguins to nest in and look up from the beach where you're likely to see a single penguin contemplating life from the top of a boulder. Every visitor gets a leaflet telling the story of the colony – it started from just two breeding pairs in 1985 and now numbers some 3000 penguins – and the shop sells all things 'penguiney'. If you want to swim, go to the adjoining Seaforth Beach, which is a lovely sandy cove with a picnic lawn and you may bump into a stray penguin in the water.

SIMON'S TOWN

This is the most popular town on False Bay, with a pleasant atmosphere and numerous Victorian buildings lining Main Street. If you want a break from Cape Town, this makes for a good alternative base from which to explore the southern peninsula. It's also a good place to spot whales in False Bay and notice the statue of a real-size southern right whale on the quayside of the waterfront. For information, there's a **tourist office** ① *Simon's Town Museum (below), T021-786 3046, www.simonstown.com, Mon-Fri 1000-1600, Sat 1000-1300.*

Take some time to wander up the hill away from the main road – the quiet, bougainvillea-bedecked houses and cobbled streets with their sea views are a lovely retreat from the bustling beaches. The main swimming spot is **Seaforth Beach**, not far from Boulders. To get there, turn off St George's Street into Seaforth Road after passing the navy block to the left. The swimming is safe, as there is no surf due to offshore rocks which protect the beach. For children there is a water slide and a wooden raft in the water. Look out for some giant pots, a legacy from whaling days, when they were used for melting whale blubber.

Simon's Town is named after Simon van der Stel, who decided that an alternative bay was needed for securing ships in the winter months as Table Bay suffered from the prevailing northwesterly. However, because of the difficult overland access, the bay was little used in the early years. It was not until 1743 that the Dutch East India Company finally built a wooden pier and some barracks here. In 1768 the town transferred into British hands, and following the end of the Napoleonic Wars in Europe, the British decided to turn Simon's Town into a naval base. It remained as such until 1957 and is now a base for the South African Navy. The two-day **Naval Festival** is held in March each year, when some of the ships are opened to the public.

Just before you hit the town centre, the **Simon's Town Museum** ① *Old Residency, Court Rd, T021-786 3046, Mon-Fri 1000-1600, Sat 1000-1300, entry by donation*, has displays related to the town's history as a naval base for the British and South African navies. Several displays are dedicated to Just Nuisance, a great dane who became something of a local hero in the 1930s, who is now Simon's Town unofficial mascot. Also of interest is the **Peoples of Simon's Town Exhibit**, a collection referring to the forcible removal of coloured families from the area in the 1960s and 1970s, photographs, family trees and household goods. The building itself was built in 1777 as the winter residence of the Governor of the Cape.

Nearby, the **South African Naval Museum** ① *Naval Dockyard, St George's St, T021-787 4686, 1000-1600, entry by donation*, includes a collection of model ships, gunnery displays, information on mine-sweeping, a modern submarine control room plus relics from the Martello Tower.

In the centre of town, the **Quayside Centre** is a smart development on St George's Street, next to Jubilee Square in the centre of town, which has greatly enhanced the seafront. Above the shops and restaurants is the comfortable **Quayside Hotel**. Cruises in the harbour can be booked here.

Just round the corner from Jubilee Square, and worth a quick peek, is the **Warrior Toy Museum** ① *St George's St, T021-786 1395, daily 1000-1600, entry by donation*, a tiny museum with an impressive collection of model cars, trains, dolls and toy soldiers. This is a great little place and definitely worth a stop – nostalgic for adults and fun for kids. New and old model cars are also for sale.

The nearby **Heritage Museum** ① *Amlay House, St George's St, T021-786 2302, Tue-Fri 1100-1600, Sat 1100-1300, entry by donation*, faithfully charts the history of the Muslim community in Simon's Town. The town was designated a 'white' area during the Group Area Act and over 7000 people classified as coloured were relocated. The Amlay family were the last to be forcibly removed from Simon's Town in 1975 and were the first to return in 1995. The exhibition consists mainly of pictures and artefacts dating back to the turn of the 20th century.

FISH HOEK

The centre of Fish Hoek with its cheap shops and fish and chip takeaways is fairly unremarkable, but the village is best known for its fine beach – perhaps the best for swimming after Muizenberg – which stretches almost 2 km across the Fish Hoek valley. Swimming is safe at the southern end of the bay, and boogie-boarding and kayaking are also popular. From mid-August to October, there is a good chance of catching a glimpse of whales from here. The valley which stretches behind the town joins with Noordhoek beach on the Atlantic coast. In recent geological times this was flooded and all the lands towards Cape Point were in fact an island.

KALK BAY

Kalk Bay is one of the most attractive settlements on False Bay, with a bustling fishing harbour and a bohemian vibe. The town is named after the lime kilns that produced kalk from shells in the 17th century (the name Kalk is derived from the Dutch for lime). Until the arrival of the railway in 1883, the local fishermen hunted whales, seals and small fish. Today it remains a fishing harbour, worked mainly by a coloured community which somehow escaped the Group Areas Act under Apartheid. Between June and July the harbour is busy with the snoek season – look out for returning deep-sea fishing boats around the middle of the day. In the harbour itself you can see seals, who cheekily hop up to try and get to the fish at the counters. Also at the harbour, **Kalky's**, in a colourful wooden shed, serves up great fish and chips. **Main Road** is an appealing spot, lined with bric-a-brac and antiques shops and a handful of arty cafés. A dozen shops vie for custom – **Kalk Bay Gallery**, **Cape to Cairo** and **Railway House** have the most intriguing offerings. On the other side of the road is Kalk Bay's most popular attraction, the **Brass Bell**, a pub wedged between the railway tracks and the water.

High up behind the town is **Boyes Drive**, an alternative route connecting Kalk Bay with Muizenburg, offering sweeping views of False Bay and it takes just 10 minutes to complete – look out for the signs from Main Road as you head out of Kalk Bay towards Simon's Town.

MUIZENBERG

Travelling out from the city centre on the M3, Muizenberg is the first settlement you reach on False Bay and as such has long been a popular local bathing spot. The Battle of Muizenberg was a small but significant military affair that began in June 1795 and ended three months later with the (first) British occupation of the Cape. Cecil Rhodes bought a holiday cottage here in 1899 and many other wealthy people followed, building some fine Victorian and Edwardian cottages along the back streets and attracting the likes of Agatha Christie and Rudyard Kipling to its shores. Although the resort had decayed significantly over the last decade, various recent regeneration projects have meant that the area is starting to look like its old cheerful self again. The beach certainly remains beautiful: a vast stretch of powdery white sand sloping gently to the water. It is safe for swimming as there is no backwash, and it is very popular with surfers who head out to the bigger breakers. At low tide you can walk into the shallow sea for more than 300 m without having to swim.

The walk along Main Street towards St James is known locally as the **Historic Mile** and will take you past a number of interesting old buildings. Some of these are national monuments, but most are closed to the public. The first of note is the **Station building**, a fine example of art-deco architecture built in 1912. Further along on the right is the thatched and stone squat **Het Post Huijs** (**The Post House**), thought to be the oldest building in False Bay, dating back to 1742 and built by the Dutch East India Company as a toll-house to levy taxes on farmers passing by to sell their produce to ships moored in Simon's Bay. One of the early post holders was Sergeant Muys, from whom Muizenberg is thought to have got its name.

The next building of note is **Rhodes Cottage** ① *246 Main St, T021-788 9140, 1000-1600, entry by donation*, which is surprisingly small and austere for someone as wealthy as Cecil Rhodes. It has been restored and now contains many of his personal items, including his diamond-weighing scale and the chest in which he carried his personal belongings, and there are displays on his life and achievements. It's a pleasant place to wander around, with a lovely garden around the side. This is where he died on 26 March 1902, and his body was transported by train with great ceremony to the Matobo Hills outside Bulawayo in Zimbabwe, where he was buried in a giant rock outcrop. The volunteers that keep the place open make charismatic and enthusiastic guides.

CONSTANTIA

South of Kirstenbosch National Botanical Garden and the city's southern suburbs, lies the verdant area of Constantia and its winelands. This historical district was the first site of winemaking in South Africa and today it is an attractive introduction to the country's wines, as well as offering some fine examples of Cape Dutch architecture. There are five estates here, of which Groot Constantia (see below) is the best known and definitely worth a visit. **Buitenverwachting** ⓘ *T021-794 5190, www.buitenverwachting.co.za*, is a working estate with an excellent restaurant that also offers picnic baskets during the summer (November-April) from 1200-1600. **Klein Constantia** ⓘ *T021-794 5188, www. kleinconstantia.com*, is a beautiful hilly estate with a great tasting centre, and is famed for its dessert wine, Vin de Constance, allegedly Napoleon's favourite wine. **Constantia Uitsig** ⓘ *T021-794 1810, www.constantia-uitsig.com*, has excellent wines, luxury accommodation and two restaurants. **Steenberg** ⓘ *T021-713 2222, www.steenberghotel.com*, also offers superb wines as well as having luxurious lodgings, a good restaurant and a golf course.

GROOT CONSTANTIA

ⓘ *T021-795 5140, www.grootconstantia.co.za, www.iziko.org.za, Mon-Fri 0900-1800, Sat-Sun 1000-1800, free entrance to the main estate and orientation centre, museum 1000-1700, R20, under 18s free, 2 restaurants: Jonkershuis has traditional Cape food; Simon's serves burgers, salads and seafood. Wine tastings at the sales centre, R30 for 5 wines; cheese platters available. Cellar tours every hour on the hour.*

This old wine estate has some of the finest Cape Dutch architecture in South Africa, and with its rolling, vineyard setting and wine-tasting centre is a delightful place to spend an hour or two – although it does get swamped with tour buses in high season.

The main Manor House was originally home to Cape Governor Simon van der Stel between 1699 and 1712. He named the estate after Constantia, the daughter of the company official who had granted the land to him. Before his death, van der Stel planted most of the vines, but it was not until 1778 that the estate became famous for its wines. During this period the estate was unable to meet the demand from Europe, especially France. The house is now a museum full of period furniture and a booklet is available giving a brief description of the objects on show. The magnificent wine cellar behind the main house was designed by the renowned French architect, Louis Thibault, and today has displays on brandy and winemaking. There are two impressive giant oak vats each with a capacity of over 4000 litres. The **Orientation Centre** near the car park has some interesting storyboards on the history of the estate.

CAPE PENINSULA LISTINGS

WHERE TO STAY

$$$$ Cellars-Hohenort Hotel, 93 Brommersulei Rd, Constantia, T021-794 2137, www.cellars-hohenort.com. One of the most luxurious hotels in Cape Town, set in 2 converted manor houses in 3.6 ha of beautiful gardens on a wine estate with views of False Bay. 52 individually decorated spacious suites, 3 excellent restaurants, 3 heated swimming pools, tennis court, 9-hole golf course and spa.

$$$$ Hout Bay Manor, Baviaanskloof, off Main Rd, Hout Bay, T021-790 0116, www.houtbaymanor.com. A beautifully restored manor house built in 1871, with 20 luxury a/c rooms, some with free-standing baths. The decor throughout is stunning and best described as Afro-chic with bright splashes of colour. There's a pool, gorgeous bar and lounge and celebrated **Pure**, restaurant.

$$$$ Steenberg Hotel, Tokai Rd, Constantia, T021-713 2222, www.steenberghotel.com. Luxurious country hotel with 30 elegant, traditional rooms furnished with beautiful antiques, in converted farm buildings overlooking manicured gardens and working vineyards. Swimming pool, gym, spa, and the beautiful 18-hole golf course has sweeping views of False Bay. The award-winning **Catharina's Restaurant** has an excellent reputation.

$$$$ Twelve Apostles, Victoria Rd, T021-437 9000, www.12apostleshotel.com. In a gloriously scenic spot just to the south of Camps Bay, this 70-room 5-star hotel, has a commanding position overlooking the ocean and features an award-winning spa, pool, excellent restaurant, bar that also offers afternoon tea, and a small cinema.

$$$ Quayside Hotel, Jubilee Sq, St George's St, Simon's Town, T021-786 3838, www.ahagroup.co.za/quayside. A smart, modern development in a great central location overlooking the harbour, with 26 spacious rooms, balconies and Wi-Fi, bright and sunny marine blue and white decor, good views of False Bay. No restaurant but within walking distance of restaurants in Jubilee Sq for which you get a voucher for breakfast.

RESTAURANTS

$$$ Black Marlin, Miller's Point, 2 km from Simon's Town, T021-786 1621, www.blackmarlin.co.za. 1200-1600, 1800-2100. Set in an old whaling station, this place is well known for its excellent seafood and is a good lunch stop on the way to or from Cape Point. Fabulous sea views and wide range of fresh seafood – try the delicious crayfish and oysters or the signature kingklip skewers. Great wine list. It can get busy with tour buses in summer.

$$$ La Colombe, Spaanschemat River Rd, Constantia, T021-794 6500, www.constantia-uitsig.com. Mon-Sat 1230-1430, 1930-2130. Excellent French menu with strong Provençal flavours and some Asian influences, and you can expect the likes of rabbit, duck, fish and game dishes, with emphasis on rich sauces, jus and foams. The fine food is paired with wine on the 7-course tasting menus. Also here is the **Constantia Uitsig Restaurant** and the **River Café**.

$$$ The Roundhouse, Kloof Rd, T021-438 4347, www.theroundhouserestaurant.com. Tue-Sat 1200-1600, 1830-2300. High above Camps Bay and also accessed from the city from Kloof Nek Rd, this building has its origins as a guard house built in 1786 and was later a hunting lodge for Lord Charles Somerset. Now well known for its modern French cuisine, sweeping ocean views, and impeccable service.

WHALE COAST

The evocatively named Whale Coast lives up to its title from July to November, when large numbers of whales seek out the sheltered bays along the coast for breeding. Whales can be seen close to the shore from False Bay all the way east to Mossel Bay, but by far the best place for whale spotting is Hermanus as the whales favour the sheltered Walker Bay, and daily sightings are guaranteed in August and September. Elsewhere along the coast there are opportunities to see the fearsome great white shark. There are seaside towns with miles of sandy beaches and rock pools, plus the southernmost point in South Africa, Cape Agulhas.

More than 120 ships have been wrecked along this coast (the first recorded wreck dates from 1673); there are hazardous reefs, headlands and rocks all the way to Cape Infanta and the Breede River estuary. A museum in Bredasdorp traces the misfortunes of the wrecked ships. In addition to whale watching, this coast offers some of the best fishing in South Africa and an opportunity to dive historic shipwrecks.

→ ARRIVING ON WHALE COAST

GETTING THERE AND MOVING ON

It's easiest to rent a car and self-drive from Cape Town south along the Whale Coast. It takes about 2½ hours to drive from Cape Town to Hermanus. None of the three major coach companies runs a coastal service via Hermanus, although the hop-on hop-off Baz Bus (www.bazbus.com, see page 276) runs along the N2 and stops at Bot River, which is 23 km from Hermanus.

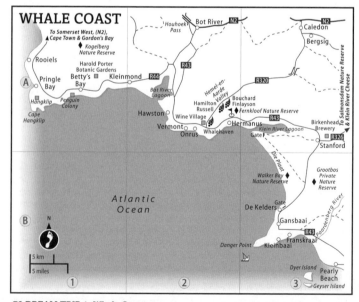

If you don't have a car, the Baz Bus comes into its own when you head further east along the Garden Route (see page 82) as the N2 hugs the coast, collecting and dropping off passengers at their chosen hostel.

→ GORDON'S BAY TO HERMANUS

The most beautiful and exhilarating stretch of the coast is between Gordon's Bay and Hermanus, where the mountains plunge into the ocean forming a coastline of steep cliffs, sandy coves, dangerous headlands and natural harbours. This route is often compared to the spectacular Chapman's Peak Drive on the Cape Peninsula, and rightly so. This is an area of much beauty and also botanical significance and along with Table Mountain National Park, is part of the UNESCO-declared Cape Floral Kingdom. It's known for its fynbos and over 1700 plant species have been recorded here.

GORDON'S BAY, ROOIELS AND PRINGLE BAY

Set in the lee of the Hottentots Holland Mountains at the eastern end of False Bay, away from the more glamorous beaches of Cape Town, is the popular family seaside resort of Gordon's Bay. There are two sandy beaches, **Bikini** (which has been awarded Blue Flag status) and **Main**, both of which are safe for swimmers. The rocky shoreline, a short walk from the seafront, is popular for fishing. The most likely catch includes mackerel, steenbras and kabeljou. The beach road is lined with a number of seafood restaurants and this is a popular lunch spot at the weekends for people from Cape Town.

Following the R44 south, the first small coastal resort after Gordon's Bay is **Rooiels** (19 km), a cluster of holiday homes at the mouth of a small river. The beach has a strong backwash, so be wary if children are swimming. There's a large troop of chacma baboons in this region that move between Rooiels and Betty's Bay and they can sometimes be seen on the beach. Continuing towards Hermanus, the road leaves its precipitous course and climbs the hills inland. After 5 km turn right to **Pringle Bay**, which is dominated by a large rock outcrop known as the Hangklip, 454 m. This is the rock you see when standing by the lighthouse at Cape Point looking across False Bay. Hangklip was formerly known as 'Cabo Falso' ('false cape'), because of its resemblance to Cape Point. It prompted sailors from the east to turn north earlier than they should have done into what is now known as False Bay. The gravel loop road around **Cape Hangklip** is a scenic distraction; another track leads to Hangklip. The road rejoins the R44 just before Silver Sands.

BETTY'S BAY

This small holiday village, midway between Strand and Hermanus, is known for its penguin colony and botanical garden. The community was named after Betty Youlden, the daughter of a local businessman who had plans to develop the Cape Hangklip area in the 1930s. Fortunately little came of the idea and today the village remains an untidy collection of holiday homes in a beautiful location. At Stony Point there is a **reserve** ① *0900-1700, R10 per person*, to protect a small breeding colony of African jackass penguins, one of the few places where you are guaranteed to see these birds breeding on the mainland. A boardwalk allows visitors good views of the penguins without disturbing them. Also here are the remains of a whaling station plus the hulk of a whaler, the *Balena*. Behind the village are the well-known **Harold Porter Botanic Gardens**, worth a visit if time permits. Along the main beach is another area of protected land, the **HF Verwoerd Coastal**

Reserve. There is safe swimming close to the kelp beds, and the dunes above Silver Sands are a popular spot for sandboarding.

HAROLD PORTER BOTANIC GARDENS

ⓘ *Off the R44, T028-272 9311, www.sanbi.org, Mon-Fri 0800-1630, Sat-Sun 0800-1700, R16, children (5-16) R10, Sugarbird Tearoom, Leopard's Kloof Restaurant, and gift shop, 0900-1630.* This garden, lying between mountains and coast, was originally acquired in 1938 by Harold Porter, a keen conservationist. In his will he bequeathed the grounds to the nation. There are 10 ha of cultivated fynbos garden and a further 191 ha of natural fynbos which has been allowed to flourish undisturbed. [Fynbos is the term given to a type of vegetation that is dominated by shrubs and comprises species unique to South Africa's southwestern and southern Cape.] The reserve incorporates the whole catchment area of the Dawidskraal River. The garden has many fynbos species, including proteas, ericas, legumes, buchus and brunias. Another draw is the chance of seeing red disa flowering in its natural habitat – this usually occurs from late December to late January. More than 88 species of bird have been identified; of special interest are the orange-breasted sunbird and the rare protea canary, which is only seen in fynbos environments.

KLEINMOND, VERMONT AND ONRUS

Kleinmond is a popular summer resort in Sandown Bay that has been frequented by the wheat farmers of the interior since 1861 and is today a sizeable resort. Exercise caution when swimming at Kleinmond as the sandy beach is steep; children should be watched at all times. The name Kleinmond refers to the 'small mouth' of the Bot River lagoon. The settlement is overlooked by the magnificent Kogelberg Mountains which in the spring are full of flowering proteas. Information is available from the helpful **Hangklip-Kleinmond Tourism Bureau** ⓘ *signposted, 14 Harbour Rd, just off the R44, T028-271 5657, www.ecoscape. org.za, Mon-Fri 0830-1700, Sat 0900-1400, Sun 1000-1400.* To the east of the town is the Bot River Lagoon, a popular sailing and canoeing area. Where the Bot River meets the sea is a large marsh which is home to thousands of waterfowl, especially at low tide. The more common species are spoonbills, herons, pelicans, gulls, terns, kingfishers and geese and a pair of fish eagles breed at the lagoon. There is also a small herd of wild horses that roam the marshlands; after several attempts to cull them in the 1950s, they are now protected.

After Kleinmond the R44 joins the R43, which then continues along the coast to the next sizeable settlements of Vermont and Onrus, these days more or less suburbs of Hermanus, before arriving in Hermanus proper. **Vermont**, named after the American state, was founded by CJ Krige who became the first speaker of the South African parliament. The beach here is sheltered by high dunes and is safe for children. **Onrus**, meaning 'restless', lying on the east bank of the mouth of the Onrus River, was named by the first European settlers because of the perpetual noise made by the waves along the rocky coastline. The Onrus River forms a small lagoon with a short sandy beach which is also safe for children to swim from. The beach is popular with surfers too.

Hermanus has grown from a rustic fishing village to a much-visited tourist resort famed for its superb whale watching. It is the self-proclaimed world's best land-based whale-watching site, and indeed Walker Bay is host to impressive numbers of whales during the calving season (July to November). However, don't expect any private viewings – Hermanus is very popular and has a steady flow of binocular-clutching visitors. While this means it can get very busy, there is also a good range of accommodation and restaurants, making it a great base for exploring the quieter reaches of the Overberg and, while you may find it far too crowded at Christmas, at other times it reverts to its small-town calm. Alternatively, being only a few hours from Cape Town, Hermanus is an easy day trip from the city.

ARRIVING IN HERMANUS

Hermanus is 120 km from Cape Town (via N2). Despite being a popular destination, none of the three major coach companies runs a service via Hermanus. One of the easiest ways to visit, if you don't have a car, is to travel on the **Baz Bus** from Cape Town to Bot River on the N2, which is 23 km from Hermanus. From here you can arrange to be collected by your hosts for a small fee, but this must be arranged in advance.

Hermanus Tourism ① *Old Station Building, Mitchell St, T028-312 2629, www. hermanus.co.za, Mon-Fri 0800-1800, Sat 0900-1700, Sun 0900-1500 (shorter hours in winter)*, is extremely helpful and has lots of information on the surrounding area, plus an accommodation booking service.

BACKGROUND

The town is named after Hermanus Pieters, an old soldier who set up camp in the bay while looking for better pastures for his animals during the hot summer months. The presence of

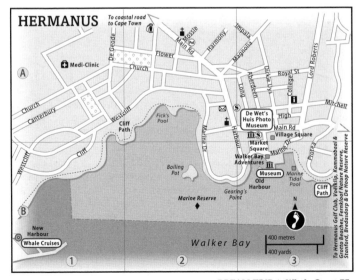

a freshwater spring persuaded him to spend the summer here. Soon other farmers arrived with their families from the interior. Almost by accident it became a holiday destination – the herds required little attention, so the men turned their attention to fishing while the women and children enjoyed themselves on the sandy beaches. When the farmers returned inland to the winter pastures, it was the fishermen who remained and settled here.

In the 1920s the town gained a reputation as an excellent location for convalescing, and even doctors from Harley Street in London were recommending the 'champagne air' of Hermanus. As it became popular with the gentry, so suitably smart hotels were built to accommodate them. After the Second World War the construction of a new harbour stimulated the expansion of the fishing industry and there are now three canning factories in Walker Bay.

PLACES IN HERMANUS

The **Old Harbour** is a national monument and a focal point for tourist activities. A ramp leads down the cliff to the attractive old jetty and a group of restored fishermen's cottages, including the **Old Harbour Museum** ① *T028-312 1475, www.old-harbour-museum.co.za, Mon-Sat 0900-1300, 1400-1700, R15, children (under 12) R10.* The displays are based on the local fishing industry and include models of fish, a whale skeleton, some shark jaws, fish tanks and early fishing equipment. One of the most interesting features is the recordings of calls between whales. There are also telescopes to watch the whales further out. An information plaque helps identify what you see. Outside the museum on the harbour ramp is a collection of small restored fishing boats, the earliest dating from 1855. Also on show are the drying racks for small fish and cement tables which were once used for gutting fish.

The **De Wet's Huis Photo Museum** ① *Market Sq, T028-313 0418, Mon-Fri 0900-1300, 1400-1700, Sat 0800-1300, 1400-1600, entry fee to the Old Harbour Museum covers this, and you can also pay the fee here,* houses an interesting collection of photography depicting the historical development of Hermanus. The building is interesting in itself as it was a Sunday school next to the Dutch Reformed Church, and it was carefully dismantled stone by stone and re-erected in Market Square.

Outside the old harbour is a memorial to those who died in the First World War. Set in the stonework is a barometer and the words "to help to protect the lives of present and future fishermen". Either side of the beehive-shaped monument are two ship's cannons. The new harbour, to the west of the old harbour in Westcliff, is still a busy fishing port. It's a great idea to head down to the dockside to buy fresh crayfish, mussels or line-caught fish from the fish shop. The staff will be happy to advise you on how best to cook your selection.

WALKS AROUND HERMANUS

The excellent **Cliff Path** starts at the new harbour in Westcliff in the west and follows the shore all the way round Walker Bay to the mouth of the Klein River in the east, a distance of just over 10 km. Between cliffs the path goes through stands of milkwood trees and takes you around the sandy beaches. The most popular viewpoints are Dreunkrans, Fick's Pool, Gearing's Point, the Old Harbour, Die Gang, Siever's Punt, Kwaaiwater and Platbank. On an ideal day allow at least a morning for the walk. Bench seats are provided at the prime viewpoints, which make them good spots for a picnic.

ON THE ROAD

The WWF acknowledges Hermanus as one of the 12 best places in the world to view whales. It is the ideal destination if you wish to see whales from land without bobbing around in a boat. The town promotes itself as the 'heart of the Whale Coast', and during the season most visitors should not be disappointed. The town's advantage is that whales can come very close to the shore. The combination of low cliffs and deep water at the base of the cliffs means that you are able to look down from above into clear water and see the outlines of whales from as close as 10 m.

To add to the excitement there is a whale crier who between 1000 and 1600 during September and October strolls around the town centre blowing a kelp horn to announce the arrival of each whale in Walker Bay. The whale crier is easily identified: he wears a giant Bavarian-style hat and carries a sandwich board which records the daily sightings of whales from different vantage points around Walker Bay. You can phone him directly on his cell phone, T079-301 4665 to ask if there are whales in the bay.

The first southern right whales start to appear in Walker Bay from June onwards. By the end of December most have returned to the southern oceans. The whales migrate north to escape heavy winter storms in the oceans around Antarctica. In August and September most of the calves are born in the calm sheltered bays, where the cows then stay with their young for a further two months. They can travel up to 2000 km to and from Antarctica on this continuous annual cycle. Out of an estimated world population of only 7000 southern right whales, up to 80 have been recorded mating and calving in Walker Bay. The best months are September and October when daily sightings are almost guaranteed. You would be unlucky not to see some sign of whale action during this period, though of course they are just as likely to be in the middle of the bay as up close to one of the vantage points along the cliff path.

The southern right whale is distinguished from other whales by its V-shaped 'blow', produced by a pair of blowholes, and callosities which appear randomly on and around the oval head. The callosities are growths of tough skin in patterns which help to identify individuals. Southern right whales are basically black with occasional streaks of grey or white on the back. Their flippers are short, broad and almost square. They are thought to live for up to 100 years, and a fully grown adult can weigh as much as 80 metric tonnes.

They are so-named because they were regarded as the 'right' whale to catch. The carcass yielded large quantities of oil and baleen, and the task of collecting the booty was made all the more easy by the fact that the whale floated in the water when killed. The northern right whale is virtually extinct, and the southern right has shown only a slight increase in numbers since international legislation was introduced to protect the species. The South African coastline is the most likely place in the world to see them in coastal waters.

BEACHES

There are some good beaches a short distance in either direction from the town centre. The best beaches to the west are found at Onrus and Vermont (see page 74). Heading east towards Stanford and Gansbaai, there are long, open beaches or secluded coves with patches of sand and rock pools. **Grotto Beach** is the largest, best developed and most popular for swimming and is one of South Africa's many Blue Flag beaches. The fine white sands stretch beyond the Klein River Lagoon, and there are changing facilities, a restaurant

FESTIVALS
Hermanus

August Hermanus Food and Wine Festival, www.hermanuswineandfood. co.za. Wine tasting from over 70 vineyards, plus cheese, olives and sushi in the gourmet food tent, and a coffee and brandy tasting lounge.

September Hermanus Whale Festival, T028-313 0928, www.whalefestival.co.za. Primarily an arts festival which attracts theatre and singing acts along with children's events and a craft market, and also the best time of the year to spot whales in Walker Bay.

and a beach shop. Slightly closer to the town centre is **Voëlklip Beach**, a little run down, but with well-kept lawns behind the sand. Conditions are good for swimming and surfing. The most popular spot for surfers is **Kammabaai** next door to Voëlklip beach. There are braai facilities under the shade of some milkwood trees.

FERNKLOOF NATURE RESERVE
① *T028-313 8100, www.fernkloof.com, 24 hrs, free. The visitor centre, 500 m from the entrance, has a display of the most common plants you are likely to see when walking in the reserve. All the hiking trails start from here.*

Set in the hills behind Hermanus, the reserve has a 60-km network of trails through an area rich in protea and coastal fynbos. Access is from the east end of Hermanus – just before the Main Road crosses Mossel River, turn up Fir Street. The reserve gates are just beyond the botanical society buildings. The diversity of plants in the reserve is due to the long period it has been under protection, plus its range of elevation from 60 to 850 m. With such a varied plant population, there is also a wide range of bird and animal species including mongoose, dassie and baboon. Higher up in the mountains, look out for breeding black eagles. Small patches of indigenous forest remain in some of the moist ravines.

HERMANUS WINE ROUTE
Hidden away in the **Hemel-en-Aarde Valley** behind Hermanus are a few vineyards producing some surprisingly good wines, mostly Burgundy varieties based around Pinot Noir and Chardonnay grapes. Rarely crowded, three vineyards are open to the public and have tastings in their cellars. **Hamilton Russell Vineyards** ① *T028-312 3595, www. hamiltonrussellvineyards.com, sales and tastings: Mon-Fri, 0900-1700, Sat-Sun 0900-1300*, is the oldest and one of the more picturesque estates and dubs itself both the most southerly wine estate in Africa and the closest to the sea. The cellar and tasting room are set beside a small trout lake. To get there follow the R43 out of Hermanus towards Cape Town, after 2 km turn towards Caledon, R320, then turn right 5 km along this gravel road.

→SWELLENDAM AND AROUND

Founded in 1745, Swellendam is the third oldest European town in South Africa, and it is also one of its most picturesque. The main centre bears witness to its age with an avenue of mature oak trees and whitewashed Cape Dutch homesteads. Unfortunately, before the town fully appreciated their inherent charm and tourist potential, many of the trees and older buildings were knocked down in 1974 to widen the main street. Nevertheless, the town is very pretty and has an appealing, quiet atmosphere, which, combined with the rural setting and beautiful views, makes it a very pleasant spot to spend a day or two. Swellendam also acts as an important base for exploring the region, with the Breede River Valley, the Little Karoo and the coast all within easy reach, and it is roughly halfway between Cape Town and the Garden Route.

Tourist information is available at **Swellendam Tourism** ① *Oefeningshuis, Voortrek St, T028-514 2770, www.swellendamtourism.co.za, Mon-Fri 0900-1300, 1400-1700, Sat 0900-1200*. This office produces a leaflet called *Swellendam Treasures*, which outlines the interesting Cape Dutch buildings still standing today.

BACKGROUND

Swellendam started as a trading outpost for the Dutch East India Company. The new settlement was named after Governor Hendrik Swellengrebel and his wife, Ten Damme. Once established, all sorts of characters passed through looking for their fortunes or more land. One of the most successful was Joseph Barry who, in the 1800s, had a virtual monopoly on all trade between Cape Town and the new settlements in the Overberg and Little Karoo.

In 1795 a particularly strange event took place. Just at the point when British soldiers were bringing an end to Dutch rule in the Cape, the burghers of Swellendam declared themselves to be an independent republic, in a reaction to the mal-administration and corruption of the Dutch East India Company. Hermanus Steyn was president from 17 June to 4 November 1795 but, once the British had set up a new regime in Cape Town, the republic was quietly forgotten about. During the 19th century the town prospered and grew as the agricultural sector gradually expanded. This came to an abrupt halt in May 1865, when a fire that started in a baker's destroyed 40 of the town's finest old buildings. Even greater harm was caused by a prolonged drought and when, in 1866, the influential Barry Empire was declared bankrupt the whole region's fortunes declined. Today the town is a prosperous community, and many of the old buildings are still standing, or have been restored.

PLACES IN SWELLENDAM

Of all the old Cape buildings in town the **Drostdy Museum** ① *18 Swellengrebel St, T028-514 1138, www.drostdymuseum.com, Mon-Fri 0900-1645, Sat-Sun 1000-1545, R15, children (6-16) R8, under 6 free, which covers entrance to a number of buildings*, is the most impressive and is often described as one of the country's great architectural treasures. The main building dates from 1747, built as the official residence and seat for the local magistrate or *landdrost*. Originally built in the shape of a T, the addition of two wings changed the form to an H. Inside, some of the floors have been preserved; what was the lounge has a lime-sand floor, while the kitchen floor is made from cow dung, which helps keep the room cool. The museum concentrates on local history, with a well-preserved collection of 18th- and 19th-century furniture. Within the grounds is a restored Victorian cottage, **Mayville**, which has an antique rose garden plus the original gazebo and is today home to a coffee shop.

Close by is an open-air display, on the Crafts Green, of many of the early farm tools, charcoal burners, wagons and a horse-driven mill complete with threshing floor. Opposite the museum is the **Old Gaol** ① *T028-514 3847*, which housed both prisoners and local government officials, including the jailer who was also the postmaster. In the middle of all the cells was one without windows, known as the 'black hole'. Today, this is a local arts and crafts centre, with a good café.

Not far from the town centre are more restored buildings from the town's early days. The **Oefeningshuis** (1838) first served as a place for the religious instruction of freed slaves;

it now houses the tourist office. Note the painted plaster clock face, which reads 1215, set above a working clock. This was designed for illiterate churchgoers – if the painted face was the same as the clock's, it was time for service. Worth a look is the fine, domineering **Dutch Reformed Church**. This large whitewashed building has a tall central clock tower and a mix of architectural styles. Just next to the church, on **Church Square**, are some fine examples of early two-storey town houses built by wealthy farmers who used to visit the town for holy communion. The square had to be large enough to hold their ox wagons. Another grand town house is the **Auld House** dating from 1802 which for many years was the family home for the Overberg trader, Joseph Barry. Inside is some furniture, originally fitted on a steamer which used to sail between Cape Town and Port Beaufort. Also worth a visit is the small **Church of St Luke** built in 1865. Finally, look out for the shop **Buirski & Co**, built in 1880. It has one of the finest examples of Victorian wrought-iron balconies and fittings in the town.

Swellendam is an ideal base for exploring this part of the Overberg. Close by is the small Bontebok National Park, and the larger Marloth Nature Reserve. They have only simple accommodation and both can easily be visited on a day trip.

BONTEBOK NATIONAL PARK

ⓘ *6 km from Swellendam, the turning off the N2 is clearly signposted, on the George side of Swellendam and there is a 5-km gravel road from the highway to the entrance, T028-514 2735, www.sanparks.org, Oct-Apr 0700-1900, May-Sep 0700-1800, R60, children (under 16) R30.*
Although this is one of South Africa's 21 national parks, it has less of interest than other parks. Nevertheless, it is a good place to spot several species of antelope, and has a pleasant riverside setting. Most of the park is accessible by car and the two loops can be driven within an hour or two, and there are two 2-km self-guided nature trails from the rest camp. Swimming and fishing are both possible in the Breede River, but only within the confines of the campsite. An angling licence must be shown.

Background At the beginning of the 20th century the bontebok was the rarest species of antelope in Africa. It had been hunted and driven off its natural habitat by the settler farmers in the Overberg. Fortunately, something even scarcer came to their rescue – a group of local conservation-minded farmers, who recognized the need to set up a protected area to save the remaining animals. In 1931 the first reserve was established, but it was not until the herd was moved to a more suitable environment beside the Breede River in 1960 that the numbers started to recover significantly. This has proved to be a success but, although no longer endangered, there are still not many places where the bontebok can be seen in the wild. Today, there are about 200 bontebok in the park and other antelope indigenous to the Overberg have been introduced to the reserve, including red hartebeest, steenbok and duiker plus the rare Cape mountain zebra. Furthermore, the Breede River provides a perfect setting for the Cape clawless otter. Bird species number about 200, and include blue crane, spurwing goose, secretary bird, Stanley's buzzard, and sunbirds and cuckoos may be seen around the office and rest camp.

WHALE COAST LISTINGS

WHERE TO STAY

Hermanus

$$$$ The Marine, Marine Drive, T028-313 1000, www.marine-hermanus.co.za. Part of the **Relais & Chateaux** group, a historic hotel and one of the finest in the country. 42 luxurious rooms, some with stunning ocean views, all with exceptionally fine furnishings – silk curtains, plush carpets, 4-poster beds and marble bathrooms. Also has a spa, heated pool, shop, internet and 2 restaurants; the seafood restaurant has won many awards.

$$$ Quarters, 5 Harbour Rd, T028-313 7700, www.quarters.co.za. Contemporary boutique hotel overlooking the old harbour and ocean, 18 smart rooms with a/c, Wi-Fi and DSTV, most with balconies and some with kitchenettes, rooftop wooden deck and pool, spa treatments in rooms, breakfast and an easy stroll to restaurants.

Swellendam and around

$$$ Klippe Rivier Country House, from the N2 take the R60, left at crossroads, 2 km, T028-514 3341, www.klipperivier.

com. Restored Cape Dutch homestead (1820) with 6 large rooms with brass beds, wooden floors, some with cosy fireplaces and under thatch, superb restaurant, swimming pool, no children under 8.

$$ Lang Elsie's Kraal Rest Camp, Bontebok National Park, reservations through **SANParks**, T012-428 9111, www.sanparks.org. For cancellations and bookings under 72 hrs, and campsite reservations, contact reception, T028-514 2735. Pleasant location next to the Breede River, 10 self-catering chalets sleeping 4, 2 of which are wheelchair accessible, good views of the Langeberg Mountains from the outside terraces, shop at reception sells some groceries and beer but stock up on fresh food in Swellendam.

$$ Old Mill Guest House, 241 and 243 Voortrek St, T028-514 2790, www.oldmill.co.za. A beautiful listed building set in a spacious garden with a stream flowing through, 6 characterful rooms with DSTV and fireplaces set in outbuildings such as the old watermill, superb meals served in the restaurant.

RESTAURANTS

Hermanus

$$$ The Burgundy, Market Sq, Marine Drive, T028-312 2800, www.burgundy restaurant.co.za. 0830-1700, 1900-2200. Restored rural cottage set back from the old harbour. One of the top restaurants in town but relaxed, with tables spilling onto a shady terrace outside. Excellent seafood including superb grilled crayfish and good poultry too like chicken stuffed with dates or duck with orange sauce.

$$ Bientang's Cave, access is via steps from the car park on Marine Drive, between the Market Sq and **The Marine**, T028-312 3454, www.bientangscave.com. Year-round 0900-1600, whale season (Jul-Nov) 1900-2130. The name doesn't lie, it's an actual

cave with an extended deck overlooking the waves. Superb spot for whale watching during season. Excellent seafood buffets and famous bouillabaisse soup, simple wood benches and long tables, very popular, book ahead.

Swellendam and around

$$$ Herberg Roosjie van de Kaap, 5 Drostdy St, T028-514 3001, www.roosjevan dekaap.com. Tue-Sun 1900-2130. Opposite the Old Drostdy and Swellendam's original inn, with cosy atmosphere in a candlelit room with thick walls and a low reed ceiling, superb gourmet South African fare, steaks and seafood, fine wines. Also has 6 comfortable B&B rooms (**$$**) around a pool.

GARDEN ROUTE

The Garden Route is probably South Africa's most celebrated area, a stretch of coast heralded as one of the country's highlights. The publicity it receives has made it hugely popular and few visitors to Cape Town miss it. The area is undeniably beautiful: a 200-km stretch of rugged coast backed by mountains, with long stretches of sand, nature reserves, leafy forests and tourist-friendly seaside towns. Officially the route runs from Heidelberg in the west to the Tsitsikamma Forest in the east, though the most popular stretch is the coastal section from Mossel Bay to the Garden Route National Park (Tsitsikamma Section). The region is separated from the interior by the Tsitsikamma and Outeniqua mountain ranges. In contrast to the dry and treeless area of the Karoo on the interior side of the mountains, rain falls all year round on the Garden Route, and the ocean-facing mountain slopes are covered with luxuriant forests. It is this dramatic change in landscape, which occurs over a distance of no more than 20 km, that prompted people to refer to the area as the Garden Route.

The larger towns, such as Plettenberg Bay and Knysna, are highly developed tourist resorts, while other areas offer untouched wilderness and wonderful hikes, including one of the most famous in the country, the Otter Trail. If hiking isn't your scene, the beaches are stunning, offering a mix of peaceful seaside villages and livelier surfer spots, and there are various attractions hugging the N2 to distract the motorist. Finally, the Garden Route is coming into its own as an adventure destination and there are numerous activities on offer from bungee jumping to mountain biking.

→ARRIVING ON THE GARDEN ROUTE

GETTING THERE AND MOVING ON
The Garden Route is served by George Airport at the western end and Port Elizabeth Airport at the eastern end. Flights link both these with Cape Town and Johannesburg. If time is limited you could, drive from Cape Town, drop off the car in Port Elizabeth and fly back or onwards from there. Otherwise, you can head back on R62 via Oudtshoorn, the Breede River valley and the Winelands.

By road, the most direct route from Cape Town to the Garden Route is along the N2; it's an easy 365-km drive and, if you aren't stopping off at Hermanus and the Whale Coast, you can break your journey for lunch in the attractive town of Swellendam.

GETTING AROUND
To get the most out of the Garden Route you really need a car, and whilst it's quite easy to drive the full length of the Garden Route in a day, most visitors either choose a base for exploring the area, or spend a day or two in several places of interest along the way. Many of the attractions are in between the major resorts so it's good to have the flexibility to stop when you want. The **Baz Bus** offers a very adequate service and drops and picks up at Garden Route backpackers' hostels every day. Mainline buses also operate a daily service, but most departures and arrivals are in the middle of the night and it's not as economical as the **Baz Bus**.

BEST TIME TO VISIT
The area's popularity means that good-value accommodation is difficult to find, and gets booked up months in advance, especially during peak season. It is advisable to avoid the

There are a number of organized tours for exploring the Garden Route which start and finish in Cape Town. For those on a budget and short of time, the **Bok Bus**, T082-3201979, www.bokbus.com, offers comprehensive three- to seven-day budget tours of all the major attractions along the Garden Route. Accommodation is in hostels or you can upgrade to a guesthouse. Prices start at R4250 for the standard five-day tour and includes breakfasts, most dinners and entrance fees. There are numerous other coach and minibus operators running short tours from Cape Town along the Garden Route that appeal to a wide range of age groups and offer a variety of accommodation alternatives depending on budget. These include: **African Eagle**, T021-464 4266, www.daytours.co.za. **Cape Rainbow**, T021-551 5465, www.caperainbow.com. **Eco-Tours**, T021-788 5741, www.ecotourssa.co.za. **Springbok Atlas**, T021-460 4700, www.springbokatlas.co.za.

area during the two weeks over Christmas and the New Year, and at Easter. For the rest of the school holidays most of the self-catering accommodation might be fully booked, but hotels and bed and breakfasts should have a free room – call in advance to be sure. For more information about the Garden Route visit www.gardenroute.co.za or www.gardenroute.org.za. The regional towns have tourist offices, and the branches of Cape Town Tourism can provide comprehensive information (see page 36).

→MOSSEL BAY

Built along a rocky peninsula which provides sheltered swimming and mooring in the bay, Mossel Bay is one of the larger and less appealing seaside towns along the Garden Route. Nevertheless, during the school holidays, the town is packed with domestic visitors. A fact often overlooked in promotional literature is that since the discovery of offshore oil deposits, Mossel Bay is also the home of the ugly Mossgas natural gas refinery and a multitude of oil storage tanks. The town has a number of Portuguese flags and names dotted around, thanks to the first European to anchor in the bay – Bartolomeu Dias, who landed in February 1488, followed by Vasco da Gama, who moored in the bay in 1497. The bay's safe anchorage and freshwater spring ensured that it became a regular stopping-off point for other seafarers. The town was named by a Dutch trader, Cornelis de Houtman, who in 1595 found a pile of mussel shells in a cave below the present lighthouse.

ARRIVING IN MOSSEL BAY
Getting there All mainline buses stop at the Shell Truck Stop at Voorbaai, on the N2 7 km from Mossel Bay. The **Baz Bus** is the only service that goes right into town.

Tourist information Mossel Bay Tourism Bureau ① *corner of Church and Market streets, T044-691 1067, www.visitmosselbay.co.za, Mon-Fri 0800-1800, Sat-Sun 0900-1600*, provides information and acts as a central reservations office for accommodation.

PLACES IN MOSSEL BAY
Bartolomeu Dias Museum Complex ① *T044-691 1067, www.diasmuseum.co.za, Mon-Fri 0900-1645, Sat-Sun 0900-1545, R2, children (under 12) R5.* Here you'll find the Culture

Museum, the Shell Museum, an Aquarium, the Maritime Museum, some Malay graves, and the original freshwater spring that attracted the early sailors and which still flows into a small dam. There's also a tea shop on site in a restored 1830s cottage. The displays in the Maritime Museum are arranged around a full-size replica of Bartolomeu Dias's caravel (which you can climb aboard for an extra fee). Also here is a tree with a fascinating past, the **Post Office Tree**, a giant milkwood situated close to the freshwater spring. History relates that in 1500 a letter was left under the tree by a ship's captain. A year later it was retrieved by the commander of the Third East India Fleet en route to India. Messages were also left carved in rocks and left in old boots tied to the branches. The tree has been declared a national monument and it is still possible to send a postcard home from here – all mail dispatched from the Post Office Tree is franked with a special commemorative stamp and makes a great souvenir.

In the middle of the bay is **Seal Island** which can be visited by cruises departing from the harbour. The island is inhabited by colonies of African penguins and Cape fur seals (the best month to see seal pups is November). Between September and November the warm waters of the bay are often visited by southern right, humpback and Brydes whales while calving. Another vantage point for viewing whales and dolphins is **The Point** at the end of Marsh Street. Close by is the 20-m-high **Cape St Blaize Lighthouse** ① *Montague St, T044-690 3015, Mon-Fri 1000-1500, R14, children (under 12) R7, for details on sleeping in the lighthouse, call T021-449 2400, or visit the National Ports Authority website, www. transnetnationalportsauthority.net*, built in 1864, one of only two remaining continuously manned lighthouses in South Africa.

ST BLAIZE TRAIL
The St Blaize Trail is a perfect introduction to the stunning coastline that you are likely to encounter along the Garden Route. This is a 13.5-km walk along the cliffs and rocky coast west from Mossel Bay. The official trail starts from Bats Cave, just below the lighthouse; the path is marked by the white image of a bird in flight. As you walk further from the town the scenery becomes more and more spectacular. You can leave the coast at Pinnacle Point, and follow a path inland to Essenhout Street. This cuts about 5 km off the walk. The path ends by a group of houses in Dana Bay. From here you will have to organize your own transport back into town, so it helps to have a mobile phone to call a taxi from Mossel Bay. A helpful map is available from the tourism office. You are rightly warned to be careful in places during strong winds, as there are some precipitous and unprotected drops from the cliff tops.

BOTLIERSKOP PRIVATE GAME RESERVE
① *T044-696 6055, www.botlierskop.co.za. To get there turn off the N2 on to the R401 to the northeast of Mossel Bay, the Klein Brakrivier turn-off, and follow signs for 25 km.*
This private reserve is situated on a 2400-ha game farm, which is home to 24 different species of animals and a wide variety of birds. A former farm, the land has been restocked and wildlife includes the rare black impala, rhino, elephant, lion, buffalo, giraffe, mountain zebra and eland. Activities include game drives, nature walks, picnics and helicopter rides. The most exciting activity is elephant riding, which costs R550, children (under 12) R275, no children under six. The two elephants are orphans who survived a culling program in the Zambezi Valley in Zimbabwe. There is luxurious accommodation available or you can visit for the day, though booking is essential. Check out the website for prices and programmes.

This appealing little town is an ideal base for exploring the Garden Route and has a superb swathe of sandy beach. Check locally for demarcated areas for swimming and surfing. Children should be supervised in the sea as there are strong rip currents. One of the safest spots for swimming is in the Touw River mouth. Except for the few hectic weeks at Christmas and New Year, Wilderness is generally very relaxed and has an excellent range of accommodation. The advantage of staying here is that you are also within a day's drive of all the interesting sights of the Little Karoo. The highlight, however, is the Wilderness Section of the Garden Route National Park, a quiet, well-managed area of the park, with three levels of self-catering accommodation and a campsite.

The town itself doesn't have much of a centre, but stretches instead up the lush foothills of the Outeniqua Mountains and along leafy streets by the lake and river. The supermarket, restaurants, post office and tourist office are by the petrol station, where the N2 crosses the Serpentine channel.

TOURIST INFORMATION
Wilderness Tourism ① *Milkwood Village, Beacon Rd, T044-877 0045, www.tourism wilderness.co.za, Mon-Fri 0800-1700, Sat 0900-1300,* is a very helpful office, especially when it comes to finding good-value accommodation during the peak season.

BACKGROUND
The first European to settle in the district was a farmer, Van der Bergh, who built himself a simple farmhouse in the 1850s. But it was in 1877 that the name was first used, when a young man from Cape Town, George Bennet, was granted the hand of his sweetheart only on condition that he took her to live in the wilderness. He purchased some land where the present-day **Wilderness Hotel** stands and promptly named it 'wilderness' (of dense bush and forest) to appease his new father-in-law. At this time the only road access was from the Seven Passes Road between George and Knysna, and Bennet cut a track from this road to his new farmhouse. In 1905 the homestead was converted it into a boarding house, and when the property changed hands in 1921, the farmhouse/boarding house underwent further alterations and the Wilderness Hotel came into being.

GARDEN ROUTE NATIONAL PARK (WILDERNESS SECTION)
① *Off the N2, 4 km east of Wilderness, reception, T044-877 1197, www.sanparks.org, 0700-2000, R96, children (2-11) R48. There are two rest camps and the nearest supermarkets and restaurants are in Wilderness.*
This section of the Garden Route National Park stretches from the Touw Rivermouth to the Swartvlei Estuary, covers 2612 ha and incorporates five rivers and four lakes as well as a 28-km stretch of the coastline. The four lakes are known as Island, Langvlei, Rondevlei and Swartvlei, and are situated between the Outeniqua foothills and sand dunes which back onto a beautiful, long sandy beach. The main attractions are the dense hardwood forest, the water and the birdlife in the reed beds affording the opportunity to encounter the brilliantly coloured Knysna lourie, or one of the five kingfisher species that occur here. During spring, a carpet of flowers on the forest floor further enhances the verdant beauty of the park.

There are two ways in which to enjoy the surroundings; on foot or in a canoe. You can cover more ground by walking, but canoeing is ideal for seeing birds. There are five trails in the park from 2-10 km. The longest is the **Pied Kingfisher Trail**, a 10-km circular route, which can be completed in three or four hours and goes via Wilderness village. It follows the river in one direction and the beach on your return. The other walks are also forest walks, except for the 3-km **Dune Molerat Trail** which takes you through dune fynbos where you may see proteas in flower in season. Maps are available at reception.

The rest camps have canoes for hire – these should be arranged through **Eden Adventures** ① *T044-877 0179, www.eden.co.za*, who have an office at reception. One of the more interesting short routes is to continue up the Touw River past the Ebb and Flow Camps. This quickly becomes a narrow stream and you have to leave your canoe. A path continues along the bank of the stream through some beautiful riverine forest and a 2-km boardwalk takes you to a waterfall where you can swim. Eden Adventures also have mountain bikes, some with child seats, to rent out for use on the trails in the park.

→SEDGEFIELD AND AROUND

Unless you turn off the N2, all that can be seen of Sedgefield is a collection of curio shops, supermarkets and snack bars. Between the main road and the beach is the **Swartvlei Lagoon**, South Africa's largest natural inland saltwater lake, most of which lies on the inland side of the N2. The lake is a popular spot for watersports and birdwatching, although the two pastimes don't always go well together. Around Sedgefield's lakes and forests look out for the secretive starred robin, the blue mantle flycatcher, the difficult-to- see Victorian warbler and the rare African finfoot.

The village itself is of little interest, but the country around the lakes is spectacular and very peaceful. On the Knysna side of Sedgefield is another lake, **Groenvlei**, a freshwater lake lying within the Goukamma Nature Reserve. **Sedgefield Tourism** ① *30 Main Rd, T044-343 2010, www.visitknysna.co.za, Mon-Fri 0800-1700, Sat 0830-1300*, has good information on accommodation.

GOUKAMMA NATURE RESERVE
① *T044-802 5310, www.capenature.org.za, 0800-1800, entry for day visitors R30, children (2-13) R15.*
The reserve was established to protect 2230 ha of the hinterland between Sedgefield and Buffalo Bay. This includes Groenvlei or Lake Pleasant, a large freshwater lake, and a 13-km sandy beach with some magnificent sand dunes covered in fynbos and patches of forest containing milkwood trees. The **Goukamma River** estuary in the eastern part of the reserve has been cut off from the sea by the large sand dunes. The lake is now fed by natural drainage and springs, and is surrounded by reed beds which are excellent for bird-watching; more than 75 species have been identified. To get there, look out for the turning for the **Lake Pleasant Hotel**, just east of Sedgefield. Beyond the hotel the road divides; take the left turning by the dunes to the bushcamp and the Groenvlei office. A 4-km hiking trail starts close by which runs along the lake shore. If you are feeling energetic, there is a 14-km trail starting from the same point, which takes you across the reserve to the Goukamma River in the eastern sector, although this leaves you with the problem of return transportation. On any of the walks in the reserve, always carry plenty of drinking water and keep an eye out for snakes, especially among the sand dunes. The second point of access is much closer to Knysna. Look out for the Buffalo Bay signpost where the N2 crosses the

Goukamma River, and the railway crosses the N2. There is Cape Nature accommodation in both the western and eastern ends of the reserve.

→KNYSNA AND AROUND

Knysna (the 'K' is silent) is the self-proclaimed heart of the Garden Route. It is no longer the sleepy lagoon-side village it once was – far from it – but is nevertheless a pleasant spot to spend a day or two. The town itself is fully geared up for tourists, which means a lot of choice in accommodation and restaurants, as well as overcrowding and high prices. It remains quite an arty place, though, and many of the craftspeople who have gravitated to the region display their products in craft shops and galleries. Nevertheless, development is booming, with a slick waterfront complex, complete with souvenir shops and fast-food outlets, setting the pace. If you're trying to choose between Knysna and Plettenberg Bay as a base, Knysna offers more amenities and activities, while Plett is far more relaxed and has the better beach. Both get very busy during high season.

ARRIVING IN KNYSNA

Getting there and around Knysna can easily be accessed by road as it lies on the N2 between Cape Town (500 km) and Port Elizabeth (260 km). **Baz Bus** has a daily service between Cape Town and Port Elizabeth, from where it continues to Durban five times a week. Mainline buses stop at Knysna daily on the route between Cape Town and Durban. **Translux** has a service between Knysna and Johannesburg and Tshwane (Pretoria) via

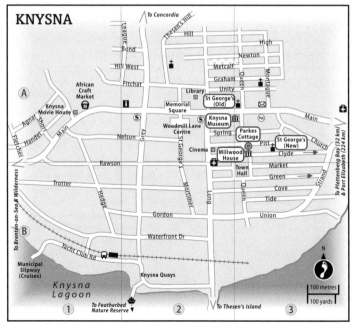

KNYSNA

Bloemfontein. The centre of town is compact and it is easy to find your way about on foot, but you'll need transport to see the outlying sights.

Tourist information Knysna Tourism ① *40 Main St, T044-382 5510, www.visitknysna. co.za, Mon-Fri 0800-1700, Sat 0830-1300, hours extended in high season,* can make reservations for accommodation, tours and public transport. It's a helpful and professional office, well clued-up on the region.

BACKGROUND

The Hottentots named a local river in the area by a word that sounded like Knysna to the early Europeans, and it's generally believed to mean a place of wood or leaves. In 1804 George Rex, a timber merchant, purchased the farm Melkhoutkraal, effectively taking ownership of all the land surrounding the lagoon. It was rumoured he was the first and illegitimate son of England's King George III. By 1817 the Knysna Lagoon was being used by ships to bring in supplies, and later to take away timber. The vast, indigenous forests just outside Knysna became an invaluable source of timber for buildings, ships and wagons. In 1870, Arnt Leonard Thesen and his family moved from Norway to Knysna and set up the first trading store and counting house, and by 1881 the settlements of Melville and Newhaven united to form the new town of Knysna. The timber industry continued well into the 20th century and unfortunately wiped out much of the natural forest on the coast, so whilst there are still tracts of Knysna forest with yellowwoods and stinkwoods towering over forest ferns, much of the region has been given over to pine plantations and looks very different to what it did 150 years ago.

PLACES IN KNYSNA

Although there are a couple of sights and museums in the town, Knysna's highlights are its natural attractions. The **Knysna National Lakes**, a broad largely undefined region of protected areas, is wonderful to explore, comprising lakes, islands, seashore and beach. This fragile ecosystem is bound to suffer from the ever-expanding tourist industry; of particular concern is the rich variety of aquatic life in the lagoon. This has not been helped by the construction of large retirement residential suburbs, such as Belvidere Estate, Thesen's Island and Leisure Isle – the latter two should never have been built upon.

Nevertheless, the Knysna National Lakes, along with Wilderness and Tsitsikamma, are now administered by SANParks as part of the newly proclaimed Garden Route National Park, and this region is now referred to as the **Knysna Lakes Section**. The most accessible area, and the main feature of the town is the **lagoon**, around which much of Knysna life revolves. **The Heads**, the rocky promontories that lead from the lagoon to the open sea, are quite stunning. More than 280 species of bird are listed in the area and the tidal lagoon and open estuary of the Knysna River provides an excellent place to view waders in the summer months, and plovers, gulls, cormorants and sandpipers are common. Large species like African fish eagle and osprey should also be watched out for.

The area also incorporates the remaining tract of Knysna forests on the southern slopes of the Outeniqua Mountains behind Knysna, which first attracted white settlers to the region. No longer a single expanse, the patches go under a variety of names and include Diepwalle Forest and Goudveld Forest. They are noteworthy for the variety of birdlife and their magnificent trees. Species of special interest include the yellowwood, assegai, stinkwood, red alder, white alder and the Cape chestnut. A variety of short walks has been laid out in the forests. In some areas horse riding and mountain biking is allowed.

One of the striking features of Knysna is the location of the sprawling township, which is at the top of the hills above the town. From a boat trip on the lagoon you can look back at the town; all the sleek modern and luxurious development in the foreground and, quite by contrast, the tight cluster of shacks at the very top of the hill.

The **Knysna Museum** ① *Queen St, T044-302 6320, Mon-Fri 0930-1630, Sat 0930-1230, free but donations accepted*, is housed in the Old Gaol – the first public building erected by the colonial government in the 1870s. Most of the collection focuses on fishing methods used along the coast, with a variety of nets and tackle on display. Unless you are a devoted angler this is not going to take up too much of your time. The highlight is in fact a fish, or to be more precise, a coelacanth. This is a prehistoric fish that was believed to be extinct, but a live specimen was famously caught by a fisherman in 1938. There is also an art gallery, tearoom and gift shop.

Millwood House ① *T044-302 6320, Mon-Fri 0930-1630, Sat 0930-1230, free but donations accepted*, is a single-storey wooden building similar to those that once made up the gold-mining community of Millwood. The house was originally built in sections and re-erected here. It is now a national monument and houses the local history museum, including a display depicting the goldrush days. Next door is **Parkes Cottage**, a similar wooden house, which was moved three times before arriving at its present site. Originally erected in Millwood village, it was moved into Knysna when the gold ran out. In 1905 it was moved to Rawson Street, and then finally in 1992 it was moved to its present site.

There are two **St George's** churches in Knysna, the old and the new. Both ran into financial difficulties during construction. To complete the old church the Bishop of the Cape Colony, Robert Gray, persuaded six local businessmen to come up with the necessary £150. The church was consecrated in October 1855. The interior has a timbered ceiling and a fine yellowwood floor. In the 1920s it was decided that a second church needed to be built to accommodate the local congregation. It was 11 years between the foundation stone being laid and the church being consecrated by Bishop Gwyer of George in April 1937. Construction had been delayed due to lack of funds. The community was very proud of the fact that all the materials used in the construction were local – the stone for the walls was quarried from the other side of the lagoon in the Brenton hills. Most of the interior fittings are made from stinkwood, and commemorate local worthies.

Mitchell's Brewery ① *Arend St, Knysna Industria, T044-382 4685, www.mitchellsknysna brewery.com, Mon-Fri 0830-1630, tours 1000 and 1500, Sat 0930-1230, tour 1000, R50*. This produces a range of home-made lagers and bitters (the latter being very rare in South Africa), and visitors can take a tour of the fermentation cellars, which includes tasting, and the brews are also available from many hotels and restaurants along the Garden Route. The most popular are the Forester's Draught pilsner-type lager, the Bosun's Best Bitter, and the heavily spiced Scottish-type traditional ale known as Ninety Shilling.

Featherbed Nature Reserve ① *T044-382 1693, www.knysnafeatherbed.com, daily 1000, 1115, 1230, R395, children (4-10) R180 (including lunch), 1430, R275, children (4-10) R80 (without lunch)*, is a private nature reserve in the unspoilt western side of the **Knysna Heads**. It can only be reached by the **Featherbed Co** ferry, which runs from the John Benn Jetty, at the Knysna Quays. The reserve is home to South Africa's largest breeding herd of blue duiker (*Cephalophus monticola*), an endangered species. Also of interest is a cave once inhabited by the Khoi, which has been declared a national heritage site. This four-hour excursion includes return ferry trip, 4WD vehicle ride up the western promontory of the Knysna Heads and an optional 2-km guided nature walk through the forest, onto the cliffs, into the caves and along the spectacular coastline. It ends with a buffet lunch under some milkwood trees before returning to Knysna. This is an excellent family excursion. The Featherbed Co also offers 1½-hour cruises around the lagoon on the double-storey John Benn at 1230 and 1800 (1700 in winter) for R120, children (4-15) R50, which has a cash bar, and on a paddle cruiser at 1230 for R150, children (4-15) R65, with lunch, or at 1800 (1700 in winter), which includes a three-course buffet dinner, R350, children (11-15) R180, (4-10) R80. In addition, they run the Cruise Café at the boat departure point at the Knysna Quays.

KNYSNA ELEPHANT PARK
ⓘ *On the N2, 20 km from Knysna and 10 km before Plettenberg Bay, T044-532 7732, www. knysnaelephantpark.co.za, 0830-1630, 1-hr tours depart every 30 mins, R190, children (3-12) R100, bookings not required; elephant riding 0930, 1030, 1500, 1600, R815, children (6-12) R390, children under 6 not permitted, booking essential.*

This small park is a refuge for orphaned elephants. Visitors are taken on tours around the forest area and are allowed to touch and play with the little elephants. Although the animals are 'free range' they are very used to human contact, making it a wonderful experience for children. Longer walks with the elephants can also be arranged and the elephant riding is a two-hour excursion through the bush ending with refreshments. Sleeping with the elephants is also on offer, and six rooms have been built above the elephants' boma where they sleep at night. This is also the only realistic chance you'll have of seeing elephants in the area – the fabled indigenous ones are far too elusive. The restaurant serves breakfast, light lunches and afternoon teas. There's another similar elephant experience at **The Elephant Sanctuary** further along the N2 at The Crags, 19 km east of Plettenberg Bay.

→PLETTENBERG BAY

Plettenberg Bay, or 'Plett', as it is commonly known, is one of the most appealing resorts on the Garden Route. Although it is modern and has little of historical interest, the compact centre is attractive and the main beach beautiful. Plett has now become fashionable and, during the Christmas season, the town is transformed. Wealthy families descend from Johannesburg and the pace can get quite frenetic – expect busy beaches and long queues for restaurant tables. For the rest of the year it is calmer and the resort becomes just another sleepy seaside town. There are three beaches that are good for swimming, and a number of attractions along the N2 to the east of 'Plett', particularly around the settlement of The Crags, where visitors could easily spend a full day visiting the wildlife sancturies.

ARRIVING IN PLETTENBERG BAY
Getting there For short trips to other towns along the Garden Route the Baz Bus represents the best value and most convenient schedule and has a daily service in either direction between Cape Town and Port Elizabeth. Mainline buses stop at the Shell Ultra City out of town on the N2.

Tourist information Plettenberg Bay Tourism ① *Melville's Corner shopping centre, Main St, T044-533 4065, www.plettenbergbay.co.za, Mon-Fri 0900-1700, Sat 0900-1300, slightly longer hours during the peak summer season*, is a helpful office with a detailed website.

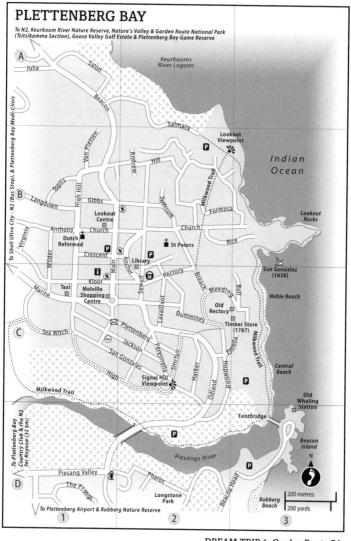

PLETTENBERG BAY

To N2, Keurboom River Nature Reserve, Nature's Valley & Garden Route National Park (Tsitsikamma Section), Goose Valley Golf Estate & Plettenberg Bay Game Reserve

BACKGROUND

In 1630 a Portuguese vessel, the **San Gonzalez**, was wrecked in the bay. This was 20 years before Jan van Riebeeck's arrival at the Cape. The survivors stayed here for eight months, during which time they built two smaller boats out of the wreckage, and one of the boats managed to sail up the coast to Mozambique. The survivors were eventually returned home to Lisbon, but they left behind a sandstone plaque on which they had inscribed the name *Baia Formosa*. Today a replica can be seen in Plett in the same place that the first was left by the sailors. (The original is now on show in the South African Museum in Cape Town.) The Portuguese had a number of names for the bay, but none stuck for very long. Later the Dutch also gave the bay several different names, such as Content Bay and Pisang River Bay; it was only in 1778 when Governor Joachim van Plettenberg opened a timber post on the shores of the bay, and named it after himself, that a name stuck.

Plettenberg remained an important timber port until the early 1800s when the Dutch decided to move operations to Knysna since it was a safer harbour. For a period the bay became famous as a whaling station but all that remains is a blubber cauldron and slipway near the **Beacon Island Hotel**.

PLACES IN PLETTENBERG BAY

While there are a few old buildings still standing which represent a little of the town's earlier history, including the remains of the Old Timber Store (1787), the Old Rectory (1776), and the Dutch Reformed Church (1834), most of the buildings were destroyed in a fire in 1914, and today the main streets are just a collection of modern shopping malls and restaurants. The real attraction of this area is the sea and the outdoors. Aside from the three beaches, **Robberg**, **Central** and **Lookout**, there is excellent deep-sea fishing and, in season, good opportunities to spot whales and dolphins, particularly southern right whales from June to October. Plett climbs up a fairly steep hill; there are many elevated land-based vantage points as well as regular boat tours offering closer encounters with the marine life. The nearby **Keurbooms River lagoon** (see below) is a safe area for bathing and other watersports, and the dunes around the lagoon are now part of the **Keurboom River Nature Reserve**.

The **Milkwood Trail** is a 3-km circular trail in and around the town. Follow the yellow footprints. You can start the walk anywhere along the route and it takes you via Piesangs River lagoon, Central Beach, and Lookout Rocks, and in the centre of town, past some of the historic buildings.

There are also some recommended walks in the **Robberg Nature Reserve** ⓘ *8 km south from Plett on Robberg Rd, T044-533 2125, www.capenature.org.za, Feb-Nov 0700-1700, Dec and Jan 0700-2000, R30, children (2-13) R15.* There are three possibilities ranging from 2-9 km on this loop along the Robberg Peninsula which forms the western boundary of Plettenberg Bay. Follow the 'seal' markers. Walking is easy thanks to boardwalks, and there are plenty of prominent viewpoints from which it is possible to see whales, seals and dolphins in the bay, but beware of freak waves along the coastal paths. Allow at least four hours for the full route. **Eden Adventures** ⓘ *T044-877 0179, www.eden.co.za*, based in Wilderness can also arrange 45-m abseiling in the reserve.

PLETTENBERG BAY GAME RESERVE

ⓘ *12 km north of Plett, leave town on the N2 east and turn on the R340 to Uplands, T044-535 0000, www.plettenbergbaygamereserve.com, 2-hr game drives May-Sep 1100 and 1500,*

Oct-Apr 0830, 1000, 1100, 1230, 1500 and 1600, R345, children (under 12) R95, 2-hr horse safaris 1000 and 1500, R345 per person.

This private reserve is located on 2200 ha spread across the hills above the Garden Route coastline with good views of Plettenberg Bay and offers open 4WD safaris or guided horse-riding trails. The reserve boasts a diversity of natural biomes, including fynbos, grasslands and indigenous forests, and on the property is the natural confluence of the Keurbooms and Palmiet Rivers. The reserve has been stocked with over 35 species of game, including lion, rhino, giraffe, hippo, crocodile, buffalo and a large variety of antelope, and 101 species of bird have been recorded. Accommodation is in a luxury lodge or visit for a game drive/ horse ride followed by a drink and light meal in the bar.

→EAST OF PLETTENBERG BAY

Getting around The N2 continues east from Plettenberg Bay, but don't expect to travel too fast as there are a number of attractions and sights that are worth stopping for.

KEURBOOMS RIVER NATURE RESERVE

ⓘ *On the east side of the Keurbooms River Bridge on the N2, 7 km east of Plett, T044-533 2125, www.capenature.co.za, 0800-1800, R30, children (2-13) R15, canoe hire R90 per day, if you just want to picnic next to the river at the reserve entrance near the bridge it's R5 per person.*

First up is the 750-ha Keurbooms River Nature Reserve. The headwaters of the Keurbooms River come from the Langkloof, north of the main Tsitsikamma mountain range. Its gorge is spectacular and well worth a voyage upstream to enjoy the unspoilt, unpolluted beauty. A variety of habitats are conserved, including the relatively unspoilt riverine gorge, patches of Knysna forest along the flood banks and in protected kloofs, coastal fynbos, and dune fields. The reserve is named after the Western Keurboom (*Virgilia oroboides*) or choice tree, which grows in the coastal forest edges. The environment attracts a number of birds; look out for the Knysna lourie, malachite and giant kingfisher, Narina trogon fish eagle, white-breasted cormorant and various sunbirds. You can hire canoes from the **Cape Nature office**, but taking a sailing trip upstream on the **Keurbooms River Ferry** ⓘ *T083-254 3551, www.ferry.co.za*, is the best way to spend a few hours. You are ferried 5 km along the river through a spectacular gorge overhung by indigenous trees and other flora.

TENIKWA WILDLIFE AWARENESS CENTRE

ⓘ *Before Monkeyland and Birds of Eden take the signposted left road for 2 km, T044-534 8170, www.tenikwa.co.za, 1-hr Wildcat Experience; tours depart every 30 mins 0900-1630, R150, children (6-13) R70, under 6 free, bookings not required; 1½-hr Cheetah Walk; 0730 and 1630, R400 per person, height restriction 1.5 m, booking essential.*

At the same turn-off to Monkeyland and Birds of Eden is this centre for orphaned, abandoned and injured wildlife, which it endeavours to rehabilitate and return to the wild whenever possible. Many of the animals are brought to the centre by **Cape Nature** from their protected reserves along the Garden Route, and when released are returned to these sites, while some are introduced back into the wild on some of the private game reserves in the Eastern Cape along the N2 around the Addo Elephant National Park (see page 184). In accordance with Cape Nature's regulations, the public cannot interact with any animals scheduled to be rereleased as this would reduce their chances of rehabilitation. But the resident species can be viewed at close quarters. The one-hour

Wildcat Experience starts with a visit to the educational centre before a short walk to meet servals, caracals, leopards, African wildcats, black-footed cats and cheetahs in enclosures. The Cheetah Walk takes visitors for a walk with two semi-tame cheetahs through large tracts of fynbos and indigenous forest at either sunrise or sunset when they are exercised. The experience lasts around 1½ hours and includes refreshments; it can be combined with the Wildcat Experience (discounted rate). Other animals on display include meerkats and tortoises, and birds such as marabou storks and blue cranes (South Africa's national bird). African penguins can be seen through glass in the penguin pool; many of them have been washed ashore by strong currents from colonies on the islands along the Garden Route, and after they are stabilized, they are returned to sea.

NATURE'S VALLEY

If you are in a hurry, stay on the N2 – this is a good stretch of road, although there is a toll of around R10. The more spectacular route is via the village of Nature's Valley along the old R102 that branches off the N2 just after The Crags, about 30 km east of Plettenberg Bay. This approach by road is particularly spectacular. The R102, dropping 223 m to sea level via the narrow Kalanderkloof Gorge, twists and turns through lush green coastal forest. Look out for ververt monkeys in the trees. At the bottom is a lagoon formed by the sand dunes blocking the estuary of the **Groot River**. A right turn leads into the village, which is surrounded on three sides by the western section of the **Garden Route National Park (Tsitsikamma Section)** (see page 95), and is made up of a collection of holiday cottages and the **Nature's Valley Restaurant & Trading Store**, an all-in-one shop, restaurant, bar, takeaway and **tourist information bureau** ① *T044-270 6835, www.natures-valley.com, 0830-1700*. Note that there are no banks in Nature's Valley. There are several braai spots on the sandy beach, but be warned that swimming in the sea is not safe. Canoes, rowing boats and yachts can all be used on the Groot River and lagoon, but powerboats are prohibited.

GROOT RIVER AND BLOUKRANS PASSES

As the road starts to climb out of the Groot Valley on the Groot River Pass, built in 1880 by Thomas Bain, it passes the **Nature's Valley Rest Camp** on the right. This is the only camp at the western end of the Garden Route National Park (Tsitsikamma Section). Many visitors will find themselves here because it is one end of the Garden Route's most spectacular hiking trails, the **Otter Trail** (see box, page 96). From the top of the Groot River Pass the road continues for 6 km before crossing a second river valley, the Bloukrans Pass. Here it descends 183 m into the narrow gorge before crossing the river and climbing up again. The R102 rejoins the N2 highway 10 km further on and crosses the **Bloukrans Bridge**, built in 1984, 217 m above the Bloukrans River, and reputedly the highest single-span arch bridge in Africa. Just after the bridge is a turning to the left that leads to a viewpoint at the top of the Bloukrans Gorge.

The main reason for stopping here is the **Bloukrans Bungee Jump** ① *40 km from Plett, T042-281 1458, www.faceadrenalin.com, 0900-1700, booking not essential but recommended, bungee jump R690, which includes the bridge walk, bridge walk only R10, DVDs and T-shirts available*. At 216 m this is the highest commercial bungee in the world. The first rebound is longer than the previous holder of the record, the 111-m bungee jump at Victoria Falls. It's a hugely exhilarating experience and the free fall once you've leapt from the bridge lasts seven seconds, travelling over 170 kph before you reach the maximum length of the bungee cord. The minimum age is 14 and there is no upper age limit; a 96-year-old has previously jumped. If you cannot muster the courage to jump, you can go on a guided bridge walk, which involves walking out to the bungee platform along the caged walkway underneath the road surface of the bridge, where a guide tells you how the bridge was built and a little bit about the surrounding area. This is not for anyone who suffers from vertigo, but if you want to support a mate who's doing a jump, it's a great way to feel some of the fear they are experiencing when standing on the lip of the bungee platform. Also at the top of the gorge is the **Tsitsikamma Forest Village Market**, a sustainable initiative to help local people make and sell curios to the many passing tourists. Shops are in a collection of attractive reed Khosian huts, and you can buy items such as candles or home-made paper.

STORMS RIVER BRIDGE

Storms River Bridge is a further 5 km along the N2 from Bloukrans. There is a viewing platform to look down into the river gorge. Next to the bridge is the **Petro-Total Village**, a popular stopover with petrol pumps, curio shops, a restaurant, small museum and the **Tsitsikamma Information office** ⓘ *T042-280 3561, www.tsitsikamma.info, daily 0830-1630.* It is worth stopping here briefly to pick up some local tourist leaflets, especially if you have plans to hike in the region. It is a helpful office and can provide information and local bookings for a whole variety of adventure activities. This is also an official stop for the mainline buses that travel along the Garden Route. Note that Storms River Village is a further 8 km along the N2, not to be confused with Storms River Mouth which is in the Garden Route National Park (Tsitsikamma Section).

→GARDEN ROUTE NATIONAL PARK (TSITSIKAMMA SECTION)

Tsitsikamma is a khoi word meaning 'place of abundant or sparkling water', and this section of the Garden Route National Park consists of a beautiful 80-km stretch of lush coastal forest between Nature's Valley and Oubosstrand. At the western end, where the Otter Trail (see box, page 96) reaches the Groot River estuary, the park boundary extends 3 km inland, but for most of its length it is no more than 500 m wide, though the park boundaries reach out to sea for more than 5 km in parts. The main administrative office is at Storms River Mouth Rest Camp, which is almost the midpoint of the park.

ARRIVING IN THE GARDEN ROUTE NATIONAL PARK

Getting there The Tsitsikamma Section is 68 km from Plettenberg Bay and 195 km from Nelson Mandela Bay (Port Elizabeth). There are two access points into the park depending on which rest camp you are staying in, although day visitors generally enter through the Storms River Mouth entrance, where there are better facilities for those on day trips. The turn-off for **Storms River Mouth Rest Camp** is on a straight stretch of the N2, about 4 km after the Storms River Bridge, and if you are approaching from the Port Elizabeth side, the turning is 4 km after the small village of Storms River. A surfaced road leads down to the reception centre on the coast. The last part of this drive is a beautiful, steep descent through lush rainforest, a marked contrast to the coniferous plantations along the N2 toll road.

The Nature's Valley Rest Camp is 40 km west of Storms River Mouth and can only be reached from the R102; when approaching from Knysna take the Nature's Valley turning at Kurland (R102). If you miss this turning you cannot turn off the N2 toll road until it meets with the other end of the R102, at which point you are only 8 km from the turning for Storms River

ON THE ROAD
Otter Trail

This is one of South Africa's best hiking trails, managed by South African National Parks (SANParks), T012-426 5111, www.sanparks.org. The 42.5-km, five-day/four-night trail, marked with painted otter footprints and named after the Cape clawless otter that occurs in the region, runs between Storms River Mouth and Nature's Valley in the Tsitsikamma Section of the Garden Route National Park. Only 12 people can start the trail each day and groups must consist of a minimum of four. It costs R860 per person, which includes four nights in the hiking huts as well as the permit. Due to its popularity, bookings are open up to 13 months in advance.

None of the sectors is that long, but it is still fairly strenuous in parts since you have to cross 11 rivers and there are steep ascents and descents at each river crossing. The Bloukrans River crossing presents the most problems. Check tide tables; you will at least have to wade, or even swim across. Waterproofing for your rucksack is vital. If you are unable to cross the river, you can take the escape route, which branches to the right of the trail, where it climbs steeply to the top of the plateau and leads to the N2. At each overnight stop there are two log huts, each sleeping six people in bunk beds; mattresses and firewood are provided. Each hut has a braai place with a sturdy steel grill but hikers need to provide their own pots for cooking. There are numerous streams and springs throughout the length of the Otter Trail that are suitable for drinking. However, it may be wise to use purification tablets.

The trail traverses some spectacular landscape and never strays far from the coastline. Vegetation varies from fynbos plateaux to densely forested valleys and in parts goes along rocky cliffs and boulder-strewn beaches. Apart from the natural beauty and the birdlife, the trail passes some fine waterfalls and Strandloper caves. Look out for the fine old hardwood trees which have escaped the dreaded axe, and in spring, an abundance of wild flowers.

Camp. When approaching from Port Elizabeth look out for signs for Nature's Valley, R102. Nature's Valley Rest Camp is clearly signposted 3 km outside the village of the same name.

Best time to visit The best time to visit is between November and February. Bear in mind that, although this is midsummer, you can expect rain at any time. Annual rainfall is in excess of 1200 mm; June and July are the driest months, while May and October are the wettest.

Park information Gates 0600-1930, office 0730-1800, overnight visitors arriving after 1800 should arrange to pick up keys from the gate, T042-281 1607, www.sanparks.org, R120, children (2-11) R60. At the Storms River Mouth Rest Camp there's a shop, 0800-1800, which stocks gift items as well as groceries, wine and beer, and a restaurant, 0730-2130, and other facilities include a swimming pool, and short boat trips on the *Spirit of Tsitsikamma*, which runs every 45 minutes, 0900-1600, and goes up the Storms River Gorge from the jetty below the suspension bridge.

VEGETATION AND WILDLIFE

A cross-section of the coastlands would reveal the Tsitsikamma Mountains (900-1600 m), whose slopes level off into a coastal plain or plateau at about 230 m, and then the forested cliffs which plunge 230 m into the ocean. The slope is only precipitous in a few places;

elsewhere along the coast it is still very steep, but there is enough soil to support the rainforest which the park was in part created to protect. The rainforest is the last remnant of a forest which was once found right along this coast between the ocean and the mountains. The canopy ranges between 18 m and 30 m and is closed, which makes the paths nice and shady. The most common species of tree are milkwood, real yellowwood, stinkwood, Cape blackwood, forest elder, white pear and candlewood, plus the famous Outeniqua yellowwood, a forest giant. All are magnificent trees which combine with climbers such as wild grape, red saffron and milky rope to create an outstandingly beautiful forest.

The mammal species that live in the park include caracal, bushbuck, blue duiker, grysbok, bushpig and the Cape clawless otter, but given the steep slopes and dense forest, sightings are very rare. Birdwatching, however, is very rewarding, and over 220 bird species have been identified. The most colourful bird in the forest is the Knysna lourie (*Tauraco corythaix*). Its call is a korr korr korr, and in flight it has a flash of deep red in its wings, with a green body and distinctive crest. In the vicinity of the Storms River and Groot River estuaries you will see an entirely different selection of birds: over 40 species of seabird have been recorded here. The most satisfying sighting is the rare African black oystercatcher, with its black plumage and red eyes, beak and legs.

HIKING IN THE PARK

There are four different trails in the vicinity of the Storms River Mouth Rest Camp. The most popular is a 1-km walk along a raised boardwalk from the restaurant to the mouth of the Storms River. The last part of the walk involves a steep descent – there is a solid handrail, but the wooden steps can be slippery after rains, as can other parts of the walk. At the bottom is the suspension bridge which appears in many pictures promoting the Garden Route. The views from this point are excellent, especially at midday when there is a clear view of the narrow river gorge extending back inland. The path continues on the other side of the bridge, and from here you can climb the hill for superb views; there are over 300 steps and the path is narrow and steep. Look out for identification labels on the trees as the path winds through the forest. This is a great opportunity to see the trees which a century ago were in great demand for household furniture and building projects – much of the reason for the extensive deforestation in the area. Allow at least an hour for the walk to the bridge and back.

The other trails close to the camp are the **Lourie Trail**, 1 km through the forested slopes behind the camp; the **Blue Duiker Trail**, 3.7 km further into the forest; and the **Waterfall Trail**, a 3-km walk along the first part of the Otter Trail (see box, opposite); hikers without a permit have to turn back at the waterfall.

In addition to the Otter Trail is the **Dolphin Trail** ① *information and reservations T042-280 3588, www.dolphintrail.co.za*, a three-day guided trail to the east of Storms River Rest Camp. This is a more upmarket hike – luggage is transported from one night stop to the next, accommodation is in luxurious lodges, all meals are included and the hike is professionally guided. It is also much more expensive, at R4200 per person for three days.

GARDEN ROUTE LISTINGS

WHERE TO STAY

Mossel Bay

$$$-$$ Protea Hotel Mossel Bay, corner of Church and Market St, T044-691 3738, www.oldposttree.co.za, www.proteahotels. com. This is part of the museum complex and was formerly known as the **Old Post Office Tree Manor**, with 31 comfortable rooms and self-catering suites in a smart manor house dating to 1846, making it the third-oldest building in Mossel Bay. Meals at **Café Gannet**, with views across the bay, small swimming pool, popular with tour groups.

Wilderness

$$ Moontide Guest Lodge, Southside Rd, T044-877 0361, www.moontide.co.za. An award-winning and well-run guesthouse set under milkwood trees in a beautiful and tranquil garden right on the edge of the lagoon, with 8 delightful thatched cottages, one of them a honeymoon suite, each with tasteful decor with kilims and fine furniture. A short walk from the beach and a good spot for birdwatchers. Highly recommended.

$ Fairy Knowe Backpackers, Dumbleton Rd, just off Waterside Rd, T044-877 1285, www.wildernessbackpackers.com. A great set-up in 2 farmhouses with tight staircases and creaking wooden floors surrounded by gardens and milkwood trees, spotless dorms and doubles, camping space in the garden, bar, great breakfasts, nightly camp fires and braais. **Baz Bus** stops here.

Knysna

$$$$ Pezula Resort Hotel & Spa, Lagoon View Drive, follow George Rex Drive to The Heads and turn left along Wilson St, T044-302 5332, www.pezula.com. **Zachary's** for gourmet food, cigar, champagne and whisky bars, award-winning spa, indoor and outdoor heated pools, and championship 18-hole cliff-top golf course among many other sporting facilities. Pezula's 3 private castles

on the beach offer one of South Africa's most exclusive accommodation experiences.

$$$$ Phantom Forest Eco-Reserve, 7 km from Knysna on Phantom Pass Rd, T044-386 0046, www.phantomforest.com. Ultra-stylish accommodation in 14 luxurious and eco-friendly 'tree suites' connected by walkways, set in the forest high above the lagoon. Each has private terrace and luxurious bathroom open to the trees, excellent restaurant, bar, spa and stunning pool on the edge of a wooden deck.

$$$ Rex Hotel, 8 Grey St, T044-302 5900, www.rexhotel.co.za. Super stylish in an architectural gem of a modern building, with 30 spacious luxury rooms, in muted browns and creams, with kitchenettes, a/c, DSTV, DVD players, Wi-Fi and balconies. The **Dish Restaurant** is well regarded for its gourmet food including oysters, the bar is popular with Knysna's elite.

Plettenberg Bay

$$$$ Hunter's Country House, 10 km towards Knysna, T044-532 7818, www.hunterhotels.com. A top country hotel and another **Relais & Chateaux** property, with 21 luxury thatched cottages with fireplace, antique furnishings and private patios in gardens full of wild flowers, 2 swimming pools, conservatory, antique shop, 2 superb restaurants, and gourmet picnics on the estate can be arranged.

$$$$ The Plettenberg, 40 Church St, Lookout Rocks, T044-533 2030, www. plettenberg.com. A **Relais & Chateaux** property and everything you would expect of an exclusive top-class, 5-star hotel. Located on a headland overlooking the bay with 40 luxury a/c rooms with contemporary decor, though you pay much more for sea views, superb food and wine, rim-flow pool and spa. Rates double in high season.

East of Plettenberg Bay
$$$$ Hog Hollow Country Lodge, 18 km east of Plettenberg Bay at The Crags off the N2, T044-534 8879, www.hog-hollow. com. Set in a private nature reserve, with 15 suites decorated with locally made wall hangings and woodcarvings, each with its own wooden deck with hammock overlooking the Matjies River gorge and Tsitsikamma Mountains. Good evening meals, swimming pool with stunning views, library/lounge in the main house, plenty of walks which are ideal for birdwatching.

Storms River Bridge
$$ Tsitsikamma Village Inn, Darnell St, T042-281 1711, www.tsitsikammahotel. co.za. Central original Cape Dutch homestead dating from 1845 with 49 rooms in the gardens in recreated colonial-style buildings: terraced Georgian cottages, woodcutter's log cabins, or a Drostdy (magistrate's house), for example. All have comfortable furnishings, many with brass beds. Good restaurant and the **Hunter's Pub** is the focal point of the village.

$$-$ Storms River Mouth Rest Camp, off the N2 between the Storms River Bridge and Storms River village. This is the main camp on a narrow strip of land between the ocean and forested hills, and is one of the most beautiful settings of all the national parks. It's a real thrill to watch the waves crashing on the rocks right in front of you but it is exposed when the wind blows. There are a number of wooden fully equipped self-catering chalets sleeping up to 6, and basic forest cabins sleeping 2 and sharing communal kitchen and ablutions with campers. Swimming pool, shop selling some groceries and restaurant.

RESTAURANTS

Knysna
$$$-$$ Cruise Café, 400 m west of the Knysna Quays, T044-382 1693. Mon-Sat 0800-2200, Sun 0800-1700. Great views of fishing boats on the lagoon, best known for seafood, plus good breakfasts and simple lunches such as fish and chips; more sophisticated and pricier menu in the evening such as prawn and crab risotto or roast duck, long wine and cocktail list.

$$ Knysna Oyster Co, Thesen's Island, T044-382 6942, www.knysnaoysters.co.za. 1000-2100, closes 1700 in off-season. Next to the oyster farm that has been in operation since 1949; drive across the causeway from town. The seafood restaurant is perhaps the best place to try a dozen of Knysna's famous raw or cooked oysters washed down with a glass of champagne. It's one of Kynsna's must-dos.

Plettenberg Bay
$$-$ The Lookout Deck, perched on the Lookout Rocks, T044-533 1379, www.lookout.co.za. 0900-2300. Popular family restaurant, excellent seafood, soups, salads and steaks, also has a busy bar, lively, bustling atmosphere. Perfect location; from the terrace you can watch surfers share a wave with a dolphin.

WHAT TO DO

Storms River Bridge
Tsitikamma Canopy Tour, the office is on Darnell St in the middle of the village, T042-281 1836, www.canopytour.co.za. This, the original canopy tour, is a fantastic way to see the forest from a different angle, which involves climbing up into the giant yellowwood trees and gliding between 10 different 30-m-high platforms on a steel rope, the longest of which is 100 m. Excellent for birdwatching, and the Knysna loerie may be spotted. Suitable for all ages from 7 years old. Departures are every 45 mins Sep-May 0700-1600, Jun-Aug 0800-1530, the excursion lasts around 3 hrs, costs R450 and includes light refreshments.

ROUTE 62

Unlike the Great Karoo to the north, the Little Karoo is not a flat, dry and empty landscape; instead, it is made up of a series of parallel fertile valleys, enclosed by the Swartberg Mountains to the north and the Langeberg and Outeniqua Mountains to the south. It is an especially rewarding region to explore and much of it is hardly visited by tourists. The Cango Caves are a big attraction, as are the ostrich farms, but further afield lies spectacular and peaceful countryside, dotted with a multitude of small, historic villages. Here are some of the most dramatic kloofs and passes in South Africa with excellent hiking and the springtime allure of bright patches of flowers.

The main road through the Little Karoo to the west of Oudtshoorn is the R62, a beautiful stretch, now marketed as Route 62 (www.route62.co.za).

The Breede is one of the most important rivers in the Cape, and its valley is a beautiful boundary zone. Fed by streams from the mountains, the river is a major source of water for a large number of orchards and vineyards. Worcester is the principal town of the region. Along the broad valley are important farming centres such as Bonnievale and Robertson and the picturesque villages of McGregor and, further north, Tulbagh. These old settlements are surrounded by vineyards and fruit farms that undergo beautiful colour changes through the seasons. Like the Breede River Valley (see page 106) this region is also mostly part of the Route 62 tourist initiative; www.route62.co.za.

→OUDTSHOORN

By far the largest settlement in the Little Karoo, this is a pleasant administrative centre which still retains much of the calm of its early days. It is a major tourist centre and the two major reasons for coming here are the countless ostrich farms that surround the town and the superb Cango Caves. There are also several nature reserves and scenic drives, which are introductions to the diversity of the landscape. Oudtshoorn itself is appealing, with broad streets, smart sandstone Victorian houses, many of which are now B&Bs, and a good choice of restaurants.

Oudtshoorn Tourist Bureau ⓘ *Baron van Rheede St, T044-279 2532, www.oudtshoorn.com, Mon-Fri 0800-1800, Sat 0830-1300*, has a well-informed, enthusiastic and helpful team and is worth a visit for details on accommodation and the less well-known sights of the Karoo.

GETTING THERE AND MOVING ON

Oudtshoorn is 55 km north of George and the junction with the N2 coastal road. The quickest route from the Garden Route is to drive from George and head north over the Outeniqua Pass (N12), but another route goes from Mossel Bay over the Robinson Pass (R328). Alternatively, Cape Town is roughly 450 km from Oudtshoorn via the scenic Route 62 east to Worcester and then the N1. **Greyhound** and **Intercape** buses stop at Oudtshoorn daily on the route between Mossel Bay and Johannesburg via Bloemfontein.

The centre of town is compact and it is easy to find your way about on foot, but you'll need transport to see the outlying sights such as the Cango Caves and ostrich farms.

BACKGROUND

In 1838 a small church was inaugurated on the Hartebeestrivier Farm to serve the farmers who had settled along the banks of the Olifants and Grobbelaars rivers. Nine years later the village of Oudtshoorn was founded when land was subdivided and sold by the surveyor J Ford. The town was named after Baron Van Rheede van Oudtshoorn, who died on his way to the Cape to take up the post of governor in 1773. In 1858 the first group of British immigrants settled in the village.

When visiting during the dry season it is easy to see how for many years the supply of water to the new settlement restricted its growth. A severe drought in 1865 persuaded many established farmers to move on and most made the long trek to the Transvaal. In its early days, water was brought to the town in barrels and then sold to households at sixpence a bucket. But the local farmers learnt to cope with this handicap and many of South Africa's early irrigation experts came from the region. When you cross the Grobbelaars River in the centre of town during the dry season, all the bridges and culverts seem redundant but they provide ample evidence of how much water can pass through when it rains. If you have time, walk across the Victorian **Suspension Bridge** where Church Street crosses the river; this is now a protected national monument.

It was the advent of two ostrich-feather booms (1865-1870 and 1900-1914) that truly established the town, and led to the erection of the fine sandstone buildings and 'ostrich palaces' that now line Oudtshoorn's streets. For a period of almost 40 years it was the

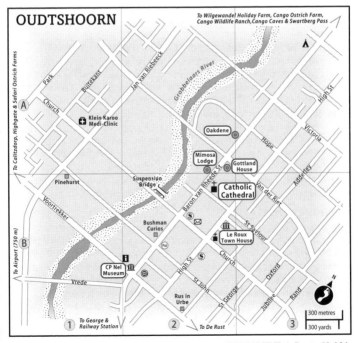

most important settlement east of Cape Town. At the peak of its fortunes, ostrich feathers were selling for more than their weight in gold – little wonder that so many birds were bred. While ostrich farming no longer brings in as much wealth, it remains an important business in the Karoo. Today, it is the production of specialized agricultural seed which contributes most to the region's wealth.

PLACES IN OUDTSHOORN

Within the town limits there is little to see aside from appreciating the sandstone Victorian buildings. There are several **ostrich palaces** in town, which unfortunately are not open to the public, but are still worth a look from the outside for their ornate exteriors. Most examples are in the old part of town on the west bank of the Grobbelaars River. Look out for **Pinehurst**, on St John Street, designed by a Dutch architect, and **Gottland House**, built in 1903 with an octagonal tower. Other buildings of note include **Mimosa Lodge**, **Oakdene** and **Rus in Urbe**. Unfortunately, many fine Victorian buildings were demolished in the 1950s.

The **Catholic Cathedral**, on Baron von Rheede Street, is a fascinating modern cruciform building with splendid stained-glass windows and a chapel beneath the main altar. The cathedral houses two notable works of art: the first is a painting given by Princess Eugenie in memory of her brother – the last of the Bonapartes, who died fighting with the British against the Boers. The second is a replica of a Polish icon incorporating childhood items from refugee children sent to Oudtshoorn during the Second World War; the children returned bearing the gift to celebrate the 50th anniversary of their evacuation.

In the centre of town, the **CP Nel Museum** ① *3 Baron van Rheede St, T044-272 7306, www.cpnelmuseum.co.za, Mon-Fri 0800-1700, Sat-Sun 0900-1700, R12, children (under 16 R3,* is fine sandstone building with a prominent clock tower and was originally built as a boys' high school. The masons who designed the building had been brought to Oudtshoorn by the 'feather barons' to build their grand mansions. The displays include a reconstructed trading store, synagogue and chemist, plus an interesting section on the history of the ostrich boom and the characters involved. The rest of the collection of historic objects was bequeathed to the town by CP Nel, a local businessman. A short walk away is **Le Roux Town House**, at 146 High Street, which is part of the CP Nel Museum and the entry fee covers both. This classic town house was built in 1908 and provides a real feel for how the wealthy lived in the fine ostrich palaces of Oudtshoorn. The interior and furnishings are in art nouveau style and the furniture was shipped from Europe between 1900 and 1920. During the summer, teas are served in the garden. **Arbeidsgenot**, Jan van Riebeeck Road, is the former home of Senator Cornelius Langenhoven, a leading figure in the history of the Afrikaans language who wrote the old national anthem of South Africa.

AROUND OUDTSHOORN

Visiting an ostrich farm in the area can be great fun, although the appeal of riding ostriches, feeding ostriches, buying ostrich eggs and leather, or eating ostrich-egg omelette can fade quickly. To keep visitors for longer, some farms have introduced different species. Visiting the farms or the Cango Caves without your own transport can be surprisingly tricky. There are no tour companies that organize daily trips, although it is possible to find a guide through the tourist office. Otherwise, you might want to hire a car for the day.

Cango Ostrich Farm ① *in the Shoemanshoek Valley 14 km from Oudtshoorn, T044-272 4623, www.cangoostrich.co.za, 0800-1630, R65, children R35, 45-min tours depart every*

20 mins, is particularly convenient as it is on the way to and from the Cango Caves. The farm attractions are also within walking distance of each other. You can interact directly with the birds, sit on or ride them, buy local curios and sample Karoo wines and cheeses.

Wilgewandel Holiday Farm ① *in the Shoemanshoek Valley, 14 km from Oudtshoorn, T044-272 0878, www.wilgewandel.co.za, 0800-1500, camel rides R35, children (3-13) R20, other activities R5-10 per person*, offers you the chance to ride a camel around the farm – a pleasant change from all those ostriches. There are also lots of attractions for children such as farmyard animals, a pet area, trampolines, bumper boats, donkey cart rides, and a restaurant serving anything from tea and scones to crocodile and ostrich steaks.

Highgate Ostrich Farm ① *10 km from Oudtshoorn off the R328 towards Mossel Bay, T044-272 7115, www.highgate.co.za, 0800-1700, R66, children (under 16) R32, 1½-hr tours depart every 15 mins*, a very popular show farm named after the London suburb of Highgate, has been owned by the Hooper family since the 1850s and opened its gates to visitors in 1938. You will learn everything there is to know about the bird, and can then try your hand at riding (or even racing) them. Snacks and drinks are served on the porch of the homestead.

Safari Ostrich Farm ① *6 km from Oudtshoorn on the Mossel Bay road, T044-272 7311, www.safariostrich.co.za, 0730-1700, adults R70, children (under 16) R35, 1-hr tours depart every 30 mins*, has the usual array of ostrich rides, educational exhibits and curio shops. There is also a smart homestead known as Welgeluk. The house was built in 1910, and is a perfectly preserved example of an ostrich palace. There are roof tiles from Belgium, teak from Burma and expanses of marble floors, proof of the wealth and influence the short-lived boom brought to Oudtshoorn families. Unfortunately, the house is closed to visitors; the closest you can get is the main gate.

Cango Wildlife Ranch ① *3 km from Oudtshoorn along the R328 towards Cango Caves, T044-272 5593, www.cango.co.za, 0800-1700, R110, children (4-15) R65, 1-hr tours every 40 mins*, provokes mixed opinions as it is, in effect, a zoo which stocks animals including white lions, leopards, cheetahs and, oddly, jaguars, pumas and rare white Bengal tigers. There is even an albino python. However, the ranch is a leading player in conservation and breeding, particularly with cheetah and wild dog, and the enclosures are very spacious. After walking safely above the animals, you have the choice of paying a little more to pet a cheetah, or you can visit the restaurant. A new attraction here is the **Valley of the Ancients**, a well-forested string of lakes and enclosures connected by boardwalks that are home to a number of unusual animals. The pools are home to Nile crocodiles, pygmy hippos, monitor lizards and otters, while birds include flamingos and marabou storks. You can watch the crocodiles being fed by hand and this is probably the only place in the world that offers cage diving with crocodiles (R280; children must be over 10).

Following the R328 north, the road passes several ostrich farms and then follows the Grobbelaars River Valley towards the Cango Caves (see below). The little village of **Schoemanshoek**, 15 km from Oudtshoorn, is in a lush valley with small farms and homesteads and has some good places to stay.

CANGO CAVES

① *On the R328 28 km north of Oudtshoorn, T044-272 7410, www.cangocaves.co.za. 0900-1700, standard 1-hr tour departs every hour on the hour last tour 1600, R69, children (5-15) R33, 1½-hr adventure tour, half past every hour 0930-1530, R90, children (6-15; minimum age is 6) R55, restaurant, curio shop.*

Tucked away in the foothills of the Swartberg Mountains 28 km from Oudtshoorn, the Cango Caves are a magnificent network of calcite caves, recognized as among the world's finest dripstone caverns. In 1938 they were made a national monument. Despite being seriously hyped and very touristy, they are well worth a visit. Allow a morning for a round trip if based locally; if you have a car it is possible to visit them and Oudtshoorn on a day trip from towns along the Garden Route such as Mossel Bay, George and Wilderness.

The only access to the caves is on a guided tour. The standard one-hour tour is a good introduction to the caves and allows you to see the most impressive formations. It is, however, aimed at tour groups, so visitors with a special interest may find it rather simplistic. During the tour, each section is lit up and the guide points out interesting formations and their given names. Although one small chamber is lit in gaudy colours, the rest are illuminated with white light to best show off the formations. These are turned off behind you as you progress further into the system as research has shown that continued exposure to light causes damage to the caves. The adventure tour lasts for 1½ hours, is over 1 km long and there are over 400 stairs. This can be disturbing for some people, since it involves crawling along narrow tunnels, and at the very end climbing up the Devil's Chimney, a narrow vertical shaft. It leads up for 3.5 m and is only 45 cm wide in parts – definitely not for broad people. If at any stage you feel you can't go on, inform the guide who will arrange for you to be led out. Although strenuous, this tour allows you to see most of the caves, and gives a real feeling of exploration. The caves are usually around 20°C, so a T-shirt and shorts will be fine. Wear shoes with reasonable grip, as after rain the floors can become a little slippery. During the holidays it gets very crowded and nearly 200,000 people pass through the caves each year. Each tour has a maximum number of people, so you may have to wait an hour or more. It's a good idea to get here early in the morning to avoid queues, or alternatively pre-book.

→LITTLE KAROO

CALITZDORP
The main road through the Little Karoo to the west of Oudtshoorn is the R62, a beautiful stretch, and after 52 km you reach the small village of Calitzdorp. Until the branch line from Oudtshoorn arrived in 1924, this settlement remained a small service stop for farmers. The village is now a successful agricultural centre and an important area for port production in South Africa. It is possible to visit a couple of port farms, and a port festival is held every May. At harvest time, fresh fruits are sold along the wide roads of the village. When the first farms were established in the area, the surrounding plains were full of game. Sadly today only the early farm names survive as a reminder. The helpful **tourist office** ① *Voortrekker St, T044-213 3775, www.calitzdorp.co.za, Mon-Fri 0900-1700, Oct-Apr also open Sat-Sun 1000-1500*, has some good leaflets on the area as well as information about the wineries.

MONTAGU AND AROUND
Although Montagu is very much a Karoo town, it is usually visited by people exploring the Breede River Valley. It is 245 km from Oudtshoorn, the administrative centre for the Little Karoo, and only 15 minutes' drive from Ashton and the Breede River. It is a delightful place in a stunning setting, its long streets lined with oak trees and whitewashed Cape Dutch houses, sitting humbly beneath jagged mountain peaks. Founded in 1851, the

settlement was named after John Montagu who, as the colonial secretary from 1843 to 1853, had been responsible for the first major road-building programme in the Cape. The greatly improved road network enabled previously remote settlements such as Montagu to thrive and grow. The climate and fertile valley are ideal for vines and growing fruit such as apples and pears.

In 1980 Montagu suffered a tragic setback when continued heavy rains in the Langeberg resulted in a flash flood down the Keisie River. It was a local catastrophe and 13 people were killed. Again in 2008 Montague and to some extent Ashton, Barrydale and Robertson, witnessed severe flooding when bridges were washed away, which for a while left the village stranded, and there was extensive damage at the Avalon Springs Resort. These have since been repaired.

Montagu Tourism ① *24 Bath St, T023-614 2471, www.montagu-ashton.info, Mon-Fri 0830-1730, Sat-Sun 0900-1700*, has several useful leaflets including one about the historic homes in the area. The **Montagu Market** ① *Bath St, opposite the tourist office, Sat 0980-1300*, is good for crafts, food and collectables.

Joubert House ① *25 Long St, T023-614 1774, Mon-Fri 0900-1300, 1400-1630, Sat-Sun 1030-1230, R5, children (under 16) R3*, the oldest building in the town, is now part of the museum (housed further along Long Street at No 41). The house has a collection of late 19th-century furnishings and ornaments and part of the garden has been turned into an indigenous medicinal plant collection.

Long Street, a popular attraction, has 14 national monuments along its length. With so many well-preserved buildings, it is easy to get a vivid impression of how the settlement would have looked in its early days and the tourist office sells a booklet about the houses.

Just 3 km from the town centre are the hot mineral springs at the **Avalon Springs Resort** ① *T023-614 1150, www.avalonsprings.co.za, day visitors 0800-2300, R60, children (under 12) R40*, which have been used for over 200 years for their healing powers. There are two indoor pools and five outdoor pools, all at different temperatures. At the weekends and holidays it gets very busy so try to go early in the morning or in the evening when it's cooler. The waters are radioactive and have a steady temperature of 48°C. There are picnic sites and a café.

Tractor rides ① *Protea Farm, from Montagu, take the R318 towards Matroosberg, after 30 km the road descends the Burger Pass into the Koo Valley T023-614 3012, www.proteafarm. co.za, or book at the tourist office, R90, children (under 16) R45, 2½-hr trips usually go Wed and Sat 1000 and 1400 if there are enough takers*, to the top of the Langeberg mountains are on offer from a farm in the **Koo Valley**. There are impressive views across the Karoo and down into the Breede River Valley from the summit. For an extra R100 (R70 for children) you get an excellent meal of *potjie*, home-baked bread and a drink. Note that the tractor does not operate in October. Wear warm clothes.

The vineyards around Montagu are best known for producing white wines with the Muscadel grape, which tend to be fairly sweet, fortified dessert wines. There are several wineries in the district which can be visited for tastings and sales. For further information visit www.kleinkaroowines.co.za.

BONNIEVALE

This small town is known for its wines and cheese, and is the site of the main Parmalat dairy factory, a brand that becomes very familiar to visitors in South Africa. The settlement was founded by one of the first farmers to appreciate fully the agricultural potential of the area, Christopher Rigg, who arrived in the valley and immediately set about building an ingenious system of canals to irrigate it. Most of the land is devoted to grape and wine production today, but you will also find several fruit orchards, including peaches, navel oranges, clementines and apricots. The **Bonnievale Tourism Office** ① *Main St, T023-616 3563, www.bonnievale.co.za, Mon-Fri 0800-1700*, is a well-organized and helpful office covering the whole Breede River region.

In the town itself the only real tourist attraction is the **Myrtle Rigg Memorial Church**, which is kept locked but keys can be obtained from the tourist office during working hours. This church has a rather sad story behind it. Two of the Rigg's children died when they were still very young, and their third child, Myrtle, died at the age of seven, in 1911. Before her untimely death, Myrtle asked that her parents build a small church to remember her by. This little Gothic-style building was constructed using the finest materials from around the world, including roof tiles from Italy and a fine carved door from Zanzibar. It was consecrated in 1921, but fell quickly into disrepair after the Riggs' deaths. Fortunately, the municipality saw fit to restore it in 1977. The **Parmalat cheese factory**, which produces 40 tonnes of gouda and cheddar each day, is another legacy of Mr Rigg and today many Parmalat dairy products are found on South African supermarket shelves. The shop sells cheese, butter, milk, yoghurt and cottage cheese.

The wine estates close to Bonnievale, open for tastings and purchases, are members of the Robertson Valley wine route (see page 107 for further details). Of these, as well as wine-tasting, **Viljoensdrift** ① *on the R317 halfway between Bonnievale and Robertson, T023-615 1901, www.viljoensdrift.co.za, Mon-Fri 0830-1700, cruise R40, children (3-16) R15*, also offers a one-hour cruise on a raft on the Breede River that departs at 1200 and you can make up a picnic from items on their deli menu to take with you.

MCGREGOR

This picturesque village surrounded by olive groves and vineyards lies off the beaten track in the lee of the Riviersonderend Mountains. The village is made up of a collection of perfectly preserved, whitewashed thatched cottages which radiate out from a **Dutch Reformed Church** which is in turn surrounded by a neat, colourful garden. Originally, McGregor was known as Lady Grey, after the wife of Sir George Grey, a former governor of the Cape Colony. In 1903 it was renamed, as there was another town in the province with the same name. The new name came from the Reverend Andrew McGregor, a Scottish minister who had worked in the district during the formative years of the village. In recent years, McGregor has attracted a creative population and there are a number of artists, potters and craftsmen living in the small cottages. The **McGregor Tourism Bureau** ① *T023-625 1954, www. tourismmcgregor.co.za, www.mcgregor.org.za, Mon-Fri 0900-1300, 1400-1630, Sat-Sun 0900-1400*, is on the corner of Church and Voortrekker Street and rents out bikes and can organize guided tours of the local fruit and dairy farms. They also issue permits for the Boesmanskloof Trail a beautiful 14-km trail which links McGregor with the village of **Greyton** on the northern side of the Riviersonderend Mountains. The trail follows forested valleys rich in protea and erica species and antelope can sometimes be seen. In the spring this area is covered with a beautiful display of wild flowers. It takes about a day to hike, but part of it, to the Oakes Falls where you can swim, takes about three hours there and back from McGregor.

ROBERTSON

This small, prosperous town has a vaguely time-warped feel to it, with tidy jacaranda-lined streets, orderly church squares and neat rose gardens. It is the centre of a large area of irrigated vineyards, and the high-quality dessert wines and liqueurs produced here have ensured the town's continued prosperity, as has the large brandy distillery. The town itself was founded in 1852 as a new parish to cope with the growing population of Swellendam further down the Breede River Valley. Conditions are ideal for agriculture as there is an abundant water supply from the Langeberg Mountains to the north and the Riviersonderend hills to the south. The lime-rich soil here provides good grazing for horses and there are a number of stud farms in the region. While there isn't a great deal to see in town, it is a pleasant place to spend a day exploring the sleepy centre and nearby vineyards. **Robertson Tourism** ① *T023-626 4437, www.robertsonr62.com, Mon-Fri 0800-1700, Sat 0900-1400, Sun 1000-1400*, is on the corner of Reitz and Voortrekker streets, and is also the office for the **Robertson Wine Valley** ① *T023-626 3167, www.robertsonwinevalley.co.za*. Outside a farmers' market is held on the second and last Saturday of the month (0900-1200).

   Robertson Museum ① *50 Paul Kruger St, T023-626 3681, www.robertsonmuseum.org, Mon-Sat 0900-1200, free*, or 'Druids Lodge', remained in the hands of the same family for nearly 100 years. The original house was built circa 1860, only a few years after the grid pattern for the town had been first laid out. In 1883 the resident magistrate, Mr WHD English, bought the house and it remained the property of the family until 1976, when the last living member, Miss Violet English, died. The municipality bought the house and set up a museum. Most of the collection is devoted to the lives of William Henry Dutton English and his offspring, as well as the history of Robertson and the area. Of particular note is a beautiful collection of lace. Here you can pick up a useful guide for a historical walk around the village that takes in the villas built during the ostrich feather boom.

   Klipdrift brandy is as iconic to South Africa as biltong is and few South African's have not heard of or use regularly the expression 'klippies and coke'. It was first distilled by Kosie Marius on his farm in 1938 and the distillery in Robertson opened in the 1940s. **Robertson Klipdrift Distillery** ① *4 Voortrekker Rd, T023-626 3027, www.klipdrift.co.za, Mon-Fri 0800-1700, Sat 0900-1600, Sun (Oct-Apr) 1000-1500, tastings and snacks R35, distillery tour Mon-Sat 1000, 1200 and 1400, Sun 1100 and 1400 R10*, has an interesting visitor centre which displays the history of the popular tipple and you can go on tours of the distillery and see the giant copper vats, which spend up to 21 years maturing, and the blending process. You can of course taste the brandy, of which there are four varieties, and is accompanied by either braaied meat nibbles marinated in brandy, or traditional sweet items like baked brandy truffles or *koeksisters*. The good **Brandewyntuin** restaurant serves breakfast and lunch.

ROBERTSON VALLEY WINE ROUTE

The Robertson Valley is home to 10% of South Africa's vineyards, and produces excellent Chardonnays and several good Muscadets. The **Wacky Wine Weekend,** held every June, is an excellent time to be in Robertson and is very popular with people from Cape Town.

This wine route follows the Breede River Valley and embraces the districts of Robertson, McGregor, Bonnievale and Ashton. In total there are 48 cooperatives and estates open to the public. The greatest concentration is found along the R317 as it follows the Breede River between Robertson and Bonnievale.

One of the most welcoming estates along the wine route is **Van Loveren** ① *T023-615 1505, www.vanloveren.co.za, Mon-Fri 0830-1700, Sat 0930-1330*. Try their Blanc de Noir wines. Tastings are conducted in a restored rondavel set in the middle of a colourful garden and can be accompanied by cheese platters.

The **Bon Courage Estate** ① *9 km from Robertson along the R317, T023-626 4178, www. boncourage.co.za, Mon-Fri 0800-1700, Sat 0900-1500*, is best known for its award-winning Chardonnays and wine tasting is in an old Cape Dutch whitewashed building or on the lawns. **Café Maude** is open for lunch. **Robertson** ① *T023-626 3059, www.robertsonwinery. co.za, Mon-Fri 0800-1700, Sat-Sun 0900-1500*, is the oldest winery in the area. The shop and processing plant are located on Voortrekker Road. During the harvest time you can see tractor loads of grapes being delivered to the town.

→ WORCESTER AND AROUND

This medium-sized farming centre is the capital of the Breede River Valley, a prosperous town with many interesting historic buildings and museums. The excellent Karoo Desert National Botanical Garden is well worth visiting, particularly during the flowering months of August to October, and there's a wine route to explore.

ARRIVING IN WORCESTER
Tourist information Worcester Wine and Tourism ① *25 Baring St, T023-348 6244, www.worcestertourism.com, Mon-Fri 0800-1700, Sat 0830-1230*.

BACKGROUND
The first Europeans to settle in the region were farmers, and when it became necessary to build a settlement, their land had to be acquired. The streets were laid out and the first plots were sold in 1820; the new settlement was named after the Marquess of Worcester, the eldest brother of the Governor of the Cape, Lord Charles Somerset. One of the first buildings to emerge was the local *drostdy* (magistracy), which was one of the finest Cape buildings in South Africa. Today it is part of the Drostdy Technical High School. The wealth in the region is almost entirely derived from agriculture, a fact that is easy to appreciate while travelling past the numerous vineyards and orchards of the valley. Many of the neat farms visible from the roadside depend upon irrigated waters. The highly fertile neighbouring Hex River Valley is in effect the last of the productive Cape farmlands. In contrast, driving east from the valley one quickly comes to the dry and arid Karoo.

PLACES IN WORCESTER
If time permits, a short walk around the centre is very pleasant. The main sights are central and close together, and the grid street pattern makes it easy to find your way about. There are some fine Victorian town buildings, although the main road is made up of mostly modern shops and fast-food outlets. Many of the old buildings are along **Church Street**, most of which were built between 1840 and 1855. Also in Church Street is the **Congregational Church**, housing some fine original examples of wooden church furnishings and standing in a well-

kept garden. The **Dutch Reformed Church** dates from 1832, a Gothic-style building which dominates the town skyline. Its spire has an interesting history: the original was considered to be too squat and was replaced by a cheap tin version in 1899. The current spire was built in 1927 after the tin one had twice been blown down by the summer gales from the southeast.

Worcester is well known throughout South Africa as being the home of two important institutes for the disabled set up by the Dutch Reformed Church. In 1881 an **Institute for the Blind** ① *126 Church St, T023-347 2745, www.blind-institute.org.za*, was opened, and a few years later an **Institute for the Deaf** ① *30 De la Bat St, T023-342 5555, www.deafnet. co.za*, was founded. Both the institutes welcome visitors who wish to learn more about the pioneering work undertaken with blind and deaf people. Unusually, the pedestrian crossings in Worcester emit sounds for the blind.

There are 18 cooperative wine cellars, three wine estates, and several brandy distilleries in the Worcester region. **KWV Brandy Cellar** ① *Church St, T023-342 0255, www.kwv.co.za, Mon-Fri 1000-1500, for tastings, guided tours of the distillery 1000 and 1400*, is the largest in the world under a single roof. There are 120 copper pot stills producing 10- and 20-year-old brandies.

WORCESTER MUSEUM
① *Robertson Rd, T023-342 2225, www.worcestermusuem.co.za, Mon-Sat 0900-1630, R12, children (under 16) R5, café and craft shop.*

This is an open-air museum depicting the lifestyle of the early pioneer farmers. It comprises 26 farm buildings which have been furnished or equipped in the styles of the period 1690-1900. Only the tobacco shed is an original structure, dating from 1900; all the other buildings are reconstructions, but good ones. Several rural skills are demonstrated using traditional methods and tools. You can watch an ironmonger at work, or view the grinding of flour and baking of bread, plus cheese- and candlemaking. Walking around the buildings gives one the feel of being on an old working farm: there are horses, cattle, pigs and geese in pens, not to mention all the farmyard smells and sounds. Inside, most of the displays are of old farm implements and home industry pieces. A couple of items worth a closer look include the early example of a fruit grader, and a mean-looking self raker from the 1860s which was used in the wheat industry. The painted Voortrekker wagon near the entrance illustrates what the living conditions were like.

In addition, the museum is the home of **Worcester Winelands** ① *T023-342 8710, www. worcesterwineroute.co.za*, which is very helpful in giving information on the surrounding winelands, as well as offering tastings and sales of local wines. There are 22 estates listed as part of the Worcester wine route, and some offer tastings, tours and sales to visitors. However, unlike many of the more visited wineries around Stellenbosch, most of the cellars here were founded in the 1940s – the farm buildings therefore lack much of the history and beauty found elsewhere, and the countryside is not as dramatic. Two of the more interesting ones to visit are:

Bergsig Estate ① *T023-355 1603, www.bergsig.co.za, sales and tastings: Mon-Fri 0800-1700, Sat 0900-1700, cellar tours: by prior arrangement, 40 km along the R43 towards Ceres*, his is the oldest estate in the region and Bergsig has belonged to the Lategan family for six generations – the first vine was planted in 1843. It is a friendly estate with some good off-dry and semi-sweet whites. The **Bistro** offers breakfast, tea and cake and light lunches.

Conradie Private Cellar ① *T023-342 7025, www.conradie-vineyards.co.za, sales and tastings: Mon-Sat 0900-1700, Sun 1000-1400, cellar tours: by appointment, 19 km from Worcester along the R60 towards Robertson.* This young cellar is well known for its reds including Cabernet Sauvignon, Shiraz and Merlot and an affordable range of whites. You can eat at the restaurant and enjoy their wine in the **Nuy Valley Guest House** across the road.

KAROO DESERT NATIONAL BOTANICAL GARDEN

① *Off Roux St beyond the golf club on the north side of the N1, T023-347 0785, www.sanbi. org, 0900-1900, free, R17, children (under 16) R7 in the flower season, Aug-Oct. Plant shop and Kokerboom Restaurant (1000-1700).*

This garden, hidden away from the commercial centre of town, combines 144 ha of natural semi-desert plants and 11 ha of landscaped gardens filled with plants from similar arid regions within South Africa. The collection was originally started at Whitehill near Matjiesfontein in 1921, but moved to Worcester in 1946 to make the gardens more accessible to visitors from Cape Town.

Visiting during a time of year when many of the species are in flower allows you to appreciate how colourful deserts can be when it rains. August, September and October are good months to go, assuming the rains have been good. Stapelias bloom from the New Year through to mid-March, and June is the ideal period to see the exotic aloes in flower. In the formal gardens there are a few greenhouses which display a collection, world-famous among botanists, of stone plants, *conophytum*. Two common plants of the region to look out for are the Namibian wild grape, *Cyphostemma juttae*, and the Karoo bush, *Pteronia paniculata*. Given that the collection comprises over 400 species of flowering plants (*aloes, lampranthus, lithops, conophytum*) it is not surprising to find that the local birdlife is exceptionally rich. Over 70 species have been recorded in the gardens. There are also several short trails, including an excellent 1-km-long **Braille Trail**, and much of the gardens are wheelchair accessible. Children will especially enjoy the porkwood plant maze.

FAIRY GLEN PRIVATE GAME RESERVE

① *5 km north of town beyond the golf club off the N1, T021-424 9173 (Cape Town), www. fairyglen.co.za.*

Set at the foot of the Brandwacht Mountains surrounded by Cape fynbos vegetation, and roughly an hour's drive from Cape Town, this is a 20,000-ha private reserve where a number of game species have been introduced including the Big Five plus wildebeest, giraffe, bontebok, hartebeest, zebra, springbok, klipspringer, nyala, steenbok and rhebok, among others, and a good variety of birdlife, including the endangered black eagle. The two elephants were relocated from Kruger. Apart from game drives, there are a number of activities for overnight visitors, and there are programmes for day visitors. The normal drill is a pickup from Cape Town 0630-0700 to get to the reserve in time for breakfast followed by a two- to three-hour game drive with perhaps a stop to look at some San rock paintings, and then lunch before being transferred back to Cape Town in the mid-afternoon; R1455 for self-drive visitors, R2155 with transfers, children (5-12) half price. There is the option to supplement the game drive with a horse safari; check out the website for all the packages.

GOING FURTHER
Tulbagh

Tucked away in the Tulbagh Valley, surrounded by the Winterhoekberg, Witsenberg and Saronsberg Mountains, is this small village with a beautifully preserved centre of traditional Cape buildings, one of the best examples of a rural Victorian settlement in South Africa. However, the state of the buildings is somewhat artificial because much of the settlement was destroyed by a sudden earthquake on 29 September 1969: the village underwent massive restoration and became the fine settlement you see today.

The first settlers arrived in the valley on 31 July 1700 but it was another 40 years before permanent structures appeared and a village took shape. As with many settlements in the Cape, Tulbagh is named after a former Governor of the Cape, Ryk Tulbagh (1751-1771). Today Tulbagh is a prosperous and peaceful settlement.

The office of **Tulbagh Tourism** ① *4 Church St, T023-230 1348, www.tulbaghtourism.org. za, Mon-Fri 0900-1700, Sat 0900-1500, Sun 1000-1500*, is enthusiastic and friendly, with some interesting and useful leaflets covering the area. There is an attached restaurant and coffee shop with outdoor seating overlooking beautiful Church Street. The office is in one of the houses which is part of the museum; tickets for all the museum buildings are sold here.

The main attraction is the delightful tree-lined **Church Street**; 32 of its original buildings were restored after the earthquake, and the whole street feels like a living museum. The majority of the buildings are in private ownership, but three are part of the town museum (see below) and a couple have been converted into B&Bs. The old slave lodge is now the **Paddagang** ('frog passage') **Restaurant**, overlooking lush lawns. In complete contrast, the main commercial centre, Van der Stel Street, is a straight line of dull modern buildings saved by a colourful municipal garden.

If your time is short, the one place to visit in Tulbagh is the **Oude Kerk Volksmuseum** ① *2 Church St, T023-230 1041, Mon-Fri 0830-1700, Sat 0900-1500, Sun 1100-1500, R10, children (under 16) R2*, which has one of the most interesting collections of Victorian furniture and objects in the Cape. The high ceiling and good light of the church makes it an ideal display case and it's a popular venue for weddings. There is also interesting information about the 1969 earthquake.

The **Old Drostdy Museum** ① *follow Van der Stel St north of town for 4 km, T023-230 0203, www.drostdywines.co.za, Mon-Fri 1000-1700, Sat 1000-1400, R7 per person, wine tasting R8*, is built on one of the early settler farms. Designed by Louis Thibault, it has been restored and now houses a fine collection of sherry vats in the cellars, plus a museum devoted to antique furniture upstairs. Nearby is the **Drostdy Wine Cellar**, where local wines and sherries are made. The Old Drostdy building appears on their wine labels. For a small extra fee, their fortified wines can be tasted in the atmospheric, candlelit cellars.

If you want to stay near Tulbagh, we recommend **Morgansvlei Country Estate** (3 km southeast of town off the R44, T023-230 8877, www.morgansvlei.com), a historical wine farm dating to 1710 in a beautiful location with mountain views and surrounded by giant oak trees. It has 15 spacious rooms with Victorian baths and vine-covered stoeps are set in Cape Dutch buildings overlooking a dam, with a peaceful grassy pool area, breakfast room and bar in the old wine cellar. Also recommended is the **Tulbagh Hotel** (22 Van der Stel St, T023-230 0071, www.tulbaghhotel.co.za), which dates from 1859 and has six air-conditioned B&B rooms, a restaurant, bar and pool in a secluded courtyard.

For information about the vineyards in this region visit www.tulbaghwineroute.com.

ROUTE 62 LISTINGS

WHERE TO STAY

Oudtshoorn
$$$ Queen's Hotel, 5 Baron van Rheede St, T044-272 2101, www.queenshotel. co.za. Elegant and historic central hotel (1880) next to the **CP Nel Museum**, with 40 a/c stylish and comfortable rooms with antiques, a/c, Wi-Fi and DSTV, impressive marble foyer, excellent restaurant, café and deli, bar, pool in courtyard.

$$$ The Robertson Small Hotel, 58 Van Reenen St, T023-626 7200, www.the robertsonsmallhotel.com. Very stylish boutique hotel with 10 exquisite rooms, startlingly all-white decor, luxurious satin and velvet fabrics, a chrome and glass bar, the excellent **Reuben's** restaurant, pool and spa, and can pack off guests for the day with a gourmet picnic basket.

$$-$ Nuy Valley Guest House, 19 km from town off the R60 towards Robertson, T023-342 7025, www.nuyvallei.co.za. A large, well-kept guesthouse in an 1871 Cape Dutch building close to the river on a wine estate, 18 individually decorated rooms, restaurant, self-catering kitchen, pool in neat gardens with rose trees and ornamental ponds. A walk will take you to a refreshing waterfall. The wine cellar has been converted into cheaper rooms with shared bathrooms, which are outstanding value.

Montague
$$$-$$ Avalon Springs, 3 km from town centre, Uitvlucht St, T023-614 1150, www.

avalonsprings.co.za. A well-developed resort centred on the hot springs with a range of self-catering apartments and chalets and hotel rooms, 2 restaurants, 3 bars, shops, several hot and cold swimming pools, 60-m water slide, jacuzzis and spa baths, gym and sauna, tennis courts. Ideal for families and you really need at least 2 nights to enjoy the facilities. Day visitors permitted.

Robertson
$$$ The Robertson Small Hotel, 58 Van Reenen St, T023-626 7200, www.the robertsonsmallhotel.com. Very stylish boutique hotel with 10 exquisite rooms, startlingly all-white decor, luxurious satin and velvet fabrics, a chrome and glass bar, the excellent **Reuben's** restaurant, pool and spa, and can pack off guests for the day with a gourmet picnic basket.

Worcester
$$-$ Nuy Valley Guest House, 19 km from town off the R60 towards Robertson, T023-342 7025, www.nuyvallei.co.za. A large, well-kept guesthouse in an 1871 Cape Dutch building close to the river on a wine estate, 18 individually decorated rooms, restaurant, self-catering kitchen, pool in neat gardens with rose trees and ornamental ponds. A walk will take you to a refreshing waterfall. The wine cellar has been converted into cheaper rooms with shared bathrooms, which are outstanding value.

RESTAURANTS

$$-$ Cango Caves Restaurant, at the Cango Caves, T044-272 7313. Open 0900-1700. Caters for tour groups but surprisingly good food and has terrace tables with views of the Swartberg Mountains. Breakfasts, light lunches, teas, the menu has a distinctive ostrich flavour – burgers, kebabs, steaks, or try the ostrich *potjie* with ginger and wild herbs or ostrich tempura with noodles.

$ Clarke of the Karoo, on the R62 as it goes through Barrydale, T028-572 1017, www.clarkekaroo.co.za. 0730-1630. Famous Route 62 lunch stop at a rambling farm stall, great traditional Karoo food like lamb curry, bobotie, plus oysters and yellowfin tuna from the West Coast, and snacks like home-made soup and burgers. The shop sells local preserves and olive oil.

THE WINELANDS

The Winelands is South Africa's oldest and most beautiful wine-producing area, a fertile series of valleys quite unlike the rest of the Western Cape. It is the Cape's biggest attraction after Cape Town, and its appeal is simple: it offers the chance to sample several hundred different wines in a historical and wonderfully scenic setting.

This was the first region after Cape Town to be settled, and the towns of Stellenbosch, Paarl and Franschhoek are some of the oldest in South Africa. Today, their streets are lined with beautiful Cape Dutch and Georgian houses, although the real architectural gems are the manor houses on the wine estates. While the wine industry flourished during the 18th and 19th centuries, the farmers built grand homesteads with cool wine cellars next to their vines. Most of these have been lovingly restored and today can be visited as part of a Winelands tour – many have even been converted into gourmet restaurants or luxury hotels.

→GETTING THERE AND MOVING ON

Paarl and Wellington are best accessed along the N1 from Worcester in the Breede River Valley. For Franschhoek and Stellenbosch, head south from Paarl on the R44.

To visit the Winelands on a self-drive trip from Cape Town you can follow this N1 route in reverse to Paarl and Wellington. Alternatively, you can take the N2 highway past Cape Town International airport, 22 km east of the city, and then continue along the northern fringes of the Cape Flats, home to the sprawling townships of Mitchells Plain, Nyanga and Khayelitsha. Beyond these the R310 left turning is the quickest route to Stellenbosch, the heart of the Winelands, 16 km from the N2.

The wine estates in the region are far too numerous to list in full, but on an organized tour or a self-drive trip (with a designated driver), there is ample opportunity to visit several estates in one day.

Tourist information Tourist offices in Cape Town (see page 36) can provide brochures and maps; also visit www.tourismcapewinelands.co.za. There are also tourist offices in the regional towns. Wine estates charge a small tasting fee of about R5-20, which often includes a free wine glass.

BACKGROUND

The Cape's wine industry was started in earnest by Simon van der Stel in 1679. Previously, vines had been grown by Van Riebeeck in Constantia, Company's Garden and in the area known today as Wynberg. The first wine was produced in 1652, and there was soon a great demand from the crews of ships when they arrived in Table Bay as red wine was drunk to fight off scurvy and it kept better than water. As the early settlers moved inland and farms were opened up in the sheltered valleys, more vines were planted. Every farmer had a few plants growing alongside the homestead, and by chance the soils and climate proved to be ideal. Van der Stel produced the first quality wines on Constantia estate, with the help of Hendrik Cloete. These were mostly sweet wines made from a blend of white and red Muscadel grapes, known locally as *Hanepoot* grapes. The industry received a boost in 1806 when the English, at war with France, started to import South African wines.

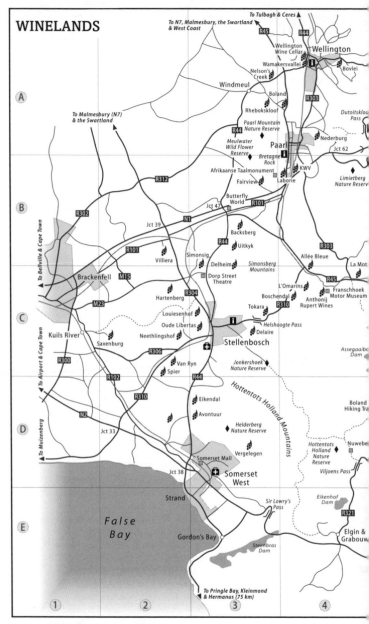

WINELANDS

To Tulbagh & Ceres ▲

To N7, Malmesbury, the Swartland & West Coast

R45   R44

Wellington Wine Cellar

Wellington 🚉

Wamakersvallei

Nelson's Creek

Bovlei

A

To Malmesbury (N7) & the Swartland ▲

Windmeul

Boland   R303

Rhebokskloof

Dutoitskloof Pass

R312

Paarl Mountain Nature Reserve

R44

Meulwater Wild Flower Reserve

Nederburg

Paarl 🚉

Jct 62

Bretagne Rock

Afrikaanse Taalmonument

KWV

Fairview   Laborie

Limietberg Nature Reserve

Butterfly World

B

R302

Jct 47   R101

Jct 39   N1

Backsberg

R303

R101

R44   Uitkyk

Allée Bleue

La Mot

Villiera

Simonsig

Delheim   Simonsberg Mountains

L'Omarins   Franschhoek Motor Museum

Brackenfell

M15

Dorp Street Theatre

Boschendal   Anthonij Rupert Wines

R45

R310

To Bellville & Cape Town ▲

M23

Hartenberg   R304

Tokara

C

Louisenhof

Helshoogte Pass

Oude Libertas   Delaire

Kuils River

Saxenburg   Neethlingshof

Stellenbosch ℹ

Assegaaibo Dam

R306

R300

Van Ryn

Jonkershoek Nature Reserve

To Airport & Cape Town ▲

R102

Spier   R44

Boland Hiking Tra

Eikendal

D

R310

Avontuur

Helderberg Nature Reserve

Hottentots Holland Nature Reserve

Nuwebe

Jct 33

Vergelegen

Viljoens Pass

To Muizenberg ▲

N2

Somerset Mall

Eikenhof Dam

Jct 38

Somerset West

R321

Strand

Sir Lowry's Pass

Elgin & Grabouw

E

False Bay

Gordon's Bay

Steenbras Dam

Hottentots Holland Mountains

To Pringle Bay, Kleinmond & Hermanus (75 km) ▼

① ② ③ ④

To Ceres via
Bain's Kloof Pass

Rawsonville

To Worcester & Great Karoo

Huguenot
Tunnel

Vemmershoek
Dam

Franschhoek
Cape Chamonix
Franschhoek
Pass
Paradise
Stables
Mont   Joubertsgat
Rochelle   Bridge

Villersdorp

Theewaterskloof
Dam

N2

To Caledon &
Swellendam

5   6

Today, all major wine grape varieties
are grown in South Africa, plus the fruity
red Pinotage, a variety produced in
Stellenbosch in 1925 by crossing Pinot
Noir and Cinsault. Wine is now produced as
far north as the Orange River Valley in the
Northern Cape, and South Africa produces
some 800 million litres of wine each year.

→PAARL WINELANDS

PAARL
While Paarl is home to two of South
Africa's better-known wine estates, KWV
and Nederburg (see page 118), the town
itself is fairly staid and is not as interesting
as Stellenbosch or as fashionable as
Franschhoek. All of the attractions and
restaurants are strung out along Main Street
at the base of Paarl Mountain. When the
first European arrival, Abraham Gabbema,
saw this mountain in October 1657 it had
just rained; the granite domes sparkled in
the sunlight and he named the mountains
paarl (pearl) and *diamandt* (diamond).
The first settlers arrived in 'Paarlvallei' in
1687 and, shortly afterwards, the French
Huguenots settled on four farms, **Laborie**,
Goede Hoop, **La Concorde** and **Picardie**.
The town grew in a random fashion along
an important wagon route to Cape Town.
Several old buildings survive, but they are
spread out rather than concentrated in
a few blocks as in Stellenbosch. There is a
helpful **tourist office** ① *216 Main St, T021-
877 0860, www.paarlonline.com, Mon-Fri
0800-1700, Sat 0900-1400, Sun 1000-1400.*

Places in Paarl The 1-km walk along Main
Street will take you past some of the finest
architecture in Paarl. Here you'll find one of the
oldest buildings, the **Paarl Museum** ① *303
Main St, T021-876 2651, Mon-Fri 0900-1700,
Sat 0900-1300, R5, children (under 16) free.* This
18th-century U-shaped Cape Dutch former
parsonage houses a reasonably diverting

DREAM TRIP 1: The Winelands 115

collection of Cape Dutch furniture and kitchen copperware plus some more delicate silver. There is also a small section outlining Paarl during Apartheid, although the fact that Nelson Mandela spent his final years in prison near Paarl is barely mentioned. Only a few hundred metres away, in Gideon Malherbe House, the **Afrikaans Language Museum** ① *Pastorie St, T021-872 3441, www.taalmuseum.co.za, Mon-Fri 0900-1600, Sat 0900-1300, R12, children (under 16) R5*, gives a detailed chronicle of the development of the Afrikaans language and the people involved. The house itself was built in 1860 by a wealthy wine farmer of the same name and the downstairs rooms have been decorated with period furniture donated by his descendents.

On the east bank of the Berg River is a 31-ha **arboretum** ① *open during daylight hours*. From Main Street, go down Market Street and cross the river; the arboretum is on the right. It was created in 1957 to mark the tercentenary of the discovery of the Berg River Valley. To help establish the parkland the town treasurer asked other municipalities in South Africa to contribute trees and shrubs from their region. The response was excellent and when the arboretum was inaugurated there were trees from 61 different regions. Today there are over 700 different species and around 4000 trees.

PAARL MOUNTAIN NATURE RESERVE
① *Jan Philips Mountain Drive, T021-872 3658, Nov-May 0700-1900, Apr-Oct 0700-1800, free, small entrance fee to the reserve but only at weekends.*

Paarl runs along the eastern base of Paarl Mountain, a giant granite massif, which in 1970 was declared the Paarl Mountain Nature Reserve. Within the 1900-ha reserve is a network of footpaths, a circular drive and a couple of dams. The vegetation differs from the surrounding countryside because of the bedrock – the granite mass is not as susceptible to veld fires and many of the fynbos species grow exceptionally tall. The domed summit is easy to climb, and near the top is an old cannon dating from the early days of the Cape Colony. Just below the summit a mountain stream flows through the **Meulwater Wild Flower Reserve**. This garden was created in 1931, and contains specimens of the majority of flowers found around Paarl Mountain including 15 species of protea.

Set high on the slopes of Paarl Mountain amongst granite boulders and indigenous trees stands the controversial **Afrikaanse Taalmonument** ① *Gabbema Doordrift St, follow signs off Main St just after the R45 enters the south of town from the N1, T021-872 3441, 0800-1700, Oct-Mar 0800-2000, R15, children (under 16) R10, coffee shop 0800-1700*, three concrete columns linked by a low curved wall. This is the Afrikaans Language Monument, inaugurated in October 1975 and designed by Jan van Wijk. Built to celebrate 100 years of Afrikaans being declared as a different language from Dutch, it is thought to be on the only monument in the world dedicated to a language. Each column represents different influences in the language. The phrase *Dit is ons erns*, roughly meaning 'this is our earnestness' is inscribed on the pathway leading up to the monument. There are excellent views across the Berg River Valley from here, and on a clear day you can see False Bay, Table Mountain and all the vineyards.

Those with little children in tow may wish to visit **Butterfly World** ① *on the R44 at junction 47 of the N1, T021-875 5628, www.butterflyworld.co.za, 0900-1700, R43, children (3-16) R25, family of 4 ticket R111*, the largest such park in South Africa, with butterflies flying freely in colourful landscaped gardens. They are at their most active on sunny days. There are also spiders, scorpions and meerkats to see and you can buy packets of seeds for children to feed the goats, ducks and chickens in the garden. There is a craft shop and the **Jungle Leaf Café** on site.

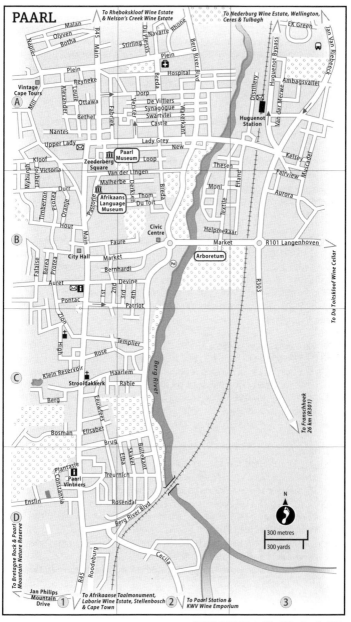

PAARL

PAARL WINE ROUTE

ⓘ *Maps and information can be picked up at the tourist office or visit www.paarlwine.co.za.* The route was set up in 1984 by local producers to help promote their wines and attract tourists into the area. The programme has been a great success and some of the estates have opened their own restaurants. All of the estates have tastings and wine sales on a daily basis. Today there are 30 members, but only the largest estates conduct regular cellar tours. Below is a short selection.

Fairview ⓘ *Suid-Agter-Paarl Rd, off the R101, T021-863 2450, www.fairview.co.za, wine and cheese sales and tastings and restaurant: 0900-1700.* This popular estate has a rather unusual attraction in the form of a goat tower, a spiral structure which is home to two pairs of goats. In addition to a variety of good wines (look out for the popular Goats do Roam and Bored Doe blends – a humorous dig at French wines) visitors can taste delicious goat cheeses, which are now produced from a herd of over 700 goats and sold in South African supermarkets. Their Camembert consistently wins awards as the best in the world at the annual World Cheese Awards. Meals are served in **The Goatshed** restaurant.

The Laborie ⓘ *Taillefer St, T021-807 3390, www.laboriewines.co.za, sales and tastings: Oct-Mar daily 0900-1700, Apr-Sep, Mon-Sat 0900-1700, Sun 1100-1500; restaurant: 1100-1530, Wed-Sun 1800-2200.* Part of KWV (see below), this is a beautifully restored original Cape Dutch homestead – in many ways the archetypal wine estate, and developed with tourism firmly in mind. It's an attractive spot, with a tasting area overlooking rolling lawns and vineyards, and a highly rated restaurant. As well as a good range of wines they produce an award-winning brandy.

KWV Wine Emporium ⓘ *Kohler St, T021-807 3007, www.kwv.co.za, sales and tastings: Mon-Sat 0900-1600, Sun 1100-1600; cellar tours: Mon-Sat 1000, 1015 (in German), 1030, 1415.* A short distance from the Laborie estate is the famous **KWV Cellar Complex** which contains the five largest vats in the world. The **Ko-operative Wijnbouwers Vereniging van Zuid-Afrika** (Cooperative Wine Growers' Association) was established in Paarl in 1918 and is responsible for exporting many of South Africa's best-known wines. They are also well known for their brandy and tastings are served with Belgian chocolates.

Nederburg ⓘ *Sonstraal Rd, T021-862 3104, www.nederburg.co.za, sales and tastings: Mon-Fri 08-1700, Sat 1000-1600, Nov-Mar Sun 1100-1400; cellar tours Mon-Fri 1030 and 1500, Sat-Sun 1100; Nov-Mar picnic lunches (vegetarian and children's menu available).* This is one of the largest and best-known estates in South Africa. Their annual production is in excess of 650,000 cases. As such a large concern they are involved in much of the research in South Africa to improve the quality of the grape and vine. Every April the annual Nederburg Auction attracts buyers from all over the world and is considered one of the top five wine auctions in the world. The homestead was built in 1800, but throughout the 19th century the wines were not considered to be anything special. This all changed in 1937 when Johann George Graue bought the estate. Riesling and Cabernet Sauvignon vines were planted, and the cellars completely modernized. Today their wines win countless annual awards.

Nelson's Creek ⓘ *R44, T021-869 8453, www.nelsonscreek.co.za, sales and tastings: Mon-Fri 0900-1700, Sat 0900-1400.* This is a very pleasant estate and the Nelson family has been successfully producing wines since 1987. In 1996, they donated part of the estate to the farm labourers who now produce wines under the 'New Beginnings' label. Picnic baskets are available in summer. A mountain-bike challenge is held on the estate in September.

Rhebokskloof ⓘ *Northern Agter-Paarl Rd, T021-869 8386, www.rhebokskloof.co.za, sales and tastings and restaurant: 0900-1700.* This old estate is now a thoroughly modern outfit. Informal tastings are accompanied by cheese and biscuits; pre-booked formal guided tastings are accompanied by a variety of snacks to bring out the flavours of the wines and a cellar tour. The terrace café is popular with tour groups and on Sundays they offer a family buffet lunch with children's entertainment; picnic baskets are available in summer.

→FRANSCHHOEK VALLEY

FRANSCHHOEK

This is the most pleasant of the Wineland's villages, with a compact centre of Victorian whitewashed houses backed by rolling vineyards and the soaring slopes of the Franschhoek Mountains. It does, however, have an artificial feel to it as most of the attractions here have been created to serve the tourist industry. The outlying wine estates all have their individual appeal, but the village itself is made up of restaurants and touristy craft shops. Nevertheless, Franschhoek is famed for its cuisine and dubs itself the 'gourmet capital of South Africa', so a visit here should guarantee an excellent meal accompanied by a fine glass of wine.

Arriving in Franschhoek Franschhoek is 71 km from Cape Town (via the N1), 26 km from Paarl and 31 km from Stellenbosch. There is no regular public transport so you will need a car. Most of the tour operators offering Winelands tours don't usually include Franschhoek. The **tourist office** ⓘ *70 Huguenot Rd, T021-876 3603, www.franschhoek.org.za, Mon-Fri 0900-1800, Sat 1000-1700, Sun 1000-1600,* has helpful staff with a good knowledge of accommodation and restaurants. The office also has the Franschhoek wine route desk (see below) and a wine- and cheese-tasting area, and there's a plant nursery at the back.

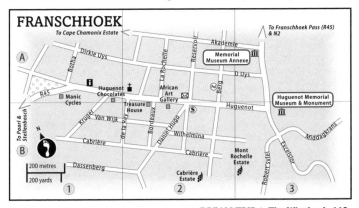

Background Although the first Huguenots arrived at the Cape in 1688, the village of Franschhoek only took shape in 1837 after the church and the manse had been built. The first immigrants settled on farms granted to them by Simon van der Stel along the Drakenstein Valley at Oliphantshoek in 1694. Franschhoek is built on parts of La Motte and Cabrière farms. The village became the focal point of the valley but the oldest and most interesting buildings are to be found on the original Huguenot farms and estates.

Places in Franschhoek The **Huguenot Memorial Museum** ① *T021-876 2532, www. museum.co.za, Mon-Sat 0900-1700, Sun 1400-1700, R10, children (under 16) R5*, is housed in two buildings either side of Lambrecht Street. The main building, to the left of the Huguenot Monument, is modelled on a house designed by the French architect, Louis Michel Thibault, built in 1791 at Kloof Street, Cape Town. The displays inside trace the history of the Huguenots in South Africa. There are some fine collections of furniture, silverware and family bibles, but the most interesting displays are the family trees providing a record of families over the past 250 years. One of the roles of the museum today is to maintain an up-to-date register of families, so that future generations will be able to trace their ancestors.

Next door to the museum is the rather stark and unattractive **Huguenot Monument**, a highly symbolic memorial built to mark 250 years since the first Huguenots settled in the Cape. It is set in a peaceful rose garden with the rugged Franschhoek Mountains providing a contrasting background. The three arches represent the Trinity, and the golden sun and cross on top are the Sun of Righteousness and the Cross of Christian Faith. In front of the arches, a statue of a woman with a bible in her right hand and a broken chain in her left symbolizes freedom from religious oppression. If you look closely at the globe you can see objects carved into the southern tip of Africa: a bible, harp, spinning wheel, sheaf of corn and a vine. These represent different aspects of the Huguenots' life, respectively their faith, their art and culture, their industry and their agriculture. The final piece of the memorial, the curved colonnade, represents tranquillity and spiritual peace after the problems they had faced in France.

FRANSCHHOEK WINE ROUTE

All the vineyards lie along the Franschhoek Valley, making it one of the most compact wine routes in the region. There are now 42 wine estates on the route, and again many estates have opened their own excellent restaurants and several also offer luxury accommodation. Maps and information on all the estates are available at the tourist office.

Allée Bleue ① *R45, T021-874 1021, www.alleebleue.com, sales and tastings: 0900-1700; restaurant 0900-16*. This estate is a good place to drop in for some quick wine tasting if you haven't the time to see a whole vineyard. Tastings include four wines accompanied by four cheeses to offset the flavours. There is a small fashionable bistro and picnic baskets are available.

Anthonij Rupert Wines (L'Ormarins) ① *R45, T021-874 9000, www.rupertwines.com, sales and tastings: Mon-Fri 0900-1630, Sat 1000-1500*. The original land was granted to the Huguenot, Jean Roi, in 1694, who named the farm after his village in the South of France. The present homestead was built in 1811 – from its grand marble halls and staircases you look out across an ornamental pond and neat gardens. Among the classic range of wines, is the Italian varietal range, Terra del Capo. Also here is the **Franschhoek Motor Museum** ① *Mon-Fri 1000-1600, Sat-Sun 1000-1500, T021-874 9000, www.fmm.co.za, R60 per person,*

One of the popular recommended day drives from Cape Town is known as the Four Passes route. This takes you through the heart of the Winelands, and, as the name suggests, over four mountain passes. It is a wonderful day out from Cape Town, especially if combined with fine wine and gourmet food in Franschhoek. The first stop on the drive is Stellenbosch. From here you take the R310 towards Franschhoek. Driving up out of Stellenbosch you cross the first pass – **Helshoogte Pass**. After 17 km you reach a T-junction with the R45: a left turn would take you to Paarl, 12 km, but the route continues to the right. This is a pleasant drive up into the Franschhoek Valley. The road follows a railway line and part of the Berg River. After passing through Franschhoek, take a left in front of the Huguenot Monument and climb out of the valley via the **Franschhoek Pass**. This pass was built along the tracks formed by migrating herds of game centuries earlier, and was originally known as the Olifantspad (elephant's path). One of the more surprising aspects of this drive is the change in vegetation once you cross the lip of the pass, 520 m above the level of Franschhoek. As the road winds down towards Theewaterskloof Dam, you pass through a dry valley full of scrub vegetation and fynbos – gone are the fertile fruit farms and vineyards.

Take a right across the dam on the R321 towards Grabouw and Elgin. An alternative but much longer route back to Cape Town is to take a left here, onto the R43. This is the road to Worcester, 50 km, the principal town in the Breede River Valley (see page 106). From Worcester follow the N1 back to Cape Town.

The Four Passes Route continues across the Theewaterskloof Dam and then climbs **Viljoens Pass**, the third of four. To the right lies the Hottentots Holland Nature Reserve, a popular hiking region. The country around here is an important apple-growing region. At the N2 highway turn right and follow the road back into Cape Town. The fourth and most spectacular pass is **Sir Lowry's Pass**, which crosses the Hottentots Holland Mountains. From the viewpoint at the top you will be rewarded with a fine view of the Cape Flats with the brooding Cape Peninsula behind.

which has over 80 vintage and classic cars on display plus other vehicles such as an 1898 tricycle. Any car enthusiast will enjoy a visit here and the valuable cars are displayed in chronological order from pre-1900 models up to a 2003 Ferrari.

Boschendal ① *R310, T021-870 4272, www.boschendal.com, sales and tastings: daily 0830-1830; vineyard and cellar tours: 1030 and 1130, by appointment; restaurants 1000-1700.* Boschendal has been producing wine since 1687 and is today one of the most popular and beautiful estates in the region, not least for its excellent food and pleasant wine-tasting area underneath a giant oak. The restored H-shaped manor house (1812) is one of the finest in South Africa, and is open as a museum to the public. The restaurant serves an excellent buffet lunch, Le Pique Nique offers picnic hampers in the gardens between November and April, and Le Café has light meals and afternoon teas.

Cape Chamonix ① *Uitkyk St, T021-876 2494, www.chamonix.co.za, sales and tastings: 0930-1630; cellar tours: by appointment.* This is one of the largest farms in the valley, with an underground cellar providing pleasantly cool tours at the height of summer. Wine tastings are held in the Blacksmith's Cottage; you can also try their fruit schnapps or the Chamonix mineral water. The **Mon Plaisir** restaurant is family friendly and highly rated. Food is prepared on a stove built in Paris in 1908. Accommodation is in 13 comfortable whitewashed self-catering cottages (**$$**).

Mont Rochelle ⓘ *Dassenberg Rd, T021-876 2770, www.montrochelle.co.za, sales and tastings: 1000-1900; cellar tours: Mon-Fri 1100, 1230 and 1500; restaurant 1200-1500, 1900-2130.* This estate has one of the most attractive settings in the region with beautiful views of the valley and it produces some good full-bodied red wines and a couple of whites. Tastings are informal and friendly and picnic baskets are available. The estate is also home to a hotel and restaurant.

La Motte ⓘ *R45, T021-876 3119, www.la-motte.co.za, sales and tastings: Mon-Sat 0900-1700, restaurant Tue-Sun 1100-1700, Thu-Sat 1830-2230.* The original manor house was built in 1752 and the grand old cellars can be viewed through glass walls from the tasting room. The museum and gallery has interesting exhibits on Cape Dutch architecture and some valuable local art. The restaurant with its pleasant conservatory has a good choice of traditional South African dishes.

→ STELLENBOSCH

Stellenbosch, the centre of the Winelands, is the oldest and most attractive town in the region, with a large university giving it a liveliness which is lacking in other nearby towns. The centre has a pleasing mix of architectural styles: Cape Dutch, Georgian, Regency and Victorian houses line broad streets, dappled with shade from centuries-old oak trees, and furrowed with water ditches which still carry water to the gardens. It's a fairly large place but, with its handful of good museums and fun nightlife, is a perfect base for visiting the wine estates.

ARRIVING IN STELLENBOSCH

The town is served by the suburban Metro railway from Cape Town, but for safety reasons, this is best avoided. Hiring a car is the best way of getting here as you then have the freedom to explore the surrounding wine estates. The trip from Cape Town takes about an hour, either along the N1 or the N2. Stellenbosch itself is perfect for exploring on foot as many of the interesting sights are concentrated in a small area along Church, Dorp and Drostdy streets. **Stellenbosch Tourist Office** ⓘ *36 Market St, T021-883 3584, www.stellenboschtourism.co.za, Mon-Fri 0800-1800, Sat 0900-1700, Sun 1000-1600 (in Jun and Aug the office opens 1 hr later and closes 1 hr earlier),* is a professional and helpful office, which provides maps and can help with accommodation bookings, tour information and wine routes. **Stellenbosch On Foot** ⓘ *T021-887 9150, or book at the tourist office, R90 per person (minimum 3 people),* offers 90-minute guided walks that leave from the tourist office every day at 1100 and 1500.

BACKGROUND

In November 1679, Governor of the Cape Simon van der Stel left Cape Town with a party of soldiers in order to explore the hinterland. There was already a great need for additional land to be brought under cultivation to supply both Cape Town and passing ships calling for fresh supplies. On the first night the group camped beside a stream they named the Kuilsrivier. The stream turned out to be a tributary of a much larger river, the Eersterivier. As they followed the Eersterivier towards the mountains they found themselves in a fertile alluvial valley. There was no sign of human habitation, the waters were cool and clean and everything seemed to grow in abundance – exactly the type of land Van der Stel had been sent to discover. Several days after entering the valley the group camped under a large tree on an island formed by two branches of the Eersterivier. The camp was named Van der Stel se Bosch (Van der Stel's Wood).

Six months later, in May 1680, eight families from Cape Town moved into the area, tempted by the offer of as much free land as they could cultivate, and by the summer of 1681 Stellenbosch was a thriving agricultural community. This became the first European settlement in the interior of southern Africa. By the end of 1683 more than 30 families had settled in the valley, a school had been built and a *landdrost* (magistrate) had been appointed. Throughout his life, Simon van der Stel maintained a close interest in the development of the town. One of his greatest legacies was to order the planting of oak trees along the sides of every street. Canals were also built to bring water to the town gardens. Today, a number of the original oaks are still standing and some have been proclaimed national monuments.

It is difficult to picture it today, but at the end of the 17th century this new settlement was a frontier town. For the next 100 years the magistracy had dealings with the explorers, hunters, adventurers and nomadic peoples who lived beyond the Cape, and the authority extended over 250,000 sq km. In the meantime, the town prospered as an agricultural centre and also emerged as a place of learning. In 1859 the Dutch Reformed Church started a Seminary which in 1866 became the Stellenbosch Gymnasium, renamed Victoria College in 1887. After the creation of the Union of South Africa in 1910, there was pressure on the new government to establish a single national university. By this stage Victoria College had emerged as a respected Afrikaner school, and Stellenbosch itself was regarded as an important centre of Afrikaner culture. In 1915 a local farmer, Johannes Marais died and left £100,000 towards higher education in Stellenbosch. This bequest finally persuaded the government to yield to public pressure and in April 1918 the Victoria College became the University of Stellenbosch.

PLACES IN STELLENBOSCH

Stellenbosch offers two approaches to sightseeing: walking around the town centre viewing public buildings, oak-lined streets and stately homes; or going on a wine tour, visiting any number of the roughly 130 wineries and private cellars. Spend a couple of days in Stellenbosch and you'll get to do both. No other town in South Africa has such an impressive concentration of early Cape architecture. However, like Swellendam (see page 78), many of the earliest buildings were lost to fires in the 18th and 19th centuries; what you see today is a collection of perfectly restored buildings. Following each fire, the destroyed buildings were recreated with the help of photographs, original plans and sketches, although the technology and materials of the day were used. This is perhaps why they appear to have survived in such good condition. This restoration process is not unusual: the town of Tulbagh in the Breede River Valley was completely destroyed by an earthquake in 1969, but today it has the look and feel of an unspoilt quaint Victorian village.

Dorp Street, which runs east–west in the southern part of town, has all the classic features – an avenue of oak trees, running water in open furrows and carefully restored white-walled buildings. A walk from the **Libertas Parva** building to the Theological College takes you through the oldest parts of town and past some of the best-preserved old buildings. Libertas Parva (No 31), is a beautifully restored classic H-shaped manor house built in 1783, though the present front gable and twin front doors date from the late Georgian period. Today it serves as the **Rembrandt van Rijn Art Gallery** ① *T021-886 4340, Mon-Fri 0900-1245, 1400-1700, Sat 1000-1300, 1400-1700, free*, with pictures of Cape Town. The cellar behind the house has a small wine and cork museum. Continue east along Dorp Street, where you'll pass the famous **Oom Samie se Winkel (Uncle Samie's Store)** ① *No 84, T021-887 0797, 0830-1700*, a Victorian-style general store that is still functioning as a shop today. It became most famous between 1904 and 1944 when the store was owned and run by Samuel Johannes Volsteedt, when he stocked virtually anything and everything the townspeople could possibly need. The shop still sells a wide range of goods and retains it character with items hanging from all corners, and old cabinets full of bits and pieces. Also of particular note on Dorp Street are the town houses just past the junction with Helderberg Street. **Hauptfleisch House** (No 153), **Bakker House** (No 155), **Loubser House** (No 157), and **Saxenhof** (No 159), are regarded as the best-preserved street façades in old Stellenbosch.

Branching off from Dorp Street is Drostdy Street, dominated by a building with a tall tower. Also in this street is the town church, the **Moederkerk**; its current steeple church was designed by Carl Otto Hagen and built in 1862. Inside, it is worth admiring the pulpit and the unusually thick stained-glass windows.

Turn right at the top of Drostdy Street into Van Riebeeck Street, then left into Neethling Street to reach the **Botanical Gardens** ① *0800-1700, free, tea room 1000-1700*. These were established in the 1920s and are part of the University of Stellenbosch, with a fine

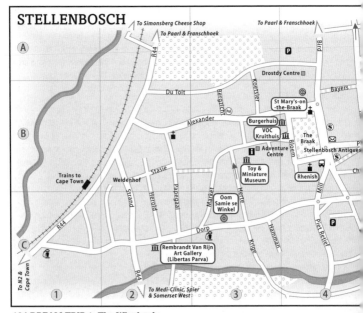

collection of ferns, orchids and bonsai trees. One of the more unusual plants to look out for is the *Welwitschis* from the Namib Desert.

Heading west back along Van Riebeeck Street brings you to Ryneveld Street, where you'll find the entrance to the engaging **Village Museum** ① *T021-887 2948, www.stelmus.co.za, Mon-Sat 0930-1700, Sun 100-1700, R20, children (under 14) R5*. The complex currently spreads over two blocks in the oldest part of town. If you follow the guide numbers you will be taken through four houses, each representing a different period of the town's history. The oldest of these is **Schreuderhuis** (1709), one of the earliest houses to be built in Stellenbosch. The simple furniture and collection of household objects are all of the same period. The house was built by Sebastian Schreuder, a German. **Blettermanhuis** (1789) is a perfect example of what has come to be regarded as a typical H-shaped Cape Dutch home. The furnishings are those of a wealthy household between 1750 and 1780. The house was built by Hendrik Lodewyk Bletterman, the last *landdrost* to be appointed by the Dutch East India Company. Notice the contrast in furnishings between Schreuder the messenger and Bletterman the magistrate. The third building in the museum to have been restored is **Grosvenor House** (1803), in Drostdy Street. This is an excellent example of the two-storeyed town houses that once dominated the streets of Cape Town. The home was built by Christian Ludolph Neethling, a successful farmer, in 1782. The fourth and final house is the fussy **OM Bergh House** (1870), which once had a thatched roof. All four houses are set in neat kitchen gardens which have been recreated to reflect the popular plants of each period. Guides dressed in period clothes are at hand answer any questions and point out interesting details.

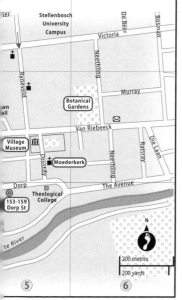

Much of the town's activity today takes place around the **Braak**, at the western end of Church Street. This is the original village green, and one-time military parade ground. On the western edge by Market Street is the **VOC (Vereenigde Oost-Indiesche Compagnie) Kruithuis** ① *T021-887 2948, www.stelmus.co.za, Sep-May, Mon-Fri 0930-1300, R2*, or Powder House, built in 1777 as a weapons store. Today it is a military museum. A short distance north, on the corner of Alexander Street, is the **Burgerhuis** ① *T021-887 0339, Mon-Fri 0800-1630, Sat 1000-1300, 1400-1600, free*, a classic H-shaped Cape Dutch homestead built by Antonie Fick in 1797, that is now decorated to represent the house of a well-to-do Stellenboscher in the Victorian era.

Two churches overlook the Braak, **Rhenish Church**, built in 1832 as a training school for coloured people and slaves, which has a very fine pulpit, and **St Mary's-on-the-Braak**, an Anglican church completed in 1852. A little to the west, on

Market Street just behind the tourist office, is the **Toy and Miniature Museum** ① *T021-887 2948, www.stelmus.co.za, Mon-Sat 0930-1700, Sun 1400-1700, R5*, a small but fairly diverting collection of antique toys including a working model of the Blue Train, and a set of rooms devoted to miniatures. Most interesting are the tiny replicas of furniture, clothes and household items for dolls' houses that you can buy in the shop.

STELLENBOSCH WINE ROUTE

① *Maps and brochures on the wine route can be picked up at the tourist offices in Stellenbosch and Cape Town or visit www.wineroute.co.za. Remember the drink-drive laws in South Africa; when wine tasting, you may be offered up to 15 different wines to sample at each estate, so make sure one of you stays sober.*

This was the first wine route to open in South Africa, in April 1971. It was the idea of three local farmers: Neil Joubert, Frans Malan and Spatz Sperling. It has been hugely successful, attracting tens of thousands of visitors every year, and today the membership comprises more than 200 private cellars. It's possible to taste and buy wines at all of them, and the cellars can arrange for wine to be delivered internationally. Most of the estates have excellent restaurants as well as providing very popular picnic lunches with wine – at weekends it is advisable to book in advance – and many also have guest accommodation.

Delaire ① *R310, T021-885 8160, www.delairewinery.co.za, sales and tastings: Mon-Sat 0900-1700, Sun 1000-1600; restaurant: Tue-Sat 1200-1430, 1830-2100*. This small estate on the crest of the Helshoogte Pass has some of the best views in the valley, and on a clear day visitors are rewarded with views of the Simonsberg Mountains. Their flagship Merlot is very popular, while the Chardonnay remains a favourite export label. The estate provides accommodation in 10 private luxury houses (**$$$$**).

Delheim ① *Knorhoek Rd, off the R44, T021-888 4600, www.delheim.com, sales and tastings: 0900-1700, cellar tours: 1030 and 1430, restaurant: 0930-1630*. The restaurant has a beautiful setting with views towards Cape Town and Table Mountain, and serves breakfasts, lunches and teas, and offers picnic baskets to eat at benches next to the river. Tastings are conducted in a cool downstairs cellar. There are nine comfortable suites for accommodation (**$$$**).

Eikendal ① *R44, T021-855 1422, www.eikendal.com, sales and tastings: 1000-1600; cellar tours: Mon-Fri, 1000 and 1430*. The microclimate on the western slopes of the mountain is ideal for viticulture, and there is a wide selection of both whites and reds. Lunch is served in the wine-tasting room or the gardens; Swiss-owned so expect unusual European dishes on the menu. There are nine comfortable suites for accommodation (**$$$**).

Hartenberg ① *Botterlary Rd, T021-865 2541, www.hartenbergestate.com, sales and tastings: Mon-Fri 0900-1715, Sat 0900-1500; cellar tours: by appointment; lunches: 1200-1400*. The first vines on this estate were planted in 1692, and today is best known for its Gravel Hill Shiraz. During the summer, lunches are served in the shade and peace of the gardens; come winter the tasting room doubles up as a restaurant with warming log fires. Picnic baskets are available to enjoy on the lawns, or picnic backpacks can be taken on a short walking trail through a wetland area on the estate.

Neethlingshof ⓘ *R310, T021-883 8988, www.neethlingshof.co.za, sales and tastings: Mon-Fri 0900-1700, Sat-Sun 1000-1600; cellar and vineyard tours: by appointment; lunches: Tue-Sun 1000-1530.* With its fine Cape Dutch buildings and grand pine avenue (which features on the labels of the wines), this estate is a very pleasant one to visit. The first vines were planted here in 1692 and the manor house was built in 1814 in traditional Cape Dutch H-style. Today this has been converted into the **Lord Neethling** restaurant renowned for its venison and veal. The **The Palm Terrace** has outside tables with beautiful views of the gardens.

Saxenburg ⓘ *Polkadraai Rd, T021-903 6113, www.saxenburg.co.za, sales and tastings: Mon-Fri 0900-1700, Sat 1000-1700, Sun 1000-1600; restaurant: Wed-Sun 1200-1500, Wed-Sat 1800-2030.* Saxenberg has a long history, starting in 1693 when Simon van der Stel granted land to a freeburgher, Jochem Sax. Sax planted the first vines and built the manor house in 1701, and the estate has been producing ever since. It produces a small number of cases each year; its Private Collection of red wines is very good. The **Guinea Fowl** restaurant is in part of the original wine cellar and accommodation is in three small guest rooms on the estate (**$$**).

Spier ⓘ *R310, T021-809 1100, www.spier.co.za, sales and tastings: 1000-1630; meals are available throughout the day and evening at 2 restaurants; picnics and a deli are also available.* This is the Winelands' most commercial wine estate, offering an array of activities as well as wine tastings. Their Private Collection Chenin Blanc and Chardonnay are especially good and frequently win awards. There is a Cheetah Outreach programme (although the creatures seem rather lacklustre) and a birds of prey area, plus horse riding, fishing, an 18-hole golf course and the Camelot spa. **Moyo**, is one of the best restaurants in the Winelands and accommodation is at the **Spier Hotel**.

Simonsig *Kromme Rhee Rd, M23, T021-888 4900, www.simonsig.co.za, sales and tastings: Mon-Fri 0830-1700, Sat 0830-1600; cellar tours: Mon-Fri 1000 and 1500, Sat 1000; restaurant: Tue-Sat 1100-1500, Wed, Fri and Sat 1900-2200, Sun 1100-1400.* This large estate has been in the Malan family for 10 generations, and in recent years has produced some exceptionally fine wines. There is an attractive outdoor tasting area with beautiful views out over the mountains. One wine worth looking out for is the Kaapse Vonkel, a sparkling white considered the best of its kind in South Africa. The **Cuvée**, restaurant has a more modern menu than most and a terrace under oak trees.

THE WINELANDS LISTINGS

WHERE TO STAY

Paarl Winelands

$$$$ Grande Roche, Plantasie St, T021-863 5100, www.granderoche.co.za. A T-shaped manor house dating to 1707 which has established itself as one of the top hotels in South Africa, with 35 luxury a/c suites set in a collection of restored farm buildings in peaceful gardens surrounded by vineyards, 2 floodlit tennis courts, 2 swimming pools, gym. **Bosman's** restaurant is regarded as one of the best in the country.

Franschhoek Valley

$$$$ Le Quartier Français, 16 Huguenot Rd, T021-876 2151, www.lequartier.co.za. A superb hotel and impeccable service with 17 enormous luxury rooms with fireplaces, beautiful bathrooms, plush furnishings and views over the pool and peaceful, shady courtyard, some have private splash pools and lofts for children.

The Screening Room, is a private cinema, and **The Treatment Room**, an intimate spa. The attached restaurants, **The Tasting Room**, and **The Common Room** are considered Franschhoek's best.

Stellenbosch

$$$$ Lanzerac Manor, Jonkershoek Rd, 2 km from town centre T021-887 1132, www.lanzerac.co.za. Very expensive but fittingly luxurious hotel set around an 18th-century Cape Dutch manor house on a wine estate, tastings and cellar tours on offer. 48 spacious and plush suites with private patios and all mod cons, 2 restaurants: the formal **Governor's Hall**, and the more relaxed **Lanzerac Terrace** for alfresco dining during summer. There's an extensive spa with a separate pool overlooking the vines which is also popular with non-guests for a day of pampering.

RESTAURANTS

Paarl Winelands

$$$ Laborie, Taillefer St, off the R45 south of town, T021-807 3095, www.laborie restaurant.co.za. Daily 1100-1530, Wed-Sun 1800-2200. Gourmet restaurant on wine estate with pleasant seating under giant oak trees. Delicious Mediterranean dishes, lots of contemporary choices, as well as Cape specialities like bobotie and Karoo lamb loin, and some vegetarian options. Smart but relaxed atmosphere, good service.

$$-$ The Goatshed, Suid-Agter-Paarl Rd, off the R101, T021-863 2450, www.fairview. co.za, T021-863 3609, www.goatshed.co.za. 0900-1700. At the popular wine and cheese farm, which can sometimes be overrun with tour groups, but don't let that put you off as the food is excellent. Cheese platters with freshly baked bread are the highlight, but the mains of duck, lamb, veal and trout

will appeal to the hungrier. Naturally the baked cheesecake is superb.

Stellenbosch

$$$ Moyo, Spier, on the R310, T021-8091133, www.moyo.co.za. 1200-1600, 1800-2300. Consistently fully booked so make a reservation at least a week ahead. Superb restaurant in a beautiful location and a highlight of a trip to South Africa. Arranged in Bedouin tents with outside tables in delightful tree houses or wrought-iron gazebos lit by candles. The vast buffet has just about everything imaginable from hot mussels to fine cheese and pan-African food. Each table is entertained by women who decorate your face with traditional Xhosa white paint, Zimbabwean musicians, jazz bands and township opera singers.

DREAM TRIP 2:
Durban→Battlefields→Drakensburg→Nelson Mandela Bay 21 days

GOING FURTHER

DREAM TRIP 2
Durban→Battlefields→Drakensburg→Nelson Mandela Bay

KwaZulu Natal manages to squash the country' greatest diversity into a wedge of land between the towering Drakensberg Mountains and the long sweep of sub-tropical coastline. Here, visitors can go on safari, hike through dramatic wilderness, surf the country's best beaches and experience South Africa's strongest African culture.

The province's principal city, the sprawling conurbation of Durban, boasts an extensive beachfront and a steamy tropical climate. Inland, the Battlefields region still bears the scars of the Zulu Wars: the Zulu-Boer War, the Anglo-Zulu War and the Boer War, and there are dozens of battlefield sites; the most evocative are those at Isandlwana, Rorke's Drift and Blood River.

The Drakensberg Mountains soar to 3000 m and extend 180 km along the western edge of KwaZulu Natal, forming the backbone of the uKhahlamba-Drakensberg Park and determining the border with Lesotho. The mountains offer the country's finest hiking and there are numerous remote trails and points from which to explore, ranging from luxury hotels to campsites.

The Eastern Cape, although far less visited than many parts of South Africa, is a fascinating region where most of the people live in rural settlements and work on the land. The former homeland of the Xhosa people, the Wild Coast boasts a rugged, virtually deserted coastline dotted with small seaside villages, while to the southeast is a variety of game reserves and national parks, including the Addo Elephant National Park.

On this itinerary there is the option of flying onwards from Nelson Mandela Bay (Port Elizabeth), a major industrial centre that has surprisingly good beaches, or continuing along the Garden Route, the lush coast stretching towards Cape Town.

DURBAN

The sprawling conurbation of Durban is Africa's largest port and although its appeal is not immediately apparent – few original buildings survive and it can feel hectic and overcrowded – it boasts wide beaches, an extensive beachfront and a steamy tropical climate. The city also has one of the country's most interesting cultural mixes – it is home to substantial Zulu and white communities and South Africa's largest Indian population. Away from the Central Business District (CBD) are attractive suburbs, where tropical foliage spills from ornate balconies and the fast pace of city life is all but forgotten.

ARRIVING IN DURBAN

Getting there Opened in 2010 to replace the old airport to the south of the city, the new **King Shaka International Airport** ① *La Mercy on the Dolphin Coast, 35 km north of the city centre off the N2, T032-436 6000, www.acsa.co.za, www.kingshakainternational.co.za*, has regular domestic flights to and from South Africa's other principal cities. However, with the exception of **Emirates**, there are few international flights and most people change in Johannesburg. There are numerous facilities in the terminal building including restaurants, shops, banks with ATMs and foreign exchange services, several mobile phone rental shops and a **tourist information desk** ① *Mon-Sat 0800-2100, Sun 0900-2100*. Taxis and car hire offices can be found outside the terminal building, and many hotels and backpacker hostels offer airport transfer services. The **King Shaka Airport Shuttle Bus** ① *T031-465 5573, www.airportbustransport.co.za*, departs and arrives at the dedicated stop outside the terminal, 0500-2200, R50 one way to Umhlanga and R70 to Durban city centre, tickets are bought on the bus. From the airport, buses depart every 30 minutes and go to all the large hotels in Umhlanga and in Durban's city centre and beachfront, as well as the Gateway Mall in Umhlanga and Durban's central bus station in the CBD. In the other direction the buses must be pre-booked (so they know which hotels to stop at) and again they run at 30-minute intervals. **King Shaka Airport Shuttle Services** ① *T084-231 1363, www.kingshakashuttles.co.za*, has a desk in the arrivals hall (among other shuttle companies) and provides shuttle buses to Umhlanga, R180, and Durban CBD, R280, for one to four passengers. They can also go to Durban's outlying suburbs. The **Margate Mini Coach** (see page 164) also stops at the airport on its service to the south coast.

Durban **railway station** is on Masabalala Yengwa Road (M12) to the north of the CBD. Behind is the **motorcoach terminal** for major long-distance buses run by **Translux**, **Intercape** and **Greyhound**.

Moving on From Durban, Dream Trip 2 takes you via the Valley of 1000 Hills (40 minutes, see page 144), round the Battlefields Route (page 144) and then through the Drakensburg Mountains and back to Durban.

Once in Durban, you can head south and spend some time on the coast en route to East London or Nelson Mandela Bay (Port Elizabeth). From either of these places it is possible to fly on to Cape Town. With more time, you could spend a week or so travelling overland to Cape Town via the Garden Route and the Whale Coast.

Getting around Durban has developed into South Africa's largest sea port and is also one of its main tourist centres. The approach to Durban passes through coastal tourist resorts, industrial areas, townships and eventually reaches the Central Business District (CBD). The extensive beachfront and the most important landmarks are within easy walking distance in the city centre, but the CBD is now a pretty rough-and-ready district and you'd be advised to take a taxi between the sites. Confusingly, the street names in the CBD were changed in 2008 and presently signs feature the old and new names. **Mynah**, T031-307 3503, is a frequent local bus service that runs between the city centre bus terminal, opposite the Workshop Shopping Mall on Commercial Road, the beachfront and Berea and Morningside, R4; it's very useful if you want to get to town from the suburbs, or from the north or south of the city centre. The **People Mover** is a useful (and wheelchair accessible) bus service that runs up and down the beachfront every 15 minutes between Suncoast Casino and Entertainment World in the north and uShaka Marine World in the south (0630-2300, R4, day ticket R10).

Tourist information Durah Africa ⓘ *Tourist Junction, Station Building, 160 Monty Naicker Rd (formerly Pine St), T031-304 4934, www.durbanexperience.co.za, Mon-Fri 0800-1630, Sat 0900-1400, Sun 0900-1300,* is the city tourist information service, which is very helpful and produces a range of brochures, including accommodation, restaurant and

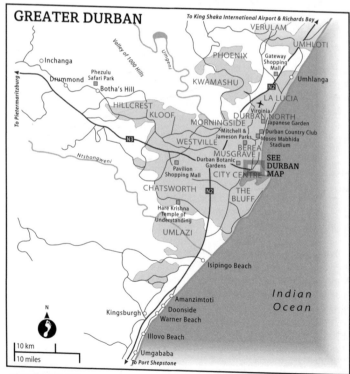

events guides. It also offers hotel and tour bookings, bus and rail bookings, a curio shop, a café and runs extremely good city tours. They have other tourist information desks in the uShaka Marine World, Gateway Mall and at King Shaka International Airport.

Safety Safety has been a long-standing issue in downtown Durban. Although safety standards plummeted in the late 1990s, a number of initiatives in recent years, such as an increased police presence, the installation of CCTV cameras and upgrading of local housing, has improved the situation a great deal. Nevertheless, it's sensible to keep your wits about you – stick to busy areas, don't carry valuables and avoid looking like a tourist. Most importantly, avoid the CBD at night unless you take a taxi. The suburbs by contrast are relatively safe.

→PLACES IN DURBAN

The main areas of interest to tourists are the **city centre** around Farewell Square, the **Indian district** around Queen and Grey streets, and the beachfront **Golden Mile**.

CITY CENTRE

The small area surrounding City Hall between Dr A B Xuma Street and Anton Lembede Street in central Durban is one of the city's more interesting spots. The colonial buildings and gardens offer a striking contrast between Durban's past and the present. High-rise office blocks tower over the remains of Durban's colonial history, where pastel-coloured art deco buildings are dwarfed by mirrored skyscrapers. The city centre's eclectic mixture of architectural styles is the responsibility of Lord Holford, the town planner who developed the city centre during the 1970s. Lord Holford was originally from South Africa but became one of England's most notorious town planners when he created many of the soulless city centres built in England during the 1960s. He returned to South Africa to help redesign city centres as part of the Apartheid programme; his work destroyed the bustling Indian atmosphere of the city centre when thousands of Indians were moved out. The original plans for the new centre involved the demolition of the City Hall and the old railway station, but vociferous protests by conservationists prevented this.

Francis Farewell Square is the hub of this area and is named after the first British settler who built his home here out of wattle and daub in 1824. Today the square has a busy street market, but at night it resembles, rather incongruously, a Victorian cemetery as this is where most of Durban's commemorative statues have been placed. There is a cenotaph to those who died in both world wars, a memorial to the dead of the Boer War and statues of Queen Victoria, in commemoration of her diamond jubilee, and Natal's first two prime ministers.

The City Hall, on Anton Lembede Street, faces directly onto the Francis Farewell Square. This is one of Durban's most impressive buildings and reflects the town's municipal might at the turn of the 20th century. The neo-baroque building was completed in 1910 and in its day was one of the British Empire's finest city halls in the southern hemisphere. The main entrance is on Farewell Square and the hall inside is decorated with an interesting collection of portraits of Durban's mayors. What is particularly appealing about the building are the palms lining the street outside. You will also find the Natural Science Museum and Durban Art Gallery here.

The **Natural Science Museum** ① *T031-311 2256, Mon-Fri 0830-1600, Sat 0830-1200, Sun 1100-1600, free, gift shop and coffee shop*, has a grand colonial entrance adorned with palm trees. Inside is an assortment of scientific displays, including a huge gallery of stuffed African mammals. More interestingly, the museum also houses an extremely rare Dodo

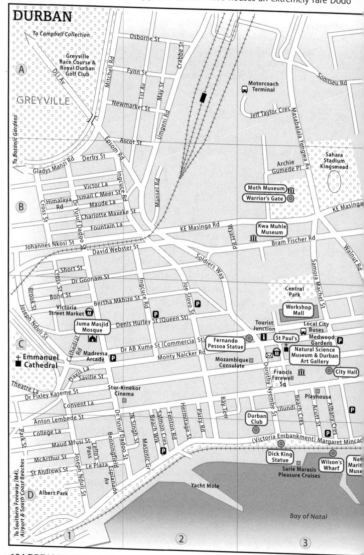

skeleton and South Africa's only Egyptian mummy. The **KwaZuzulwazi Science Centre** has an excellent series of displays dedicated to the Zulu culture.

The **Durban Art Gallery** ① *T031-311 2265, Mon-Sat 0830-1600, Sun 1100-1600, free,* on the upper floor of City Hall, has a superb collection of work by South African artists

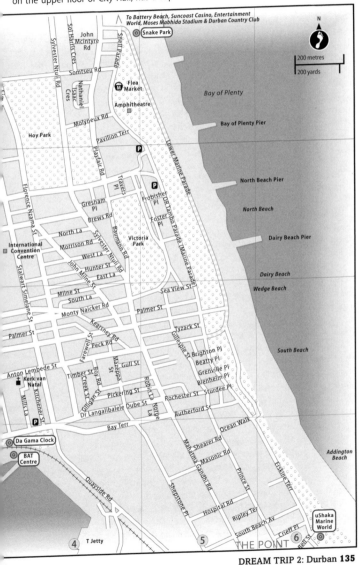

dating from the beginning of this century. This was one of the first galleries in South Africa to collect black art, and it remains an important cultural centre. It also hosts regularly changing exhibitions of contemporary art and handicrafts.

The Playhouse is directly opposite the Anton Lembede Street entrance to the City Hall. It was built in 1935 and was originally used as a bioscope, which seated 1900 people. The lounge bar became popular with visiting sailors during the 1970s and was notorious for its heavy drinking sessions and occasional fights. The cinema was eventually forced to close after a fire and has now been restored and converted into an arts complex with five theatres.

St Paul's Church was originally built in 1853, and was rebuilt in 1906 after a fire. The church is purely British in architectural style and inside there are commemorative plaques to Durban's early settlers. The chapel of St Nicholas on the left side of the aisle was part of the Mission to Seamen between 1899 and 1989. Reverend Wade, who was rector of the church between 1952 and 1961, was the father of tennis one-hit-wonder Virginia Wade, who won the ladies singles title at Wimbledon in 1977.

The **post office**, built in 1885, was originally Durban's first town hall. There is a plaque on the southern corner of the building, which commemorates Winston Churchill's speech after his escape during the Boer War.

The grand structure that is now home to **Tourist Junction** is Durban's old railway station. The building, modelled on a traditional British Victorian railway station, was completed in 1899 and is one of the few left standing in South Africa.

The **Fernando Pessoa Statue** is directly opposite Tourist Junction on the other side of Dorothy Nyembe Street. The bronze statue commemorates Fernando Pessoa who lived in Durban during the early years of his life between 1896 and 1906. On his return to Portugal he lived in poverty while teaching English in Lisbon but went on to become Portugal's most celebrated and complex modern poet.

The Workshop, also on Dr A B Xuma Street, lies directly behind the old railway station and is an enormous shopping mall that has been built inside the old train sheds. With the transition of major shops to the Pavilion and Gateway malls in the suburbs, the Workshop has suffered a decline in recent years and is starting to look very shabby and doesn't have very many interesting shops. You can get authentic Indian snacks at the food court though.

Around 500 m north of the Workshop, on Bram Fischer Road near Warrior's Gate, is the **Kwa Muhle Museum** ① *T031-311 2223, Mon-Sat, 0830-1600, Sun 1130-1600, free*, housed in the Old Pass Office. It's a fascinating and moving exhibition of what it was like to be an African under the old regime and is also known locally as the **Apartheid Museum**. There is a collection of waxwork figures in hostels along with a series of photographs of incidents and riots of the past 25 years. Another display features the Indian merchants of (formerly) Grey Street; here you can learn more about the first trade union, the Grey Street mosque, Bertha Mkhize Street beer hall, the Bantu Social Centre and bunny chow. One of the exhibits is on the 'Durban System', a method for Durban's city council to raise revenue to finance the administration of African affairs during Apartheid without using a penny of white taxpayers' money: they gave themselves the monopoly on brewing sorghum beer, which they sold for a fine profit in African-only public beer houses.

The **Warrior's Gate Moth Museum** ① *K E Masinga Rd, T031-307 3337, Tue-Sun 1100-1500, free*, has a large collection of military memorabilia from the First and Second World Wars and battlefield relics from the Anglo-Boer and Zulu wars.

INDIAN DISTRICT

The area around Bertha Mkhize Street, Denis Hurley Street and Grey Street is one of the oldest areas of Durban still standing. It is a good 20-minute walk west from the centre down Dr A B Xuma Street or Monty Naicker Road, or take a taxi to Bertha Mkhize Street. The pastel-coloured shopping arcades were built in the 1920s and 1930s by Indian traders. Originally they were designed so families could have their homes over their shops. In 1973, however, legislation was introduced which prohibited Indians from living in the area, though not from trading. Family labour living above the shops was seen as integral to their success and the legislation was deliberately introduced in an effort to reduce their competition with white-owned businesses. With the new legislation, much of the residential population was forced to move out to Chatsworth or Phoenix; the wealthier traders moved to Westville.

Thankfully the new residential rules did not succeed in destroying the Indian-owned businesses and many have continued to prosper. A number of original shops are still here, selling spices, saris and other goods from India, but it is now very much a commercial, rather than residential, area.

Victoria (effectively now **Bertha Mkhize**) **Street Market** ① *Mon-Sat 0600-1800, Sun 1000-1600*, is on the corner of Denis Hurley Street and Bertha Mkhize Street. The original market was destroyed in 1973 by fire and has been replaced by a modern market. The new concrete building is rather dingy, but there are over 170 stalls inside selling curios, leather goods, fabrics, copper and spices. The main attraction of the stalls here are the spices and dried beans imported from India. Upstairs are a variety of food stalls serving up delicious snacks such as bunny chow, samosas and Durban curries. It gets extremely busy, so beware of pickpockets and don't take anything valuable with you.

The entrance to the **Madressa Arcade** is on Grey Street. The bazaar-like arcade was built in 1927 and houses shops selling luggage, CDs and Indian fabrics.

The **Juma Masjid Mosque** ① *corner of Denis Hurley St and Grey St, T031-306 0026, open to all Mon-Fri 0900-1600 but not during prayer times*, was also built in 1927 and claims to be the largest mosque in the southern hemisphere, despite the fact that Muslims are a minority in Durban, which is largely Hindu. It sports gilt-domed minarets and a peaceful marble hall. The dress code must be adhered to: no shorts for men and women should wear long skirts or trousers and cover their shoulders; leave your shoes at the door.

MARGARET MNCADI AVENUE (VICTORIA EMBANKMENT)

The Victoria Embankment was originally built in 1897 and was a grand and desirable residential area facing a beautiful stretch of beach. Very little of this remains today, and at first glance the Embankment seems like any other busy road lined with skyscrapers. There are still a few sights worth seeking out, though. At the eastern end of the Embankment is the ornate **Da Gama Clock**. A good example of late-Victorian design, this large cast-iron clock was erected to commemorate the 400th anniversary of Vasco da Gama's discovery of the sea route to India in 1487.

A short walk further on at the junction of Dorothy Nyembe Street and the Victoria Embankment is the **Dick King Statue** which commemorates Dick King's epic 10-day ride to Grahamstown in 1842 whilst Durban was under siege. The **Durban Club** is on the opposite side of the embankment and was built in 1904. This is one of the few original buildings left on the Victoria Embankment, a grand edifice which gives an inkling of what the Victoria Embankment once looked like.

Wilson's Wharf is a modern development overlooking the harbour, home to a couple of cafés, a fish market and three boats which house the **Port Natal Maritime Museum** ① *entrance is on the docks opposite the junction of Samora Machel St and the Margaret Mncadi Av, T031-311 2230, Mon-Sat 0830-1600, Sun 1100-1545, small entry fee*. Visitors can walk through the minesweeper, the *SAS Durban*, and the two tugs, the *Ulundi* and the *JR More*.

Just beyond the Maritime Museum is the excellent non-profit making **BAT (Bartle Arts Trust) Centre** ① *on the harbour front, T031-332 0451, www.batcentre.co.za*. This is a popular arts centre with a concert hall and a bar and restaurant, as well as several little shops selling excellent contemporary Zulu crafts.

BEACHFRONT

The most popular seafront area extends along the length of Marine Parade (now OR Tambo Parade). Traditionally known as the **Golden Mile**, it's a favourite with South African holidaymakers. The beachfront is lined with high-rise hotels, gardens and a promenade; behind is a built-up urban area which had become distinctly insalubrious. Developments over the last few years, however, have upgraded housing, brought in investment and improved safety here, although it's still best avoided at night. There's a police station on the promenade and a high police presence.

The beaches, all of which are impressive stretches of long, golden sand, are divided into areas designated for surfing, boogie boarding and swimming. All are protected with shark nets and lifeguards are on patrol daily 0800-1700. At the northern end of the Lower Marine (OR Tambo) Parade is a **flea market**, a hive of activity at weekends, with stalls selling Indian snacks and curios.

The promenade along Lower Marine (OR Tambo) Parade and Snell Parade has numerous tourist attractions. Running from north to south, the entertainment starts with the flea market and the **Snake Park** ① *T031-563 6395, 0900-1630, small entry fee*. The park has a large collection of snakes from around the world with daily snake-handling demonstrations several times daily and feedings at weekends. Nearby are several stands where extravagantly dressed rickshaw drivers wait for tourists. The options are either a quick and painless photograph with the driver, or a photograph and ride up and down Marine (OR Tambo) Parade, usually costing around R20.

The leading attraction here, however, is **uShaka Marine World** ① *1 Bell St, T031-328 8000, www.ushakamarineworld.co.za, 0900-1700, Wet 'n' Wild closed Mon-Tue Apr-Oct, free entry to the shops and restaurants in the Village Walk, which has access to the promenade and beach*; **Wet 'n' Wild** ① *R110, children (3-12) R85, SeaWorld R110, children (3-12) R85, combined ticket R150/110, under 3s free*. To get here drive down Mahatma Gandhi Road (formerly Point Road) from the city centre and it's on the beach at The Point (see below). This enormous waterpark is the largest in Africa, and has the fourth largest aquarium in the world. The park is split into three areas: SeaWorld is an impressive underground aquarium; Wet 'n' Wild has a huge choice of impressive waterslides and rides; and Village Walk is a retail village that is filled with shops and restaurants. The highlight in SeaWorld is the phantom ship, where visitors walk through glass tunnels surrounded by ragged-tooth sharks and game fish. Each corridor has a different theme, and there is a range of presentations in pools surrounding the ship throughout the day. There's also a dolphinarium, a seal pool, dive tank and a snorkel reef. Another free zone is the uShaka Beach, which hosts a variety of activities such as beach volleyball and surfing, and has 24-hour security.

BATTERY BEACH

Heading 1 km north of Snell Parade and the Golden Mile, Battery Beach is perhaps the most attractive of Durban's beaches, with good swimming and fewer crowds. It's also the location of the **Suncoast Casino and Entertainment World**, with slot machines, cinemas, a selection of bars, takeaway joints, themed restaurants and a car park for 2000 vehicles. Directly in front of the complex is the beach where you can sunbathe or rollerblade on the promenade.

The newest attraction behind Battery Beach is the impressive **Moses Mabhiba Stadium** ① *Masabalala Yengwa Av (M12), 1 road back from the beachfront, T031-582 8242, www. mosesmabhida.co.za; 30-min tour of the inside of the stadium, Mon-Fri 1100 and 1600, Sat and Sun 0900 and 1600, R20, children (under 12) R15*, which was built for the 2010 FIFA World Cup™, and named after anti-Apartheid activist Moses Mabhida, who was both general secretary of the South African Communist Party and vice-president of the South African Congress of Trade Unions. With its 'arc of triumph' constructed over the top, this has, unlike some of the other stadiums built in South Africa for the tournament, become somewhat of an attraction in its own right. The 350-m-long, and 105-m-high arc which holds up the roof of the 62,000-seater stadium is not only a striking feature to admire (and beautifully lit at night), but provides some entertaining activities. On the north side is the **Adventure Walk** ① *Sat and Sun 1000, 1300 and 1600, R80 per person, no children under 10*, when visitors can go on a guided climb while attached to a safety harness up and down the 550 steps to the top of the arch. On the south side is the **SkyCar** ① *0900-1800, R50, children (6-12) R25, under 6s free*, a funicular railway car that carries up to 20 passengers and also climbs the curve to the top of the arc. These can be followed by the **Big Rush Swing** ① *R595*, a bungee-like 220-m swing beneath the arc. The excellent views from the top of the stadium take in the sweeping Golden Mile and ocean, the high-rises of the CBD and inland towards the hilly suburbs. There are a number of restaurants and an attractive landscaped piazza at the base of the stadium.

GOING FURTHER
Dolphin Coast

The area north of Durban, between Umhlanga and Tugela Mouth, is known as the Dolphin Coast, thanks to the bottlenose dolphins that frolic in the waves year-round. It is also known as the Sugar Coast, thanks to the rolling sugar plantations backing the sea. It is possible to miss many of the sights and small coastal settlements if you remain on the N2 highway.

The old coast road runs parallel to the sea passing through the beach resorts of Umhlanga, Ballito and Salt Rock attracting vast crowds of holidaying South Africans in summer. North of Umhlanga, most of the resorts are less developed and appeal to more upmarket holidaymakers than those found closer to Durban.

UMHLANGA

Seventeen kilometres north of the Durban CBD, Umhlanga was once no more than a sleepy holiday resort. These days, with its sprawl of high-rises, office and shopping parks, and modern housing developments, it is the wealthiest and most upmarket suburb of the city. **Umhlanga Tourism** ① *Chartwell Drive, T031-561 4257, www.umhlanga-rocks. com, Mon-Fri 0800-1630, Sat 0900-1200*, can book accommodation and has maps and brochures to pick up.

Places in Umhlanga In high season, wealthy South Africans flock to Umhlanga, a beautiful stretch of wave-lashed sand with a belt of high-rise hotels and condominiums. Access to the water is almost exclusively through the resort and hotel complexes, although there is a 3-km stretch of promenade that spans the front of these, which has been attractively landscaped with indigenous plants along the dune belt next to the beach. The **Umhlanga Lagoon** lies just to the north of town at the end of the promenade, where a trail continues through a beautiful expanse of wetland and forest to an unspoilt, open beach yet to be concreted by the developers.

A popular local landmark is the **Umhlanga Lighthouse**. The distinct red and white circular concrete tower stands 21 m above the beach and acts as a fixed point to help ships waiting to dock in Durban harbour confirm their exact position in the outer anchorage. The lighthouse tower has stood here since November 1954, occupying the centre point on the beach, right in front of the Oyster Box Hotel. The lighthouse has never had a keeper; instead it was operated by the owner of the Oyster Box Hotel from controls in the hotel office, though now its fully automated.

The **KZN Sharks Board** ① *Herrwood Drive, T031-566 0400, www.shark.co.za, display hall and curio shop Mon-Fri 0800-1600, tour and film Tue-Thu 0900 and 1400, Sun 1400, R35, children (4-12) R20*, set inland from the resort, studies the life cycles of the sharks that inhabit the sea off the coast of KwaZulu Natal and investigates how best to protect bathers with various forms of netting. Umhlanga became the first beach to erect shark nets in 1962, following a series of attacks along the whole coast in December 1957. Today the Sharks Board is responsible for looking after more than 400 nets, which protect nearly 50 beaches. Tours at the Sharks Board begin with a 25-minute audio-visual show on the biology of sharks and their role as top predators in the marine food chain. This is followed by an (optional) stomach-churning shark dissection. The display hall has a variety of replicas of sharks, fish and rays, including that of an 892-kg shark. It is also possible to accompany researchers on the **Sharks Board boat** ① *T082-403 9206 (booking essential), R250 per person, no children under 6, min 6 people, max 12 people, 2 hrs*, as they conduct daily servicing of the shark nets off Durban's Golden Mile. The boat goes from Wilson's Wharf back in Durban at 0630. You won't necessarily see sharks in the nets, but you have a good chance of spotting dolphins and sea birds and there are good views back across to Durban. The ride out beyond the harbour walls can be bumpy.

Hawaan Nature Reserve is 4 km north of Umhlanga at the end of Newlands Drive. During the 1920s, William Alfred Campbell, son of Sir Marshall who had founded the sugar estates, used to stage a hunt every year in this unique forest environment. It was not until 1980 that 60 ha were protected as part of the nature reserve. Within the reserve there are 4 km of leisurely guided walks through an unusual area of mature coastal forest. The trails are not open to the public but you can join the 0800 Saturday morning **guided walk** ① *T031-566 4018*. The area is rich in birdlife and you can also see bushbuck, duiker and vervet monkeys.

BALLITO AND AROUND

The small-scale, largely low-rise resort of Ballito is far more attractive than Umhlanga, further south, with easy access to the long beach and attractive accommodation nestled in lush vegetation stretching up the hillside. At the south of town, just off the coast road, is the **Dolphin Coast Publicity Association** ① *T032-946 1997, www.thedolphincoast.co.za, Mon-Fri 0830-1700, Sat 0900-1300*, a useful stop-off with information on the Dolphin Coast area. Most visitors to Ballito are South African holidaymakers, who settle in for a bucket-and-spade holiday every summer. If you're passing through, it's a pleasant enough spot for a day or two by the beach, but stick to the southern, less developed end.

North of Ballito, the resort of **Salt Rock** is named after a rock where the Zulus used to collect salt and is similar to Ballito, while nearby **Shaka's Rock** is named after the cliff from which Shaka is said to have thrown his enemies to their foamy deaths. There is good snorkelling at Tiffany's Reef and Sheffield Reef, but neither resort holds much appeal other than for those after a sand and sea holiday.

WHERE TO STAY

Umhlanga
$$$$ Teremok Lodge, 49 Marine Drive, T031-561 5848, www.teremok.co.za. A boutique lodge set in a tropical garden, contemporary and stylish decor and design, 8 luxury a/c suites with stand-alone baths, rain showers, Wi-Fi, spacious lounge, pool, spa, lovely breakfast room with picture windows opening on to a giant milkwood tree. No children under 16.

Ballito
$$$ Boathouse, 33 Compensation Beach Rd, Ballito, T032-946 0300, www.boathouse. co.za. Upmarket guesthouse on the beach, 22 a/c beautifully decorated rooms with floor-to-ceiling windows, balconies and DSTV, the bar is a great place to have a sundowner and spot dolphins, lovely pool on a wooden deck, restaurant specializing in seafood.

DURBAN LISTINGS

WHERE TO STAY

$$$ Protea Hotel Edward, 149 OR Tambo Parade, T031-337 3681, www.proteahotels.com. The most luxurious of the beachfront hotels with a restored art deco façade, 101 elegant a/c rooms, with DSTV and minibar, most have sea views, lavish lobby and lounge, 2 restaurants, bar, small rooftop pool and deck, excellent service.

$$$ Quarters, 101 Florida Rd, Morningside, T031-303 5246, www.quarters.co.za. 4 historic homes have been converted to create this boutique hotel, with a refreshingly modern feel, 23 rooms, with luxury fabrics on the walls, DSTV and Wi-Fi. Excellent restaurant, shaded courtyard, modern bar. Good location close to restaurants.

$$$ Riverside Hotel & Spa, Northway, Durban North, T031-563 0600, www.riverside hotel.co.za. Large modern hotel overlooking the Umgeni River, a good spot for birdwatching in the estuary, 169 spacious a/c rooms with DSTV, friendly service and a great cafe/restaurant and popular bar, pool and spa.

$$$ Royal Hotel, 267 Anton Lembede St, T031-333 6000, www.theroyal.co.za. The hotel originally built on this site in 1842 was made of wattle and daub; it now has 204 smart a/c rooms, with Wi-Fi, DSTV, pleasant decor, some with great harbour views, attractive outdoor pool, gym, sauna, bars and 2 excellent restaurants.

$$ The Benjamin, 141 Florida Rd, Morningside, T031-303 4233, www.benjamin.co.za. Classy boutique hotel in a great location close to restaurants on Florida Rd. 43 tastefully decorated rooms with a/c, Wi-Fi and DSTV, centred around a nicely restored historic building, pleasant lounge with antiques, sunny breakfast room overlooking the pool.

$$-$ Tekweni Backpackers, 169 Ninth Av, Morningside, T031-303 1433, www.tekweni backpackers.co.za. One of the liveliest, most popular hostels in Durban, with dorms and double rooms set across 2 rambling houses, space for a couple of tents, kitchen, bar, small pool, internet access, travel desk, all meals available. Often in a party mood, easy stroll to restaurants on Florida Rd.

RESTAURANTS

$$$ Cargo Hold, uShaka Marine World, see page 138. Open 1200-1500, 1800-2200. Great location, popular with families, spread over 3 floors in the phantom ship, with a glass wall looking into the shark tank – ragged tooth sharks sidling by as you eat. Impressive menu, including good seafood, steaks, warm salads and Mediterranean starters. Reservations essential.

$$$ Jewel of India, Southern Sun Elangeni, 63 Snell Parade, North Beach, T031-362 1300. Open 1200-1500, 1800-2200. Large restaurant with traditional Indian decor, serving tasty North Indian dishes served with tandoori breads, each dish is cooked from scratch and the waiters are knowledgeable about the menu and make recommendations.

$$$ Moyo, uShaka Marine World, T031-332 0606, www.moyo.co.za. 1100-2230. Part of the successful Moyo chain (other branches in Johannesburg and Stellenbosch) with good ocean views from the pier at uShaka Marine World, a pan-African menu with dishes from Morocco tagines to Mozambique curries and traditional South African *potjieko*, live music, Xhosa face painting, fantastic atmosphere and professional service.

$$$-$$ New Café Fish, Yacht Mole, Margaret Mncadi Av, T031-305 5062. Open 1200-1500, 1830-2200. Set right on the water with yachts moored within arm's reach, upstairs bar is great for a sundowner, a basket of calamari and view of the working harbour. Downstairs is a more formal restaurant, seafood a speciality, very popular, outdoor deck in summer. **$$ Bean Bag Bohemia**, 18 Lilian Ngoyi (Windermere) Rd, Morningside, T031- 309 6019, www.beanbagbohemia.co.za. 1000-2400. Hugely popular set-up, with a vibey bar on the ground floor and smarter tatty-chic restaurant upstairs, in an old converted Durban town house. Quirky decor, great Mediterranean-based menu of mezze platters, pasta and steak, plus Asian dim sum, and the bar stays open late.

WHAT TO DO

Boat trips

Ocean Ventures, on the promenade, uShaka Marine World (page 138), T086-100 1138, www.oceanventures.co.za. Offers numerous boat trips including dolphin watching, 1 hr, R300, children (5-15) R150; whale watching in season (Jun-Dec), 2 hrs, R450, children (5-15) R300; and exciting speed-boat trips, 30 mins, R150 per person. Also surfing and ocean kayaking lessons and hires out boards and kayaks from R100.

Sarie Marais Pleasure Cruises, T031-305 4022, at the Gardiner Jetty, Margaret Mncadi Av (Victoria Embankment) www. sariemaraiscruises.co.za. A good way to get a grip on the size and workings of Durban Harbour is to go on a short harbour cruise on an engine-powered ferry boat, which departs every 30 mins 0900-1600 from the jetty, R50, children (under 12) R30. The little boats are able to get right beneath the hulls of the massive container ships moored at the docks.

Tour operators

Expect to pay in the region of R400 for a half-day city tour, and R600-800 for a full-day tour to the outlying regions such as Valley of 1000 Hills. **Durban Africa** at the Tourist Junction (see below) can recommend numerous tour operators.

Catchet Tours, T031-205 7502, www. cachettours.co.za. Good range of ½- and full-day tours including Durban city, Valley of the 1000 Hills, overnight trips to St Lucia and the Drakensberg.

Durban Africa, Tourist Junction, T031-304 4934, Station Building, 160 Monty Naicker Rd (formerly Pine St), www. durbanexperience.co.za. The tourist office runs walking tours Mon-Fri, from R100, children (under 12) R70. The 3-hr tours must be booked a day in advance and are a good, safe way of getting to know the city. There's a choice of an Oriental/Indian or a history theme.

Jikeleza Tours, T031-702 1189, www. jikelezatours.co.za. Township tour starting at the Kwa-Muhle Museum to explain the nature of Apartheid, before visiting the Umlazi or Nanda township. Also evening trips with local guides for drinks at the township shebeens, plus wider city tours.

Strelitzia Tours, T031-579 5681, www.strelitziatours.com. A comprehensive range of tours in the province 1-3 days with regular departures. City tours and day trips to townships and Valley of 1000 hills.

Tekweni Ecotours, T082-303 9112, www.tekweniecotours.co.za. Excellent cultural tours including a half-day city tour which includes a visit to the Hare Krishna Temple of Understanding and the Indian township of Chatsworth, and to the Victoria Street Market and a traditional healer. Also Valley of 1000 Hills, and overnight tours to Hluhluwe-Imfolozi and Sani Pass in the Drakensberg.

BATTLEFIELDS ROUTE

The vast, open landscapes of northern KwaZulu Natal are as evocative as one would hope, with rolling plains and savannah grasslands stretching to the horizons and studded with flat-topped acacias, mysterious rock formations and granite koppies. This landscape forms the stage upon which three major wars have been fought, and the battlefields of the clashes between Boers, Britons and Zulus can all be visited. Don't expect self-explanatory sights, however – many of the battlefields are marked by little more than small commemorative plaques, and you'll need a good guide to really bring the history of the region to life. This area also provides an eye-opening glimpse into the lives of rural Zulus, the out-of-the-way roads passing numerous traditional subsistence kraals, with their thatched rondavals, herds of goats and waving children.

The best way to appreciate the history of the battles is to go on an organized tour; with a decent guide it can be very moving. The major sites can be visited in a day. Two of the best museums are the Siege Museum in Ladysmith and the Talana Museum in Dundee. Of the wars fought between the Voortrekkers and the Zulus, the most interesting battlefield site is Blood River, east of Dundee. Two of the most interesting historical sites of the Anglo-Zulu War are Isandlwana and Rorke's Drift; the latter has a good museum, making it the best site to visit without a guide. The most interesting Boer War sites to visit are Talana, the Siege of Ladysmith and Spioenkop.

VALLEY OF 1000 HILLS

The Valley of 1000 Hills is a peaceful area, supposedly named at the end of the 19th century by the writer Mark Twain after the dozens of hills which fold down towards the Umgeni River. It is an easy 35-km drive from Durban. Follow the N3 north out of the city and leave at the Westville/Pavilion Mall exit. Join the old Pietermaritzburg road (R103) and drive through the suburbs of Kloof and Hillcrest. Here you will pick up signs for the Valley of 1000 Hills Meander which runs through the villages of Botha's Hill, Drummond, Monteseel and Inchanga. The **Comrades Marathon**, a gruelling 90 km between Pietermaritzburg and Durban, follows this route in June. For information contact **1000 Hills Tourism** ① *Old Main Rd, Botha's Hill, T031-777 1874, www.1000hills.kzn.org.za, Mon-Sat 0900-1600.*

Between Durban and Pietermaritzburg the landscape quickly climbs some 700 m over a series of rolling hills characteristic of the suburbs around the two cities. From Botha's Rest, there are many viewpoints on the R103 from where you can see the valley unfold. The fertile hills are dotted with villages, farms and encroaching townships closer to Durban. The valley has historically been a Zulu stronghold and, in the early 19th century, it became a refuge for dispossessed Zulus who had lost their farmland through battle further north.

The R103 runs along the lip of the valley; tourism has gone into overdrive along this route, with a variety of craft shops, restaurants, B&Bs, guesthouses, farm stalls and several Zulu cultural villages. The most popular of these is **PheZulu Safari Park** ① *5 Old Main Rd, Botha's Hill, T031-777 1000, www.phezulusafaripark.co.za, Zulu shows daily 1000, 1130, 1400, 1530, R120, children (under 12) R90, additional 1-hr game drives R205, children (under 12) R100.* There are commanding views of the valley from here, a reptile farm, a small game park with zebra and antelope, curio shops, and the **Croctilians** restaurant which specializes in croc steaks. The main attraction here is the Zulu show, where visitors are taken into traditional beehive-shaped huts and Zulu beliefs, rituals and artefacts are explained. There follows an impressive dancing display.

The Umgeni Steam Railway's **1000 Hills Choo-Choo** ⓘ *Kloof Station, Village Rd, T082-353 6003, www.umgenisteamrailway.co.za, 2 daily departures on the last Sun of each month, 0845 and 1230, R150, children (2-12) R120 return*, is a vintage 1912 steam train that runs along a line built 1877-1880. On departure days there are two round trips, between Kloof and Inchanga stations, and it's a leisurely way to enjoy the scenery. At Inchanga Station is a tea room and small railway memorabilia museum to visit before the return journey.

→LADYSMITH AND AROUND

Ladysmith is a quiet rural town surrounded by cattle and sheep ranches, with little more than a run-down shopping complex, a handful of Victorian buildings and the Siege Museum – a good place from which to start a visit to the Battlefields Route. The siege aside, Ladysmith is perhaps best known as being the origin town to Ladysmith Black Mambazo, the phenomenally popular South Africa band. The region lying to the south of Ladysmith is where many of the Boer War Battlefields are located. The Siege Museum in Ladysmith will help to arrange tours or provide a detailed map of the battlesites.

ARRIVING IN LADYSMITH
Getting there Ladysmith is 247 km northwest of Durban on the N11. It is well connected to the highway network and, some 26 km south of Ladysmith, the N11 connects with the N3, which in turn leads north into the Free State and south to Durban. Mainline buses stop in Ladysmith on the Bloemfontein—Durban and Johannesburg—Durban routes.

Moving on The N11 heads north where after 26 km the R602 leads to Dundee (70 km from Ladysmith), while to the southwest at the junction where it joins the N3, the N11 also connects to the R616 leading to the Northern Drakensberg.

Tourist information Ladysmith Tourism ⓘ *Siege Museum, Murchison St, T036-637 2992, www.ladysmith.kzn.org.za, Mon-Fri 0900-1600, Sat 0900-1300*, has a good selection of maps and leaflets on the battlefields, and is also very helpful with accommodation suggestions and advice on battlefield tours.

BACKGROUND
The Voortrekkers first arrived in 1847 and established a small republican settlement on the banks of the Klip River. However, it was only a matter of months before the area fell under the British sphere of influence. British settlers began to arrive during the 1850s to farm in the area. Ladysmith grew in importance as a trading centre because it was on the trail connecting the diamond and gold mines of the interior, Kimberley and Barberton, with Port Natal on the coast. Ladysmith is most famous for being besieged by General Piet Joubert for 118 days during the Boer War (see box, page 146). The British garrison of 12,500 men was cut off from the outside world for the duration of the siege.

PLACES IN LADYSMITH
Ladysmith's historical monuments are on the main square by the town hall on Murchison Street. The **town hall**, on the corner of Murchison and Queen streets, is a classic Victorian municipal building which was completed in 1893. During the siege, it was converted into a hospital until the clock tower was hit by a six-inch shell. The **Siege Museum** ⓘ *Murchison*

ON THE ROAD
The siege of Ladysmith

The siege of the British in Ladysmith by Boer forces lasted from early in the Anglo-Boer War, October 1899, until February 1900, 118 days in total. The British forces in northern Natal, under General White, had been forced to withdraw into Ladysmith after a series of defeats at the hands of Boers from both the Free State and Transvaal. The Boer forces had taken up positions in a six-mile radius around the town but made few decisive attempts to defeat the 10,000 remaining British troops.

The Boers, under the command of Piet Joubert (ably assisted by his tactically minded wife), did make one major assault on the British defences at Bester's Ridge on 6 January 1900. But the British were able to repulse the Boer attack, although it succeeded in placing a further strain on their already stretched resources.

The Boer forces decided to concentrate on starving out the British or shelling them into submission, while they held off any British attempts to relieve the town from the south by securing defensive positions in the hills overlooking the Tugela River.

For the besieged British troops the defence of Ladysmith required patience and organization, rather than heroics. In December 1899 General White had been ordered to try to break out and join up with the British forces under Buller who was attempting an advance through Colenso. But details of the advance were never relayed to White and the first he knew of the attack was when he heard the artillery fire. After the losses sustained in the defence of Bester's Ridge in January 1900, White was unable to offer any support to General Buller's forces in their attempts to relieve Ladysmith and all his troops could do was sit tight and survive the bombardment as best they possibly could.

Conditions for the town's inhabitants, whether military or civilian, were harsh. Food and other provisions were in short supply and what was available became exceptionally expensive. Tins of condensed milk, for example, could fetch up to a pound and bottles of whisky seven pounds. One source of comfort for the civilians and wounded was that the Boer commanders allowed them to set up a camp and hospital at Intombi, some four miles southeast of the town, so that they were spared the heavy artillery bombardment of the town centre. News of Buller's numerous blunders at Colenso, Spion Kop and other battles along the Tugela did nothing for morale, however, and many inhabitants felt it was only a matter of time before they had to give in to the Boers.

In February 1900 Buller's substantial army at last had some success in its assaults on the Boer positions along the Tugela. On 27 February the British succeeded in taking Pieter's Railway and Terrace Hills overlooking the railway crossing of the Tugela at Colenso; the Boer forces surrounding Ladysmith rapidly lost morale. As news of the decisive defeat of General Conje's forces in the northern Cape filtered through to the Boer military lines, their resolve snapped and they fell back towards Elandslaagte, many in fact returning home, leaving the path clear for Buller's troops to at last relieve the beleaguered troops and citizens at Ladysmith.

St, T036-637 2231, Mon-Fri 0900-1600, Sat 0900-1300, R11, children (under 14) R6, is next to the town hall. This is a fascinating museum, with one of the country's largest collections of South African military memorabilia, including reconstructions of scenes from the Siege of Ladysmith and the Boer War. There are displays of weapons, uniforms and household goods that were used during the siege, with explanations in English, Afrikaans and Zulu.

There are four field guns on Murchison Street just outside the museum: **Castor** and **Pollux** are the two guns sent from Cape Town at the outbreak of the Boer War for the defence of the town; **Long Tom** is a replica of the Creussot Fortress Guns, which were used by the Transvaal Republic to bombard Ladysmith from the surrounding hills. The Boers destroyed the original gun at Haenertsburg when Kitchener's Fighting Scouts threatened to capture it. The last gun is a German **Feldkanonne**, which was captured in German Southwest Africa and sent back as a war trophy.

Walking south down Murchison Street will take you past two historical hotels. The **Royal Hotel** was built before the siege, at the time of the gold and diamond rushes of the interior. During the siege it was used by the press corps as a base. The **Crown Hotel** is the site of Ladysmith's first hotel, built of wattle and daub. The earliest battlefield tours, on horseback, could be booked here in 1904. Further down Murchison Street, on the corner with Princess Street, is the **Old Toll House** where wagon drivers paid a toll before entering town.

At the northern end of Murchison Street is the **Central Mosque**, which was completed in 1922, and has a beautiful fountain and courtyard surrounded by palm trees. To the east of the town centre off Queen Street is the Hindu **Vishnu Temple** and, next to it, the life-size **Statue of Mahatma Gandhi**, which was erected in 1993 by the Hindu community in Ladysmith to celebrate the centenary of Gandhi's arrival in Natal. He was a stretcher-bearer during the Anglo-Boer War, and trained some 1100 other Indians in this dangerous task.

WEENEN GAME RESERVE

ⓘ *20 km south of Colenso off the R74, from Durban take the N3 to Estcourt and follow the Colenso road for 25 km, T036-354 7013, www.kznwildlife.com, Oct-Mar 0500-1900, Apr-Sep 0600-1800, R30, children (under 12) R20, car R20.*

This 5000-ha reserve has succeeded in converting heavily eroded farmland into an area where the flora and fauna indigenous to the Natal Midlands have been re-established. The vegetation is mostly grassland, interspersed with acacia woodland. One of the great attractions are the black and white rhino. More common species include giraffe, red hartebeest, eland, zebra, kudu, ostrich and common reedbuck. This is a good reserve for birdwatchers; more than 250 species have been recorded including korhaans, blue crane and the scimitarbilled woodhoopoe. There are some short walking trails from the campsite, picnic sites, and a 47-km network of game-viewing dirt roads.

→DUNDEE AND AROUND

The R602 leaves the N11 26 km north of Ladysmith and shortly passes the village of **Elandslaagte**, where there is a signpost leading to the site of the Battle of Elandslaagte. On 21 October 1899, British forces abandoned the village and the railway station. They had kept it open to enable the Dundee garrison to retreat to Ladysmith. The R602 continues to Dundee through a vast treeless plain with plateaux rising up in the distance. The small mining and farming town of **Glencoe**, just before Dundee, is named after the town in the Highlands of Scotland, from where some of the first miners originated.

The modern town of Dundee grew up around the coal mining deposits which were first exploited here on a large scale in the 1880s. The town centre unfortunately fell victim to South Africa's town planners, and is today a rather dull grid of modern streets lined with sleepy shops. Although it provides a convenient base from which to explore the battlefield sites at **Isandlwana**, **Rorke's Drift** and **Blood River**, it might be preferable to stay at one of the more remote lodges away from town.

ARRIVING IN DUNDEE
Tourist information Tourism Dundee ① *Civic Gardens, Victoria St, T034-212 2121, www. tourdundee.co.za, Mon-Fri 0900-1630*, is a helpful office with information on accommodation and excellent advice on how best to view the battlefields depending upon your time, budget and level of interest. Contact them in advance to book a local personal battlefield tour guide.

PLACES IN DUNDEE
The **MOTH Museum** ① *corner of Beaconsfield and Wilson streets, open by appointment through the tourist office*, is one of the best private collections of military memorabilia in South Africa and includes pieces from the Anglo-Zulu War. The museum can usually only be visited on an organized tour. MOTH stands for Memorable Order of Tin Hats and refers to the British ex-servicemen of the Anglo-Boer War.

The **Talana Museum** ① *1 km north of town on the R33, T034-212 2654, www.talana.co.za, Mon-Fri 0800-1630, Sat and Sun 1000-1630, R15, children (under 16) R2*, has been built on the site of the Battle of Talana Hill, which took place on 20 October 1899 and was the first major battle of the Boer War. British forces had been sent to Dundee to protect the coal field from the advancing Boers. General Lucas Meyer, moving down from the Transvaal, took the hill and began bombarding the British. The counter attack succeeded in forcing the Boers off the hill but only at great cost to the British, who lost 255 soldiers including their commanding officer, General Penn Symons. A self-guided trail visits the remains of two British forts and the Boer gun emplacements, passing a cairn where General Penn Symons was wounded.

The main building is a modern museum with good displays on the Zulu Wars and the Anglo-Boer War. The industrial section includes the **Consol Glass Museum**, which has an extensive display of glass products, which were once produced here, illustrating the changes in taste from highly decorative Victorian vases to the crisp designer products of today. The **Chamber of Mines Coal Museum** has re-created scenes of early mining in Dundee with many of the original tools on display. The **Miner's Rest** restaurant and curio shop is housed in a typical miner's cottage of the 1920s in the gardens behind the new building.

Many outlying buildings are original. The **Peter Smith Cottage** has been restored and decorated with period furniture, while the workshop and stables outside have a collection of original blacksmith's tools and several wagons. **Talana House** has historical displays on the lifestyles of the Zulus and the early settlers in Dundee, with interesting bead collections. Both these buildings were used as dressing stations during the Battle of Talana Hill.

BATTLEFIELD EXCURSIONS
The battlefield sites around Dundee can easily be visited on day trips. The major sites are clearly signposted and can be reached from Dundee or Ulundi. However, the sites themselves are often little more than a war memorial in a windswept field; they are isolated and accessed along dirt roads. Allow enough time to return in daylight as the bad roads and wandering cattle make it dangerous to drive at night. The best way to appreciate the sites and the epic events that took place in this region is to take a guided tour with a qualified historian.

ON THE ROAD
Blood River

The year 1838 had been a difficult one for the Voortrekkers in Natal. In February their leader Piet Retief was beaten to death at the Zulu king Dingane's kraal and shortly afterwards about 500 members of a Voortrekker party at Bloukrans River were killed in a Zulu ambush. The majority of the dead were in fact 'coloured' servants but subsequent generations of Boers honoured the defeat by naming the site Weenen – meaning 'weeping'. Voortrekker attempts at reprisals against the Zulus similarly failed and in a battle near the Buffalo River Piet Uys, another Voortrekker leader, was killed. It was only with the arrival later in the year of Andries Pretorius and a party of 60 experienced commandos that Voortrekker fortunes began to take a turn for the better.

On 9 December Pretorius set out with 468 men and three cannon to confront Dingane's army. Before setting out he reportedly stood on a gun carriage and made the famous vow that if God gave them victory "we would note the date of victory to make it known even to our latest posterity in order that it might be celebrated to the honour of God". Many historians doubt if the vow was ever really made; certainly it was not commemorated until many years after the event. Nevertheless the vow has taken on an important place in Afrikaner traditions.

On 15 December Pretorius' scouts reported a heavy Zulu presence nearby and he ordered the column to move their wagons into the tried and tested Voortrekker defensive laager. The method involved lashing all the wagons together into a ring and protecting all cattle, horses and stores in the centre. This allowed trekkers to hide in and under the wagons and fire out at any approaching attackers. Pretorius had formed his laager on the banks of the Ncome River with a deep gully to the rear and an open plain to the front. He placed the three cannon at points along the perimeter of the laager to give them a clear line of fire across the open ground. Early in the morning of 16 December the Zulu army, estimated at about 10,000, began its attack.

Wave upon wave of Zulu soldiers charged the laager but their short spears, so effective in hand-to-hand combat, were useless against the trekkers' rifles and the grapeshot from the cannons. Finally the Zulu attack faltered and Pretorius sent out a party of mounted commandos to pursue the shattered Zulus. The trekkers were merciless and shot every Zulu in sight, including more than 400 hiding in a small ravine. No prisoners were taken and around 3000 people were killed. No trekkers had been killed and only three were injured – including Pretorius who was stabbed in the hand. So many Zulu soldiers were shot whilst trying to flee back across the Ncome River the waters ran red – hence the name Blood River.

Ncome-Blood River ⓘ *43 km from Dundee, take the R33 northeast as far as Dejagersdrif, where there is a turning on the right leading to Blood River, the last section of the journey is on a dirt road, T034-271 8121, www.ncomemuseum.co.za, 0800-1630, free.* This is the site of a replica *laager* that commemorates the dreadful battle between the Zulus and the Boers on 16 December 1838 (see box, above). The 64 wagons are made of bronze and include replica bronze spades, lamps and buckets, all slightly larger than life size, and there is a small museum, the **Ncome Museum**, which is dedicated to the Zulu role in the battle. It is designed in the shape of a pair of buffalo horns, which was the formation in which the Zulu army attacked. The museum garden has a Zulu *isivivane* (cairn) and a 'reed garden', which is used to explain the symbolic importance of reeds to the Zulu people. To the east of the complex is a mountain called **iNtaba kaNdlela** (Ndlela's Mountain). Ndlela was the chief commander of the Zulu army during the battle, and his warriors rested on this mountain before crossing the Ncome River to the iNtibane Mountain, which is west of the museum. iNtibane is known as Vegkop (Battle Hill) in Afrikaans. There is also a café selling historical leaflets.

Isandlwana ① *80 km southeast of Dundee, take the R68 west, passing through Vant's Drift and Nqutu; the dirt road leading to Isandlwana is clearly signposted south of Nqutu, T034-271 8165, Mon-Fri 0800-1600, Sat-Sun 0900-1600, R20, children (under 12) R10.* This is where the 24th Regiment was defeated by 25,000 Zulu warriors on 22 January 1879. It is the most epic of the great Zulu War stories: the Zulus sat silently in a valley watching a small British regiment (which thought the Zulus were elsewhere), waiting for the signal to attack. A British patrol stumbled across them, upon which the impis leapt to their feet and stormed over the lip of the hill, descending upon the small regiment in the characteristic 'horns of the buffalo' manoeuvre. Within two hours, 1329 of the 1700 British soldiers were dead. Today, it is an atmospheric spot, with white-painted cairns marking the places where British soldiers were buried, and a self-guided trail taking in the memorials, starting with the relatively new memorial to the Zulu dead, a giant bronze replica of a Zulu victory necklace.

Rorke's Drift ① *42 km from southeast of Dundee, clearly signposted off the R68 between Dundee and Nqutu, T034-642 1687, open 0900-1600, R20, children (under 12) R10.* Made famous by Michael Caine and his memorable performance in the movie *Zulu*, this site was a Swedish mission next to a ford over the Buffalo River. In 1879, the mission consisted of two small stone buildings, a house and a storeroom, which was also used as a church, and these were commandeered by the British at the start of the war and converted into a hospital and a supply depot. Only 110 men were stationed there on 23 January 1879, when two survivors of Isandlwana arrived warning of an imminent attack. Four thousand Zulus arrived 1½ hours later and launched the assault on the mission station. The British refused to surrender, and succeeded in defending the mission from behind a makeshift barricade of grain bags and biscuit boxes. The ferocious attack was resisted for 12 hours before the Zulu impis withdrew, losing around 400 men; 17 British officers were killed. The mission station has been converted into a fascinating little **museum**, which illustrates scenes from the battle and outlines the lives of the men who were awarded the Victoria Cross. Just beyond the museum there is a cemetery and a memorial to those who died.

BATTLEFIELDS ROUTE LISTINGS

WHERE TO STAY

Ladysmith and around
$$$$ Nambiti Plains Private Game Lodge, 25 km east of Ladysmith and 2 km after the turning off the N11 on to the R602 to Dundee, T071-680 4584, www.nambitiplains.conm. An expensive private 20,000-ha Big Five game reserve and one of the few safari options in the Battlefields region, with 5 secluded luxury bush suites with verandas and outside showers set in a tract of acacia trees, thatched bar and boma, pool and deck. Rates include all meals and 2 game drives; the reserve has been stocked with a number of plains species, lion and cheetah and an expanding herd of elephant. They can also arrange battlefield tours or recommend self-drive routes and provide packed lunches.

Dundee and around
$$$$ Fugitive's Drift Lodge, approximately 50 km south of Dundee towards Greytown on the R33, T034-642 1843, www.fugitivesdrift.com. Home to the Rattray family, this lodge offers traditional accommodation and excellent guided tours. Rooms are stylish and comfortable and have private verandas. The lounge and dining room is filled with Battlefields memorabilia. Very sadly, the Battlefields finest historian David Rattray died in 2007 but prodigies Rob Caskie and Joseph Ndima now take tours, and, like David Rattray, are superb storytellers bringing the history alive. The original Battlefields experience. Rates include all meals.

$$$ Isandlwana Lodge, Islandlwana, 74 km southeast of Dundee, accessed off the R68, T034-271 8301, www.isandlwana.co.za. Superbly constructed luxury lodge with awesome views over Isandlwana and the rolling grasslands. The stunning wood, thatch and stone double-storey building sensitively blends in with the landscape and is built into the rock that the Zulu commander stood on at the start of the Isandlwana battle. 13 tastefully decorated rooms, with stone bathrooms and balconies with views over the battle site. Rob Gerrard, the resident historian, offers excellent tours – his storytelling will provide a startlingly moving insight into the battles. Rates include all meals.

$$$ Penny Farthing, 14 km south of Dundee on the R33 towards Greytown, 2 km off the main road on the right, T034-642 1925, www.pennyf.co.za. This farm has a choice of 1 room in a restored old fort with its own lounge and fireplace, or 5 rooms in the colonial sandstone farmhouse, decorated with antiques and French doors leading to the garden. Meals are taken communally at the 16-seater table and battlefield tours are with resident guide Foy Vermaak, a descendent of a Voortrekker family who fought in the Zulu and Anglo-Boer wars.

WHAT TO DO

Most of the lodges provide excellent battlefield tours and they can also be organized in advance by the tourist offices in Ladysmith, page 145, and Dundee, page 148, and at the Talana Museum in Dundee, page 148. These can recommend several characterful guides in the region.

The website for the Provincial Tour Guides of KwaZulu Natal: www.battlefieldsregionguides.co.za, is also a good resource for organizing a guide. Costs are in the region of R700-900 for a full-day guided tour in your own car.

UKHAHLAMBA-DRAKENSBERG

The Drakensberg Mountains, which rise to 3000 m and extend 180 km along the western edge of KwaZulu Natal, form the backbone of the uKhahlamba-Drakensberg Park, and determine the border with Lesotho. This formidable mountain range is one of South Africa's most staggeringly beautiful destinations, and in 2001 it was awarded the status of a World Heritage Site by UNESCO, both for its diverse flora and fauna and its impressive San rock paintings. The greater uKhahlamba-Drakensberg Park extends from the Royal Natal National Park in the north to Sehlabathebe National Park, part of Lesotho, in the south. The protected area is 180 km long and up to 20 km wide. Almost the entire range falls within protected reserves managed by KZN Wildlife (T033-845 1000, www.kznwildlife.com). There are numerous points from which to explore the Berg, ranging from fully equipped holiday resorts and luxury hotels to campsites, mountain huts and isolated caves.

ARRIVING IN UKHAHLAMBA-DRAKENSBERG PARK

Getting there The most popular resorts in the Drakensberg are within two to three hours' drive of Durban, accessed from the N3 and then a network of minor roads heading west into the mountains. The Northern Drakensberg resorts and reserves around Monk's Cowl and Cathedral Peak are signposted from Winterton and Bergville, off the N3, along either the R74, the R600 or the R616. The Battlefields Route lies to the northeast of this region (see page 144). The Central Drakensberg reserves such as Kamberg and Giant's Castle can be reached from the N3 and the Midlands towns of Nottingham Road, Mooi River and Estcourt. Those in the far south are best approached from Pietermaritzburg and the N3 via the R617 and Underberg.

Getting around Baz Bus ① *T021-439 2323, www.bazbus.com*, runs through the Drakensberg three times a week en route between Durban and Johannesburg, stopping at Winterton and Oliviershoek Pass. In the southern Drakensberg, the **Underberg Express** ① *T033-701 2750, www.underbergexpress.co.za*, runs to and from Durban, Pietermaritzburg and Underberg. There is little in the way of public transport between the Battlefields and the Drakensberg, so the best way of exploring the area is by car.

Best time to visit The weather in the Drakensberg can be divided into two main seasons: summer and winter. Although the weather tends to be pleasant all year round, the altitude and the mountain climate shouldn't be underestimated. Climatic conditions can change rapidly and snow, fog, rain and thunderstorms can develop within minutes, enveloping hikers on exposed hillsides.

Winter (May to August) is the driest time of the year and also the coolest. There will always be some rain during the winter months which, when it's cold enough, will occasionally fall as snow. Daytime temperatures can be as high as 15°C, while at night temperatures will often fall below 0°C. Despite the risk of snow, this the best season for hiking.

Summer (November to February) is the wettest time. The mornings tend to be warm and bright, but as the heat builds up clouds begin to collect in the afternoon. The violence of the thunderstorms when they break is quite spectacular, usually accompanied by short bursts of torrential rain. Daytime temperatures average around 20°C and the nights are generally mild with temperatures not falling much below 10°C. The summer is a less popular season for hiking, although then the landscape is greener and the wildlife more abundant.

Tourist information There are a number of tourist offices in the area. The **Drakensberg Tourism Association** ① *Municipal Building, Thatham Rd, Bergville, T036-448 1557, www. drakensberg.org.za, Mon-Fri 0900-1700*, provides information on the whole region. The **Central Drakensberg Information Centre** ① *Thokozisa, on the R600, 13 km west of Winterton, T036-488 1207, www.cdic.co.za, daily 0900-1700*, is an arts, crafts and tourist centre, which has a coffee shop and restaurant, and stocks useful maps and brochures. It can also help arrange accommodation.

Safety There have been a number of carjacking incidents in the Drakensberg. Beware when driving down isolated roads and always take local advice.

Entry fees An entry fee, which includes a community levy and an emergency rescue levy, is payable each time you enter a protected area administered by **KZN Wildlife**. This fee is included in the cost of accommodation within the parks so only day visitors pay an entry fee at the gate. Current rates for day visitors are R20-40, children R10-20 depending on the park, and in some cases there's a fee for a car of about R25.

WHAT TO DO

Hiking, horse riding and mountaineering are the traditional Drakensberg activities. and many of the larger resort hotels also offer a wide range of sporting facilities such as tennis, golf and swimming.

STAYING IN THE PARK

There is a huge choice in the area, including within KZN Wildlife accommodation and in private establishments on the fringes of the park. KZN Wildlife offers a wide range of facilities, from luxury lodges and chalets through to campsites, mountain huts and caves. All of the KZN Wildlife camps are basically self-catering and, although there are some camp shops which sell food, the choice is limited. It is far better to come prepared and buy your food beforehand in the nearest large town.

The areas bordering the national park have a number of privately run self-contained holiday resorts. These tend to offer numerous sporting and entertainment facilities, and while they are sometimes rather distant from the mountains themselves, most offer outstanding views of the Drakensberg.

Reservations for **KZN Wildlife** ① *T033-845 1000, www.kznwildlife.com*. Bookings can be made by telephone or online; camping reservations must be made directly with the officer in charge of the campsite, see individual areas for details.

→NORTHERN DRAKENSBERG

The scenery of the Northern Berg is exceptional in its grandeur, and is perhaps the most photographed section of the range. The Royal Natal National Park is the most popular of all the resorts in the Drakensberg, and although there are some good hikes outside the park, they don't really compare with the sheer majesty of those within its boundaries.

ARRIVING IN NORTHERN DRAKENSBERG

Access from Durban is via the N3, a 2¾-hour drive to Bergville, and four hours to the Royal Natal National Park.

BERGVILLE

This quiet country town is in the centre of a maize and dairy farming area. It was established and named after a retired sea captain in 1897, and two years later at the onset of the Anglo-Boer War a blockhouse was built by the British, which today stands in the grounds of the local courthouse. Most visitors will either be passing through en route to the resorts in the Northern Drakensberg or be heading northeast towards Ladysmith and the Battlefields. The main reason for stopping is to visit the helpful **Drakensberg Tourism Association** (see page 153).

ROYAL NATAL NATIONAL PARK

ⓘ *The park can be reached from the R74 from both Harrismith (60 km) or Bergville (45 km), the turn-off is 8 km south of the Oliviershoek Pass from where it is a further 14 km to the park gate, the routes are well signposted from the N3, T036-438 6411, gates Oct-Mar 0600-1900, Apr-Sep 0600-1800, office 0800-1630, R30, children (under 12) R20.*

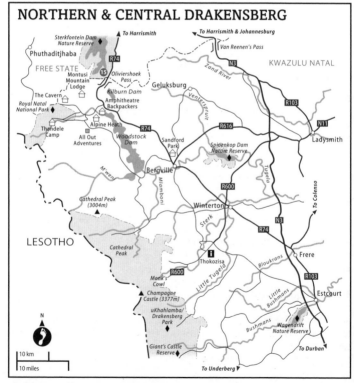

NORTHERN & CENTRAL DRAKENSBERG

The highlight of a visit to the park is the first view of the massive rock walls that form the **Amphitheatre**. The **Eastern Buttress** (3009 m) is the southernmost peak of the 4-km of cliff face, which arcs northwards towards the **Sentinel** (3165 m) forming an impressive barrier. On the plateau directly behind the Amphitheatre is **Mont-aux-Sources** (3299 m) named by French missionaries in 1836. This mountain is the source of five rivers: the **Elands** which flows into the Vaal; the **Khudeda** and the **Singu** leading into the Orange/ Gariep River in the Free State; and the **Tugela** and the **Bilanjil** which lead into Natal.

The most impressive of these is the Tugela which plunges over the edge of the Amphitheatre wall, dropping around 800 m through a series of five falls. The gorge created by the waters of the Tugela is a steep-sided tangle of boulders and trees which at a point near the Devil's Tooth Gully has bored straight through the sandstone to form what appears to be a tunnel around 40 m long.

The national park was established in 1916 when farms around the Amphitheatre were bought by the government to protect the land. Tourism started around this time and the park has been popular since then. Queen Elizabeth II visited the park in 1947, five years before she became queen; since then, the national park and the (now closed) hotel are prefixed by the word 'Royal' in memory of this visit.

Hiking There are over 130 km of walking trails around the Royal Natal National Park, many of which are easy half-day strolls. Even the hikes that don't climb up to the top of the escarpment wind through beautiful countryside of grassland dotted with patches of yellowwood forest and proteas set against the stunning backdrop of the Amphitheatre. The office sells hiking maps and a leaflet describing the many possible walks around the park.

The 20-km hike up to **Mont-aux-Sources** (3299 m) can be completed in a strenuous day's walk. The path starts at **Mahai Campsite** and heads steadily uphill following the course of the Mahai River. The path climbs steeply around the eastern flank of the Sentinel (3165 m). Just after the Sentinel Caves is the notorious chain ladder, built in 1930, which takes you up a 30-m cliff face. Once on top, Mont-aux-Sources is only 3 km away and involves no more serious climbing. The views from the top of the escarpment are splendid as they stretch out over KwaZulu Natal.

The walk up the **Tugela Gorge** is a 14-km round trip which begins at the car park below Tendele Camp. The path heads up the gorge and follows the Tugela River passing through shady patches of yellowwood forest. Higher up along the valley there are rock pools which are ideal for swimming in. After around 6 km at the entrance to the gorge there is a chain ladder; from here you can either wade through the gorge or climb up the ladder and walk along the top. There are magnificent views here of the Devil's Tooth, the Eastern Buttress and Tugela Falls. Beware of heavy rain on this walk as flash flooding through the gorge is extremely dangerous.

The 8-km trail to **Cannibal Cave** heads north from the road leading to **Mahai Campsite**. The route follows the Goldie River for 1 km before crossing over and following the ridge north again until it passes close to Sunday Falls. The path then rises over Surprise Ridge and on to the Cannibal Cave. The walks from the **Rugged Glen Campsite** are over rolling hills and although there are some good views of the Amphitheatre, they don't compare with the hikes from the Thendele and Mahai camps.

OLIVIERSHOEK PASS

The 1730-m Oliviershoek Pass was named after Adriaan Olivier who was one of the first Voortrekkers to descend from the Orange Free State in the 1830s. He claimed a farm for himself at the foot of the pass. As the R74 ascends to the top of the pass from the north it begins to climb through pine forests. Although the mountains here aren't as spectacular as Mont-aux-Sources (see below), they do have their own quiet charm and it is worth stopping off at one of the few restaurants on this road. The R74 in this area also provides access to numerous private resorts bordering the Royal Natal National Park.

→CENTRAL DRAKENSBERG

The Giant's Castle Nature Reserve is the most spectacular of the Central Berg resorts. It has two camps: Giant's Castle and Injisuthi. Here, the basalt cliff faces rise up to 3000 m and stretch out to the north and south for over 30 km. Further north, the road to Monk's Cowl, with its string of resorts, curio villages and golf courses, is one of the most heavily developed areas of the Drakensberg. While you may see more tourists in this region, the scenery is no less spectacular and access is easier than in other areas of the park. This is also home to the internationally famous Drakensberg Boys' Choir.

Arriving in Central Drakensberg Two roads from Winterton lead towards the central Drakensberg resorts: heading north the R74 goes via Bergville, 22 km, to the **Royal Natal National Park**, 62 km. Two kilometres south of Winterton on the R600 there is a signposted turning to **Cathedral Peak**, 43 km. The R600 continues on to **Monk's Cowl** (Champagne Valley), 35 km. To reach **Injisuthi**, take the turning to Loskop off the R600, before reaching Loskop there is a dirt road on the right. Follow the signposts to Injisuthi from here. Heading southeast, the R74 crosses the N3 to **Estcourt**, 43 km.

WINTERTON

This small village with tree-lined streets is an important centre for dairy farms as well as being the last place to stock up on supplies for visitors to Cathedral Peak or Monk's Cowl. The petrol station and the supermarket are on the junction of the R74 with the road leading into the centre of village. Nearby, in Thokosiza, is the **Central Drakensberg Information Centre**, a major arts, crafts and tourist centre.

SPIOENKOP DAM NATURE RESERVE

① *14 km north of Winterton on the R600, office T036-488 1578, Oct-Mar 0600-1900, Apr-Sep 0600-1800, R20 per person.*

This 6000-ha game park is a popular tourist resort for boating and fishing. Almost all the game here has been reintroduced and there is a good chance of seeing white rhino and buffalo. With this in mind visitors must be careful when walking in the open around their campsite. Other animals you can expect to see include giraffe, kudu, mountain reedbuck, waterbuck, blesbok, impala, zebra, eland, duiker and steenbok. The area is particularly rich in birdlife and more than 270 species have been recorded here. Anglers can fish the reservoir from the dam or from the shore.

The **Battle of Spion Kop**, 24 January 1890, was yet another embarrassing defeat for the British at the hands of the Boers and had a marked impact upon British public opinion. In order to relieve the beleaguered British troops at Ladysmith (see box, page 146), General

Warren attempted a direct assault on the Rangeworthy Hills to dislodge the Boer positions. He decided to occupy the highest peak on the ridge – Spion Kop. However, this meant that the shallow British defences were exposed to Boer gunfire from all sides and soon suffered heavy losses. A brigade under General Lyttelton came to Warren's assistance but General Buller disastrously reversed the decision, ordering all British forces to retreat down from Spion Kop and back across the Tugela. Some 1750 British troops were either killed, wounded or captured at Spion Kop compared to about 300 Boers. The famous battlefield overlooks the dam and is clearly visible from the reserve. It can be reached on one of the self-guided trails.

CATHEDRAL PEAK

ⓘ *Signposted from Bergville (48 km) and Winterton (41 km), T036-488 8000, 0700-1900, R30, children (under 12) R15, or R50/25 with a visit to the Rock Art Centre, vehicles to Mike's Pass R60.* Cathedral Peak is the main point of access to some of the wildest areas of the central Drakensberg, and provides some of the most spectacular scenery for hikers. Driving into the area, the road passes traditional Zulu villages and dips through leafy valleys, with the views gradually opening up as you get closer to the park. The park itself is ringed by dramatic peaks with views of the Cathedral Spur and Cathedral Peak (3004 m), the Inner and Outer Horns (3005 m) and the Bell (2930 m). An alternative to hiking round the peaks is to drive up Mike's Pass, suitable for saloon cars (although it says 4WD only), from where there are spectacular views of the Little Berg (R60 per car).

Hiking There is a good network of paths heading up the Mlambonja Valley to the escarpment from where there are trails heading south to Monk's Cowl and Injisuthi or heading north to Royal Natal National Park. There are designated caves and mountain huts on the longer trails. Didima Camp or the **Cathedral Peak Hotel** are good bases from which to set out exploring the area on a series of day walks and maps are available. The 10-km hike to the top of **Cathedral Peak** (3004 m) is one of the most exciting and strenuous hikes in this part of the Drakensberg, and the views from the top of the Drakensberg stretching out to the north and south are unforgettable.

Cave paintings The sheltered valleys in this area are thought to have been one of the last refuges of the San, and this is one of the best places to see a large number of San cave paintings in the Drakensberg. An excellent introduction is just past the entrance to the park, at the **Rock Art Centre** ⓘ *Didima Camp, T036-488 8025, open 0800-1300, 1400-1600, coffee shop and craft centre.* The stylish thatched building holds a series of displays interpreting the art found in the surrounding mountains. A key thread in the museum is the eland, a vital aspect in San mythology and culture, with some life-size replicas in the entrance. The museum begins with an introduction to the culture and lifestyle of the San, with a look at archaeological finds, quotes from some of the last San descendants, and descriptions of the symbolic meaning of some of the most famous paintings. At the back of the museum is a replica of an open-topped cave, complete with starry sky and fake camp fire, where recordings of San folklore stories are played. This leads to the auditorium, an impressive structure built to look like a rock overhang, where you can watch an interesting 15-minute audio-visual show on the history of the San and their cave paintings.

ON THE ROAD
Cave paintings

The sandstone caves of the Drakensberg are one of the best places in the world to see rock art. Most of the surviving paintings are on the walls of rock shelters. There are traces of paintings on exposed rocks but they have been heavily weathered. The paintings tend to be quite recent and are probably only 200 to 300 years old, but they do form part of a long-standing tradition. The earliest cave paintings in Southern Africa date from 28,000 years ago.

The pigments used by the San were made from natural ochre mixed with blood, fat or milk. Artists would carry their pigments in antelope horns hanging from their belts. The San here were particularly prolific and there are hundreds of caves throughout these mountains which are covered with layer upon layer of paintings. Some of the most beautiful of South Africa's cave paintings can be found in the Drakensberg.

There have been numerous attempts at interpreting the meaning of these paintings. One of the more outlandish theories held by European archaeologists at the beginning of the last century was that they had been drawn with the help of migrating Carthaginians. Other more recent theories hold that the paintings are either little more than well-executed graffitos illustrating scenes from daily life or that they were used in sympathetic magic.

The most recent research has drawn from ethnographic records from the end of the last century and interviews with the remaining San people in this century. The eland features largely in San mythology and is one of the most frequently painted subjects. It seems unlikely that the eland were painted as part of a hunting ritual using sympathetic magic as the eland is not often found in food debris from archaeological excavations. It is thought that the eland in some way represented god.

The most prevalent current theory holds that the paintings of human figures dancing, which show people with nose bleeds hallucinating geometric patterns, are people taking part in shamanic rituals who are in a state of trance.

There are also other paintings which seem to deal with more mundane matters. The scenes of San collecting wild honey, hunting pigs or being chased by a leopard reveal aspects of a way of life which has now disappeared.

MONK'S COWL AND CHAMPAGNE VALLEY

The R600 road to Monk's Cowl passes through one of the most developed areas of the Drakensberg. Looking down from Monk's Cowl the view of KwaZulu Natal is dotted with hotels, golf courses and timeshare developments and the area is locally dubbed 'Champagne Valley'. However, **Champagne Castle**, **Monk's Cowl** and **Cathkin Peak** are still impressive features in this landscape. The entrance to Monk's Cowl is 32 km west of Winterton where there is a KZN Wildlife campsite and several interesting hikes. On the way there are numerous resorts and attractions in the valley off the R600.

Drakensberg Boys' Choir School ① *on the right of the R600 towards Monk's Cowl, T036-468 1012, www.dbchoir.info,* has one of the most beautiful locations for a school in the whole of South Africa. The school is highly accredited in its own right, but is most famous for the choir that has performed all over the world in the last three decades. Boys aged between nine and 15 have performed in front of the Pope and 25,000 people at the Vatican City, sung with the Vienna Boys' Choir in Austria, and have been proclaimed top choir at the World Festival of Choirs. The choir has even received a special award at Disney's Magic Kingdom.

During term time the choir performs (anything from Beethoven to Freddy Mercury) on Wednesday at 1530 in the school's impressive auditorium (booking essential).

Just before the **Champagne Castle Hotel**, turn off the R600 to reach **Falcon Ridge** ① *T082-774 6398, 1-hr bird shows Sat-Thu 1030, R40, children (under 12) R15*, a rehabilitation centre for rescued birds of prey, mostly injured from flying into power lines. The daily falconry show is a big attraction, and you can don a glove and have your photo taken with a large raptor.

Drakensberg Canopy Tour ① *on the right of the R600 just after the turn-off to the Champagne Sports Resort, T036-468 1981, www.drakensbergcanopytour.co.za, departure every 45 mins, Apr-Sep 0800-1700, Oct-Mar 0600-1600, R450, no children under 7, includes refreshments*, is set in a patch of indigenous forest in the shadow of Cathkin Peak. It is one of many canopy tours now around South Africa (see www.canopytour.co.za for the other locations). It's a great way to see the forest canopy from platforms in the trees and on rock faces some 40 m above the ground. The platforms are connected by steel cables that you swing across on a harness. The experience lasts about three hours.

Monk's Cowl ① *at the end of the R600, 32 km west of Winterton, T036-468 1103, gates Oct-Mar 0700-2000, Apr-Sep 0600-1800, office 0800-1230, 1400-1630, R35, children (under 12) R18*, taking its name from the peak between the Champagne Castle and Cathkin peaks, is a popular part of the uKhahlamba-Drakensberg Park for camping, day hikes or a stop at the tea room at the reserve's entrance, and is usually visited on a day excursion from the resorts in Champagne Valley.

Hiking Maps are available from the office for the short hikes around Monk's Cowl and the paths are clear and well signposted. Places to visit include **Nandi's Falls** (5 km), **Sterkspruit Falls** (2 km) and **The Sphinx** (3 km). The paths cross areas of proteas and some woodland and some go past gloriously refreshing rock pools.

The route up to **Champagne Castle** (3377 m) is a 20-km, two-day hike which involves a steady slog uphill, but no climbing skills are needed.

GIANT'S CASTLE RESERVE
This reserve was established in 1903 when there were only 200 eland left in the whole of KwaZulu Natal. Over the years, the reserve has successfully helped the eland population in the Drakensberg to recover and at present there are around 600 in the reserve. Blesbok, mountain reedbuck and oribi are some of the other mammals you are likely to see. Rolling hills of sourveld grasslands dominate the landscape of the reserve, with the Drakensberg escarpment towering over the main camp. A wall of basalt cliffs rises up to over 3000 m and the peaks of **Giant's Castle** (3314 m), **Champagne Castle** (3248 m) and **Cathkin Peak** (3149 m) can be seen on the skyline. The grasslands below the cliffs roll out in a series of massive hills, which give rise to the Bushman's River and the Little Tugela River.

Arriving in Giant's Castle Reserve The road to Giant's Castle is signposted from Mooi River (64 km) and Estcourt (65 km) on the N3.

Giant's Castle camp and around ① *T036-353 3718, gates Oct-Mar 0500-1900, Apr-Sep 0600-1800, office 0800-1800, R30, children (under 12) R15*. The area around the camp has a network of short paths through riverine forest and wetlands which supports many species of bird. The malachite kingfisher, Gurney's sugarbird and the various sunbirds are often spotted here and grey duiker can sometimes be seen walking around the camp.

There are numerous interconnected hikes crossing the reserve. The shorter walks explore the forests and river valleys within a few kilometres of the camp, whilst the longer ones take up to three days and can reach areas as far afield as Injisuthi. A comprehensive leaflet detailing the hiking choices is available from the camp office.

The **Main Cave** is half an hour's walk from the camp and has a large wall covered in paintings and a simple display on the archaeology of the cave and the San who lived there. The cave must be visited with a guide; book at the main office (see above).

The 7-km hike up to **World's View** (1842 m) follows a path north along a ridge overlooking the Bushman's River. The climb up to the top is not too strenuous and the views looking over Wildebeest Plateau to Giant's Castle and Cathkin Peak are well worth the effort. The best time to see the peaks of the mountains is early in the morning as clouds tend to descend in the afternoon.

The more challenging walks to **Langalibalele Pass**, 12 km, **Bannerman Pass**, 20 km, and **Giant's Castle** involve a long uphill struggle to reach the top of the escarpment. The hike up to Giant's Castle at 3314 m takes three days and means using Giant's Hut as a base camp for two nights. The second day's hike from the hut to Giant's Castle Pass, 12 km, rises up through scree slopes and loose rubble. From the top of the pass it is a further 1 km to the peak. Giant's Hut is 10 km from the main camp and there are several well-marked paths which lead to it.

Injisuthi camp and around ⓘ *Signposted from Winterton and Loskop, the last 30 km of the journey are on a poor dirt road, T036-431 7848, gates Oct-Mar 0500-1900, Apr-Sep 0600-1800, office 0800-1230, 1400-1630, R20, children (under 12) R10.* Injisuthi is an isolated camp high up in the Giant's Castle Reserve. The valley is covered with large areas of yellowwood forest and grassland, and looming over the camp are the awe-inspiring mountain peaks of **Champagne Castle** (3248 m), **Monk's Cowl** (3234 m) and **Cathkin Peak** (3149 m). **Mafadi** (3446 m), **Injisuthi Dome** (3410 m), and the **Injisuthi Triplets** – Eastern Triplet (3134 m), Western Triplet (3187 m) and Injisuthi Buttress (3202 m) – are some of the highest peaks in South Africa and have become magnets for South Africa's climbers. The game in Injisuthi Valley used to be abundant and the Zulu word *Injisuthi* actually means 'well-fed dog' as hunting parties here were often so successful. San also thrived here and left many cave paintings.

There is a selection of trails for day hikes beginning at the campsite and following the Injisuthi Stream to the southwest. Poacher's Stream is a tributary of the Injisuthi and this path leads off Boundary Pool (3 km) where it is possible to swim. Following the Injisuthi further up the valley are Battle Cave (5 km), Junction Cave (8 km) and Lower Injisuthi Cave (8 km). There is a daily guided walk (7 km), to **Battle Cave** and other San sites, which should be booked the day before. Battle Cave is named after one its cave paintings, which shows two groups of San attacking each other. Figures are shown running into the fight with arrows flying between them. There are hundreds of other paintings on the cave walls of animals that used to live here, including lions, eland, rhebok, an elephant and an antbear.

Giant's Castle is a three-day hike from Injisuthi following the contour path south. The trail can be exhausting but it does pass through spectacular mountain scenery including Popple Peak. Reservations for sleeping at Lower Injisuthi Cave and Bannerman Hut have to be made in advance.

KAMBERG NATURE RESERVE

ⓘ 48 km from Nottingham Rd travelling via Rosetta; the route is well signposted and only the last 19 km are on dirt roads. If travelling from Mooi River (42 km) on the N3, take the turning to Rosetta, T033-263 7312, gates Oct-Mar 0500-1900, Apr-Sep 0600-1800, office 0800-1130, 1400-1530, R30, children (under 12) R15.

This reserve is at relatively low altitude, the highest point being **Gladstone's Nose** at 2265 m, and is therefore known for its birdlife, with over 200 species recorded here. However, the scenery is not as spectacular as at some of the other reserves, although the Clarens Sandstone around Kamberg does have its own special appeal, and there is some good San rock art within the reserve.

Kamberg is probably best known for its trout fishing; there is a hatchery open to the public and several dams stocked with brown and rainbow trout which can be fished all year round. The Mooi River can only be fished during the season between September and April.

The trails around Kamberg are quite leisurely and involve no steep climbs. The **Mooi River Trail**, 4 km, has been designed with wheelchair access in mind, and is a relaxing stroll past willows and eucalyptus trees along the banks of the Mooi River. Longer trails, such as the hike up to **Emeweni Falls**, are detailed in a booklet available in the camp office.

There are several rock art sites in the reserve, but the two main sites worth visiting for the variety and quality of the paintings are Game Pass Shelter and The Kranses. The sheer number of paintings at **Game Pass Shelter** (about a 7-km walk from Kamberg) is impressive. Among the many scenes on the rock wall is one of a human with hooves instead of feet holding the tail of a dying eland. This is thought to have shamanic meaning and to be connected to a trance-like state. Just outside the shelter there are some fossilized dinosaur footprints. An impressive **San Rock Art Interpretation Centre** *ⓘ T033-263 7312, 0900-1600, R20, children (under 12) R10*, provides visitors with an insight into the lifestyle of the San. There's an audio-visual presentation followed by a guided walk to the Game Pass Shelter that takes about 2½ hours. The centre also has a small restaurant.

The walk to the **Kranses** group of caves is a 12-km round trip. Apart from these there are also several other interesting caves to visit. The Kranses has a long sheltered rock wall covered in paintings of eland. Among these are some smaller scenes showing a group of people, some of whom are carrying shields. It is known that the San didn't use shields so they must be paintings of cattle herders, possibly the Amazizi, who moved up into the Drakensberg and lived peacefully with the San.

UKHAHLAMBA-DRAKENSBERG LISTINGS

WHERE TO STAY

Northern Drakensberg

$$$$ Montusi Mountain Lodge, follow signs along R74 towards Royal Natal National Park, T036-438 6243, www.montusi.co.za. Attractive series of luxury thatched chalets surrounded by lawns, with large bedrooms, plush sitting rooms and private terrace with staggering views towards the amphitheatre. Good restaurant and small bar, guided walks in the Royal Natal National Park, including to San rock art and the top of the amphitheatre, fly-fishing, horse riding, swimming pool, and Zulu village visits. Smaller and not as family orientated as other resorts.

$$$ Alpine Heath, below Oliviershoek Pass, follow signs along the R74 (Cavern Berg Rd), T036-438 6484, www.alpineheath.co.za. A fully self-contained and well-established resort with 100 self-catering chalets with 3 bedrooms, 2 bathrooms, lounge with fireplace and DSTV, and patio with mountain views. Facilities include 2 pools, gym, spa, tennis, shops, restaurant and pub, and horse riding and mountain biking can be arranged.

$$$ The Cavern, 10 km, follow the signs heading off the R74 towards the Royal Natal National Park, T036-438 6270, www.cavern.co.za. Large complex set among gardens and woodland offering accommodation in 55 comfortable thatched cottages. Wide range of activities including horse riding, bowls, pool, spa, and evening entertainment. Rates include all meals and guided hikes. A superb location and good choice for families.

$$$-$ Thendele Camp, KZN Wildlife, T033-845 1000, www.kznwildlife.com. Stunning location with unrivalled views of the amphitheatre from a cluster of chalets, cottages and a lodge sleeping 6. The cottages and lodge have cooks who prepare food supplied by the guests, while the chalets are self-catering with fully equipped kitchens, fireplace, terrace and braai. The camp's setting makes it one of the most popular in the entire Drakensberg, so must be booked months in advance. The shop sells maps, books and souvenirs.

$$ Sandford Park Country Hotel, R616 to Ladysmith, T036-448 1001, www.sandford.co.za. Charming country hotel dating back to 1852, with 50 rooms, some in separate rondavels, with DSTV and tasteful furnishings, neat gardens, large pool, horse riding, hiking and canoeing, and a popular restaurant and bar. Good base from which to explore both the Drakensberg and the battlefields.

$ Amphitheatre Backpackers, 21 km northwest of Bergville on the R74, T036-438 6675, www.amphibackpackers.co.za. Excellent backpackers, the main building is a converted sandstone house with log fires, dorms, doubles and camping, hearty home-cooked meals, packed lunches to take with you on over 30 hikes in the area. If you don't have your own transport, this is a perfect introduction to the mountains. Daily guided hikes to the top of the amphitheatre and day trips into Lesotho. On the **Baz Bus** route.

Central Drakensberg

$$$ Cathedral Peak Hotel, at the end of the road past the entry gates, T036-488 1888, www.cathedralpeak.co.za. All-round resort in a stunning location close to the high peaks of the Drakensberg, popular as a base for hikers and for weddings in its own stone chapel, with 90 luxurious rooms, several restaurants and bars, 3 pools, 9-hole golf course, horse riding, mountain biking, squash and tennis, 10-m climbing tower, gym and spa. Rates include meals.

$$$ Champagne Castle, 2 km, T036-468 1063, www.champagnecastle.co.za. Traditional Drakensberg family resort in a spectacular mountain setting, with 72 smart rooms, set in the main lodge and annexes with thatched roofs, surrounded by attractive leafy grounds. Restaurant, bar, horse riding, trout fishing, tennis, pool, spa. Rates include all meals.

$$$-$$ Didima Camp, on the road leading into Cathedral Peak, just before **Cathedral Peak Hotel**, KZN Wildlife, T033-845 1000, www.kznwildlife.com. Large camp themed around the art of the San people and the thatched chalets have been designed to look like caves, with 28 double/twin chalets, 38 self-catering units sleeping 2, built back to back so can be converted into 4-bed units, 1 6-bed chalet and a honeymoon suite. All have DSTV and fireplace, and there's a restaurant, bar, small shop and pool. The conference centre/wedding chapel has a full-height glass wall framing a view of Cathedral Peak. Also here is the **Rock Art Centre** (see page 157).

$$$-$$ Giant's Castle camp, KZN Wildlife, T033-845 1000, www.kznwildlife.com. 44 chalets sleeping 2-6, with lounge, TV and fully equipped kitchen. Shop sells a wide range of books and curios but only a limited selection of dried and frozen food. **Izimbali** restaurant and pub if you don't want to self-cater. Swimming in summer is permitted in the Bushmen's River below the camp. There are also 4 mountain huts for hikers about 4-5 hrs' walk from Giant's Castle camp.

WHAT TO DO

All Out Adventures, near the entrance to the **Alpine Heath resort**, off the R74, below Oliviershoek Pass, T036-438 6242, www.alloutadventures.co.za. 0900-1630, closed Tue out of season, no need to pre-book but phone ahead in quieter seasons. Fun activities for young and old; a flying trapeze (R100 for 2 flights), a bungee bounce (R60), where you're put in a bungee harness and then bounce very high from a trampoline, a big swing (R150) from the top of a pine tree, a zip-liner slide (R100), and a canopy cable tour (R375) to various platforms in the trees. Children's combo tickets are available. Also organize paintballing and quad-biking. Coffee shop serving snacks.

Climbing
The website of the KwaZulu Natal section of the **Mountain Club of South Africa**, www.kzn.mcsa.org.za, is a useful source of information for experienced rock climbers. **Peak High**, T033-343 3168, www.peakhigh.co.za. Contact Gavin Raubenheimer for details of guided climbs in the Drakensberg, and about the possibility of ice climbing the **Lotheni Falls**, which are usually frozen from mid-Jun to mid-Aug. Strictly for experienced mountaineers only, with full equipment, including an ice pick.

Fishing
Trout were introduced into the rivers of the Drakensberg around 1900 and over the years fly-fishing has become popular. Fishing licences are available from some of the offices at the camps, and some rent out rods and tackle. Enquire with **KZN Wildlife**, T033-845 1000, www.kznwildlife.com. Many of the private resorts also arrange trout fishing.

Helicopter flights
There is an airfield at the **Dragon Peaks** resort from where you can take short helicopter flights over the mountains. Bookings can also be made at the **Cathedral Peak Hotel**, or the **Champagne Sports Resort**, or call **Westline Aviation**, T083-652 7493. A 20-min scenic flight costs around R900 per person.

DURBAN TO EAST LONDON

The landscape south of Durban includes a fertile subtropical region stretching from the southern tip of the Drakensberg Mountain Range to the Indian Ocean. The Umzimkulu, the Umkomaas and the Elands rivers wind their way from the Drakensberg escarpment through the rolling hills of KwaZulu Natal to the sea. This was one of the first areas to be settled by the British during the 19th century and continuous agricultural development has left its mark on the landscape. Some of South Africa's largest pine and eucalyptus plantations extend for mile after mile around Harding, while, nearer to the coast, sugarcane and banana plantations dominate the scenery. A strip of subtropical forest runs down the coast bordering the beach.

A typical sun, sea and sand holiday is the main activity of this region and it is among South Africa's most popular domestic holiday destinations. Dolphin watching and scuba-diving on the Aliwal Shoal and on the reefs south of Port Shepstone are additional distractions, and a wide range of sporting facilities, including numerous golf courses, are available at the resorts. The main attractions inland are the nature reserves at Oribi Gorge and Umtamvuna.

The coastline region that stretches roughly 280 km from East London to the Umtamvuna Nature Reserve next to Port Edward in KwaZulu Natal was once the Transkei, meaning 'across the Kei River' in isiXhosa), an independent homeland during the Apartheid years. These days it is known as the Wild Coast and is a largely rural area of rolling grasslands wedged between the Great Kei River in the south and the Umtamvuna River in the north. Its inland borders are the Drakensberg and the Stormberg mountains, and dotted between are small villages, brightly painted kraals and endless communal pastureland. It remains a traditional area populated by the Xhosa, some of whom still practise customs such as dowry payments and initiation ceremonies. The Great Kei River was originally the border between South Africa and the Transkei and, as the N2 crosses the Kei River 65 km north of East London, the difference in the standard of living between the two areas is striking. Years of overpopulation and under-investment have taken their toll in the former Transkei. The landscape is deforested and seriously eroded and, away from the N2 and the roads leading to the resorts, the roads are in poor condition compared to the rest of the country. There are few tourist amenities here and you will get a more realistic picture of the poverty that still blights South Africa. Nevertheless it is a beautiful region and the coastline itself is rugged and peaceful, with a number of caves, beaches, cliffs and shipwrecks to explore.

GETTING AROUND

The route from Durban southwest to East London follows the N2 over 655 km. The highway firstly follows the coast as far as Port Shepstone (120 km from Durban), before heading inland via Kokstad, after which it runs through the interior of the Eastern Cape and joins the coast again at East London. The mainline buses and the Baz Bus stick to the N2. Another option to get to the southern resorts is the **Margate Mini Coach** ① *T039-312 1406, www.margate.co.za/minicoach.htm*, which runs between King Shaka International Airport, Durban Station, Amanzimtoti, Scottburgh, Hibberdene, Port Shepstone and Margate.

→AMANZIMTOTI TO SCOTTBURGH

The Strelitzia coast is one of the more built-up areas south of Durban. Driving down the N2, the road first goes through an extensive industrial belt and then to Amanzimtoti, or 'toti', only

22 km south of Durban, which is effectively a suburb and an unattractive high-rise holiday resort with little appeal. The Zulu name translates as 'sweet waters', as described by Shaka. **Inyoni Rocks** and **Pipeline Beach** are the two main beaches for swimmers and sunbathers.

Between Amanzimtoti and Umgababa are a series of coastal resorts known collectively as Kingsburgh. This 8-km stretch is known for its good beaches and is popular with surfers and jet-skiers. Travelling down the coast from Amanzimtoti, the first beach you reach is **Doonside**; across the Little Manzimtoti River is **Warner Beach**. **Winkelspruit** is one of the more developed parts of the area. Across the Lovu River is **Illovo** beach, which is backed by a lagoon at the mouth of the river. **Karridene** is at the mouth of another river, the Msimbazi. **Umkomaas** is the last resort in this area, which is 48 km south of Durban and is where the Umkomaas River spills into the sea at the largest estuary on the south coast. The source of the 300-km-long river is just south of Giant's Castle in the Drakensberg, where it begins its journey at over 3000 m.

SCOTTBURGH

Scottburgh, 58 km south of Durban, is one of the busiest resorts on the Strelitzia coast. The popular beach by the estuary of the Mpambanyoni is protected by shark nets. The beaches are connected by a miniature seafront railway. There's a **tourist office** ① *Blue Marlin Hotel, Scott St, T039-978 3361, www.scottburgh.co.za, Mon-Fri 0900-1630.*

The **Aliwal Shoal** lies just north of Scottburgh, and after Sodwana Bay is one of South Africa's most popular diving areas. The shoal is a haven for marine life and has good dives on wrecks and the reef. The caves attract ragged-tooth sharks each winter.

→HIBISCUS COAST

There is less industrial development along this coast, which stretches from Scottburgh to Port Edward, but the overall impression as you drive down the coast is of a long line of caravan parks and holiday homes, set in a lush subtropical strip of forest. The ocean is the highlight here. During the warm winter months millions of sardines travel close to the beaches, known locally as 'The Sardine Run', attracting dolphins, sharks, game fish and birds, and the ocean teams with life.

UMZUMBE

This small, pleasant village 100 km south of Durban has a great backpackers' place to chill out at by the sea. It's also a good spot for dolphin watching and scuba-diving. From Durban, turn off the N2 at Hibberdene and follow the R102.

PORT SHEPSTONE

Located at the mouth of the Umzimkulu River, Port Shepstone is the largest town on the south coast and is more of an industrial centre than a tourist resort. **Hibiscus Coast Tourism** ① *16 Bissett St, T039-682 7944, www.tourismsouthcoast.co.za, Mon-Fri 0900-1700, Sat-Sun in season.*

SOUTH OF PORT SHEPSTONE

The towns and villages on this southernmost stretch of coast are the last of the chain of resorts that feel like seaside holiday camps before the R61 enters the Wild Coast (see page 166). Hiking in Umtamvuna Nature Reserve, diving on Protea Banks and the reefs off Shelly Beach, and whale and dolphin watching are the highlights of this region.

Shelly Beach is 5 km south of Port Shepstone on the R61. It is quite a large suburb with one of the region's biggest shopping malls, and the beach here is a popular launch site for fishing and diving charter companies. Activities at the **Pure Venom Reptile Park** ① *off the Izotsha Rd, T039-685 0704, www.purevenom.com, 0900-1700, R60, children (under 12) R40,* include having your photo taken with pythons, mambas, cobras or vipers. The park is home to nine species of American rattlesnake, plus crocodiles and other reptiles. There's a restaurant and petting farm for kids.

Uvongo, 12 km south of Port Shepstone, is built on cliffs looking out to sea and is one of the more pleasant resorts on the south coast. The beach, protected by shark nets, is safe for swimming and surfing. The waterfall at the nearby **Uvongo River Nature Reserve**, open from sunrise to sunset, is a pleasant place for a picnic. This 23-m-high waterfall tumbling over cliffs into the beachside lagoon is the reserve's main feature. At the rear of the beach are some steps to a viewpoint overlooking the falls.

MARGATE AND RAMSGATE

Originally a palm-fringed stretch of sand, the town began to expand in 1919 and is now a highly developed family resort, popular with holidaymakers from Gauteng. The beach is excellent and was awarded the Blue Flag a few years ago. From the junction with the N2 South Coast Toll Road, the link road immediately enters the tourist zone passing the mini-golf and holiday homes on the way into town. In the centre, high-rise flats are crammed in towards the beachfront, which can get very crowded during the school holidays. Contact the **Hibiscus Coast Publicity Association** ① *Panorama Parade, Margate Beachfront, T039-312 2322, www.hibiscuscoast.kzn.org.za, Mon-Fri 0830-1630, weekends in season, for further information.*

Ramsgate is 2 km south of Margate and is now practically a suburb, but the beach here is a little quieter and has shark nets so is popular for surfing. It has a tidal pool for swimming and some pedalos and canoes available for hire.

→WILD COAST

ARRIVING ON THE WILD COAST

Getting there and around The N2, the Wild Coast's main road, is well surfaced. However, it doesn't run along the coast but rather from East London up to 100 km inland until it meets the coast again at Port Shepstone in KwaZulu Natal, from where it heads north to Durban. The towns along the N2 have thriving economies based around transport. There are abundant petrol stations, basic supermarkets and one or two small hotels, but these are mainly for commercial clientele so there are very few frills. Consequently the towns along the N2 are utilitarian and scruffy and always thronged with traffic. The long-distance buses stick to the N2, and the **Baz Bus** only deviates to Port St Johns. The coast itself is the area's main attraction and there is a fine selection of isolated seaside accommodation between East London and Port St Johns. A number of roads lead from the N2 to the coastal resorts, often by way of ramshackle villages, and although there has been a lot of road resurfacing going on in the Eastern Cape in the last few years, many of these are gravel. If driving, it is always a good idea to check on the latest state of the road, as the region is prone to seasonal flooding. **Note** Before heading for the coast from the N2, remember to stock up on petrol, food, cash and everything you think you will need – the nearest shop or bank could be 100 km away.

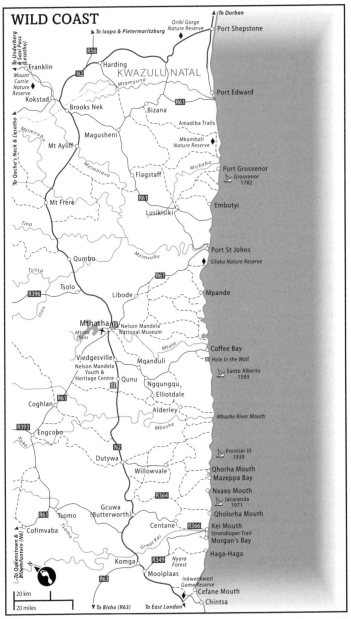

Tourist information Arriving at a resort without a reservation is not a good idea as they are often at the end of long and difficult roads. Remember most resorts are fully booked during the holiday season. All towns along the N2 have public telephones, so even with a last-minute decision it is possible to phone ahead and check on the condition of the road. For more information visit www.wildcoast.co.za.

Wild Coast Holiday Reservations ① *T043-743 6181, www.wildcoastholidays.co.za*, is an excellent central reservations service that can advise on and book accommodation and hiking trails along the coast. This can be very useful when trying to find out about some of the more remote hotels. A great way of seeing the most inaccessible areas of the Wild Coast is by doing a tour of the rural regions.

→PORT ST JOHNS

This small, peaceful coastal town is 94 km east of Mthatha on a tarred road and lies on the banks of the Mzimvubu River. It has a laid-back atmosphere and its bohemian feel has attracted many artists and, more recently, backpackers. Consequently, there's a good selection of budget accommodation here, much of which is self-catering. There aren't many restaurants but local produce such as papaya, avocado, pecans, macadamia nuts and fresh fish is sold on the beach.

Portuguese ships stopped here to pick up water on their journeys up the coast and the town itself is named after the *São João*, which was wrecked here in 1552. A trading post was built in 1846, and in 1878 the British established a military outpost here and built Fort Harrison. When the Transkei was an independent homeland, Port St Johns was a major cannabis-growing area, and much of the 'green gold' was sent to the gold mines of Johannesburg.

First Beach is at the mouth of the Mzimvubu River but swimming is not advised as there is the threat of sharks which are attracted to the calmer waters of the estuary. The Cape Hermes Lighthouse is here and looks out over the river mouth and was built using local granite in 1903 and named after the survey ship, HMS Hermes, which charted the local waters. **Second Beach** is the most attractive beach: a beautiful stretch of soft sand, backed by smooth, forested hills. It is safe for swimming as it has a very gentle slope, and there are lifeguards present. There are two nature reserves within easy reach of town: Silaka (see below) and **Mount Thesiger**, which has a small herd of wildebeest belonging to an unusual subspecies which has no mane. The warm, sulphurous springs at **Isinuka** are just outside town.

The **tourist office** ① *T047-564 1187, www.portstjohns.org.za, Mon-Fri 0830-1600, Sat 0900-1300*, is on Town Entrance Square, just to the right as you enter the town.

SILAKA NATURE RESERVE

This reserve is on a gravel road 6 km south from Port St Johns and lies in a forested valley that stretches from Second Beach to Sugarloaf Rock. Although the reserve is small, the tropical atmosphere of the trails weaving through the tangle of thick forest is unmissable. Blesbuck, blue wildebeest and Burchell's zebra have been reintroduced. There is a beautiful stretch of rugged coastline and just off the beach is Bird Island, a breeding colony for sea birds. Interesting rock pools occur on the shore surrounding the island, which may be reached at low tide. At the estuary opposite Bird Island, an attractive pebble beach is surrounded by driftwood and aloes, which grow almost to the sea.

ON THE ROAD
The wildest coast

The Wild Coast partly derives its name from its hauntingly beautiful wilderness character, but also from the ferocious seas when stormy conditions prevail. The Indian Ocean off the Eastern Cape is notorious for being capable of creating 20-m-high freak waves. These are formed because (near Port St Johns in particular), the 3000-m-deep continental shelf is extremely close to the shore, and the swiftly flowing Agulhas current, which moves in a southwesterly direction, is accelerated further by strong winds from the northeast. This can increase the surface speed of the water to over seven knots.

Over the centuries, these extreme conditions have sent countless ships crashing onto the shore, and there are numerous rotting hulks of shipwrecks along the Wild Coast. Additionally, many other ships plunged to the ocean floor and vanished without trace, yielding nothing but an occasional small treasure for the beachcomber, and coins, pottery, and other artefacts from wrecks are sometimes still washed up along the shoreline.

Some of the doomed ships have left their legacy. The name of Coffee Bay supposedly comes from a ship that was wrecked in the bay in 1893 with a cargo of coffee beans; Port St Johns reputedly comes from the wreck of the 16th-century Portuguese ship *São João*; and Mazeppa Bay's name comes from the ship *Mazeppa*, which ran aground in 1842.

→MTHATHA

The former capital of the Transkei straddles the N2, 22 km northeast of East London. It is believed that a clan of the Tembu tribe had a custom interring their dead by casting them into the river with the entreaty '*mThate Bawo*' (Take him, Father) and that this was the origin of the name of the river on which Mthatha was founded. Today Mthatha is an impoverished, sprawling, unattractive modern town full of cheap supermarkets and discount liquor stores with a small grid of historical buildings at its core. Founded in 1871, it was the capital of Transkei from 1976 to 1994 and has grown to be a busy administrative centre. The N2 passes through the city centre where some of the oldest buildings are located, including the City Hall built in 1908 and the Bhunga (parliament) Building dating from 1927. The latter is now home to the **Nelson Mandela National Museum**, the town's only sight, but definitely worth a stop for an understanding of how homelands such as the Transkei were created under the Apartheid system, and to learn more about the man.

PLACES IN MTHATHA

The former site of the Transkei parliament, is the **Nelson Mandela National Museum** ⓘ *Bhunga Building, Owen St, T047-532 5110, www.nelsonmandelamuseum.org.za, Mon-Fri 0900-1600, Sat-Sun 0900-1300, free, museum shop.* It was officially opened by the great man himself on 11 February 2000, to coincide with the 10th anniversary of his release from prison. The displays provide a moving insight into Mandela's life and his struggle against Apartheid, focusing on his autobiography, *Long Walk to Freedom*. There are extracts of the book complemented by photography, personal items, letters and video footage, including a short excerpt from a rare interview he gave in 1961 before being imprisoned. Other displays include international awards and honorary degrees that he received, portraits and sculptures of him and diplomatic gifts he received during his term of office. There's even a boxing glove signed by Mohammed Ali and George Foreman (Mandela used to box in his youth).

The other component of the museum is the **Nelson Mandela Youth and Heritage Centre** (same information as above), in the tiny rural village of **Qunu**, on the N2, 32 km southwest of Mthatha, where Mandela lived as a youth. In later life, he fondly recalled his days playing in the fields around the village, stick-fighting with other boys and sliding down rock faces. He was also a herd boy, taking care of sheep and calves. His former **school** consists of two rondavels and a hut, where there are exhibits of his early life, and the graves of his parents and his son and daughter are also here, along with his new house, which can be photographed from the outside but not visited. A guide can be picked up at the information centre and crafts are on sale.

→SOUTH TO KEI MOUTH

There are two possible routes leading on from Kei Mouth. The **Pont** is a car, passenger (and cattle) ferry (0630-1730, R30 per car), which crosses the Kei River. After crossing on the Pont, the gravel R366 road heads uphill for 9 km where it joins the R48/1 at Centane. The road then divides, heading inland to Gcuwa (Butterworth) on tar or seawards to Qholorha Mouth on gravel.

COFFEE BAY

There are some very rough tracks further north from Qhorha Mouth to Coffee Bay which are only suitable for a 4WD. Instead you'll need to go back to Dutywa on the N2, then 67 km towards Mthatha, take the right turn on to a tarred road and it's 75 km to Coffee Bay. At the mouth of the Nenga River, Coffee Bay is well known for its good surf, making it a major stop on many backpacker routes. Nevertheless, development has been low key and it remains a quiet and laid-back place. The name Coffee Bay comes from the coffee trees which grew here briefly in the 1860s after a ship ran aground with a cargo of coffee beans. The **Hole In The Wall** is a famous natural feature and well worth a visit. An enormous tunnel has been eroded by the sea through a cliff which lies just offshore. The local Xhosa call it *izi Khaleni*, which means 'place of thunder'. At high tide the sound of the waves clapping can be heard throughout the valley. You can drive there; about 10 km to the south of Coffee Bay, or the amazing hike from Coffee Bay to the Hole in the Wall traverses high sea cliffs and rolling green hills and is approximately three hours in either direction. Along the way, you pass Xhosa villages and are treated to spectacular views of the coastline.

QHORHA MOUTH

The N2 highway continues north from Gcuwa (Butterworth) until it reaches Dutywa. There is a turning at Dutywa to Willowvale, 32 km, from where there is a road which passes the village of Nyokana and leads to Qhorha Mouth, 66 km from Dutywa. This road is tarred as far as Willowvale. Despite what some maps say, there is no road from Mazeppa to Qhorha Mouth. To get between the two, you have to go via the N2. Qhorha Mouth is a small collection of houses, hardly large enough to be called a village, and is known for its kob fishing. The rivermouth here marks the ecological boundary between the sundu palms whose habitat lies to the south of the river and are characteristic of KwaZulu Natal, and the lala palms which only grow to the north. At the mouth of the river is a lagoon and a fine swathe of beach.

MAZEPPA BAY

This small holiday resort 48 km from Centane is named after the *Mazeppa*, a coastal trading ship that ran aground here in 1842 on its way from Port Natal. There is a suspension footbridge to the island from where you can see Clan Lindsay Rocks, the site where the *Clan Lindsay* was wrecked in 1898. **First Beach** is good for swimming, and the waves on this stretch of coast attract local surfers. Just back from the beach are the shell middens left by strandlopers. August is a busy month here when many people come for the shark fishing. The nearby **Manubi Forest** has 7 km of trails passing through patches of yellowwood and sneezewood trees. A 4-km hike north along the coast leads to the grounded wreck of the *Jacaranda*, a 2000-ton Greek ship that ran aground in 1971.

NXAXO MOUTH

The road heading north from Centane goes 28 km to the one resort at Nxaxo Mouth, which lies at the confluence of the Nxaxo and Nqusi rivers. The area has a lagoon and is dotted with swamps and islands. The estuary is rich in birdlife and there are hiking trails through a small strip of coastal forest to a colony of crowned cranes. Listen for the distinctive calls of groups of trumpeter hornbills which inhabit the forest.

QHOLORHA MOUTH

Qholorha Mouth is 16 km from the Pont over the Kei River or come directly from Gcuwa (Butterworth). There are two holiday resorts here on a beautiful stretch of headland overlooking a spacious beach. The Qholorha (meaning steep place) River takes its name from the gorge it has carved on its way to the sea. The river forms a pretty lagoon at the mouth as it is held back by a wide beach, frequented by herds of cattle that go there to sleep, relax and chew the cud. There is a hike up the **Gxara River Heads**, 4 km inland, to the pool where Nongqawuse, a young Xhosa girl, saw visions and communed with her ancestral spirits. She heard voices telling her that the dead would rise and destroy the European invaders if the Xhosa destroyed all their cattle and crops. This disastrous prophesy lead to the deaths of thousands of people through starvation, and Nongqawuse had to spend the rest of her life in hiding. She is buried on a farm near Alexandria.

GCUWA (BUTTERWORTH)

Recently renamed with a Xhosa name, this is the first town that the N2 passes on its way through the old Transkei. It is a hectic and unappealing stretch of supermarkets and discount stores, and has little to keep you there for long. Founded as a Wesleyan mission station in 1827, it is the oldest town in the Transkei, although little of its history is evident today. At the end of the Frontier Wars in 1878, traders began to settle here and the town has grown to become a small industrial centre. Just outside of town, there is one attraction worth stopping for: the **Bawa Falls** on the Qholorha River are spectacular after the rains when the water drops over 100 m. From Gcuwa (Butterworth), the N2 continues north to Mthatha, 135 km.

→ KEI MOUTH TO EAST LONDON

The coast immediately to the north of East London has been named the 'Romantic Coast' by the local tourist board, and its relative wildness makes the statement ring true. Although the coast is being developed for tourism there are still considerable stretches of the coastline which are protected nature reserves. There are thick dune forests and windswept open beaches stretching to wild waves. The coastal resorts nearest to East London can get crowded during the South African school holidays, but for the rest of the year it is quite surprising how isolated and quiet this coast really is.

ARRIVING IN EAST LONDON

Getting around The resorts of Gonubie, Chintsa, Haga-Haga, Morgan's Bay and Kei Mouth are all within an hour's drive of East London. Public transport to these resorts is virtually non-existent, but as the hoteliers on the coast regularly visit East London to collect supplies, you can often get a lift to the coast by phoning ahead. The **East Coast Shuttle** ① *T043-740 3060*, runs a service from East London to the coastal resorts as far as Kobb Inn but requires a minimum of six passengers.

KEI MOUTH

This quiet seaside resort has a collection of shops, a petrol station, post office, a couple of resorts and a clutch of holiday homes. It's 90 km from East London and 44 km from the N2 on the newly tarred R349.

The **Kei River** used to be the border between the two former homelands of Ciskei and Transkei, now all part of the Eastern Cape. The river is navigable upstream for a short distance by boat or canoe, although sandbanks make it difficult at times. The fully automated Cape Morgan Lighthouse was built in 1964, and the lantern sits on top of a 12-m lattice tower and emits two white flashes every 10 seconds with a range of 24 sea miles. It's a 3-km walk southwest along the coast from Kei Mouth and a path leads down from there to some good fishing spots.

MORGAN'S BAY

This is a perfect resort, 90 km from East London and 42 km from the N2, for a peaceful beach break and a taste of the Wild Coast. A newly tarred road runs from the N2 to Kei Mouth (below), and from there the turn-off to Morgan's Bay is a 6-km good gravel road. It was named in 1822 after AF Morgan, who was master of a British Royal Navy survey ship. The village itself is tiny and somewhat isolated and has little more than a couple of resorts and campsites, the local store, a bottle shop, a couple of curio shops and a petrol pump. The surrounding countryside is a nature reserve and is a great place for hiking along the cliffs or strolling along the miles of white sandy beach where deep currents wash up unusual shells. The bay is regarded as one of the most beautiful in the country. Called **Double Mouth**, it consists of a lagoon formed by two small rivers backed by a line of sandstone cliffs. The beach with a lighthouse was voted one of the top 10 beach walks of South Africa by the South African outdoor magazine *Getaway*.

HAGA-HAGA

Further along the coast lies this tiny seaside resort, 72 km from East London and 27 km from the N2. The road travels through fields of pineapples, and can be potholed and corrugated at times, but is never impassable. There are two theories on how this resort got its name. One is that it is derived from the sound the waves make as they wash the shoreline. The other is that the village was settled in the early 1920s when farmers from the hinterland would bring their livestock here for winter grazing, the smaller animals by ox wagon. To cross the beach they would unspan one team of oxen and hook them onto the other team, hence the word *haka*

haka, which is isiXhosa for 'hook on'. The rocky coastline, good beaches and lagoon where you can swim make it ideal for hiking and fishing and, with only about 70 houses, one shop and a hotel, this is a peaceful spot to spend a few days and lose track of time.

CHINTSA

The combined villages of Chintsa East and Chintsa West nestle on lush hills rolling down to a lagoon and a wide stretch of deserted beach. (It takes about 10 minutes to walk from Chintsa West to Chintsa East along the beach, but nearly 30 minutes to drive between them around the lagoon.) Although popular during the Christmas holidays, the resort is blessedly isolated for the rest of the year and offers relaxing outdoor activities such as canoeing and horse riding, though the main appeal here is lazily exploring the shell-strewn beach, forests and tranquil lagoon. Construction of the large Chintsa River Golfing Estate on the west bank is underway and the project is to include an 18-hole golf course, 350 holiday/time-share homes and a large hotel. Time will tell how it will change the face of this peaceful coastal settlement.

INKWENKWEZI GAME RESERVE

ⓘ *T043-734 3234, www.inkwenkwezi.com, 33 km from East London, take the N2 towards Mthatha and after 25 km out of East London, turn right at the Inkwenkwezi/Chintsa signpost, the reserve is 8 km on the right.*

This private 100-sq-km coastal game reserve has a combination of forest dunes and bushveld, and is home to an impressive range of imported game, including rhino, elephant, lion, wildebeest, giraffe, warthog, Eastern Cape kudu and an abundance of birdlife. The best time of year for spotting birds is from September to November; the wild flowers are best from August to September. Accommodation is available, and a range of activities can be organized for overnight guests, including night drives, horse riding, mountain and quad-biking, and walking trails. Day visitors are welcome and a four-hour game drive with lunch costs R695 and departs at 0800 and 1400, and a four-hour sunset drive with dinner can be arranged for four or more people for R895 per person. Additionally, the reserve offers an elephant experience when guests get to interact with two tame elephants (one hour costs R125, children aged 4-9 R60, under 3s free) or ride them (a one-hour ride is R500 per person).

DURBAN TO EAST LONDON LISTINGS

WHERE TO STAY

Amanzinimoti to Scottburgh

$$$ The View, 9 Hillside Rd, Amanzimtoti, T039-903 1556, www.theviewguestlodge. com. Smart small modern hotel high on the hillside with sweeping ocean views, 20 sea-facing individually decorated rooms with patios, 2 pools, spa, excellent terrace restaurant with an Italian-inspired menu, relaxing tropical gardens.

$$ Cutty Sark, beachfront, Scottburgh, T039-976 1230, www.cuttysark.co.za. Slightly dated but good-value family hotel in a lovely beachside location, with 55 rooms with TV, 2 restaurants, rates include breakfast and dinner, bar, swimming pool, tennis and squash courts, gym, in 6 ha of well-kept tropical gardens. Horse riding and diving can be arranged.

Port St Johns

$$$ Umngazi River Bungalows and Spa, about 25 km west of the town, off the R61 back towards Mthatha, T047-564 1115, www.umngazi.co.za. Thatched luxury bungalows facing the estuary surrounded by mangrove forest, restaurant, bar (dine in the wine cellar), shop, spa and pool. A wide range of watersports, including sunset cruises up the river and night fishing. Award-winning resort, good value for families, full-board rates. Check out the website for off-season 3-night specials.

$$ The Spotted Grunter Resort, off the R61, 3 km from the town centre by the river, T047-564 1279, www.spottedgrunter.co.za. A small, peaceful resort with attractive timber cabins with TV, kitchenette and braais, sleeping 4-6. Set in beautiful gardens with swimming pool on a bank of the Umzimvuba River, full of avocado and lychee trees where the rare Cape parrot feeds. If you don't want to cook, all meals are available from the **Angler's Arms**. The owners can organize fishing.

Coffee Bay

$$$-$ Hole In The Wall Hotel and Holiday Village, 8 km south of the village, T047-575 0009, www.holeinthewall.co.za. Set by the beach, this large resort has a selection of accommodation to suit all budgets, 26 hotel rooms in garden thatched rondavels, 28 self-catering whitewashed units with 2 bedrooms sleeping up to 8, 10 pitches for camping, and a backpacker lodge with 9 cheaper doubles and 3 dorms further up the hill. Swimming pool, bar, restaurant, pool tables, volleyball court, TV lounge, nightly seafood braais. A good all-round option on the Wild Coast that can organize plenty of activities.

Mazeppa Bay

$$$ Mazeppa Bay Hotel, T047-498 0033, www.mazeppabay.co.za. Accommodation is a mix of doubles, family rooms and rondavels, all with sea views and private surrounds. The central area has a pool, restaurant, bar, TV lounge, gym, steam room and tennis court. Mountain bikes and fishing gear can be hired. The whole complex sits on a green ridge covered with tropical vegetation, overlooking a broad sandy beach. Also prides itself on having its own island. Good value and 3 meals a day are included in the rates.

Qholorha Mouth

$$$-$$ Trennery's, T047-498 0004, www.trennerys.co.za. 45 thatched chalets set in large shady gardens full of mature trees. Seafood restaurant, pool, canoeing, golf, boating, tennis, fishing, bowls, snooker table and a small shop. Breakfast and dinner are included in the rates and there are good-value weekly specials. An all-round holiday resort in one of the finest settings along this stretch of coast.

Morgan's Bay

$$ Morgan's Bay Hotel, Beach Rd, T043-8411062, www.morgan-bay-hotel.co.za. Family-run hotel which markets itself as an affordable family resort, with separate kids' dining room and child minders, 33 good-value rooms, prices vary with the tourist season but off-season is excellent value. Swimming pool, views across the bay, gardens which extend down to the beach, restaurant with an extensive breakfast buffet and an à la carte menu in the evenings, both inclusive in the rates. There is also a caravan and camping park (**$**) with 31 sites, with electricity, braais and coin-operated laundry.

Chintsa

$$$ Prana Lodge, Chintsa Drive, Chintsa East, T043-704 5100, www.pranalodge.co.za. An intimate boutique lodge in a tract of woodland and vegetated dunes, linked to the beach by a boardwalk. 7 a/c spacious individually decorated suites with DSTV, DVD, private walled gardens and plunge pools. Spa with Thai massages, restaurant serving gourmet food and good wines.

$$-$ Buccaneer's Backpackers, Chintsa East, T043-734 3012, www.cintsa.com. Superb backpacker lodge set in forests overlooking the lagoon and beach. A 2-km dirt track leads to the secluded site, with a choice of dorms, doubles, fully equipped self-catering cottages and camping on platforms beneath trees. There is a lively bar, pool, kitchen, volleyball court, climbing wall, horse riding on the beach, beauty treatments and massages, free canoes and surfboards, excellent home-cooked evening meals and free daily activities. Also home to **African Heartland Journeys** (see below). **Baz Bus** stop.

Inkwenkwezi Game Reserve

$$$$ Inkwenkwezi Tented Camp, T043-734 3234, www.inkwenkwezi.com. Luxury tents or chalets, some with fireplaces and fridges, bathrooms set in a cave-like environment with showers to look and feel like a waterfall. The **Emthombeni** restaurant and bar serves Eastern Cape cuisine overlooking the valley. Rates (mid-range/cheap) include meals, local wine and beer, and game activities.

WHAT TO DO

Amanzinimoti to Scottburgh
Aliwal Dive Centre, 2 Moodie St, Umkosaas, T039-973 2233, www.aliwalshoal.co.za. PADI 5-star dive centre, courses, snorkelling and whale- and dolphin-watching trips. Good-value accommodation for divers above dive centre with dorms, en suite doubles and meals.

Margate
African Dive Adventures, T039-317 1483, www.africandiveadventures.co.za. Dives at the Protea Banks where schools of hammerhead and Zambezi sharks are regularly seen. Can also organize 2-hr boat trips to see the Sardine Run from R550 per person.

Wild Coast
African Heartland Journeys, Buccaneer's Backpackers, Chintsa, T043-734 3012, www.ahj.co.za. Sensitively run camping tours by 4WD, bike and canoe that go right into the heartland of the Wild Coast to places you could never get to otherwise. Accommodation is in Xhosa villages. Highly recommended.
Amadiba Adventures, T039-305 6455, www.amadibaadventures.co.za. A local community-run initiative offering 1- to 6-day horse or hiking trails up the coast and inland. Accommodation is in mobile camps with eco-toilets and hot bush showers, and prices include 3 meals per day. Local guides are very knowledgeable about the area. All proceeds go back into the local community. Excellent reports and it is an organization worthy of support.

EAST LONDON TO NELSON MANDELA BAY

There are two routes to East London from Nelson Mandela Bay (Port Elizabeth). The quickest is on the N2 via Grahamstown. An alternative route is to take the R72 coastal road, but there are three very compelling reasons for following the N2: to explore the wonderful Addo Elephant National Park; to visit the string of new private game reserves, including the superb Shamwari Game Reserve; and to see the old colonial town of Grahamstown.

→EAST LONDON

East London is South Africa's only river port and a major industrial centre, with an economy based on motor assembly plants, textile and electronics industries. Nevertheless, the city centre has a handful of attractive historical buildings, and there are some good beaches which surprisingly get very busy with domestic tourists over Christmas. Nahoon Beach is best known for its excellent surfing, and the city has attracted a real surfing community in recent years. Despite this, it's not a very attractive place and most travellers only pass through on their way to other coastal resorts or to the Amatola Mountains.

ARRIVING IN EAST LONDON
Getting there East London Airport ① *11 km west of the city centre off the R347, T043-706 0306, www.acsa.co.za*, is nowhere near as busy as the other regional airports (although it is a busy hub for the exportation of Eastern Cape pineapples). SAA connects East London with a number of other cities. **East London Airport Shuttle** ① *T043-726 4844, www.elbusshuttle.com*, operates an airport shuttle service to the centre of town, Gonubie and King William's Town. **East Coast Shuttle** ① *T043-740 3060*, operates from the airport to the resorts from Gonubie to Kobb Inn on the Wild Coast. The larger car hire companies have desks at the airport. There are bus services to most South African cities with **Greyhound**, **Intercape**, and **Translux**. The **Baz Bus** also stops here.

Tourist information The main tourist office covers the region from East London to King William's Town and is known as **Buffalo City Tourism** ① *91 Western Av, Vincent, T043-721 1346, www.tourismbuffalocity.co.za, Mon-Fri 0815-1630, Sat 0900-1400, Sun 0900-1300.*

BACKGROUND
East London was originally founded as a military camp on the banks of the Buffalo River in 1847 and its strategic position as a port was soon recognized. Sir Harry Smith, the British governor, ambitiously named it London, and its two main thoroughfares are still Fleet Street and Oxford Street. Later it was renamed Port of East London, and then simply as East London – not after London's East End but because the port was on the eastern bank of the river.

PLACES IN EAST LONDON
The town centre is a modern, bustling place, though it's fairly run down so exercise caution away from the beach. However, there are several historical monuments: the **Colonial Division Memorial** is in front of the City Hall; the **German Settler Memorial** is on the Esplanade; and there are **War Memorials** on Oxford Street.

The **Ann Bryant Art Gallery** ① *90 St Marks Rd off Oxford St, T043-722 4044, www. annbryant.co.za, Mon-Fri 0900-1700, Sat 0900-1200, free, coffee shop*, is in an interesting Edwardian building dating from 1905. The collection was originally mostly of British artists but now has many fine contemporary South African works. An arts and crafts fair is held here on the first and second Sunday of every month.

The highlights of the **East London Museum** ① *319 Oxford St, T043-743 0686, www. elmuseum.za.org, Mon-Thu 0930-1630, Fri 0930-1600, Sat 1000-1300, Sun and public holidays 1000-1500, R10, children (under 16) R3, coffee shop*, include the world's only dodo egg and the coelacanth that was trawled up off the Chalumna River. The coelacanth, known as the fossil fish, was thought to have been extinct for 80 million years until it was 'rediscovered' in 1938. The museum also has some good displays on Xhosa culture and customs, and a section devoted to Nguni beadwork. In the garden is an impressive collection of cycads.

Also on Oxford Street, the **City Hall** dates from1897, and the design of the clock on **Victoria Tower** was modelled after London's Big Ben. Inside, the marble staircase was constructed from marble directly imported from Carrar in Italy. Outside, is a monument to

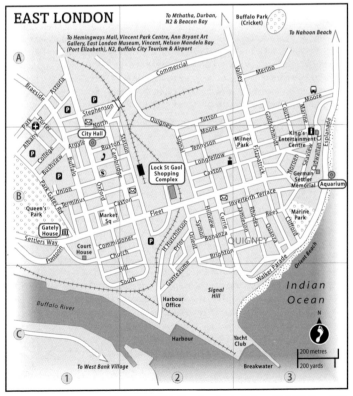

honour Steven Bantu Biko, which was unveiled by Nelson Mandela on 12 September 1997 to mark the 20th anniversary of his death while in police custody.

Gately House ① *1 Park Gates Rd, T043-722 2141, www.elmuseum.za.org, Mon, Wed-Fri 0930-1630, Sat 1100-1600, R10, children (under 16) R3,* was built in 1876 by John Gately, one of East London's first mayors. The house was donated to the city in 1966 and is now a town house museum decorated with original Victorian furnishings.

Established in 1931, the **East London Aquarium** ① *Esplanade, T043-705 2637, www. elaquarium.co.za, 0900-1700, R20, children (3-18) R13, under 3s free,* is the oldest aquarium in the country with over 400 freshwater and marine species on display. There's a seal show twice daily at 1130 and 1530, and feeding times are half an hour before. There's also a whale deck with a telescope – a blue flag flies when whales are sighted.

The **Lock Street Gaol Shopping Complex** is on Fleet Street. Built in the 1800s, this was South Africa's first women's jail, and its most famous inmates were Winnie Madikizela-Mandela (ex-wife of Nelson Mandela) and Daisy de Melker, who was accused of poisoning two husbands and a son. The original gallows can still be seen. It now houses shops and offices.

WEST BANK VILLAGE

West Bank Village is the oldest surviving area of East London with some interesting old buildings on Bank Street and near the entrance to the harbour. **Hood Point Lighthouse** ① *T043-700 3056, Mon-Fri 1000-1500, also Sat-Sun Oct-Apr, R14, children (under 12) R7,* was built in 1895 and is a typical Victorian lighthouse with a steel upper gallery and keyhole windows. **Fort Glamorgan** is a vaulted brick building on Bank Street, which now serves as a prison. The fort was built in 1848 during the Seventh Frontier War to defend the supplies that were being sent to the inland garrisons from the Buffalo River Mouth.

→KING WILLIAM'S TOWN

King William's Town, more commonly known simply as King, is 56 km northeast of East London. The London Missionary Society established a mission station here in 1826 and over the years the town has grown into an important commercial centre. It is best known as the birth and burial place of anti-Apartheid activist Steven Biko who was put under house arrest in the town from 1973 before he was arrested in August 1977 at a road block near Grahamstown, outside his restricted area. After his arrest he was taken to Port Elizabeth and intensively interrogated for 26 days, and, during a severe beating on 7 September, suffered a massive brain haemorrhage. Although police doctors urged that he go for hospital treatment, he was thrown naked in the back of a police vehicle and driven the 12 hours to the Central Prison in Pretoria, where he died alone in his cell on 12 September. He was 30 years of age. The police first claimed he had starved himself to death while on a hunger strike. They later changed their story to say Biko had hit his head against a wall in a scuffle. Finally, 20 years later, the police admitted before the Truth and Reconciliation Commission that they had killed Biko. Diplomats from 13 counties joined mourners at his funeral in King William's Town but not a single South African was made accountable for his death. His grave, with a lovingly tended polished tombstone, lies in the **Steve Biko Remembrance Garden** on the edge of town on the road to Nelson Mandela Bay (Port Elizabeth). To reach the grave, follow Cathcart Street south of King William's Town and turn left down a dirt track that is signposted to the garden. It's a moving place and the grave is much humbler than expected for such an important figure in South African history. The **Amathole Museum** ① *Alexander Rd, T043-642 4506, www.museum.za.net, Mon-Fri 0800-1630, Sat 0900-1300, R5, children (under 15) free*, is a good place to get a feel for Xhosa history with displays on how the British crushed the Xhosa during the various frontier wars. There's also some contemporary art, including bus, bikes and cars made from wire, and some dusty old stuffed mammals, including Huberta the hippo. There's a good selection of local crafts for sale in the museum shop.

→GRAHAMSTOWN

Grahamstown is first and foremost a student town. At the top end of the high street is one of the country's major centres of learning, **Rhodes University**, which has 70 major buildings on a 195-ha campus with approximately 3800 students and 1800 staff. The presence of the university has a significant impact on this small town and during term time the pubs and bars are packed with students. It is a pleasant enough place to wander around and there are a number of interesting little shops along the high street.

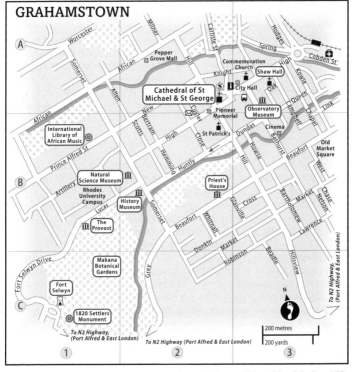

FESTIVALS
Grahamstown

June-July **National Festival of Arts**, T046-603 1103, www.nationalartsfestival. co.za. Famous 10-day festival and one of the top cultural events in the country. Over 50,000 visitors are attracted to the town to watch a range of shows, which include theatre, dance, fine art, films, music, opera and an increasing variety of traditional crafts and art, plus a huge range of fringe shows. There's something for everyone from techno raves to medieval banquets.

The centre of the festival is the 1820 Settlers Monument. During this period accommodation gets booked very quickly, so make reservations several months ahead, or phone the tourist office to check if any private homes are letting out rooms or to enquire about accommodation available at the Rhodes University's halls of residences. During the festival the whole atmosphere of the town changes, so if you are in the country at this time it is well worth a visit.

Despite the English feel to the town centre the other side of the valley is dominated by a poor, dusty and badly serviced township where the majority of the African residents live. The proximity of the two sides of town makes the contrast more apparent than in some of the bigger towns and cities, where the townships are some distance from the centre.

ARRIVING IN GRAHAMSTOWN
Getting there The town is served by some mainline buses on the route between Nelson Mandela Bay (Port Elizabeth) and Durban. The **Baz Bus** does not stop here, though, as it deviates off the N2 after Nelson Mandela Bay and goes via Port Alfred on the coast.

Tourist information Grahamstown Tourism ① *63 High St, T046-622 3241, www. grahamstown.co.za, Mon-Fri 0830-1700, Sat 0900-1300*, is a well-organized centre with accommodation-booking facilities for the entire region. The staff can arrange and book a variety of local tours. There is also a **Translux** desk.

BACKGROUND
Grahamstown was established around a fort which had been built here after the Fourth Frontier War. It was founded in 1812 and named after Colonel Graham. Within two years it was a busy border settlement. The 1820 settlers began to arrive after the end of the Fifth Frontier War, during which Grahamstown had been besieged by Xhosa warriors. Despite the continual threat of armed conflict and problems of security, the town had evolved into the second largest settlement in the whole of southern Africa by 1836.

One factor behind the town's rapid growth was that the majority of the 1820 settlers were ill-prepared to be farmers, let alone in an environment of which they had no knowledge. As soon as they realized farming was not going to bring them wealth and security they gave it up and returned to the town to take up the jobs they were trained to do. Grahamstown quickly established a thriving industry based around blacksmiths, carpenters, millers and gunsmiths. Having returned to the town, the skilled settlers quickly built a series of elegant stone buildings which remain grand specimens of the era's architecture today. Of particular note are the buildings around Church Square, but elsewhere there are churches and fine private homes. The culmination of all this is a smart town centre with a distinctly English atmosphere.

PLACES IN GRAHAMSTOWN

When you look at a map or walk about the town centre you quickly come across a variety of different museums: the Observatory Museum, Natural Science Museum and the History Museum, along with Fort Selwyn and the Provost. These displays are all part of the **Albany Museum** ① *T046-622 2312, Tue-Fri 0900-1300, 1400-1700, Sat 1000-1400, Observatory Museum also open Mon, entry to each is about R5-10*, which celebrated its 150-year anniversary in 2005. The collection has grown as the town has developed and presents a fairly complete picture of its history.

The **Observatory Museum** ① *on the right-hand side of Bathurst St, as you look up towards the City Hall*, is a unusual building. It contains a collection of Victorian furniture, household goods and silver, but the highlight is the entertaining camera obscura (a rare specimen, claimed to be the only Victorian camera obscura in the southern hemisphere), which projects an image of Grahamstown onto a screen. Visitors are led up a tiny spiral staircase to a small room on the roof, where an enthusiastic guide pivots the camera to show a 360° view, pointing out major sights. There is also an observatory and a meridian room, from which astronomical time can be calculated. The clock is a miniature of one that was made in 1883 for the Royal Courts of Justice in London. The painting on the pendulum of *Father Time* is by the well-known Frontier Artist, Frederick Timpson I'Ons. The building, which itself is loosely connected with the drawn-out identification of the *Eureka* diamond back in 1869, has a magnificent presence. There are three floors of balconies, each with ornately carved arches and railings, enough to give a hint of how it would have looked in its heyday.

At the **Natural Science Museum** ① *Somerset St*, most of the displays are aimed at children. Some of the more interesting exhibits include a large iron meteorite which came down in a shower in Namibia, a Foucault pendulum and some dinosaur fossils. There are regular temporary exhibitions, and this is one of the main venues for the **Scifest**, a science and technology festival held in March. There is a café in a courtyard at the back.

The **History Museum** ① *Somerset St, opposite the Natural Science Museum*, houses an interesting collection outlining the area's history, including beadwork displays from the Eastern Cape, traditional Xhosa dress, 1820 settler history and some art galleries, with regularly changing contemporary exhibitions.

The **Provost** ① *off Somerset St, at the western end of town in the botanical gardens*, is a quadrangular building with a double-storeyed tower at its apex. It was built in 1837 by the Royal Engineers to act as a military prison; their actual instructions were to build a "fortified barrack establishment". A lot of thought went into the overall design of the complex as the architects of the time sought to come up with a design where, from the central tower, it would be possible to view as many prisoners as possible with minimal manpower. In January 1838 the first 20 convicts were brought here. They were mutineers, and after they had shot one of their officers, Ensign Crowe, they were executed on the parade grounds. The building was proclaimed a national monument in 1937.

Fort Selwyn ① *Fort Selwyn Drive, open by prior appointment only*, is at the western end of town close to the Settlers Monument. During the sixth Frontier War in 1834 parliament decided that it would be necessary to protect the barracks. The Royal Engineers who built the fort were commanded by Major Charles Jasper Selwyn. Between 1841 and 1868 the fort was used as an artillery barracks and a semaphore link – a mast was erected in the northeast corner – but then the army gave up using the building in 1870. During the Anglo-Boer War the fort served in the defence of Grahamstown, but by the 1920s it had once more been left to become run down and overgrown. It was not until the 1970s, when it was proclaimed a national monument, that the building finally got the restoration work it deserved. Although it stands on the property of the Department of Nature and Environmental Conservation, it was given to the Albany Museum to use as exhibition space to further promote the history of Grahamstown.

The **1820 Settlers Monument** is, oddly, a large modern office block with rather a totalitarian feel to it. There is a series of rooms which includes a conference hall, theatre and a restaurant and it's another principal venue for the **Grahamstown Arts Festival**. It overlooks the city and completely dominates its surrounds on Gunfire Hill. It was opened in July 1974, but in 1994 disaster struck and fire gutted the whole complex and it was restored in 1996. The memorial is surrounded by the **Makana Botanical Gardens** ① *daily 0800-1630, free*, which were laid out in 1853 with displays of indigenous plants. The botanical garden has a recreation of a nostalgic old English garden, but more interestingly there is a huge collection of aloes, cycads, proteas and tree ferns. Assuming you're not afraid of ghosts, try to catch a glimpse of Lady Juana Smith, the Spanish wife of Sir Harry Smith who reputedly haunts the gardens.

Part of the university, the **International Library of African Music (ILAM)** ① *Prince Alfred St, T046-603 8557, www.ilam.ru.ac.za, by appointment only, Mon-Fri 0830-1245, 1400-1700*, is a university research centre for traditional African music, and houses a fascinating collection, with over 200 traditional African instruments from across the continent. To get there, follow signs from the gate opposite Rhodes University Theatre.

The Anglican **Cathedral of St Michael and St George** occupies its rightful position in the centre of town on Church Square. The style of this building is early English Gothic, a 13th-century style which the Victorians chose to revive in the late 19th century. Like similar buildings in Europe, the cathedral took generations to complete. Work started in 1824 and the first usable form was opened in 1830 as a single-room church. In 1879, the 150-foot bell tower and spire was added, and in 1952 the Lady Chapel was completed, so the cathedral had taken 128 years to build. Look out for the memorial tablets which together provide a vivid history of Grahamstown as the frontier of the empire.

The **Priest's House**, on Beaufort Street, was built as a residence for the bishop and the clergy of the Catholic church. It is one of the finer buildings in Grahamstown and like the Observatory Museum has a connection with the identification of the *Eureka* diamond. Because of this connection, the De Beers Group rescued the house in 1981, helped to partially restore the building and then oversaw the establishment of the **National English Literary Museum** ① *T046-622 7042, Mon-Fri 0830-1300, 1400-1630*. These days the research carried out behind the scenes is proving to be an important component in the understanding of the role of English as a national language of South Africa. There is a comprehensive collection of scholarly books, articles and press-clippings as well as a good bookshop. A small display gallery presents temporary exhibitions focusing on a particular writer, literary period or theme. The house is also of interest. The façade is typical of the Cape during the 1800s – flat, with a colonnaded neo-Georgian portico.

The **Shaw Hall** is behind the Observatory Museum, but still in the High Street. It was inaugurated in 1832 as a Methodist Church, with three galleries and room for over 800 members. Once the Commemoration Church had been completed in 1850, the first building was turned over for use as a meeting hall. The Reverend William Shaw was a local missionary worker. The most important role the building played was on 25 April

1864 when the Governor of the Cape Colony, Sir Philip Wodehouse, convened a session of parliament in the hall. This was part of a programme of tacit support for a movement that was trying to break away from the western part of the province and set up an independent government. Although nothing ever came of the idea, it was a clear indication of how serious the government took the threats of secession, since this was the only time that the Cape parliament ever sat outside of Cape Town.

→EAST OF ADDO

PUMBA PRIVATE GAME RESERVE
ⓘ *20 km west of Grahamstown off the N2 and 100 km from Nelson Mandela Bay (Port Elizabeth), the day visit reception is on the N2, the safari lodges are a further 5 km, T046-603 2000, www.pumbagamereserve.co.za.*
Established in 2004, this is another conservation initiative incorporating former Eastern Cape farms, and covers 6790 ha of bushveld and open plains, with views of the Zuurberg Mountains to the east and water frontage on the Kariega River floodplain. It is home to the Big Five and 40 other species of mammal and some 270 species of bird. Highlights include the free-roaming pride of white lion and, again, wild dog have recently been released. There are two luxury lodges, and day safaris begin at 1500 and include a two-hour game drive followed by dinner in a thatched boma, and another one-hour game drive back to the transfer point on the N2, for R900 per person; children under 12 get a discount but no children under eight.

LALIBELA GAME RESERVE
ⓘ *24 km east of Grahamstown off the N2, T041-581 8170, www.lalibela.co.za.*
This private game reserve covers 7500 ha and spans four ecosystems that are home to the Big Five as well as cheetah, hyena, hippo, giraffe, zebra, warthog and numerous species of antelope. Wild dog were released here in 2006. Day visitors are not permitted but there are three luxury lodges.

AMAKHALA GAME RESERVE
ⓘ *Off the N2 approximately opposite the turning for Shamwari Game Reserve (see below); the road is well signposted, T046-636 2750, www.amakhala.co.za.*
This is another of the Eastern Cape's successful new game reserves. The 6000-ha reserve was created in 1999 as a joint conservation venture between neighbouring farms and today has six independently owned lodges. All are owner-managed by the descendants of the original families who arrived here as British settlers from 1820. The lodges offer various styles of accommodation: there are two colonial homesteads, two classic bush lodges, a historic inn and a settler farmhouse. The reserve is now another Big Five destination and has been stocked with rhino, elephant, cheetah, lion, buffalo, giraffe, black wildebeest, zebra and over 16 antelope species. Leopard is on the property but is rarely seen. Day and night drives and game walks are arranged from the lodges for overnight guests. There is also the opportunity to go on a cruise or canoe trip on the Bushman's River. Day visitors are welcome and safaris commence around midday with a two-hour game drive followed by a buffet lunch and then an afternoon cruise on the Bushman's River with cheese and wine; and the excursion ends with a short early-evening game drive, all for R980 per person. The day visit is not recommended for children under six due to the long programme.

SHAMWARI GAME RESERVE

ⓘ *From Grahamstown, the R342 turning is about 58 km along the N2. From Nelson Mandela Bay (Port Elizabeth), follow the N2 towards Grahamstown. After 65 km take a left turn, signposted Shamwari. This gravel road is the R342; after 7 km take a right turn. It is then a further 2 km to the entrance. T041-407 1000, www.shamwari.com.*

This is a privately owned 20,000-ha reserve which in many aspects resembles the reserves of Mpumalanga along the boundary of Kruger National Park. In 1990 Adrian Gardiner, a successful businessman from Port Elizabeth, bought the property and read up on historical accounts of the Eastern Cape, which described the region as one of the richest wildlife zones in Africa. Reports dating back to the 18th century indicate a time when vast herds of Cape buffalo and zebra, wildebeest, black rhino, leopard and lion freely roamed the hills and valleys. However, by 1853 early settlers had wiped out most of the game and cleared vast areas of forest for farmland. When Gardiner bought the property all that remained was a dry, eroded dust bowl, but in the last 20 years natural grasses and bush flora have been planted and many species of game reintroduced. Once decimated by overgrazing and drought, the landscape has been transformed into big game country. Today the reserve has been well stocked with game from all over the region including black rhino, elephant, buffalo, leopard, lion and antelope of all sizes. Wild dog, last seen in the area over 200 years ago, have also been reintroduced. Day visitors are not permitted, but there are seven super-luxurious lodges within the reserve, and overnight packages include all meals and game activities.

SCHOTIA SAFARIS

ⓘ *To the east of Addo, 55 km from Nelson Mandela Bay (Port Elizabeth), and just north of the junction of the N2 and N10, T042-235 1436, www.schotia.com.*

This is a private game reserve on the edge of Addo with 15 types of antelope, several smaller species such as warthog, monkeys and genets, and lion, hippo, giraffe and rhino. Schotia is also known for its huge open-air dining *lapa* – reputedly the largest in South Africa – built of reed and thatch, which is supported by several large Schotia trees. The lodge here has simple accommodation units and if you are staying overnight all game activities are included; day and night game drives into Addo are also available. It is also possible to come as a day visitor between 1600-2200 and the package includes afternoon and evening game drives and a buffet dinner and drinks for R660. Alternatively, you could combine the above day visit with a morning safari to Addo for R1320. Pickups can be arranged from Nelson Mandela Bay if you don't have a car. Check the website for options.

→ADDO ELEPHANT NATIONAL PARK

The original elephant sector of the Addo Elephant National Park, was proclaimed in 1931, and covered little more than 2000 ha, and only 11 elephants remained in the area. It grew from there and, since 2000, the park has undergone a process of massive expansion with new land purchase made possible by funds from the government and overseas donors. Today the park covers 292,000 ha and is the third largest conservation area in South Africa. The park now encompasses five neighbouring game reserves and wilderness areas and stretches from the Indian Ocean to the Little Karoo and incorporates five different habitat biospheres. The weather is usually warm and dry, and visits to the park are enjoyable all year round.

At the coast is a belt of coastal dunefields and forest. The 200-m-long Alexandria Dunefield, the largest active dunefields in the world after the Namib Desert, now falls within the park and the 120,000-ha marine reserve adjoining Addo includes many islands that are home to large populations of gannets and African penguins. With the reintroduction of lion in 2003, it is now possible to see the Big Seven – elephant, rhino, lion, buffalo, leopard, whale and great white shark – in a malaria-free environment. This expansion of the park is one of the most exciting and ambitious conservation projects ever undertaken, and Addo, now home to the densest population of elephant on earth, has become a highlight of the Eastern Cape.

BACKGROUND AND WILDLIFE

Great herds of elephant and many other game species once roamed the area of the park (like much of the Eastern Cape region) before they were practically decimated by hunters in the 1700s and 1800s. The settler farmers arrived in the late 1800s when the competition for agricultural land and water also took its toll on the elephant population, reaching a head in 1919 when farmers called upon the Cape government to exterminate the elephants. Major PJ Pretorius (a descendent of Vootrekker leader Andries Pretorius) was appointed and, between 1919 and 1920 he shot and killed 114 elephants; he was said to have shot as many as five a day.

Public opinion about the protection of elephants then gradually changed, leading to the proclamation of the park in 1931, when there were just 11 elephants in the area. However, conflicts between elephants and farmers continued until, in 1954, an elephant-proof fence was constructed using tram rails, and an area of 2270 ha was fenced in. There were 22 elephants at the time.

Although the park was originally proclaimed to protect a single species, priorities have now changed to conserve the rich biological diversity found in the area. Today this finely tuned ecosystem is sanctuary to a breeding herd of over 450 elephants, 400 Cape buffalo, 48 black rhino, hippo, cheetah, leopard, lion, spotted hyena, a variety of antelope species, as well as the flightless dung beetle – unique to the park and found wherever there's elephant dung. Over 185 species of bird have also been recorded here. The relative flatness of the bush and the large number of elephant mean that they are easily seen. To add to this, there are a couple of waterholes which can be accessed by car. Visitors will often see several herds drinking at one time – this can mean watching over 100 elephant – a magnificent experience. Although you'll see them at any time of year, one of the best times to visit is in January and February, when many of the females will have recently calved.

ARRIVING IN ADDO ELEPHANT NATIONAL PARK

Getting there Most visitors head for the area where the elephants are found, which is south of the main camp at the main park entrance, 72 km from Nelson Mandela Bay (Port Elizabeth) and about one hour's drive. It can be reached by taking the R335 via Motherwell, which is well signposted off the N2 from Nelson Mandela Bay to Grahamstown. Another access road into the park feeds off the N2 highway near Colchester, and goes through the new Matyholweni Gate and Camp in the new southern block of the park before joining up with the existing network of tourist roads in the park. To get there from Nelson Mandela Bay, take the N2 highway towards Grahamstown and, after 40 km where the road crosses the Sundays River Bridge, turn left at the 'Camp Matyholweni' sign. Follow this road for about 3 km until you enter Matyholweni Gate at Camp Matyholweni. Follow the southern access road inside the park for 36 km to Addo's main camp. Coming from the Grahamstown direction, either take this southern route, or from the N2 turn on to the N10 towards Cradock/Cookhouse, 80 km east of Grahamstown. Then, after 22 km, take the R342 to the left when you get to the intersection with Paterson on your right, which leads into the park and continues on to the main camp. Within the park there is a network of good gravel roads if you are in your own car, or you can book day and night drives, game walks, and horse rides through reception. Booking ahead is essential. The coastal section and Alexandria Dunefield is south of the N2, and there are access points to the beach off the R72.

Park information Addo Main Gate and Rest Camp, T042-233 8600, www.sanparks. org, conservation fees are R160, children (2-11) R80, children under two free. Gates open

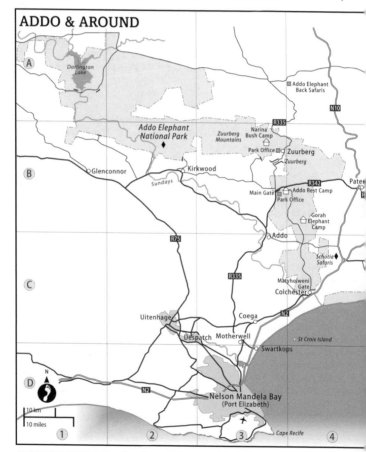

daily 0700-1900; the wildlife viewing area is open 0600-1800 in summer and 0700-1730 in winter, though times vary according to season so check with reception; office 0700-1900. There's a restaurant open 0730-2200, that serves light snacks and meals and a shop open 0800-1900 in summer and 0800-1800 in winter, selling a selection of groceries. Petrol and diesel 0730-1630. The nearest bank and ATM is in Addo, 15 km away. There is a swimming pool and tennis court at the main camp and a hide at a game-viewing waterhole that is floodlit at night. The park's other hide tends to be busier as it is near the restaurant, but it overlooks a small dam and is good for birdwatching. Note that in the elephant-watching area it is illegal to leave your vehicle anywhere other than at signposted climb-out points. Matyholweni Gate and Rest Camp, T042-468 0916, gates open daily 0700-1600, though times vary according to season so check with reception; office 0700-1900. There is no shop, restaurant or fuel, and the nearest facilities including banks are in Colchester and the other towns along the N2.

GAME DRIVES

Apart from self-driving on the good network of gravel roads, guided game drives with a game ranger can increase your chance of game spotting and provides a deeper understanding of the wilderness. Day and night drives should be booked in advance at the main rest camp and park reception as soon as you arrive. Two-hour sunrise, morning, midday and afternoon drives cost R220 per person, a sunset drive with drinks costs R330 and a night drive costs R250. Night drives are an added attraction as private vehicles are not allowed outside the camps after sundown, and unusual species like porcupines, spring hares and genets may be spotted. Children under six are not permitted on guided game drives, and children under 12 pay half price.

Alternatively, the Eyethu Hop-on Guides are local community guides which operate 0800-1700 from the main rest camp and park reception. They accompany you in your own vehicle for approximately two-hour drives for R120 per car.

ALEXANDRIA HIKING TRAIL

ⓘ *Permits for the unguided Alexandria Hiking Trail are available through SANParks, www. sanparks.org. Alternatively, contact the main reception office at Matyholweni Rest Camp, T042-468 0916. Minimum three, maximum*

12 people, R110 per person; it's a popular trail at weekends. At least one person must be able to read a map and compass and wear a reflective jacket in the event of an air rescue emergency. Take precautions against ticks.

On the coast to the south of Alexandria between the Bushman's River and the Sundays River mouths is the part of the park that is dunes and coastal forest. There are many easy trails passing along the beach and into the forest. The longest hike, for which permits are necessary, is the Alexandria Hiking Trail. It is 36 km long and is a marked two-day circular track – the first day is 19.5 km and the second day 16.5 km – be warned that the markers can be blown over in strong wind and get buried in the sand. The trail starts at the Woody Cape offices of the park, near the town of Alexandria. Just before entering the town, take the gravel road to the right, to the office, T046-653 0601.

There is no large game here but this is the habitat of the hairy-footed gerbil which is endemic to this area. The forests are good for birdwatching and along the coast it is possible to see dolphins and the Damara tern. The first day takes you from the base camp at Langebos through forest down to the coastal dunefield which extends for 120 km up the coast. The hiking can be tough along the windy dunes but worth it for the fine isolated beaches. One night is spent in the hut at Woody Cape. In the morning the trail then heads back across farmland in the Langevlakte Valley and back to Langebos.

EAST LONDON TO NELSON MANDELA BAY LISTINGS

WHERE TO STAY

East London

$$$-$$ Blue Lagoon, Blue Bend Pl, Beacon Bay, T043-748 4821, www.bluelagoonhotel. co.za. 76 recently and tastefully redecorated a/c rooms with DSTV, Wi-Fi and 24-hr room service, on the Beacon Bay headland overlooking the sea and estuary with stunning views. Some 2-bedroom apartments and 3-bedroom townhouses with kitchenette and lounge set in large grounds full of palms, 2 restaurants and bars, swimming pool, squash and tennis courts.

Grahamstown

$$ 137 High Street, 137 High St, T046-622 3242, www.137highstreet.co.za. Simple guesthouse in a restored historical building with yellowwood floors and ceilings, in a good location close to restaurants and sights, with 8 rooms, en suite bath or shower, M-Net TV, Wi-Fi. Good service, restaurant serves excellent breakfasts and freshly made cakes and scones, as well as more substantial meals for dinner.

$$ The Cock House, 10 Market St, T046-636 1287, www.cockhouse.co.za. Beautifully restored 1820s national monument with 9 double rooms with en suite bathrooms, 4 self-catering flats, special touches include electric blanket and home-made biscuits. Luxurious guesthouse with a good à la carte restaurant attached, comfortable lounge and library. Nelson Mandela has stayed here 3 times and South African author Andre Brink was a former resident. The 1st-floor veranda is a particularly fine feature.

Pumba Game Reserve

$$$$ Msenge Bush Lodge. Overlooking a waterhole with 11 glass-enclosed thatched a/c chalets, each with deck, outside shower and plunge pool. The central building has the dining room, bar, lounge, swimming pool and spacious deck overlooking a grassy plain where there is much animal activity. Very expensive.

Shamwari Game Reserve

$$$$ Lobengula Lodge. The most luxurious of the 7 complexes, with thatched roof and decorated to the highest standard. 5 rooms with outdoor shower, a/c and underfloor heating; the 6th room is the most expensive option in the whole reserve – the Chief Suite. It has a separate lounge with fireplace, private plunge pool and outdoor shower. The swimming pool has a sunken cocktail bar and there's a small gym, beauty spa and steam bath.

$$$$ Long Lee Manor, is the Edwardian manor house near the main entrance on the western side of the reserve. Largest of the 7 camps, although it never feels crowded. The 18 rooms have underfloor heating, ceiling fans, a/c, TV, telephone. Facilities include 2 swimming pools, a floodlit tennis court, a beauty spa and down by the Bushman's River at a point known as the hippo pool, is a covered *lapa* where guests can watch the animals drink while they enjoy a meal.

Schotia Safaris

$$$ Bush Lodges, see page 184, T042-235 1436, www.schotia.com. 2 double en suite chalets with fireplaces, hidden in the bush that are very private and aimed at honeymooners. A 3rd chalet has 4 beds suitable for families. No electricity, but lamps will be lit for you in the evening. There are a further 8 slightly cheaper twin/double/family rooms in a converted dairy, some with showers but shared toilets, for which there is a discount, and with electricity. All meals and game drives included in the price, transfers from Nelson Mandela Bay can be arranged.

Addo Elephant National Park

$$$$ Gorah Elephant Camp, in the main elephant section of the park, access is from the N10 towards Paterson, 4 km north of the junction with the N2, central reservations T044-5011 111, www.hunterhotels.com. This luxurious (and very expensive) camp is a **Relais & Chateaux** property covering a 5000-ha concession, with 11 huge tents with a colonial theme, 4-poster beds and terraces. Relaxing boma area with rock swimming pool, meals are served in a superbly renovated coach house, overlooking a waterhole frequented by elephant, buffalo and antelope. The price includes all meals, guided game drives and night drives.

$$$$-$$ Addo Rest Camp, next to the main entrance gate and park reception. There are 61 units in total, each fully equipped for self-catering, some have a/c and braai facilities. Some are equipped for wheelchair users. The 2 guest cottages (**$$$$**), **Hapoor** and **Domkrag**, have 6 beds with 2 en suite a/c bedrooms, a fully equipped kitchen and a living room with DSTV. The **chalets $$$** are suitable for 4 people and have a bathroom and kitchen. The **2-bed huts ($$)** are simple units with a shower, fridge and toilet, and there is a fully equipped communal kitchen. The 5 2-bed Safari Tents (**$$**) have bedding, towels, fan, fridge and braai, use of communal ablutions and kitchen. There is also **camping ($)** available, a maximum of 4 people can occupy any 1 pitch. The grounds are well grassed and there is plenty of shade. Communal kitchens have hot plates, power points and hot water. Facilities include a swimming pool, waterhole with hide, restaurant and curio shop which also sells some frozen food. Guided day and night drives and 2-hr horse-riding trails can be booked at reception.

$$ Narina Bush Camp, is next to the Witriver in the Zuurberg Mountains approximately 22 km (gravel road, 40 mins' driving) from the main rest camp and park reception. This is a tented camp with 4 tents (2-bed) and must be booked as 1 unit although the minimum is 4 persons, towels and bedding are provided, open lapa/braai area, kitchen with gas stove, fridge, paraffin lamps, cutlery, crockery and cooking utensils, 1 shower with hot water from a paraffin cylinder geyser, and 1 toilet. Because there's no electricity the guests have to arrive at least 2 hrs before sunset (and no later than 1800) as they still have to carry their food and clothing to the camp from the car park, crossing a river and walking 400-500 m through the forest.

WHAT TO DO

Addo Elephant Back Safaris, in the north of the Addo Elephant National Park in the Zuurberg Mountains, on the Toevlugt Farm, 1.5 km before Addo's main gate, turn left at the Zuurburg sign, the farm is 34 km from this turn-off, however the last 17 km up and over the pass and after the Zuurberg Mountain Village, is rough gravel road, a transfer service is offered from the Village of Addo, contact them for details, T042-235 1400, vwww.addoelephantbacksafaris. co.za, 3-hr excursion 0800, 1100, and 150, R875, children (under 12) R440 but must be accompanied by a parent on top of the elephants. There's the opportunity to ride and walk with 3 tame elephants through the bush and forest. The ride/walk is at an enjoyable pace and not strenuous and allows visitors to observe the elephants' habits close up and in their natural surroundings. The experience lasts for about 3 hrs and snacks or lunch are provided. There's comfortable accommodation in log and canvas-sided cabins, and accommodation packages (**$$$$**) include the elephant experience as well as a game drive in Addo, a game walk, all meals and some drinks, and accompanying the elephants to their stables at bedtime.

NELSON MANDELA BAY

Port Elizabeth stretches along the shores of Algoa Bay. It is a major port and industrial centre and the biggest coastal city between Cape Town and Durban. Since 2006, along with the peripheral towns, it now forms the much larger metropolitan area of Nelson Mandela Bay. The city centre, known as 'Central', is a grid of Victorian houses and green spaces (burnt brown in summer), but unfortunately it has been blighted by the urban decay seen in other South African cities in recent years, and is not as attractive or as safe as it once was. The rest of the city – a modern sprawl of shopping malls, office blocks and apartments – is not aesthetically pleasing either. Nevertheless, Nelson Mandela Bay is celebrated for its long hours of sunshine and the warm waters of the bay, making it a good place to try some watersports. The main tourist area along the long soft-sand beaches of Algoa Bay, is more enticing, despite the holiday flats and apartment blocks creeping onto the land behind them. As an industrial city it is understandable that tourists don't want to spend a great deal of time here. However, given the fact that you can fly back to Cape Town in less than an hour, and with the massive growth in tourism along the Garden Route, the city has become a convenient point for visitors to start or finish their journey.

Perhaps the city's biggest draw is its proximity to a number of game reserves. The most popular are the Addo Elephant National Park and the Shamwari Game Reserve. These offer the opportunity to see the Big Five without having to worry about malaria. Although Shamwari is a private reserve only open to guests at the very smart camps, there are other similar reserves that open for day visits as long as you book in advance.

→ARRIVING IN NELSON MANDELA BAY (PORT ELIZABETH)

GETTING THERE

Port Elizabeth Airport ① *4 km from the city centre along Alister Miller Drive, T041-507 7319, www.acsa.co.za*, receives several flights daily from major South African cities. The airport has restaurants, ATMs and a tourist information desk in arrivals. Visitors staying at Humewood Beach and Summerstrand can reach the airport without having to negotiate the city centre by way of an elaborate ring road and flyover system. Most major hotels provide a courtesy bus from the airport or alternatively, there are taxis. Several car hire groups also have a desk in the terminal. The mainline **railway station** is on the edge of the town centre on Station Street, by the harbour. Nelson Mandela Bay is served by **Greyhound, Intercape** and **Translux** buses, and it is the overnight spot for the **Baz Bus** on the route between Cape Town and Durban, which calls in at most of the backpacker hostels.

GETTING AROUND

Local buses depart from Market Square Bus Station, beneath the Norwich Union Centre Building on Strand Street. The **Algoa Bus Company** ① *T041-404 1200, 080-142 1444 (toll free), www.algoabus.co.za*, operates a regular service between the beachfront, city centre, St George's Park, Rink Street, Greenacres and the Bridge Shopping Complex – **Route O**. Timetables can be picked up at the Market Square information kiosk or can be downloaded from the website.

BEST TIME TO VISIT

Algoa Bay enjoys a subtropical climate with long hours of sunshine and some light rain throughout the year. Winters are mild, and summers are warm with an average daytime temperature of 25°C and are considerably less humid than the more northerly parts of South Africa's east coast. Moderate sea temperatures make it popular for watersports. Southern right whales visit the bay from June to November, while humpback whales calve and feed their young between May and December. Also be on the lookout for Cape fur seals, penguins, bottlenose dolphins, gannets and cormorants throughout the year.

TOURIST INFORMATION

Nelson Mandela Bay Tourism ① *Donkin Lighthouse Building, Belmont Terr, Central, T041-585 8884, www.nmbt.co.za, Mon-Fri 0800-1630, Sat-Sun 0930-1530, and in Boardwalk, Marine Drive, Summerstrand, T041-583 2030, 0800-1900*, are useful offices that can book accommodation and advise on nightlife, tours and travel throughout the Eastern Cape.

→BACKGROUND

In 1497, Vasco da Gama noted the 'Bay' on one of his voyages. It was later named Baia de Lagoa, referring to the lagoon situated at the mouth of the Baakens River. For hundreds of years, however, Nelson Mandela Bay (Port Elizabeth) was referred to on navigational charts only as "a landing place with fresh water". The city was established in 1820 when the

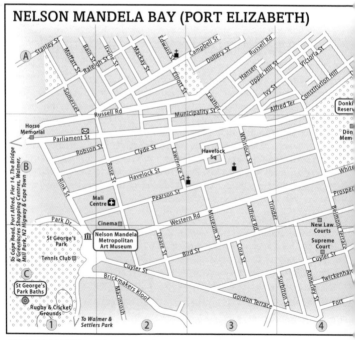

NELSON MANDELA BAY (PORT ELIZABETH)

first British settlers arrived. The town became a port and a trading centre for the early settlers who were gradually moving inland. During the first half of the 20th century, Port Elizabeth expanded and became an important trading and manufacturing city. The main exports were mineral ores, citrus fruits and wool. Ford General Motors opened its first assembly plants here in the 1920s. Today, with a population of around 1.5 million, it is South Africa's fifth largest city, and one that is currently reinventing itself as 'Nelson Mandela Bay', which is its new formal name. The Nelson Mandela Bay Stadium, built as a venue for 2010 FIFA World Cup™, is the newest addition to the city's skyline, and is around 1 km north of the city centre at North End. With its distinctive roof built of panels made to look like petals, it's locally dubbed 'The Sunflower'.

→ PLACES IN NELSON MANDELA BAY

CENTRAL NELSON MANDELA BAY
The 5-km **Donkin Heritage Trail** has been created to show visitors the most important monuments, buildings, gardens and churches around the city centre. An excellent guidebook, available from the information office, contains 47 places of historical interest. A few of the more interesting buildings are mentioned below (not necessarily in the order you might come across them on the trail). The trail starts in Market Square opposite the City Hall, simply follow the useful signs.

Market Square is probably Port Elizabeth's most attractive corner, with a couple of fine buildings and the beginning of bustling Govan Mbeki Avenue. **City Hall** was built between 1858 and 1862; the clock tower was added in 1883. While part of the hall is still used by the council, it is also now a lecture and concert hall for public performances. Look out for a replica of the Diaz Cross in Market Square. This was donated by the Portuguese Government to commemorate the arrival of Bartholomeu Diaz in Algoa Bay in 1488. The **Main Public Library** ① *T041-585 8133, Mon-Fri 0900-1700*, dominates the northwestern corner of Market Square. This fine early Victorian building, with its terracotta façade shipped out from the UK, dates from 1835 and started life as a courthouse. It was not until 1902 that it was officially opened as the public library. Outside by the road is a fine marble statue of Queen Victoria, erected in 1903. Once inside, visitors have the opportunity to view some beautiful early books.

The **Prester John Memorial** stands in Fleming Square, behind City Hall. It is dedicated to the mythical king-priest and the Portuguese explorers who discovered South Africa. It was unveiled in 1886 and is thought to be the only monument in the world depicting Prester John. The monument is in the form of a large Coptic cross.

The **Campanile** ① *Strand St, T041-506 3293, Tue-Sat 0900-1230, 1330-17, Sun 1400-1700, entry by donation*, is a 53-m bell-tower close to the docks down by the railway station. It was built to commemorate the landing of the 1820 settlers and was once the highest structure in Port Elizabeth. The views of the city and harbour remain impressive, and if you're fit you can climb up 204 stairs to the observation room at the top. It contains the largest carillon of bells in the country as well as a chiming clock, and the tower is a useful reference point on the coast. Note this is in a rough area and it's advised to visit in a group.

South of City Hall is the **Wezandla Gallery and Craft Centre** ① *27 Baakens St, T041-585 1185, www.wezandla.com, Mon-Fri 0900-1700, Sat 0900-1300*, hard to miss with its brightly painted exterior. This is an interesting collection of African art: wire and wood sculptures, woven baskets, pottery, crafts and curios. Many of the items are the work of local craftsmen and there are a reputed 25,000 items for sale.

Donkin Reserve is a public park in Central, high up on a hill with views of Govan Mbeki Avenue and the harbour. On the inland side of the park is the fine façade of the **King Edward Hotel**; on the other side is a lighthouse and an unusual pyramid. The lighthouse dates from 1861 and is today home to the **Nelson Mandela Bay tourist office**. The rest of the lighthouse building can be opened on request on weekdays, 0830-1630 (ask at the tourist office). The odd-looking pyramid is actually a memorial erected by Sir Rufane Donkin in memory of his wife, Elizabeth, after whom the city was named. Local folklore is rather more sinister and suggests that her heart was buried in the pyramid. Rufane Donkin, a British colonialist and former Cape Governor, was sent to administer Port Elizabeth in the late 19th century, but his wife Elizabeth never saw the town.

On the southeastern corner of the reserve, **The Opera House** ① *Whites Rd, T041-586 2256, www.peoperahouse.co.za*, is reputedly the only surviving example of a Victorian theatre in Africa. Built in 1872, it preceded the arrival of the railway by two years. The first performance was Gilbert and Sullivan's *The Mikado* by the newly formed Port Elizabeth Amateur Operatic and Dramatic Society. It was constructed on the site of some old gallows where public hangings took place, so ghost stories abound.

South of Donkin Reserve, **No 7 Castle Hill Museum** ① *7 Castle Hill Rd, T041-582 2515, Mon-Fri 1000-1300, 1400-1630, R9, children (under 17) R5*, is housed in one of the oldest buildings in the city. It was built in 1825 for the Reverend Francis McCleland as the Rectory. The cottage has been restored to look like an early-Victorian home, complete with a slate roof, yellowwood floors and 19th-century furniture and household goods.

Continuing south on Belmont Terrace, is **Fort Frederick** ① *daily, sunrise to sunset, free*. This was the first stone building in the Eastern Cape, completed in 1799. From its high point it overlooks the mouth of the Baakens River. It was built to stop any French troops from landing in the rivermouth but had the effect of helping the rebels at Graaff-Reinet. No shot has ever been fired from, or at, the fort.

Running through the town is the Baakens River Gorge which is surrounded by the well-kept, 54-ha **Settlers Park Nature Reserve** – not what you would expect to find in the middle of South Africa's fifth largest city. The valley runs for 7 km and is full of interesting birds, plants and even some small buck. Unfortunately, despite the tranquil setting, there are occasional muggings, so don't come alone. The reserve has three entrances: How

Avenue, just off Park Drive; Chelmsford Avenue, just off Target Kloof; and Third Avenue, Walmer. Look out for the recommended walks by each entrance, such as the 8-km **Guinea Fowl Trail**, which starts in the car park at Third Avenue. **Birdlife Eastern Cape** ① *T041-379 3201*, meet here at 0800 on the first Saturday and third Thursday of each month for birdwatching walks; visitors are welcome.

On the western fringes of the city centre on Park Drive is the 73-ha **St George's Park**. Established in 1860, this is the city's oldest park and is home to a number of sporting facilities. The bowling club was formed in 1882 and is the oldest in South Africa, while Africa's first Test Match was played at the cricket oval in 1889. The **Nelson Mandela Metropolitan Art Museum** ① *flanks the main entrance to the park at 1 Park Drive, T041-56 2000, www.artmuseum.co.za, Mon and Wed-Fri 0900-1800, Tue, Sat- Sun 1300-1700, 1st Sun of every month 0900-1400, free*. Formerly the King George VI Art Gallery; most of the collection on display is of 19th- and 20th-century British art, but there are also some good monthly contemporary exhibitions, accompanied by films and lectures. Other displays include a collection of oriental miniatures as well as pottery and sculpture.

The **Horse Memorial** standing on the corner of Russell and Cape roads was created after the Boer War. Between 1899 and 1902 thousands of horses died, more often through fatigue and starvation than from being slain in battle. The inscription on the memorial reads: "The greatness of a nation consists not so much in the number of its people or the extent of its territory as in the extent and justice of its compassion." The statue shows a man kneeling in front of a horse with a bucket in his hands making as if to feed or quench the horse's thirst.

OUTSIDE CENTRAL NELSON MANDELA BAY

Most visitors head for Nelson Mandela Bay's beaches, which lie to the east of the city centre in the suburbs of **Humewood** and **Summerstrand**, where there are a number of typical seaside attractions and facilities. There are also other beaches and a couple of game reserves within striking distance of the city.

In Humewood, **Bayworld** ① *off Marine Drive, T041-586 0650, www.bayworld.co.za, daily 0900-1630, R4, children (3-17) R25, (under 3) free, penguin and seal presentations daily 1100 and 1500, restaurant, shop*, comprises the Port Elizabeth Museum, Oceanarium and Snake Park. The Port Elizabeth Museum has exhibits on natural and cultural history. Look out for the 15-m southern right whale skeleton and the fully rigged models of early sailing ships. There is also a collection of objects collected from wrecks in and around Algoa Bay. The rest of the collection focuses on fossils and early man. The **Oceanarium** has over 60 species of fish, as well as a ragged tooth shark tank, rays, turtles and African penguins, while the snake park has a number of snakes, tortoises, lizards and baby crocodiles.

Also in Humewood is the **South End Museum** ① *corner of Humewood Rd and Walmer Blvd, T041-582 3325, www.southendmuseum.co.za, Mon-Fri 0900-1600, Sat-Sun 1000-1500, free*. This museum is dedicated to the South End suburb, which was destroyed when the Group Areas Act in 1950 led to the forcible removal of the cosmopolitan population of the area. South End was one of the prime areas of the city because it was close to the centre of town, the beachfront and the harbour. During Apartheid, not only the blacks, Indians and coloureds were forcibly relocated from the city, but the Chinese too.

Midway between Humewood and Summserstrand on Marine Drive, opposite Shark Rock Pier, is the **Boardwalk Casino and Entertainment World**, also simply known as the

Boardwalk ① *T031-507 7777, www.suninternational.com.* The complex is set around a series of man-made lakes and beautiful gardens lit by some 40,000 lights after dark. There are numerous entertainment venues in the centre, including the Supersport Arena (for televised sports), the Boardwalk Amphitheatre, a children's games arcade, ten-pin bowling alley, and five-screen cinema. The 24-hour casino offers 700 slot machines and 20 gaming tables, and there's a selection of restaurants, and specialist shops.

The 366-ha **Cape Recife Nature Reserve** ① *next to the Pine Lodge Holiday Resort, Marine Drive, Summerstrand, the turn-off is just beyond Humewood Golf Club, T041-584 0238, 0800-1600, free,* is a 366-ha area encompassing a wide expanse of unspoilt beach, vegetated dunes, and rocky outcrops on the very southern tip of Algoa Bay. A walking trail leads from the car park and entrance gate. There are a number of pools and concrete pipes in the reserve which are part of the Cape Recife water reclamation works, and will be of interest to birdwatchers as they attract a number of plovers, waders and ducks. There are tours of the red and white candy-striped **Cape Recife Lighthouse** ① *www.transnetnationalportsauthority. net, Mon-Fri 1000-1500, T041-507 2484, R14, children (under 12) R7,* which sits on an attractive swathe of beach scattered with shells right on the tip of the reserve at Cape Recife Point. Built in 1851 and 24 m high, it marks the turning point for ships from the ocean into Algoa Bay and warns mariners of the offshore **Thunderbolt Reef**, the graveyard of numerous ships, the most recent being the *Kapodistrias* which sank in 1985.

TOWNSHIPS

The townships around Nelson Mandela Bay can be visited on a tour. The New Brighton township has been in existence since the region was mostly farmland. In 1903, land 8 km north of Port Elizabeth was earmarked for the establishment of a large 'model native settlement'. The outbreak of bubonic plague in 1901 was used as an excuse to gain government assistance for forced removals to this new 'location'. Over time New Brighton became known as the Red Location and takes its name from a series of corrugated-iron barracks, brought down here from a defunct concentration camp at Uitenhage as well as the Imperial Yeomanry Hospital at de Aar. Both had been used in the South African War of 1899-1902. In time, these sheds eventually rusted and turned deep red. After the ANC's armed wing Umkhonto we Sizwe went underground in 1960, Red Location was used for hiding political fugitives. Well-hidden cells were erected between shack floors and the ground where these fugitives could hide from the security police. Today the township is home to the **Red Location Museum** ① *corner of Palme and Singaphi streets, New Brighton, approximately 8 km northeast of the city centre off the N2 towards Grahamstown, take the Burman Rd exit, turn left into Baxter St, left into Old Grahamstown Rd, and follow signs, T041-408 8400, www.freewebs.com/redlocationmuseum, Mon-Fri 0900-1600, Sat 0900-1500, R12, children (under 16) R6.* Opened in 2006, the striking, industrial warehouse-styled complex uses space, corrugated iron, wood and steel to echo its shanty town origins (it is now surrounded by small government-built houses), as well as a stark angular façade to mirror the many industrial factories in the city (South Africa's centre for the motor trade). It has won three major international architectural awards, including the 2006 Royal Institute of British Architects' inaugural Lubetkin Prize for the most outstanding work of architecture outside the UK and Europe. It tells the history of the township and its part in the struggle, and includes a series of 'memory boxes' or galleries of photos and exhibits. There's a shop and café, and outside is a vast space for public events.

Other townships surrounding the city are **Swartkops**, **Kwa-Zakhele** (meaning 'place to build yourself' in Xhosa) and **Motherwell** on the road to Addo, which is reputedly the largest township in the Eastern Cape, dating back to the 1980s when the city's population swelled with people looking for work.

GAME PARKS

Kragga Kamma Game Park ① *15 km east of Nelson Mandela Bay on the Kragga Kamma road off the N2, T041-379 4195, www.kraggakamma.com, 0800-1700, self-drive R5, children (5-18) R20, under 5s free, guided 2-hr game drives R150 per person*, is a private game reserve is in a lush tract of coastal forest where all the animals roam free. These animals include rhino, buffalo, giraffe, zebra, cheetah and a number of antelope, including the shy nyala. The resident bird of prey is the jackal buzzard and other species include fish eagles, yellow-billed kites and Knysna loeries. You can drive around the small network of gravel roads in your own car or alternatively take a two-hour guided game drive. There's a café, some picnic sites and accommodation in safari tents and log cabins.

The **Seaview Game and Lion Park** ① *25 km west of Nelson Mandela Bay, signposted off the N2, the park is 7.5 km towards the sea, T041-378 1702, www.seaviewgamepark.co.za, 0900-1700, lion feeding Sun 1200, R50, children (2-18) R20, (under 2) free*, is a wildlife park with around 40 species of animal, including giraffe, zebra, wildebeest, impala, duiker and monkeys. But it is the lions that most people come to see. In total there are 55, all hand reared, including 14 white lion and, for an extra fee, visitors can get close up to a lion cub and possibly cuddle one. The lions (and oddly a pair of Siberian tigers), can be spotted in enclosures from a boardwalk, and there are nature trails and self game drives, a restaurant and curio shop, and a few stands for caravans and tents.

NELSON MANDELA BAY LISTINGS

WHERE TO STAY

$$$$ Hacklewood Hill Country House, 152 Prospect Rd, Walmer, T041-581 1300, www.hacklewood.co.za. Luxurious guest-house in a late-Victorian manor house full of antiques and paintings, with 8 a/c tasteful rooms, with massive en suite bathrooms and DSTV. Beautiful gardens, swimming pool and tennis court, elegant dining room where you'll need to brush up on the use of silverware, and special touches like selecting wine from the impressive cellar. Advance booking essential during the peak season. No children under 14.

$$$$-$$$ Radisson Blu Hotel, Port Elizabeth, Marine Drive, Summerstrand, T041-509 5000, www.radissonblu.com. PE's 1st 5-star hotel in a distinctive 18-storey high state-of-the-art glass tower, with 173 sea-facing a/c luxury rooms, with floor-to-ceiling windows and sleek modern, minimalist decor. Well-regarded Italian restaurant, trendy cocktail bar on the pool deck, top-class facilities include spa, gym and Wi-Fi throughout.

$$$ The Beach, Marine Drive, Summerstrand, T041-583 2161, www.thebeachhotel.co.za. Luxurious, low-rise 4-star hotel right on the beach, with 58 well-appointed rooms, 3 good restaurants, bar with ocean views from the patio, large pool, tidy gardens, good service, just across the road from Shark Rock pier and adjacent to the Boardwalk.

$$ Brighton Lodge, 21 Brighton Drive, Summerstrand, T041-583 4576, www.brightonlodge.co.za. A very comfortable guesthouse where each of the 11 en suite bedrooms has been decorated from a different period, and has microwave, fridge, DSTV, Wi-Fi and private entrance and patio. Swimming pool, walking distance from the Boardwalk and the beach, and breakfast can be served in bed.

RESTAURANTS

$$$ Old Austria, 24 Westbourne Rd, Central Nelson Mandela Bay, T041-373 0299. Mon-Fri 1200-1500, Mon-Sat 1300-2230. Set in a restored Victorian whitewashed rectory, with chandeliers, polished wooden floors and grandfather clocks, the menu features Austrian fare such as schnitzel and apple strudel. There's also good fish and seafood, including poached sole and grilled prawns.

$$$ Ginger, The Beach Hotel (see above). 1100-1500, 1800-2200. The city's best gourmet restaurant, with chic stylish decor, an outside deck, sleek bar and beautifully presented and imaginative cuisine. A sample menu could be seared scallops with leek and sherry risotto, followed by roast duck with pineapple sauce and crêpes suzettes.

$$ 34' South, Boardwalk, Summerstrand, T041-583 1085, www.34-south.com. 1000-2130. Fabulous deli and sister branch to the one at the Knysna Waterfront, with all sorts of treats from olives to cookery books. Chrome-and-glass decor, you can make up meals from the counters or choose a selection of tapas and seafood snacks, tables outside on the wooden deck.

DREAM TRIP 3:
Johannesburg→Sun City→Kruger→Johannesburg
21 days

Johannesburg 4 nights, page 201

Magaliesberg Mountains 1 night,
pages 215 and 225
Self-drive from Joburg to Magaliesberg
(2 hrs) or from Tshwane via Hartbeespoort
Dam (2 hrs) and Rustenburg en route to
Sun City (140 km)

Sun City 2 nights, page 226
Hartbeespoort Dam to Sun City (1½ hrs);
Rustenberg to Sun City (45 mins)

Pilanesberg Game Reserve 2 nights,
page 228
Self-drive or guided tour (recommended)
from Sun City or long day trip from
Tshwane or Joburg (3 hrs)

Nelspruit 1 night, page 231
Flight/bus or self-drive from Joburg
(55 mins/4 hrs)

**Kruger National Park: southern and
central camps** 4 nights, pages 238
and 241
Join a tour or self-drive from Joburg
(5½/6½ hrs) or Nelspruit (1/2½ hrs)

**Kruger National Park: private game
reserves** 2 nights, page 244
Join a tour or self-drive from Joburg
(6½ hrs) or Nelspruit (2 hrs)

Panorama Region: Blyde River Canyon
1 night, page 252
Drive southwest from Hoedspruit (2½ hrs),
which is easily accessible from Kruger's
Phalaborwa Gate (1¼ hrs) and the private
game reserves

Panorama Region: Graskop 2 nights,
page 253
South of the Blyde River Canyon (1 hr)

Panorama Region: Hazyview 1 night,
page 256
South from Graskop to Sabie (30 mins) and
east from Sabie (45 mins), convenient
for southern Kruger's Phabeni Gate
(30 mins) or Paul Kruger Gate

Johannesburg 1 night, page 201
From White River take the R358 to
Nelspruit then the N4 to Johannesburg
(4½ hrs) for your flight home.

GOING FURTHER

Swaziland, Zululand and Maputaland
pages 259 and 263
With more than 3 weeks, this itinerary can
be the first or last leg of a grand tour of
South Africa, from Johannesburg to Cape
Town, which would combine all 3 trips
outlined in this book.

DREAM TRIP 3
Johannesburg → Sun City → Kruger → Johannesburg

Since its sudden birth in 1886, Johannesburg has dominated the country, morphing from a rough frontier town into a financial metropolis. Although in the past, Joburg has suffered from much-publicized high crime rates, it is now successfully dusting off its dodgy reputation and drawing back visitors in droves. Crime-busting regeneration programmes have seen formerly run-down areas transformed into places to visit, live in and enjoy, while recent additions to tourism attractions include some of South Africa's finest museums, such as the celebrated Apartheid Museum or the Cradle of Humankind.

Just 50 km north, South Africa's recently renamed capital, Tshwane (Pretoria) couldn't be more different. Unlike Joburg, Tshwane is staid and conservative, with wide streets lined with jacaranda trees which bloom a regal purple in spring.

North West Province is known as the home of Sun City, a huge entertainment complex and one-time gambling haven. Adjoining it is the Pilanesberg Game Reserve, which offers the chance of seeing the Big Five at a malaria-free altitude and just a few hours from Johannesburg.

To the east of Joburg, Mpumalanga province is home to the magnificent Kruger National Park, one of the best places in Africa for game viewing. West of the park, the Panorama Region is a mountainous area dotted with quiet agricultural towns, clustered along the top of the spectacular Blyde River Canyon.

An extension to this itinerary could take you south to the wildlife sanctuaries of tiny Swaziland and then west to the game reserves, wetland parks and marine reserves of Maputaland and Zululand. And, for the ultimate South Africa Dream Trip, you could continue along the coast all the way to Cape Town.

JOHANNESBURG

Johannesburg, Joburg or Jozi is the largest financial, commercial and industrial centre in South Africa. With an estimated population of four million spread over some 600 suburbs covering approximately 1300 sq km, it's the most densely populated region of the country. Barely over 100 years old, the discovery of gold transformed this deserted heartland into a vast urban sprawl and made it one of the wealthiest cities in the world. The gold rush brought in settlers from all over the world creating a multiracial and cosmopolitan city, but Apartheid changed all that. Forced relocations altered the fabric of Johannesburg, creating deep divisions in society that are still evident today. Despite Apartheid's demise, Johannesburg is still mostly segregated, albeit no longer by legal requisite. The city centre and neighbouring suburbs, such as Hillbrow, are largely home to the urban black population, a condensed area of overcrowded high-rise flats where poverty and crime are rife. Soweto is a vast, sprawling township of government housing and informal settlements, home to the majority of Johannesburg's black commuters. Most white residents, on the other hand, live in the leafy and affluent northern suburbs.

But things have been changing considerably. Soweto is now a city in its own right, with affluent suburbs, a fast-growing middle class and an excellent infrastructure serving the community. The notorious city centre, meanwhile, is undergoing extensive regeneration programmes. But while crime rates have dropped considerably, safety remains an issue, with most visitors, like most well-off locals, confining themselves to the safe suburbs and numerous shopping malls.

Joburg's today is not unlike a large American city where everything works smoothly and, for most, the standard of living is much higher than the rest of the country. Places of interest include the many museums dedicated to old Johannesburg and the city's gold-mining past as well as the Apartheid struggle, and architecture ranges from the CBD's art deco buildings and tangle of skyscrapers to Sir Herbert Baker-designed mansions dotted around the city. The city also finds time to breathe and relax in the many beautiful open spaces and parks, which are very popular at the weekend.

→ ARRIVING IN JOHANNESBURG

GETTING THERE

Johannesburg's **OR Tambo International Airport** ① *Kempton Park, T011-921 6262, flight information T0867-277888, www.acsa.co.za*, is 24 km from the city centre and 35 km from the northern suburbs on the R24, roughly halfway between Johannesburg and Tshwane (Pretoria). Outside rush hour, both cities can be reached by car in around 30 minutes. OR Tambo is Africa's busiest airport, and the most important hub for air travel in the southern hemisphere. Formerly Johannesburg International Airport, it was renamed in 2006 to honour late anti-Apartheid activist and former president of the ANC, Oliver Reginald Tambo.

To find out the status of a flight, check the website or send an SMS to T38648 with the flight number, in reply to which you'll receive up-to-date flight details.

The airport has a full range of facilities, and domestic and international arrivals and departures are linked by one long terminal. **Master Currency** and **American Express** branches are open to meet all arriving flights and there are banks and ATMs throughout the airport. You can hire mobile phones and buy local SIM cards at **Vodacom** ① *www. vodacom.co.za*, or MTN ① *www.mtnsp.co.za*, at international and domestic arrivals, which are open 0500-2400. In international arrivals, there is a post office, and there's also a branch of **Postnet** on the shopping level of the domestic terminal. The duty-free shops in international departures are extensive. Wi-Fi is available in all public areas and there are internet cafés in all terminals.

Opposite the arrivals level of the terminal is the **Parkade Centre**, a multi-storey car park and site of all car hire offices and shuttle bus companies. **Magic Bus** ① *T011-394 6902, www.magicbus.co.za*, **Airport Link** ① *T011-794 8300, www.airportlink.co.za*, and **Airport Shuttle** ① *T012-348 0650, www.airportshuttle.co.za*, drop off at the major hotels in Johannesburg and Tshwane (Pretoria). They charge around R400 per person plus R60 for each additional person from the same group. Alternatively you can pre-book one through your hotel, guesthouse or backpacker hostel.

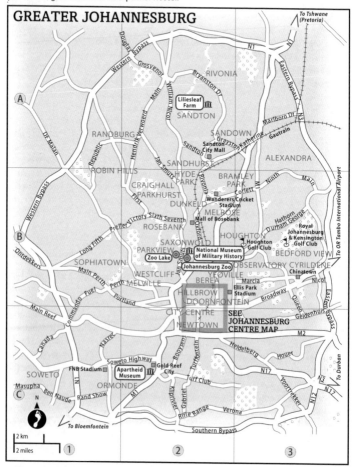

GREATER JOHANNESBURG

ON THE RAILS
The Gautrain

The Gautrain, T0800-428 87246, www.gautrain.co.za, is an 80-km high-speed railway network linking Johannesburg with Tshwane (Pretoria) with a branch line from Sandton to OR Tambo International Airport. It was built to relieve the chronic commuter traffic on the M1 and the N1 (which in the mornings and late afternoons resemble car parks). The north-south line, starting at Park Station in Johannesburg's CBD, goes in a northerly direction to Rosebank, Sandton (where it interchanges with the airport line), Midrand, Centurion, Pretoria CBD and Hatfield. The airport branch goes between Sandton and OR Tambo International Airport. The trains can travel up to 160 kph and, while part of the lines in the built-up areas are underground (Park, Rosebank and Sandton stations are underground), many of the tracks are above ground including the section in Midrand which goes over an impressively long viaduct.

Trains run Monday-Friday 0530-0830 and 1600-1900 every 12 minutes; 0830-1600 and 1900-2030 every 20 minutes; Saturday and Sunday 0530-2030 every 30 minutes. It takes 15 minutes between Sandton and the airport, and it takes 40 minutes between Johannesburg's Park Station in the CBD and Tshwane (Pretoria). A **Gautrain Gold Card** can be bought at the stations by cash, credit or debit card and a one-off R10 registration fee is applicable. They can be loaded with a single or multiple journeys, and can be reloaded at anytime. Note: you must have at least R20 loaded on to the card to enter any gate. Children under three travel free. A short fare between two stations – Sandton and Rosebank or Hatfield and Tshwane (Pretoria), for example – costs R19, rising to R46 for journeys from one end of the line to the other. The fare between the airport and Sandton is R105; the additional extra fare to your final destination is calculated from Sandton. At Sandton you can change to the main line for other destinations. All trains and stations are wheelchair-accessible.

Metered taxis can be found outside the main terminal building but tend to be more expensive than the shuttle services and drivers often do not know the way without direction to the lesser-known hotels or guesthouses. Be sure to use an approved **Airports Company South Africa (ACSA)** taxi and ignore the touts. The taxis have the ACSA logo on them.

All the hotels located near the airport offer a free pickup shuttle service, and a drop-off service for a nominal fee. Opposite the main terminal building and behind the **Intercontinental Johannesburg OR Tambo Airport** hotel are a series of hotel bus stops where the hotel shuttles come and go, but at quieter times of the day you may need to phone the hotel to tell them you are waiting.

The station for the **Gautrain** ① *call centre T0800-428 87246, www.gautrain.co.za*, is directly linked to the departures level of the terminal building (see box, above).

Gauteng's second airport, **Lanseria International Airport** ① *Randburg North, T011-367 0300, www.lanseria.co.za*, is off the R512 from Randburg in Johannesburg's northern suburbs or the N14 from Tshwane (Pretoria), 40 km from Johannesburg's CBD, 45 km from Tshwane (Pretoria) and roughly 65 km northwest of OR Tambo. Fewer airlines fly to Lanseria than OR Tambo. It is presently used by **Kulula** and **Mango**, on some of their daily flights between Johannesburg and Cape Town and Durban, as well as charter and executive jet services. With international status, air traffic is likely to increase in the future. Taxis meet flights, and shuttle bus services can be pre-booked through the same companies as OR Tambo (see page 201), or through your hotel.

Park City in the centre of the CBD is a large integrated transport terminal and is where the railway station is for long-distance trains, the Gautrain and local Metrorail services; it is also the terminus for the mainline long-distance bus companies, **Greyhound**, **Intercape** and **Translux**.

MOVING ON

The Gautrain links Johannesburg to Tshwane (Pretoria) (see page 219), 58 km to the north and 45 km north of OR Tambo airport. Alternatively, you can rent a car and head to the North West Province and the Magaliesberg Mountains via the Lion Park, Lesedi Cultural Village, the Cradle of Humankind and the Sterkfontein Caves (see pages 215-216). If you are visiting Tshwane and then heading west to Magaliesberg Mountains, Sun City and Pilanesberg Game Reserve, see page 225.

For the next stage of this trip you'll need to return from Sun City to Johannesburg and then either fly, take a bus or drive to Nelspruit and Kruger National Park (see page 231).

If you are heading east to Swaziland (page 259), about 350 km from Johannesburg, take the N17 (4½ hours).

GETTING AROUND

Although Johannesburg's public transport infrastructure has been much improved recently, and there are a few options to get around efficiently and cost effectively by bus and suburban train, the city is a sprawling conurbation and the lack of convenient public transport between the sights is still an obstacle for visitors. It is still advisable to stick to private tours, hire cars and metered taxis. If you hire a car, plan your route before setting out and always carry a map – the system of one-way streets and snaking highways can be utterly bewildering.

ORIENTATION

The once-prosperous **central business district** (**CBD**) is today a hectic muddle of abandoned office blocks, market stalls and concrete flyovers. Crime remains a problem here and most businesses have moved out to the safer northern suburbs, although recent regeneration projects are starting to draw back investment. A visit to the city centre is well worthwhile for an insight into how Johannesburg has developed over the decades, although it is recommended that you go on an organized tour.

Johannesburg's affluent northern suburbs are in the hills to the north of the CBD. Clustered around the main freeway to Tshwane (Pretoria), the M1, they feel far removed from the hectic bustle of the centre. Of these, **Sandton** is effectively a city centre in its own right, with its own clutch of gleaming skyscrapers. This is where many of the business and financial institutes (including the Johannesburg Stock Exchange) moved to from the CBD in the 1990s. These are the safest areas in the city and home to most of the city's tourist accommodation, restaurants and shopping malls.

The largest of Johannesburg's suburbs feels very different. The infamous township of **Soweto** lies southwest of the city, named because of its location – South West Township. Soweto is linked to the city by a number of freeways that carry hundreds of thousands of commuters to the city centre and northern suburbs each day. Adjoining Soweto to the south, are smaller townships where other communities were relocated during Apartheid; coloured people were forced to move to **Eldorado Park**, and Indians were moved to **Lenasia**.

BEST TIME TO VISIT

The area in which Johannesburg and Tshwane (Pretoria) are located is known as the Highveld, a high plateau with an average altitude of over 1500 m. Generally summer days are warm and wind-free and winter days are cool, crisp and clear. But the weather here can be extreme. The middle of summer, from December to February, can get very hot, and is when most of the yearly rain falls, characterized by spectacular electric storms. Temperatures drop in the middle of winter and, during July and August, evenings are cold and frosts are common.

TOURIST INFORMATION

Gauteng Tourism ⓘ *1 Central Pl, corner of Jeppe and Henry Nxumalo streets, Newtown, T011-639 1600, www.gauteng.net, Mon-Fri 0800-1700*, is responsible for information for the whole province. It has a small selection of maps and brochures, and the staff are very helpful and will advise you on sites and attractions. There are also kiosks in the Mall of Rosebank at the **African Craft Market** ⓘ *T011-327 2000, open 0900-1800*, **Sandton City** ⓘ *T011-784 9596, open 0900-1800*, and **OR Tambo International Airport** ⓘ *T011-390 3614, open 0600-2200*. All have a selection of maps and brochures and can help with accommodation. **Johannesburg Tourism** ⓘ *Grosvenor Corner, 195 Jan Smuts Av, Parktown, T011-214 0700, www.joburgtourism.co.za, Mon-Fri 0800-1700, Sat 0900-1300*, has limited information but an excellent website. The **City Council** ⓘ *www.joburg.org.za*, also has tourist information on its excellent website, which covers every aspect of the city.

→ BACKGROUND

After the discovery of gold in 1886, Johannesburg grew rapidly, and was named after two men; Johannes Meyer and Johannes Rissik, who both worked for the Pretoria government in land surveying and mapping. Capital poured into the new settlement, drawing Africans away from rural land, and by 1895 almost 100,000 people lived in Johannesburg and the mines employed more than 75,000. Building went on all over the city and the railways, electricity and telephones had all arrived by the end of the 19th century.

Much of modern Johannesburg's fabric was formed by the actions of the Apartheid regime from the mid-1950s. The thriving multiracial conurbation was changed dramatically with the advent of the Group Areas Act, which forcibly relocated the city's black population from the centre to specially built townships outside town, such as Soweto. The most infamous forced removal was the bulldozing of an area to the west of Johannesburg called Sophiatown. This was an area of slum housing near to the city centre and was home to a diverse population of Africans, coloureds and 'poor whites'. During the 1940s and 1950s there was a huge outburst of a new African urban culture in Sophiatown, based mainly on the influence of American jazz musicians. This cultural explosion attracted bohemian whites and a huge number of African writers, journalists and politicians. To the Apartheid planners, the area stood for everything they opposed. In the mid-1950s the entire population was removed and the bulldozers were sent in. A new white suburb was built over the ruins and, in a gesture that was crass even by the standards of Apartheid, they named the new suburb Triomf – Afrikaans for 'triumph'. In 2006, the name was changed back to Sophiatown.

After the mid-1980s this forced movement of Africans from the city centre to the townships was reversed. The breakdown of influx controls such as Pass Laws, which were banished in 1986, led to the rapid growth of the African population in Johannesburg's city centre, especially in Hillbrow, which has one of Africa's highest population densities. Since the end of Apartheid this trend has continued and has been bolstered by the arrival of new immigrants from outside South Africa's borders. Tens of thousands of Nigerians, Congolese and Zimbabweans have flooded, often illegally, into the centre, suburbs and townships.

The inner city suffered from much-documented soaring crime rates in the 1990s, and it became a lawless place that was often dubbed the most dangerous city in the world. It witnessed a mass migration of business and offices as they moved out to the northern suburbs, leaving the high-rise buildings in much of the CBD abandoned, or hijacked by slum landlords for use as informal housing.

But today much is being done to reverse the trend. Massive raids on apartment blocks in Hillbrow have ousted thousands of illegal immigrants, an extensive network of CCTV cameras has been installed on every street corner, a Metro police force was established and numerous regeneration projects have made the city centre far more attractive and considerably safer. The first of these regenerated areas was Newtown, where the streets were pedestrianized and Mary Fitzgerald Square upgraded; the area is now filled with restaurants and shops and is attracting businesses back to the centre. This acted as a model for other parts of town, and there have been many more city improvement projects. In 2003, Johannesburg was 'twinned' with New York. In fact, during the preparation for the 2010 FIFA World Cup™, the city enlisted the advice of former mayor of New York Rudolph Giuliani to assist in combating crime.

While improved security is drawing back visitors, it's still sensible to take common sense precautions. Johannesburg's centre cannot yet be casually explored on foot, and the best way of seeing the sights is on a guided tour.

→ PLACES IN JOHANNESBURG

CITY CENTRE
After a huge regeneration project, the **Newtown Precinct** ⓘ *www.newtown.co.za, for information contact Gauteng Tourism, page 205*, on Mary Fitzgeral Square, has once again become the cultural heart of the CBD. Newtown originally started out as a racially mixed working-class district where bricks were manufactured. In the late 1890s, the brickworks were removed to make way for the first railway marshalling yard in Johannesburg. Working-class people of all races continued to live in the area up until 1906 when the Johannesburg City Council forcibly removed the African and Indian residents. They were relocated to a camp south of Johannesburg near the sewerage works called Klipspruit, which was the first section of the township known today as Soweto. This was the first forced removal to take place in Gauteng.

Today Newtown is dominated by Mary Fitzgerald Square, which is a smart, landscaped, 11,000-sq-m square lined with shops and cafés and a number of attractions including the Market Theatre Complex, Museum Africa and Newtown Park. It is named after the first woman to become a member of Johannesburg's city council in 1921, who was also a champion for women's rights, which led to the achievement of the women's right to vote in 1930. The square has parking facilities and the best way to approach Newtown is from Braamfontein in the north by the impressive Nelson Mandela Bridge. This 284-m steel-cable bridge with its distinctive white columns spans over 40 railway lines, and was opened in 2003 by Mandela as part of his 85th birthday celebrations.

On the north side of the square next to Museum Africa (see below), is the **Market Theatre Complex**. As well as the theatre, which is one of the best and most established in Gauteng, there are a couple of popular restaurants and bars, including **Gramadoelas**, and stalls strung along the street selling Zulu beadwork, jewellery and crafts. At weekends, the market expands into the square, which also holds special events and occasional live music and can accommodate 30,000 people. It was the principal fanpark during the 2010 FIFA World Cup™. To the south of Mary Fitzgerald Square is the small but attractive **Newtown Park**. The most popular attraction here is **Bassline**, Johannesburg's premier venue for live jazz. Even if not visiting the club, outside is a lovely statue of soulful barefooted legendary singer Brenda Fassie leaning into a microphone. You can sit on the seat next to her for a photo. To the east of the square and park, look out for the enormous **Turbine Hall**, on the corner of Jeppe and

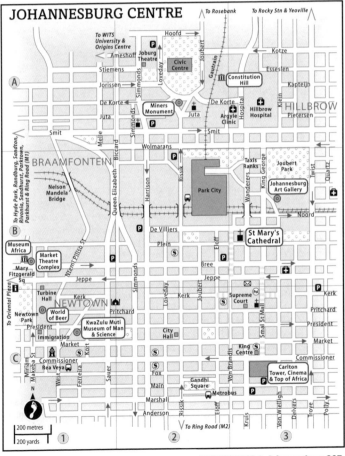

ON THE ROAD
City of gold

The high plateau on which Johannesburg was built was originally an arid place inhabited by a few Boer farmers grazing cattle and cultivating maize and wheat. This harsh and isolated landscape was transformed after the discovery of gold in 1886. During the 1880s, prospectors began arriving in the Eastern Transvaal attracted by reports of gold in Barberton and the mountains of the Eastern Drakensberg. George Harrison arrived from the Cape and travelled north to look at an abandoned gold mine on a farm in the Witwatersrand. He was employed to build a farmhouse at Langlaagte but in his free time he continued his search for gold. He discovered Main Reef in March 1886 and travelled to Pretoria to register his claim. Within weeks hordes of prospectors and fortune hunters began to arrive and officials of the Pretoria government were quickly sent to inspect the diggings and to lay out plans for a town.

Johannesburg expanded at a phenomenal rate and within three years had become the largest town in the eastern Transvaal. Confidence in Johannesburg's future was so great that traders in other regions of South Africa dismantled their wood and corrugated-iron buildings and transported the component parts to reassemble them in the new boom town. The *Star* newspaper relocated to Johannesburg from Grahamstown and transported its printing press across the veld by ox wagon. The gold rush attracted people from all over the world and Johannesburg became a cosmopolitan town where vast fortunes could be made overnight. Gambling dens, brothels and riotous canteens lined the streets and hundreds of ox-drawn wagons arrived daily to deliver food, drink and building supplies.

The mines expanded as new technologies opened up the deeper deposits of gold and Johannesburg was gradually transformed from being a gold rush boom town to being a large modern industrial city.

Miriam Makeba streets. The original building was the coal-fired Jeppe Street Power Station, which was built in 1927 and extended in 1934 to keep pace with Johannesburg's growing electricity demand. It was decommissioned in the mid-1960s, after which it fell into disrepair, but was restored in 2005 and today is a conference and event venue and HQ for one of the mining companies. It's a fine example of Johannesburg's industrial architecture.

Museum Africa ① *Old Market Building, 121 Bree St, T011-833 5624, Tue-Sun 0900-1700, free*, is housed in the city's former fruit and vegetable market, which was built in 1913. One of the city's major museums, it attempts to explain the black experience of living in Johannesburg. There are displays on the struggle for democracy and on life in the goldmines and the townships, with mock-ups of both a mine tunnel and an informal settlement. On the second floor is a gallery dedicated to San rock art and the most popular gallery is called 'Tried for Treason', with some interesting original editions of newspapers dating from treason trials in the 1960s, although the displays pale in comparison next to those of the Apartheid Museum (see page 210). Perhaps most rewarding is the ground floor gallery, with changing temporary exhibitions, including some excellent photography shows. There is a small café and gift shop by the entrance.

South African Breweries' (SAB) **World of Beer** ① *15 President St, T011-836 4900, www. worldofbeer.co.za, Tue-Sat 1000-1800, over 18 years of age, R30 including 2 complimentary beers, pub lunches available 1100-1600*, will appeal to anyone who enjoys the golden nectar. SAB dominate the African beer industry and control many local breweries throughout southern and eastern Africa and now own Miller Lite in the US. Their flagship lager, Castle, is probably the most popular beer between Cape Town and Cairo. The 90-minute tour covers the brewing process, a greenhouse that nurtures ingredients, and a variety of mock-up bars from a township *shebeen* to a honky-tonk pub from Johannesburg's mining camps.

The **KwaZulu Muti Museum of Man and Science** ① *corner of Diagonal (14) and President St, T011-836 4470, Mon-Fri 0730-1700, Sat 0730-1300*, isn't actually a museum but a *muti* shop, which has been on this site since 1897. *Muti* is a form of witchcraft practised exclusively by witch doctors, and this shop is crammed with products used in traditional herbal medicine and magic. The ingredients on sale include leaves, seeds and bark, as well as more specialized items such as monkey skulls, dried crocodiles and ostrich feet.

Further east between Marshall and Commissioner streets, Gandhi Square is the main terminus for the Metrobus in the CBD. Built in 1893 as Government Square, it was renamed after Mahatma Gandhi in 1999 and was completely refurbished in 2002. Gandhi came to Johannesburg in 1902 and worked as a lawyer and civil rights activist. There's a statue of him in his lawyer's robes, carrying a law book, and there are plaques around the square telling the history of his time in South Africa.

To get a feel for why locals call Johannesburg the Manhattan of Africa, head to the **Top of Africa** ① *Carlton Tower, access is on the 2nd floor of the Carlton Centre shopping mall, between Commissioner and Main streets, Mon-Fri 0900-1800, Sat 0900-1700, Sun 0900-1400, R15, children (under 12) R10, the mall has a multi-storey car park*. Amidst the hectic high-rises and run-down office blocks in the CBD, the soaring 223-m-tall Carlton Tower is a popular stop-off for tours. The lift whisks visitors up to the 50th floor, from where a glass-fronted lookout deck is wrapped around the building. The views are astounding, the glittering grid of skyscrapers tapering out to an endless urban sprawl. There are good views of the few remaining historical buildings left in the centre, such as City Hall (1915) and the post office (1897), and on an exceptionally clear day you can see the Voortrekker Monument on the northern horizon. There is a little curio shop and a café.

Constitution Hill ① *1 Kotze St, Braamfontein, T011-381 3100, www.constitutionhill.org. za, Mon-Fri 0900-1700, Sat 1000-1400, R30, children (under 16) R15, the complex is completely wheelchair accessible*, is the site of the notorious Old Fort Prison Complex (to the north of the centre). Opened in 2004, this is another of Johannesburg's excellent contemporary museums and, in a similar way to the Apartheid Museum, it uses multimedia tools to display its exhibits. Known as Number Four, the old prison, which only closed in the 1980s, was known for holding hundreds of blacks in appalling overcrowded conditions; most had been arrested for not carrying their pass books. Illustrious prisoners include Nelson Mandela, Mahatma Gandhi and many of the leading anti-Apartheid activists. You can wander around the complex yourself or there are regular tours, which include a film about Mandela's time here, a tour of the women's gaol and a photo exhibition of ex-inmates and wardens. You can still see graffiti on the backs of the cell doors and the giant pots that prisoners ate simple porridge from. South Africa's Constitutional Court has been built here and some of the bricks from the old prison were used in the new court to demonstrate the injustice of the past being used towards justice in the future.

Not far from Constitution Hill, at the top of Rissik Street, is the Miner's Monument. The bronze statue of three giant miners in shorts, hard hats and gum boots holding a giant drill was erected by the Chamber of Mines in 1964. The Civic Centre and Joburg Theatre are just to the north of here.

In the east of the CBD, the **Johannesburg Art Gallery** ① *Joubert Park, King George St, T011-725 3130, Tue-Sun 1000-1700, free, bookshop, café, parking in front of the gallery*, is a treasure trove of valuable art and houses collections of 17th-century Dutch paintings, 18th- and 19th-century British and European art, 19th-century South African works, a large contemporary collection of 20th-century local and international art, and a print cabinet containing works from the 15th century to the present. The initial collection was put together by Sir Hugh Lane, and exhibited in London in 1910, before being brought to South Africa. The collection is larger than that of the National Gallery in Cape Town (page 46), and notable works include those by Pablo Picasso, Claude Monet and Henry Moore.

OUTSIDE THE CITY CENTRE

Apartheid Museum ① *next to Gold Reef City, corner of Northern Parkway and Gold Reef Rd, Ormonde, T011-390 4700, www.apartheidmuseum.org, Tue-Sun 1000-1700, entry R50, children (under 16) R35 (not suitable for children under 11)*. Twenty years ago, few people would have believed that a museum about Apartheid could ever exist. Today, this is the most critically acclaimed museum in the country and an excellent insight to what South Africa – past and present – is all about. This extraordinarily powerful museum was officially opened by Nelson Mandela in April 2002 and is the city's leading tourist attraction. The museum is divided into 'spaces' which follow the birth of Apartheid to the present day. When paying your entry fee you are issued with a random white or non-white ticket that takes you through two different entry points to symbolize segregation. The building itself has an innovative design to reflect the cold subject of Apartheid – harsh concrete, raw brick, steel bars and barbed wire.

The museum begins with a 15-minute film, taking you briefly through Voortrekker history to the Afrikaner government of 1948 which implemented Apartheid. The 'spaces' are dedicated to the rise of nationalism in 1948, pass laws, segregation, the first response from townships such as Sharpeville and Langa, the forced removals and the implementation of the Group Areas Act. From here, exhibits cover the rise of Black Consciousness, the student uprisings in Soweto in 1976, and political prisoners and executions.

The reforms during the 1980s and 1990s are well documented, including President FW DeKlerk's un-banning of political parties, Mandela's release, the 1994 election, sanction lifting, and the new constitution. One of the most interesting 'spaces' is the House of Bondage, named after a book of photographs published in 1967 by Ernest Cole and banned in South Africa at the time. A white photographer, he managed to class himself as coloured in order to go into the townships and take the pictures. The black and white photographs are both tragic and beautiful. The exhibitions effectively use multimedia, such as television screens, recorded interviews and news footage, all providing a startlingly clear picture of the harshness and tragedy of the Apartheid years. Allow at least two to three hours for a visit.

Johannesburg Zoo ① *corner Jan Smuts Av and Upper Park Drive, Parkview, T011-646 2000, www.jhbzoo.org.za, open 0830-1730, last ticket 1600, R50, children (3-12) R30, golf carts can be hired, restaurant*, was established in 1904 and covers 54 ha of parkland with spacious vegetated enclosures surrounded by moats and trees. The zoo is home to over 2000 animals from 355 species. Among other animals, there are the big cats, elephants, gorillas, chimpanzees and the only polar bears in Africa. The ponds attract free-ranging aquatic birds, which come here to breed. There is also a petting farm for children and the pre-booked night tours to see the nocturnal animals are fun, ending with marshmallows and hot chocolate around a bonfire.

Across Jan Smuts Avenue from the zoo, **Zoo Lake** ① *sunrise-sunset, rowing boats, Tue-Sun 0930-1630, 6 per boat, R8 per person*, is a large, lovely well-established park with manicured lawns and lots of trees. It was first laid out 1904, and during Apartheid the park and the zoo remained open to all races. The lake's Coronation Fountain was built in 1937 to commemorate the coronation of King George VI, and in 1956, as part of Johannesburg's 70th birthday celebrations, Margot Fonteyn danced Swan Lake in front of the lake. It's popular for picnics, jogging, dog-walking and duck-feeding; the Muslim community come here each year to celebrate Eid at the end of Ramadan, and it is the venue for the annual Carols by Candlelight in December. Rowing boats are for hire, there's a large open-air swimming pool, tennis courts, a bowling club, a tea garden and a couple of restaurants including **Moyo**.

Near Johannesburg Zoo is the **South African National Museum of Military History** ① *20 Erlswold Way, Saxonwold, T011-646 5513, www.ditsong.org.za, 0900-1630, R22, children (under 16) R11*, which has exhibits on the role South African forces played in the Second World War, including artillery pieces, aircraft and tanks. There is a more up-to-date section illustrating the war in Angola with displays of modern armaments, including captured Soviet tanks and French Mirage fighter planes. In the section on Umkhonto we Sizwe (the ANC's armed wing), *CASSPIRS*, the formidable armoured personnel carriers used by security forces in the townships during black uprisings against Apartheid, are on display.

Origins Centre ① *Wits University, Yale Rd, Braamfontein, T011-717 4700, www.origins. org.za, open 0900-1700, R70, children (under 12) R35, café and book/curio shop*, is another of Johannesburg's excellent new attractions. It is run by Wits's Rock Art Research Institute, which has over the last few decades been very much involved in the archaeological sites to the northwest of the city in the Cradle of Humankind (see page 215). The museum covers archaeological and genetic materials relating to the origins of humankind. There are displays of tools made by early man that show how they were made, as well as their spiritual significance. There are also examples of South Africa's ancient rock paintings and engravings, and their supposed meanings, with a large part of the display dedicated to the beliefs of the San (Bushmen). There's a film of the San retreating into their spiritual world through trance which is both vivid and a little disturbing. The final exhibit focuses on how genetic testing can contribute to understanding our ancestry and visitors can add their own DNA to a world database.

Gold Reef City ① *Northern Parkway, Ormonde, T011-248 6800, www.goldreefcity.co.za, Wed-Sun 0930-1700, Story of Jozi, 2-hr guided tours 0900, 1000, 1100, 1400 and 1500, R230, children (under 6) R130 (excludes mine tour), theme park rides, R150, family combination tickets available*, is built on the site of one of Johannesburg's gold mining areas, but today has developed into a garish theme park with rides, amusement arcades and a gaudy casino. Of greater interest is the Story of Jozi tour, which takes you around the restored miners' cottages with staff dressed in period costume, and includes a gold-pouring demonstration and a tour of the gold mine. The tour drops to a depth of about 220 m, taking you down No 14 Shaft, which opened in 1897 and closed in 1971, and was one of the richest deposits of gold in its day.

Liliesleaf Farm ① *7 George Av, Rivonia, T011-803 7882, www.liliesleaf.co.za, Mon-Fri 0900-1700, Sat-Sun 0900-1600, guided tours take 1-2 hrs, last tour 1600, R60, children (3-16) R35*, now a museum, is where in the 1960s the most prominent leaders of South Africa's struggle from the then-banned ANC and Communist Party sought shelter and attended meetings. These included Nelson Mandela, Govan Mbeki and Walter Sisulu, among many others. Although today it's surrounded by Johannesburg's northern suburbs, it was once an isolated rural spot and the farm was fronted by 'white owners', Arthur Goldreich, a member of the Communist Party, and his family. On 11 July 1963, a meeting was held by Umkhonto we Sizwe or the MK (meaning 'spear of the nation' and the ANC's armed wing) to discuss Operation Mayibuye, a plot to overthrow the Apartheid government. However, the police had been tipped off that Walter Sisulu was at the farm and it was raided. Sisulu and just about the entire leadership of the MK were arrested (Mandela had been arrested six months earlier in KwaZulu Natal). This led to what became known as the Rivonia Trials in late 1963, and the subsequent imprisonment of the ANC's leaders. Today you can walk around the farm – there are exhibits in the main house and outbuildings – and watch a short film.

SOWETO

The most popular excursion from Johannesburg is to the (in)famous township of Soweto, lying 13 km southwest of Johannesburg city centre. Soweto has mushroomed into a city in its own right, it covers 135 sq km and is home to around one million people. Short for South West Township, people first moved here in 1904 from Sophiatown where there was an outbreak of plague. The township increased in size dramatically in the 1950s and 1960s when black people were forced to relocate from the city centre into designated areas outside the city. Since then, the population has soared, bolstered by immigrants from rural areas, as well as from Nigeria, Mozambique, Zimbabwe and other African countries.

Despite its reputation, Soweto feels remarkably ordinary. Large areas are given over to tidy rows of affluent suburban houses. As in any other South African city, there are districts and suburbs and shopping centres. The streets are well maintained, there are banks and golf courses and the giant FNB Soccer City, which was fully overhauled for the 2010 FIFA World Cup™. Yellow commuter Metrorail trains trundle to Johannesburg and Mercedes cruise

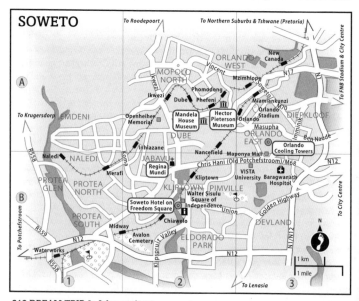

between smart homes with well-tended gardens and satellite dishes. Soweto allegedly has the highest concentration of millionaires in the country and one of the most successful BMW dealerships, and is now home to one of Johannesburg's largest shopping malls, **Maponya Mall**, on Chris Hani (Old Potchefstroom) Road. The flip-side, however, much like any other city in the country, is that there are also still areas of squatter camps and informal housing, where unemployment is as high as 90% and people have to share amenities like taps and toilets. The government is constantly trying to improve the situation by building two-room rudimentary houses to replace the shacks, but efforts are hampered by the thousands of people who flood into Soweto every month, fleeing rural poverty and desperate for jobs.

Arriving in Soweto These days it is quite feasible to visit Soweto independently – for drivers, the roads are clearly marked and the museums are well signposted and have safe parking, especially those in Orlando West, such as the Hector Pieterson Museum and the nearby Mandela House Museum. The Maponya Mall and Orlando Cooling Towers are easily accessed off the Chris Hani (Old Potchefstroom) Road, and are a short drive from its intersection with the N1. Nevertheless, a half-day guided tour is still the most convenient and productive way to visit Soweto, and most take in a handful of important historical sites, with perhaps a visit to an informal settlement and a township shebeen for lunch.

Places in Soweto Hector Pieterson Museum ① *Khumalo and Pela streets, Orlando West, T011-536 2253, Mon-Sat 1000-1700, Sun 1000-1600, R25, children (under 13) free,* is a modern museum standing two blocks away from where 13-year-old Hector Pierterson was shot dead by riot police during a school demonstration on 16 June 1976. The children had been demonstrating about the use of Afrikaans as the dominant language in education, before the police opened fire and killed more than 170 students. This event, captured on camera by a photojournalist in an image that shocked the world, sparked the final 10-year battle against Apartheid causing townships across the country to rise up in bitter revolt. (The incident is now known as the Soweto Uprising and the 16 June, Youth Day, is a public holiday. Outside the museum is a memorial to Hector, marked by the iconic photograph of his body being carried by a friend with Hector's wailing 17-year-old sister running alongside. The inscription on the memorial reads: "To honour the youth who gave their lives in the struggle for democracy and freedom".

This incredibly moving and powerful museum is similar to the Apartheid Museum in that it uses multimedia exhibits, films, newspapers, personal accounts and photographs to piece together what happened on and around that date. The exhibit route follows a loop around a central courtyard where the names of all the children who died are inscribed on a granite bed. Strategically placed windows allow visitors to look out on buildings and streets where the events of the day unfolded, including Orlando Stadium where the ill-fated demonstration was supposed to, but never did, finish. One of the tour guides is Antoinette Sithole – Hector's sister who was in the photograph. There is an excellent museum bookshop with dozens of interesting books on South Africa.

Mandela House Museum ① *8115 Vilakazi St, Orlando West, T011-936 7754, www. mandelahouse.co.za, Mon-Fri 0900-1700, Sat-Sun 0930-1630, R60, children (under 16) R20, tour guides are available at no extra charge, allow 40 mins for the tour,* is a short walk from the Hector Pieterson Museum. This is where Nelson Mandela lived before he was incarcerated. He moved into the diminutive four-roomed house in 1946 with his first wife, Evelyn Mase, and in 1958 brought his second wife, Winnie, to live with him. He was, however, to spend little time here in the ensuing years, as his role in struggle activities became all-consuming and he was forced underground in 1961 until his arrest in 1962. Winnie Madikizela-Mandela, herself imprisoned several times, lived in the house with her daughters while Nelson Mandela was in jail, until her own exile to Brandfort in 1977, where she remained under house arrest until 1986. Mandela said of the house in his autobiography, Long Walk to Freedom: *"It was the opposite of grand, but it was my first true home of my own and I was mightily proud. A man is not a man until he has a house of his own."* Mandela insisted on moving back to the house on his release from prison in 1990. But after only 11 days, its small size and the difficulty of keeping it secure put too much of a strain on him and he moved out of the township to a larger house in Houghton where he still lives with his third wife, Graca Machel who he married on his 80th birthday in 1998.

The house was opened as a museum by Winnie in 1997 and for many years it displayed an odd collection of Mandela's personal effects. It's now in the hands of the Soweto Heritage Trust who refurbished it in 2008 to what it looked like in the 1950s, with bare concrete floors and a corrugated-tin roof, and it displays information about his time in the house. Further down the street is the home of Archbishop Desmond Tutu, hidden behind high walls. **Vilakazi Street** is the only street in the world to have been home to two Nobel Peace Prize winners, Nelson Mandela and Desmond Tutu.

To the southwest, off Chris Hani (Old Potchesfstroom) Road, the **Regina Mundi Catholic Cathedral** ① *1149 Khumalo St, T011-986 2546, 0800-1700,* is also worth visiting. An ordinary 1960s-built construction, this, the largest church in Soweto, was an important site of demonstrations in the 1980s. You can still see bullet holes in the ceiling, a lasting testament to shots fired by police at fleeing school children as they tried to take refuge inside during the 1976 Soweto Uprising.

From Old Chris Hani (Old Potchefstroom) Road, turn south into Klipspruit Valley Road to reach **Walter Sisulu Square** ① *corner Klipspruit Valley and Union roads, Kliptown, T011-945 2200, www.waltersisulusquare.co.za.* This is where the Freedom Charter, calling for equality for all, was presented by the ANC to a mass gathering of people in 1955. The square, which used to be called Freedom Square, was renamed after one of the delegates, Walter Sisulu, when he died in 2003. The authorities broke up the illegal gathering but the charter was adopted as a guiding document, and it remains the cornerstone of ANC policy to this day; it is seen by many as the foundation of South Africa's 1996 Constitution. Back in 1955 it was just a dusty patch of land, but in 2003 was redeveloped into an attractive paved square housing a number of monuments. These include the 10 Pillars of the Freedom Charter: 10 giant slabs of concrete representing the clauses of the Freedom Charter, and the red-brick conical Freedom Charter Monument. Additionally, there are a few market stalls, shops and restaurants lining the square and the **Soweto Hotel on Freedom Square**.

Finally, Soweto's boldest attraction are the two 100-m-high **Orlando cooling towers** on Dynamo Street, on the north side of Chris Hani (Old Potchefstroom) Road in Orlando West. They have long been a landmark and are part of a now-disued power station that was built in the 1950s to provide central Johannesburg with electricity (even though Soweto didn't get electricity until 1986). The power station closed in 1998, long after its intended lifespan and, in 2003, the First National Bank (FNB) sponsored the painting of the towers. One is painted with the FNB's logo, while the second tower is painted with a fantastic vivid mural of life in Soweto, with cartoon characters of musicians, children playing, a woman selling her wares on a stall, minibus taxis, a Metrorail train, a football stadium, Baragwanath Hospital, a Madonna and child which represents the Regina Mundi Catholic Church, and of course a figure of a smiling and waving Nelson Mandela in one of his trademark African print shirts. The largest hand-painted mural in South Africa, it took six months to create, and the 100-m-high scaffolding around the tower was dropped into place by helicopter. The mural has become iconic, not only to Soweto but to Johannesburg as a whole.

Apart from admiring the mural, the other reason to come to the cooling towers is the **Orlando Towers Adventure Centre** ⓘ *T011-312 0450, www.orlandotowers.co.za, Fri-Sun 0900-1700, bungee jump R480, power swing R360, internal swing R360, abseil R260, viewing platform only R60.* Opened in 2008, there is a 100-m lift on one of the towers, and a number of bungee jumps and power swings inside and out. The less adventurous can go up to the viewing platform at the top. This is not for the faint-hearted – the lift is open air and the last 3 m to the top is by a sort of suspended stairway as the top of the tower curves outwards. Nevertheless the views of Soweto are unbeatable.

AROUND JOHANNESBURG

There are a number of attractions to the northwest of Johannesburg that are within 40 minutes' drive from the northern suburbs and offer an alternative to the urban sights. They are also en route from Johannesburg to the Magaliesberg Mountains (see page 225) in the North West Province. These can just as easily be visited from Tshwane (Pretoria) on a day trip.

The **Lion Park** ⓘ *on the R512, 17 km northwest of Randburg and 9 km south of Lanseria Airport, T011-691 9905, www.lion-park.com, Mon-Fri 0830-1700, Sat-Sun 0830-1800, self-drive R130, children (4-12) R70, guided game drives R195, children (4-12) R120, family discounts available, restaurant and curio shop,* en route to Lesedi (see below), is worth a stop for the excellent photo opportunities. There are over 85 lions in the park, including many cubs and a rare pride of white lions. Although they are bred in captivity, they are well cared for and have ample room in the drive-through enclosures. The lions are accustomed to vehicles and don't think twice about strolling right up to a car. Keep windows at least half closed. Other animals kept here include hyenas, cheetah and a variety of antelope. Walks and close encounters with cubs are on offer and you can climb a tower to feed giraffes.

At **Lesedi Cultural Village** ⓘ *on the R512, 12 km north of Lanseria Airport, T012-205 1394, www.lesedi.com, tours at 1130 and 1630, R390 per person including lunch or dinner, or R250 excluding lunch or dinner, children (6-12) half-price (under 5s) free,* four African villages have been recreated from the Xhosa, Zulu, Pedi and Sotho tribes. The three-hour tours include an audio-visual presentation on all aspects of tribal life of the 11 ethnic groups that live in South Africa, as well as music, singing and traditional dancing from over 60 performers around a large fire in an amphitheatre. The morning tour concludes with lunch, and the afternoon tour finishes with dinner of game meat such as impala or crocodile. Lesedi is the Sotho word for 'light'. For those who wish to extend the experience, there is mid-range accommodation in traditional bomas or rondavels decorated with Ndebele crafts.

Approximately 40 km to the northwest of Johannesburg is a region dubbed the **Cradle of Humankind** ⓘ *www.cradleofhumankind.co.za,* thanks to thousands of humanoid and animal fossils being unearthed over recent decades. It holds some of the world's most important archaeological sites, revealing over 40% of all hominid fossils ever discovered and rivals Tanzania's Olduvai Gorge in significance. The 470-sq-km area was declared a UNESCO World Heritage Site in 1999.

Seven kilometres from the Sterkfontein Caves (see below) on the R24, **Maropeng** ① *T014-577 9000, www.maropeng.co.za, 0900-1700, last boat ride 1600, R115, children (4-14) R65, combination tickets with Sterkfontein Caves R190, children (4-14) R110 (available until 1300 to allow visitors to get to both sites)*, meaning 'returning to the place of origin' in the Setswana language, is an interactive museum that tells the story of the creation of our world and the evolution of man over a four billion-year period; another of Johannesburg's excellent cutting-edge museums that uses computer wizardry and multimedia displays. The entrance has been built as a grassy burial mound, while the exit is a sleek structure of modern glass and concrete and the journey from one to the other takes the visitor from the birth of planet earth to where we are today. The first experience is a boat ride through a tunnel of erupting volcanoes, icebergs, an eye of a storm and swirling gases that made up the planet. It's rather magical and the sounds and temperatures are lifelike, but be warned that it may frighten very small children. Once off the boat the series of exhibits start from how the earth was formed, early life forms and the emergence of man, and go through to cover topics on how man has changed the environment, such as population explosion, use of the earth's resources and global appetite. Towards the end is a large display of photographs of people's faces from all over the world and a mesmerizing series of images of man's achievements are flashed on a giant screen, covering everything from man inventing the wheel to landing on the moon. Allow at least two to three hours for the experience and there are three restaurants on site.

Although the dolomite hill holding the **Sterkfontein Caves** ① *T014-577 9000, www.maropeng.co.za, 0900-1700, guided tours run every 30 mins, last tour 1600, R120, children (4-14) R70, combination tickets with Maropeng R190, children (4-14) R110 (available until 1300 to allow visitors to get to both sites)*, was discovered in the late 19th century, it was not until 1936 that the most important find was made, the first adult skull of the ape man *Australopithecus africanus* – 'Mrs Ples' for short. The skull is estimated to be over 2.6 million years old, and was found by Dr Robert Broom. Even older hominid remains have been found here since. The caves consist of six chambers connected by passages. Tours begin in the impressive multimedia visitor centre, which includes comprehensive exhibitions on our ancestors, with displays of life-sized hominid replicas and a large amphitheatre. Tours then pass through the six caves, taking in the archaeological sites. There is a craft market and a restaurant on site. **Note** Wear comfortable shoes and be prepared for a lot of stairs. The caves are off the R563, off the N14 from Randburg towards Hartbeespoort Dam.

Off the R563, 7 km to the northeast of Sterkfontein Caves, or off the R512, 2 km north of Lanseria Airport, turn left at the Kromdraai sign for 13 km for the **Rhino and Lion Nature Reserve** ① *T011-957 0349, www.rhinolion.co.za, 0800-1600, lion feeding Sat-Sun 1300, R100, children (3-12) R70*, also in the Cradle of Humankind region. This private 1600-ha game park which opened in 1985 with just two white rhinos is today home to more than 600 animals including buffalo, lion, white rhino, wild dog, cheetah, hippo, crocodile and more than 20 species of antelope. Around 200 species of bird occur here naturally. The predators are kept in separate enclosures and visitors can watch them being fed; there's a snake and reptile park and 'vulture restaurant'. Game drives in the reserve's open-topped vehicles depart from reception throughout the day.

JOHANNESBURG LISTINGS

WHERE TO STAY

$$$$ Melrose Arch, 1 Melrose Sq, Melrose Arch, T011-679 2994, www.africanpride hotels.com. Hip urban hotel with 117 stylish rooms, lots of chrome, bare-brick walls, mood-enhancing lighting, designer furniture. Smart bar and superb **March Restaurant** for gourmet food, unusual pool with underwater music. Great location.

$$$$ The Michelangelo, 135 West St, Sandton, T011-282 7000, www.michel angelo.co.za. One of the best luxury options of Sandton, with 242 super-luxury rooms, including a variety of giant suites, residents' lounge, restaurants, bar, heated pool, gym. Built around a Renaissance-style central atrium and makes up one side of the lovely Nelson Mandela Sq.

$$$$ Radisson Blu Hotel Sandton, corner Rivonia Rd and Daisy St, Sandton, T011-245 8000, www.radissonblu.com. Stylish new 5-star hotel in a commanding block with outstanding views of Sandton's high-rises. 290 rooms and 11 penthouses. The **Vivance** Italian restaurant, wine bar, spa, pool and deck are on the 8th floor.

$$$$ Saxon, 36 Saxon Rd, Sandhurst, T011-292 6000, www.thesaxon.com. Voted the 'World's Leading Boutique Hotel' every year since it opened in 2000, with 26 suites including one named after Nelson Mandela, who spent 7 months here working on his book *Long Walk to Freedom*. Beautifully decorated with African objets d'art, set in 2 ha of well-tended grounds, gigantic heated swimming pools, state-of-the-art gym, spa, restaurant, 2 wine cellars.

$ Backpackers Ritz, 1A North Rd, Dunkeld West, T011-325 7125, www. backpackers-ritz.co.za. Johannesburg's longest-established backpackers set in a large house in a leafy neighbourhood. Dorms and doubles, internet, bar, meals available, garden and pool. The travel desk can arrange all tours. Close to shops and entertainment at Hyde Park and Rosebank, all in a safe suburb, 30 mins from airport, free pickup. Call before leaving home.

$ Soweto Backpackers, 10823A Pooe St, Orlando West, T011-936 3444, www. sowetobackpackers.com. Also referred to as **Lebo's** after its charismatic owner, this is an excellent way to experience township life, especially if combined with one of their Soweto guided bike tours, and it's walking distance from the Hector Pieterson Museum and Vilakazi St. Dorms, doubles, camping in the garden, lively bar with great music, internet, kitchen, home-cooked meals.

RESTAURANTS

$$$ Browns of Rivonia, 21 Wessels St, Rivonia, T011-803 7533, www.browns.co.za. Sun-Fri 1200-1500, Mon-Sat 1800-2230. Pleasant setting in the courtyard of an old farmhouse, the menu includes roast lamb, salmon timbale, mustard sirloin and crêpes and you can choose your own cheese from the cheese room. Impressive wine list with some 30,000 bottles in the cellar.

$$$ Bukhara, Nelson Mandela Sq, Sandton City, T011-883 5555, www.bukhara.com. 1200-1500, 1800-2300. Inarguably the best Indian food in South Africa, this elegant restaurant at the entrance of the **Michelangelo Hotel** has a broad range of aromatic and flavoursome North Indian dishes, and you can watch the chefs in the glass-fronted kitchen.

$$$ Butcher Shop & Grill, Nelson Mandela Sq, Sandton City, T011-784 8676, www.the butchershop.co.za. Mon-Sat 1200-2245, Sun 1200-2145. Justifiably famous for its aged steaks served with a variety of sauces and you can choose your cut of meat from the butcher. Also seafood, vegetarian options, and a good range of starters and desserts.

There are other outlets around the country, but this is the original and gets through around 5 tons of steak each week.

$$$ Gramadoelas, Market Theatre Complex, Bree St, Newtown, T011-838 6960, www.gramadoelas.co.za. Tue-Sat 1200-1500, Mon-Sat 1800-2200. One of the best places to try African dishes is at this long-standing favourite, the ramshackle decor adds to the atmosphere. South African dishes include fried *mopani* worms, *sosaties* (spicy kebabs), and *bobotie* (sweet and spicy ground beef pie), and the menu features cuisine from as far afield as Ethiopia and Morocco. Also try home-brewed sorghum beer or *mageu* (fermented milk).

$$$ Moyo, Melrose Sq, Melrose Arch, T011-684 1477, www.moyo.co.za. Open 1100-2300. The original branch of the popular chain of upmarket African-themed restaurants appearing around South Africa. This outlet is in chi-chi Melrose Arch, and is spread over 3 floors, with rustic, candlelit ethno-fashionable decor, and pan-African cuisine, including superb Mozambique seafood, Moroccan tagines and South African game dishes. Live music in the evenings. There is also a branch in Zoo Lake Park near the zoo.

Cafés

Thrupps, corner Oxford and Rudd roads, Illovo, T011-268 0298, www.thrupps.co.za. Mon-Fri 0745-1800, Sat 0800-1400, Sun 0800-1300. Once located on President St in the CBD, Johannesburg's 'Grocers of Distinction' has been going strong since 1892 when it imported items for English immigrants – it still sells Gentleman's Relish, along with pâtés, pheasant, caviar, quail, goose, imported cheese and Scottish smoked salmon. The café does excellent breakfasts and freshly baked treats. Also does takeaway picnics.

SHOPPING MALLS

Johannesburg has more than 25 vast, modern shopping malls.

Hyde Park Corner, Jan Smuts Av, Hyde Park, T011-325 4340, www.hydeparkshopping. co.za. Mon-Sat 0900-1800, Sun 1000-1400. Luxury shopping aimed at ladies who lunch. The excellent **Exclusive Books** has its flagship outlet here, which often hosts book launches and literary events, and there are cinemas and the 132-room **Southern Sun Hyde Park Hotel ($$$)**, T011-341 8080, www.southernsun.com.

The Mall of Rosebank, between Cradock and Baker avenues, Rosebank, T011-788 5530, www.themallofrosebank.co.za. Mon-Fri 0900-1800, Sat 0900-1700, Sun 1000-1600. One of the more pleasant malls with a large open-air plaza lined with cafés. The Zone@Rosebank features stylish boutiques and music shops aimed at young people. Also home to the excellent **African Craft Market** (see above). The **Rooftop Market**, Sun 0900-1700, is upstairs in the multi-storey car park and is a very popular venue with Johannesburg residents on a Sun for its 600 stalls of crafts, jewellery, second-hand books, food and deli items.

Sandton City and Nelson Mandela Square, corner of Sandton Dr and Rivonia Rd (attached by a walkway and sky bridge), T011-883 2011, www.sandton-city.co.za; T011-217 6000, www.nelsonmandelas quare.com. Mon-Fri 0900-1800, Sat 0900-1700, Sun 1000-1600. Massive triple-storey mall featuring all of South Africa's chain stores, cinemas, African art galleries and hyper-markets. The opulent Nelson Mandela Sq has international exclusive stores and fashionable restaurants around an attractive piazza-style square, which is home to a formidable 6-m bronze statue of the great man himself. His shoes are 1 m across and children can sit on them.

TSHWANE TO SUN CITY

The name Pretoria was given to the new settlement by Marthinus Wessel Pretorius, in memory of his father, Andries Pretorius, who had led the Voortrekkers in the bloody massacre of the Zulus at Blood River. Today it is the administrative capital of South Africa and the third largest city in the country. Despite being almost joined to Johannesburg 56 km to the south by a band of green-belt towns, the atmosphere of each city couldn't be more different. While Johannesburg was built on gold and industry, Pretoria's was founded during the Voortrekker period of South Africa's turbulent past and retains a rather stern, bureaucratic atmosphere – albeit softened by a large student population. In 2000, it underwent a name change to Tshwane, which is now in common use on maps and signposts. While it is safer than Johannesburg, downtown Tshwane, like most major cities in South Africa, has gone through a transformation in recent years. With the demise of Apartheid, black South Africans are again permitted to live and work freely within the city centre, and it has much more of an African feel about it.

Stretching west to the historic town of Rustenburg are the gently rolling Magaliesberg Mountains, which, thanks to their proximity to Tshwane (Pretoria) and Johannesburg, are a popular weekend retreat. It's a scenic area for sports and outdoor pursuits and the mountains are ideal for hiking. This eastern region of the North West Province gets the lion's share of visitors, thanks to the extravagant attractions of Sun City and the excellent Pilanesberg Game Reserve, where stocks of game readily stand to attention for camera-toting safari enthusiasts.

→ ARRIVING IN TSHWANE

GETTING THERE
The centre of Tshwane (Pretoria) is 45 km from Johannesburg's OR Tambo International Airport. For details of arriving by air, see page 201. You can travel to/from the airport by using an airport shuttle bus service, or by the **Gautrain** (see box, page 203), which links both Tshwane (Pretoria) and Johannesburg and the airport via Sandton. The Pretoria Gautrain station is in the CBD adjacent to the main railway station on the corner of Scheiding and Paul Kruger streets, and Hatfield Station is on the corner of Grosvenor Road and Arcadia Street. Metrorail suburban trains run between Tshwane (Pretoria) and Johannesburg but high crime levels means you should generally avoid it. The central Metrorail station, as well as the terminal for the long-distance mainline buses (**Intercape**, **Greyhound** and **Translux**) are at the main railway station on the corner of Scheiding and Paul Kruger streets in the city centre.

MOVING ON
Most people will continue the itinerary to the Magaliesberg Mountains (see page 225) and then on to Sun City and Pilanesberg Game Reserve (see page 228) in a hired car, heading west out of Tshwane on the R104/R27.

GETTING AROUND
Most of Tshwane's sights are in the city centre or lie in the surrounding hills and can easily be seen in a day. While there is a good local bus service connecting the city centre and suburbs, it does not go to the various monuments, so the easiest way to get to these is either to hire a car or go on a guided tour. **Church Street** is Tshwane's main through road, running from east to west and, at 26 km long, is considered to be one of the world's longest streets. From

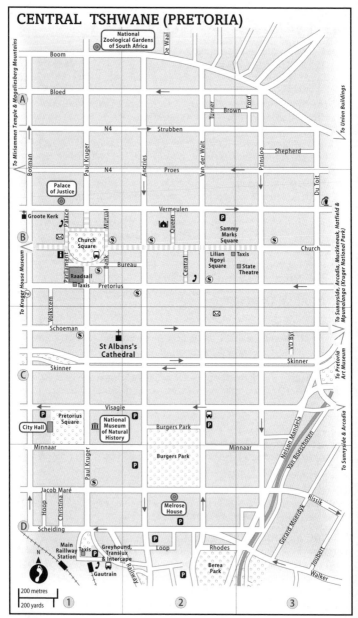

CENTRAL TSHWANE (PRETORIA)

National Zoological Gardens of South Africa

To Miriammen Temple & Magaliesberg Mountains

Boom

Bloed

De Waal

A

N4

Strubben

Turner

Ford

Brown

To Union Buildings

Paul Kruger

Bosman

N4

Andries

Proes

Van der Walt

Prinsloo

Shepherd

Du Toit

Palace of Justice

Vermeulen

Groote Kerk

Palace

Mutual

Queen

Sammy Marks Square

B

Church Square

Parliament

Bank

Bureau

Central

Church

Raadsaal

Taxis

Pretorius

Lilian Ngoyi Square

Taxis

State Theatre

Volkstem

Schoeman

St Albans's Cathedral

VD Byl

Skinner

To Kruger House Museum

C

Skinner

To Sunnyside, Arcadia, Muckleneuk, Hatfield & Mpumalanga (Kruger National Park)

To Pretoria Art Museum

Visagie

City Hall

Pretorius Square

National Museum of Natural History

Burgers Park

Nelson Mandela

Van Boeschoten

To Sunnyside & Arcadia

Minnaar

Minnaar

Burgers Park

Paul Kruger

Jacob Maré

Hoop

Christina

Melrose House

Rissik

Gerard Moerdyk

D

Scheiding

Main Railway Station

Taxis

Greyhound, Translux & Intercape

Loop

Rhodes

Berea Park

Joubert

Walker

N

Gautrain

Railway

200 metres
200 yards

1

2

3

the city centre it leads east to the suburbs of **Arcadia**, where many of the embassies and the Union Buildings are located, and to **Hatfield** and **Brooklyn**, a few kilometres further east. The city's colleges, universities and sports stadiums are located in this area, as well as the majority of the hotels and restaurants. Both are attractive suburbs, dotted with parks and gardens, and streets lined with Tshwane's distinctive jacaranda trees.

BEST TIME TO VISIT

Tshwane (Pretoria) has a pleasant climate with warm to hot summers and mild sunny winters. While still on the Highveld, the temperature is normally 3°C warmer than Johannesburg, given that it is roughly 300 m lower in altitude and closer to the Bushveld region in the north. The best time to visit is during the spring when the city is transformed by the thousands of flowering jacaranda trees, covering the parks and gardens in a mauve blanket.

TOURIST INFORMATION

Tshwane Tourism ① *Old Nederlandsche Bank Building, Church Sq, T012-358 1430, www. tshwanetourism.co.za, Mon-Fri 0800-1700, Sat 0900-1300*, doesn't have the usual desk and helpful staff found in most local tourist offices, but it does produce a couple of useful maps, highlighting the major sights. The Tshwane (Pretoria) office of **South Africa National Parks** (**SANParks**) ① *643 Leyds St, Muckleneuk, reservations T012-428 9111, www.sanparks.org*, is the head office and handles all bookings for accommodation and special long-distance hikes such as the Otter Trail in the Garden Route National Park.

→ BACKGROUND

In 1854, work began on building a church right by today's Church Square, and by the 1860s, as the city was steadily growing, Marthinus Pretorius, who had been made president of the republic, tried to unite the Orange Free State with the Transvaal. He failed, resigned as president and was replaced by the Reverand Thomas François Burgers in 1870. Under Burgers, the city developed and schools and parks were built, but the problems of administering the region remained unresolved. The British eventually annexed the Transvaal in April 1877, and their first action was to establish a garrison which attracted a large number of immigrants. New buildings were erected and the fortunes of the city began to look more promising. However, during the Transvaal War of Independence, the British withdrew and the city was taken over by the Paul Kruger who was to cause countless problems once gold had been discovered.

At the end of the Anglo-Boer War, Pretoria was named as the capital of the British colony, and as such it continued to prosper so that when the Union of South Africa was created in 1910, Pretoria was made the administrative capital of the new state. Shortly afterwards, the Union Buildings were constructed to house the new government. The growth of the town was now closely related to the expanding civil service and its status as an important city was assured. The city has remained a centre for government and today most overseas diplomats are based here. The city is also headquarters of the defence forces and home to the University of South Africa (UNISA). Today it has over 300,000 students throughout the world and is regarded as one of the largest correspondence universities in the world.

The metropolitan council has reorganized itself to unite the previously segregated areas under one administration. The greater area is now called Tshwane, meaning 'we are the same'. Like Johannesburg, Tshwane (Pretoria) has large townships to the northwest and northeast of the city.

CITY CENTRE

The oldest buildings in Tshwane (Pretoria) are clustered around Church Square, once a Voortrekker marketplace. Today, it is the heart of the city and is a popular meeting spot for locals, with suited businessmen stopping on the grass for lunch and hawkers selling roasted mealies to passersby. A rather unattractive statue of a grim-faced, grizzled Paul Kruger stands in the middle, surrounded by fluttering flocks of pigeons and flanked by late 19th-century banks and government offices. The most interesting of these is the **Palace of Justice**, where Nelson Mandela and other leaders of the ANC were tried during the notorious Treason Trials of 1963-1964. On the southwest side is the Raadsall, or parliament, and the Old Netherlands (Nederlandsche) Bank building, which now houses the tourist office.

The **National Museum of Natural History** (formerly the **Transvaal Museum**) ① *432 Paul Kruger St, T012-322 7632, www.ditsong.org.za, open 0800-1600, R25, children (3-13) R10*, is a typically dusty natural history museum that was founded in 1892 and moved into its current premises in 1912. The museum serves as a research and documentation centre for the fauna of southern Africa, and is one of the leading centres for zoological research in the country. The displays, focusing on geology and stuffed animals, are spread over a series of halls, including the Austin Roberts Bird Hall, which showcases the varied birdlife of southern Africa, and a collection of semi-precious stones. More interesting, perhaps, is the fact that the world-renowned hominid fossil, 'Mrs Ples' (*Australopithecus africanus transvaalensis*), is kept here, although sadly the public doesn't have access to her. Opposite the museum is **City Hall**, dating from 1935, a grand building fronted by broad square, with a fountain and a statue of Andries Pretorius on horseback.

The **Treaty of Vereeniging** ending the Anglo-Boer War (1899-1902) was signed in **Melrose House** ① *275 Jacob Maré St, T012-322 2805, www.melrosehouse.co.za, Tue-Sun 1000-1700, R8, children (under 16) R5, small café in the converted stables*, on 31 May 1902, between the British High Command and Boer Republican Forces. The house was originally built in 1886 for George Heys, who made his fortune from trade and a stagecoach service to the Transvaal. It is regarded as one of the finest examples of Victorian domestic architecture in South Africa; marble columns, stained-glass windows and mosaic floors all help create a feeling of serene style and wealth. The house was restored after being bombed by right-wingers in 1990. Today the grounds are used for classical concerts.

Kruger House Museum ① *60 Church St West, T012-326 9172, www.ditsong.org.za, open 0830-1700, R16, children (under 16) R10*, where President Kruger lived between 1884-1901, is now a museum that displays a fairly diverting collection of his possessions, as well as objects relating to the Anglo-Boer War. At the back of the house is the state coach and his private railway carriage.

The **National Zoological Gardens of South Africa** ① *corner of Paul Kruger and Boom streets, entrance on Boom St, T012-328 3265, www.nzg.ac.za, open 0800-1730, R55, children (2-15) R35, last ticket 1630, café and shop*, formerly Pretoria Zoo, covers 80 ha, with 6 km of walkways and just over 3100 species. Heavily involved in research and conservation, it is South Africa's largest and best-designed zoo. It is home to the only koala bear to be born in Africa. Golf carts are available to get around and there's an aerial cableway and tractor rides for kids.

Difficult to miss if you are walking about in the centre of town, and a popular meeting place at lunchtime, the sprawling **Lilian Ngoyi Square** was known until 2006 as Strijdom

Square and used to be dominated by a massive bust of JG Strijdom, covered by a curved concrete roof. The roof, considered something of an architectural feat, collapsed on 31 May 2001, 40 years to the day from when it was built. Strijdom was prime minister between 1954 and 1958 when the government started to place heavy restrictions on the ANC and banned the Communist Party – his statue doesn't seem to be missed much today. The square is now named after Lilian Ngoyi, who in 1956 led a march of 20,000 women from the square to the Union Buildings to demonstrate against obligatory carrying of pass books.

Burgers Park ⓘ *between Van der Walt and Andries streets, Apr-Sep 0600-1800, Oct-Mar 0600-2200,* is the most central of Tshwane's parks. It was first laid out as a botanical garden in the early 1870s, and is today a popular meeting place where visitors relax in the shade of rubber trees, palms and jacarandas. The 'florarium' houses a collection of exotic plants in contrasting environments, from subtropical flowers to succulents from the Karoo and Kalahari regions. Elsewhere in the garden is a statue of remembrance for the officers of the South African Scottish Regiment who were killed during the First World War.

ARCADIA

Pretoria Art Museum ⓘ *667 Schoeman St, T021-344 1807, Tue-Sun 1000-1700, www. pretoriaartmuseum.co.za, R6, children (under 16) R4,* houses a fine collection of South African art as well as a selection of run-of-the-mill 17th-century Dutch paintings. The collection includes works by Pierneef, Frans Oerder and Anton van Wouw. It also houses interesting temporary exhibitions, including photography. Teas and light meals are available.

The magnificent red sandstone complex of the **Union Buildings** ⓘ *Church St, Arcadia, T012-300 5200,* sits proudly on top of Meintjeskop overlooking the city centre. This is the administrative headquarters of the South African President, most famous for being the site of Nelson Mandela's speech after his inauguration as president on 10 May 1994, when the grounds in front of the building where packed with thousands of well-wishers. The building, designed by Herbert Baker, who also designed St George's Cathedral and Rhodes Memorial in Cape Town, was completed in 1913. Baker went on to help Edwin Lutyens in the planning of New Delhi, India. (The Union Buildings in Pretoria influenced his designs for the new Government Secretariat and the Imperial Legislative Assembly.) The formal gardens below the buildings are pleasant to walk around, but the best reason for coming here is for the city view. Look out for the statues of South Africa's famous generals: Botha, on horseback, Hertzog and Smuts. Also found on the hill is the Pretoria War Memorial, Delville Wood Memorial and the Garden of Remembrance.

VOORTREKKER MONUMENT

ⓘ *Eufees Rd (M7), Groenkloof, T012-326 6770, www.voortrekkermon.org.za, May-Aug 0800-1700, Apr-Sep 0800-1800, R40, children (under 16) R20, family of 4 R100, restaurant and tea garden.*
South of the city is the looming granite hulk of the Voortrekker Monument, a controversial Afrikaner memorial. The monument, a 40-m cube, was completed in 1949 after 11 years of work. It is a sombre and unattractive structure, a windowless block dominating the landscape, but one of particular significance to Afrikaners. It was built to commemorate the Great Trek of the 1830s, when the Afrikaners struck inland from the Cape with just their ox wagons and little idea of the trials that lay ahead of them. Inside is the cavernous Hall of Heroes, guarded by a carved head of a buffalo above the entrance (thought to be the most dangerous animal in Africa). Around the walls 27 marble friezes depict both the trek and scenes from the Zulu wars, including a seriously suspect portrayal of the Battle of Blood

River, where the Afrikaners are shown as brave soldiers and the Zulus as cowardly savages. The monument used to be the site of a huge annual celebration on 16 December, the date of the battle (known as the Day of the Covenant). At exactly midday on this date a ray of sunlight falls onto a large slab of stone in the centre of the basement (rather like a tomb), spotlighting the carved words: "Ons Vir Jou, Suid Afrika" (We are for you, South Africa). The fact that this date celebrated the bloody massacre of Zulus proved, unsurprisingly, hugely controversial, and after the end of Apartheid, this national holiday was renamed the Day of Reconciliation. Today, the celebrations for this event are held at Freedom Park (see below). For impressive views of the surrounding countryside and the city, take the lift to the viewing area around the roof. In the basement are some displays of life during the Great Trek. Outside, the surrounding wall recreates the circular laager of 64 ox wagons that can be seen at the battlefield site.

FREEDOM PARK
① *Entrance off Potgieter St, across from the Central Prison, T012-336 4000, www.freedompark. co.za, 0900-1700, R45, children (2-16) R25, 2-hr tours at 0900, 1200 and 1500, R20, children (2-16) R10, restaurant and shop.*
Freedom Park is purposefully and significantly located on a hill opposite the Voortrekker Monument. A 52-ha open-air museum, and one of the most ambitious heritage projects in South Africa, it opened in 2007 to commemorate the country's political history and to celebrate its cultural heritage. Its mission is to be a testament to the truth and reconciliation process that occurred at the end of Apartheid. The impressive sleek design and architecture uses lots of slate and granite, with neat pathways and tranquil ornamental water features linking the several components. Like the Voortrekker Monument, there are tremendous views over the city from here. While you can wander around yourself, to fully understand the significance of each element, the guided tour is highly recommended (golf carts are available for the disabled and elderly).

Tours start with an explanation of the purpose of the park and a viewing of the eternal flame and the amphitheatre, which is used for ceremonial purposes including the gathering of more than 2000 government dignitaries on Reconciliation Day (16 December). The tour then visits the massive 697-m-long **Wall of Names**, where thousands of names have been inscribed of those who lost their lives in the eight conflicts that have shaped the history of South Africa. These include the slave trade period, the Boer wars, world wars and the struggle against Apartheid. The wall can accommodate more than 120,000 names and, to date, 75,000 have been inscribed. **Isivivane** is the symbolic resting place of those who died in the struggle against Apartheid, and is represented by a circle of 11 giant boulders – one from each of South Africa's nine provinces, and two more representing the national government and international community. Each of the provinces donated a boulder that was of historical value – the boulder representing Gauteng, for example, comes from the township Mamelodi, in the east of Tshwane (Pretoria), where in 1985 the South African Security Forces killed 13 people during a peaceful protest march against rent increases.

Stretching from the west of Gauteng to the North West's historic town of Rustenburg are the gently rolling Magaliesberg Mountains, which, thanks to their proximity to the urban sprawl of Tshwane (Pretoria) and Johannesburg, are a popular weekend retreat. It's a scenic area for sports and outdoor pursuits and the mountains are ideal for hiking. The Magaliesberg are a range of flat-topped quartzite mountains, which extend roughly from Tshwane (Pretoria) to just beyond Rustenburg. The range forms the natural divide between the cool Highveld to the south and the warm bushveld to the north and is about 160 km long, reaching 1852 m at its highest point – which is actually no more than 400 m above the surrounding countryside. The difference in elevation is, however, sufficient to ensure that the hills receive a relatively high rainfall and are far greener than the plains, with some remaining stands of forest. The north-facing slopes are no more than a gentle climb, cut by mountain streams and leafy gorges. Given the proximity of both Johannesburg and Tshwane (Pretoria) (both little more than one hour's drive), the Magaliesberg Mountains are a popular day trip and weekend retreat and there are a number of attractions and places to stay.

ARRIVING IN THE MAGALIESBERG MOUNTAINS

Getting there and around To explore the Magaliesberg head out on the old Pretoria–Rustenburg road from Tshwane (Pretoria), the R104 (confusingly in parts also marked the R27), which runs along the shores of Hartbeespoort Dam via the village of Schoemansville before passing over the dam wall and continuing along the northern reaches of the Magaliesberg to join the N4 to Rustenburg, and then on to the R565 to Sun City and Pilanesburg.

From Johannesberg, the R24 or the R512 are more direct routes to the southern parts of the Magaliesberg. The option here is to also visit the attractions to the northwest of Johannesburg, including the **Cradle of Humankind**, **The Lion Park** or the **Lesedi Cultural Village** (see Around Johannesburg, page 215).

For information, pick up a map for the **Magalies Meander**, www.magaliesmeander. co.za, or the **Crocodile Ramble**, www.theramble.co.za, at the tourist offices in Gauteng or at the shops and participating venues in the Magaliesberg. Both maps (and the websites) list craft shops, accommodation, activities and restaurants in the region. If arriving from Johannesburg on the R24, there's a **tourist office** ① *T011-475 7835, www.magaliesinfo. co.za, Mon-Fri 0830-1700*, in the village of Magaliesburg (in Gauteng).

HARTBEESPOORT DAM

The Hartbeespoort Dam was built in 1923 in a narrow gorge where the Crocodile River cuts through the Magaliesberg Mountains. There are two major canals which conduct water away from the dam into a series of smaller canals that irrigate the farmlands around Brits. The old main road from Tshwane (Pretoria) runs through the village of **Schoemansville** on the north shore of the lake before crossing the dam wall and continuing to Rustenburg and Sun City. There is a **Snake and Animal Park** ① *T012-253 1162, www. hartbeespoortsnakeanimalpark.co.za, daily 0800-1730, R50, children (3-12) R20, tea garden*, which remains a popular attraction for visiting families from Gauteng but, alongside the collection of reptiles, are chimpanzees, panthers and Bengal tigers, making it unpleasant and zoo-like. Boat trips on the dam leave hourly and there are seal demonstrations at 1200 and 1500 on Saturday and Sunday. Also near here is the **Hartbeespoort Dam Cableway** ① *on the R513 towards Tshwane (Pretoria), T072-241 2654, www.hartiescableway.co.za,* daily 0900-1630, R140, children (3-14) R80, a 2.3-km link to one of the highest points of the Magaliesberg. The **De Wildt Cheetah Centre** ① *also on the R513, towards Tshwane (Pretoria), T012-504 9906, www.dewildt.org.za, R270 per person (no children under 6), extra fee for a photograph with a cheetah (when available), 3-hr tours at 0830 and 1330, booking ahead is essential*, an important breeding centre famous for being the first such place where a cheetah was successfully born in captivity. On certain mornings when they are exercised, some of the king cheetahs can be seen running at high-speed. Other species include wild dog, brown hyena and vultures. The tour begins with a talk about the centre and the genetics of cheetahs, followed by a game drive around the spacious enclosures. There is also a set lunch, but this must be booked in advance.

Once over the dam wall from Schoemansville, the road reaches the Damdoryn Crossroads, which is a hive of activity and where the Welwitschia Country Market, the Chameleon Village and a large curio market are all located. A hugely popular spot with day trippers from Tshwane (Pretoria) and Johannesburg, there are numerous shops and restaurants here. At Chameleon Village there's also a small **reptile park** ① *Tue-Sun 0900-1700, R25, children (under 12) R15*, which has snakes, crocodiles, monitor lizards and random other animals like tortoises and porcupines.

From the Damdoryn Crossroads, 2 km along the R104 is the **Elephant Sanctuary Hartbeespoort Dam** ① *T012-258 0423, www.elephantsanctuary.co.za, daily programmes start at 0800, 1000 and 1400, from R425, children (3-14) R215*, which is a sister operation of the elephant sanctuaries on the Garden Route (see page 90) and in Hazyview (see page 256). Guests can interact with the five tame elephants and ride them. Check the website for programmes, some include lunch or dinner. There's luxury accommodation (**$$$$**) and overnight guests can 'brush down' the elephants first thing in the morning.

Adjacent to the Elephant Sanctuary, is the **Bush Babies Monkey Sanctuary** ① *T012-258 9908, www.monkeysanctuary.co.za, 1½-hr tours run on the hour from 0900-1600, R195, children (4-14) R95, under 3s free, coffee shop*, a 7-ha tract of indigenous forest lying in a kloof (gorge) in the mountainside. It's home to a number of species of primate (mostly rescued pets), including bush babies, lemurs and squirrel, spider and vervet monkeys, and the guided tour follows elevated wooden walkways. **Magalies Canopy Tour** ① *Sparkling Waters Hotel & Spa, T014-535 0150, www.magaliescanopytour.co.za, Sep-May 0700-1630, Jun-Aug 0800-1530, 2½-hr tours depart every 30 mins, R450 per person (no children under 7), including refreshments and a dip in the hotel pool afterwards*, is off the R104, approximately 38 km west of the Damdoryn Crossroads or 16 km southeast of Rustenburg, then 12 km from the main road; it can also be reached from the R24 south of Rustenburg. It is part of the same operation that runs the **Tsitsikamma Canopy Tour** on the Garden Route (see page 99), among other places. The tour involves gliding on a steel rope in a harness between 11 elevated platforms that have been built into the mountain rock faces. The longest slide is 170 m and in some places the platforms are 30 m high. The guides talk through the history of the Magaliesbergs and point out the plants and birds.

→ SUN CITY

Tucked between dusty plains and rolling bushveld is the surreal highrise, neon-lit resort of Sun City. Much like Las Vegas in the US, the resort was built around gambling and today comprises a vast complex of four hotels, linked by a skytrain, and extravagant recreational facilities, including a fake sandy lagoon and a constructed tropical rainforest. The result is both staggeringly impressive and laughably tacky – all good fun if you take it with a pinch of salt.

ARRIVING IN SUN CITY

Getting there Pilanesberg International Airport, is 8 km from Sun City to the north of Pilanesberg's Kwa Maritane Gate, T014-557 1115, www.acsa.co.za, but there are no scheduled services, though it is served by charter flights. By car, follow Nelson Mandela Street straight out of Rustenburg, and then take the right turning on the R565, signposted Phokeng and Sun City. Shortly before Sun City is a left turn for Pilanesberg Game Reserve. The entrance to Sun City is just after a large shopping mall by the staff housing complex. There is an entrance fee for day visitors, R50 per person; Valley of the Waves R100, children (4-14) R50, under 3s free. The **Welcome Centre** ① *T014-557 1544, www.suninternational.com, 0800-2000*, is in the middle of the complex and is a good place to start and pick up a map. The free skytrain runs throughout the complex, and shuttle buses run to and from the car park.

Moving on Take the R565 Rustenberg road out of Sun City and turn right to the Pilanesberg Game Reserve (see page 228), 140 km from Tshwane (Pretoria).

BACKGROUND

The first part of the complex was opened in 1979, when the central features were the **Sun City Hotel** and a golf course designed by Gary Player. Much of the appeal of Sun City was its gambling licence: the hotel was in Bophuthatswana where gambling was legal. Wealthy whites travelled to what were then the designated black homelands to gamble and, like many other casino resorts from the Apartheid era, the contrasts between the luxury of the resorts and the impoverished areas around them were (and, to some extent, still are) stark.

In the same year, Pilanesberg Game Reserve opened. A year later the second phase was complete – the 284-room **Sun City Cabanas** opened, aimed at families. In 1980 the famous **Sun City Million Dollar Golf Challenge** was founded, and over the years this has attracted most of the world's top golfers. In 1984 the third hotel was opened, the five-star **Cascades**, surrounded by waterfalls, streams and a tract of forest. In 1992 came the icing on the cake: the **Lost City** and the **Valley of the Waves** (see Sights and activities, below).

With the change in gambling laws, visitor numbers dropped sharply in the 1990s, but have crept up again as the focus has switched from gambling to family entertainment, golf and conferences. Although far removed from the culture and landscapes that draw most tourists to South Africa, Sun City's glitz and garishness is fascinating and worth a day's visit.

PLACES IN SUN CITY

The complex focuses on the newest and most excessive addition to the Sun City stable, the **Palace of the Lost City**, a magnificent hotel completed in 1992. The vaguely Moorish construction is characterized by soaring dome-capped towers ringed by prancing statues of antelope. Below the hotel is the **Valley of the Waves**, reached by a bridge that trembles and spouts steam during mock earthquakes (every 30 minutes). This stunning artificial sandy lagoon, complete with desert island and palm-lined soft white sand, has a wave machine capable of creating metre-high waves. Day visitors have to pay extra to enter the Valley of the Waves, accessed from the entertainments centre, but this doesn't seem to put anyone off – the beach gets completely packed at weekends, with noisy music pumping out of loudspeakers and every large wave bringing forth a yell of jubilation from the crowds. Smaller swimming pools dotted around the lagoon are quieter.

A welcome retreat lies around the hotel and lagoon, the impressive 25-ha **man-made forest**. Remarkably lush and quiet, the forest was originally made up of 1.6 million plants, trees and shrubs, and the rainforest component includes three layers with creepers and orchids growing in the canopy. Although the moulded cement rocks and perfectly pruned paths give it a distinct Disney feel, the plants have attracted prolific birdlife and the walking trails, lasting up to 1½ hours, allow a real sense of isolation from the resort.

Elsewhere, an abundance of activities are available to guests. There are two 18-hole golf courses, including the Gary Player-designed course, home to the annual **Nedbank Golf Challenge**, one of the world's great championships with prizes valuing over US$4 million. At **Waterworld**, guests can try parasailing, waterskiing and jetskiing. There is a horse-riding centre, tennis, mini-golf, squash, a gym and spa, mountain-biking trails, jogging routes, 10-pin bowling and swimming pools (the more peaceful of which are located in the hotels).

Close to the entrance is **Kwena Gardens Crocodile Sanctuary** with over 7000 crocs, including the three biggest captive Nile crocodiles in the world. Nearby is the **Cultural Village**, where guests are shown around mock-ups of villages of eight tribal groups, with dancing and singing, and a Shebeen serving pan-African cuisine. There's also an aviary, a bird of prey centre, cinemas, a casino, slot machines, restaurants and bars.

→ PILANESBERG GAME RESERVE

ⓘ *T014-555 1600, www.pilanesberg-game-reserve.co.za, Nov-Feb 0530-1900, Mar-Apr 0600-1830, May-Aug 0630-1800, Sep-Oct 0600-1830, R45, children (under 14) R20, car R20.*

This is the fourth largest national park in South Africa, and was created in 1979 to complement the luxury development being built at Sun City. The two have been closely linked ever since.

Arriving in Pilanesberg Game Reserve From Sun City, take the R565 Rustenberg road for 5 km and turn right to the Pilanesberg Game Reserve. Tshwane (Pretoria) is about 140 km from the park. It can be visited as a long day trip from Tshwane (Pretoria) or Johannesburg, but most visitors stay at least one night in the region and combine a trip to Pilanesberg with Sun City. Visitors to Sun City can book on one of the numerous two-hour game drives that leave the Welcome Centre throughout the day.

Moving on To reach the Kruger National Park (see page 231) from Pilanesberg, you will have to drive back to Johannesberg and from there continue to Kruger either on a tour or in your own vehicle. Alternatively, you could take a bus from Joburg or Tshwane to Nelspruit (see page 231) and thence on to Kruger.

BACKGROUND AND VISITING PILANESBERG GAME RESERVE

The area earmarked for the park in the 1970s was home to a large number of Tswana people who were either coerced into leaving or forcibly removed – a hugely controversial move, but one that was not reported at the time. On a more positive note, the area's reintroduction of game has been heralded as a great success. This complex and ambitious project was known as Operation Genesis. The animals came from all over southern Africa: elephant and buffalo from Addo Elephant National Park; black and white rhino from the Natal Parks Board; eland from Namibia; Burchell's zebra and waterbuck from the Transvaal; and red hartebeest from the Northern Cape and Namibia. As a transition zone between the Kalahari sandveld and the bushveld, it was also the natural habitat for a number of rare species already in existence, including brown hyena, Cape hunting dog and sable antelope. As you drive around the 55,000-ha reserve you now have a good chance of seeing all the large animals, including rhino, elephant, lion, cheetah, buffalo and the occasional leopard. More than 8000 animals have now been successfully introduced.

The park encompasses the caldera of an extinct volcano, which is geographically similar to the Ngorongoro Conservation Area in Tanzania. The crater is surrounded by three concentric rings of hills and in the centre is a lake, **Mankwe Dam**, where you can see crocodile and hippo. The hills are broken up with wooded valleys, which gradually give way to open savannah grasslands. This variety of habitat is ideal for wild animals and it is a rewarding birdwatching environment where over 340 species have been recorded. Excellent tar and gravel roads traverse the park, and maps and game checklists are available at each of the four gates: Manyane, Bakgatla, Bakubung and Kwa Maritane – the last one being the closest to Sun City.

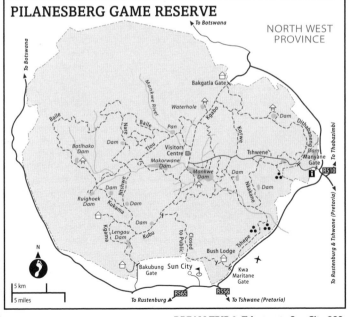

TSHWANE TO SUN CITY LISTINGS

WHERE TO STAY

Tshwane

$$$ Sheraton Pretoria Hotel, corner Church and Wessels streets, Arcadia, T012-429 9999, www.shearatonpretoria.com. A diplomats' haunt and 5-star Sheraton standards, 175 a/c rooms with marble bathrooms, DSTV and Wi-Fi, palatial lobby, heated pool, gym, restaurant, and the terrace at **Tiffins Bar** has uninterrupted views of the Union Buildings.

$$ Protea Hotel Hatfield, 1141 Burnett St, Hatfield, T012-364 0300, www.proteahotels. com. 119 a/c small but modern and good-value rooms with DSTV and Wi-Fi, pleasant decor, splash pool, restaurant and bar. Great location opposite the Hatfield Plaza and a short walk to the Gautrain.

Magaliesberg Mountains

$$$$ Mount Grace, off the R24, 3 km north of Magaliesberg village, T014-577 5600, www.mountgrace.co.za. One of the most luxurious options in the Magaliesberg, with 121 luxury rooms in thatched cottages set in 10 ha of beautiful gardens with lakes and waterfalls. Heated swimming pool, tennis, library, excellent food, sumptuous spa with hydro pools, most treatments are conducted outside beneath olive trees. No children under 12.

Sun City

$$$$ The Palace of the Lost City. Both impossibly kitsch and beautifully lavish, with 338 rooms spread across a string of airy courtyards, each overlooking fountains and sculptures of game. The entrance is marked by a super-sized sculpture of cheetahs hunting, while the lobby is a palatial hall lined with vast columns, leading to a variety of restaurants and elegant bars. The **Villa del Palazzo**, with its classic northern Italian cuisine, is an excellent restaurant overlooking the pools, **Crystal Court** has gourmet cuisine, live piano music and is surrounded by the man-made rainforest, and elsewhere there are 3 bars; a selection of shops, a beauty spa and a heated pool.

Pilanesberg Game Reserve

$$$$ Kwa Maritane Bush Lodge, near the gate of the same name, in the south of the park, T014-552 5100, www.kwamaritane. co.za. A smart bush lodge with 90 rooms with a/c, DSTV, high thatched ceilings and a private veranda. Rates (mid-range) include breakfast and dinner, game drives are extra. Nearby waterhole with underground hide reached via a 180-m tunnel from the lodge, 2 swimming pools, tennis courts, gym, and free shuttle to Sun City.

WHAT TO DO

Safaris

Game Trackers, desk at **Welcome Centre**, Sun City, T014-552 5020, www.gametrac. co.za. If visiting Sun City on a day or overnight trip, 2½-hr guided tours, R395, children (10-16) R230 (under 10) R145. 2-hr night drives, R410, children (10-16) R255 (under 10) R155. **Mankwe Safaris**, Pilanesberg's Manyane Gate, T014-555 7056, www.mankwesafaris. co.za. 2½-hr game drives in the morning, afternoon and at night, R350, children (under 10) R195.

Pilanesberg Elephant Back Safaris, pickups and booking at the **Welcome Centre**, T014-552 5020, www.pilanesberg elephantback.co.za. The 6 elephants can carry 2 riders each, plus the guide. Silently travelling through the bush on an elephant is a unique game-viewing experience. The ride takes about 1 hr but the whole excursion lasts 2-3 hrs, and includes interaction with the elephants; R1600, no children under 5.

KRUGER NATIONAL PARK

Kruger Park is the king of South African game parks and one of the best game-viewing areas in all of Africa. The figures speak for themselves: 507 bird species, 114 reptiles, 49 fish, 34 amphibians, 147 mammal and over 23,000 plant species have been recorded here. The region itself is enormous, extending from the Crocodile River in the south to the Limpopo in the north, from the wooded foothills of the eastern escarpment to the humid plains of the Lowveld. It certainly fulfils most visitors' fantasies of seeing magnificent herds of game roaming across acacia-studded stretches of savannah and, of course, is home to the Big Five. The park is 60 km wide and over 350 km long, conserving 21,497 sq km, an area the size of Wales or Israel. Despite its size, it is very well developed, with a good network covering 2600 km of roads and numerous camps, making a Kruger safari relatively hassle free.

Don't expect to have the park to yourself, however. Kruger receives over one million visitors a year and the park camps cater for up to 5000 visitors a day. Nevertheless, despite the huge number of people passing through, Kruger has managed to maintain its wild atmosphere, and only about 5% of the park is affected by the activities of the visitors.

While much of the park is designed for self-driving and self-catering, it is possible to stay in an ever-expanding choice of top-end private reserves, which are popular with first-time visitors as all game drives are led by rangers, so you can leave the animal-spotting to the experts. The fences that once split Kruger from the private reserves have now come down, so game can roam freely between the park and private concessions. Moreover, the fences between the countries bordering South Africa have also come down in the last few years: the demolition of fences between Kruger and Mozambique's Limpopo National Park and Zimbabwe's Gonarezhou have created the Great Limpopo Transfrontier Park (www.greatlimpopopark. com), a conservation area straddling a staggering 35,000 sq km. (For private game reserves along the park's western boundary, see pages 244-248.)

→ NELSPRUIT

Nelspruit developed around the railway when the line between Pretoria and Lourenço Marques (now Maputo) was completed in 1891. Briefly the capital of the Transvaal Republic after Paul Kruger abandoned Pretoria in 1900 during the Boer War, Nelspruit is now the industrial centre of the Lowveld and a processing point for the fruit, tobacco and beef farms of the surrounding region. The town has a sleepy, tropical feel with broad, modern streets lined with acacias, bougainvillea and jacaranda trees. Although there's little to keep you here, most visitors to the region pass through at some point.

ARRIVING IN NELSPRUIT

Getting there and moving on   Nelspruit has good facilities for tourists planning trips to Kruger National Park, Panorama Region (see page 251) and Swaziland (see page 259). The **Kruger Mpumalanga International Airport (KMIA)** ① *airport enquiries, T013-753 7502, www.kmiairport.co.za*, is 25 km from the centre of Nelspruit towards Kruger off the R538. Nelspruit is 355 km from Johannesburg along the N4 toll road, a smooth highway that continues east to Maputo, Mozambique's capital. **Greyhound**, **Intercape** and **Translux** all operate services from Johannesburg and Tshwane (Pretoria) to Nelspruit (en route to Maputo in Mozambique).

Getting around Nelspruit has excellent road links to Mpumalanga's major tourist attractions. The nearest entrance gates to Kruger are less than 80 km away on the N4 (east), and the R40 through White River (north), and a day trip to see the southern sector of the park is quite feasible. The mountain villages of Sabie (see page 255) and Graskop (see page 253) are equally accessible and make a pleasant change from the heat of the Lowveld. Another option is to head south of Nelspruit and explore Swaziland for a day or two. All these places have an excellent range of accommodation and there is little reason to stay in the centre of town. The shopping centres in town are convenient for stocking up on food and equipment before setting off to stay in self-catering accommodation in Kruger.

→ ARRIVING IN KRUGER NATIONAL PARK

GETTING THERE AND AROUND

Air The three principal airports serving Kruger are **Kruger Mpumalanga International Airport (KMIA)** ① *T013-753 7502, www.kmiairport.co.za*, 25 km north of Nelspruit near Kruger's Numbi and Malalane gates; **Phalaborwa Kruger Gateway Airport**, 2 km from Phalaborwa and within easy reach of many of Kruger's gates; and **Eastgate Airport**, at Hoedspruit, close to Orpen Gate. Some of the luxury game lodges also have their own landing strips for chartered flights.

Road Most people arrive in Kruger by road, either on a tour or in their own vehicle. There are nine entry gates and numerous options of approach. Which area you end up staying in will depend to a large extent on where you are coming from. Petrol is available at the larger camps during office hours, and the mark-up on litre prices is not as unreasonable as you'd expect (although note that credit cards aren't accepted). There is a speed limit of 50 kph on the surfaced roads in the park. **Kruger Emergency Road Services** is based at Skukuza, T013-735 4152. The service is not equipped to do any major repairs, but if you break down within the park they will tow you to the nearest garage outside the park.

Orientation Given its huge size, many visitors to Kruger concentrate on one area of the park on each visit. Unless you are staying for more than a couple of nights, it is impossible to combine effective game viewing and visit all the areas. For the routes followed in this guide, the park has been divided into two areas: southern (see page 238) and central (see page 241), with a description of each of the different camps within these areas.

Arriving Most of the camps are at least an hour's drive from the nearest entrance gate so always make sure you arrive in time to get to the camp. At the park gate, your reservation will usually be checked before you are allowed in, especially during the busy periods when all the accommodation, including campsites, gets booked up. You could be fined if you arrive at the camp gate after it has closed.

Moving on If you leave the park through Orpen Gate you will be able to make your way back to Johannesburg through the Panorama Region (see page 251), heading south from Hoedspruit. The Panorama Region can be accessed from the other southern gates too.

PARK OPENING HOURS AND FEES

Park gates are open sunrise-sunset. Camp receptions are open daily April to June 0800-1800; March, September and October 0800-1830; November to February 0800-1900. Conservation fees are R204, children (2-11) R102, under 2s free. South African residents get a substantial discount.

BEST TIME TO VISIT

Each season has its advantages. The park looks its best after the summer rains when the new shoots and lush vegetation provide a surplus of food for the grazers. Migratory birds are attracted and display their colourful breeding plumage, and this is a good time to see courtship rituals and nesting. The animals look their best thanks to their good diet, and mammals give birth to their young. The disadvantages of summer are that the thick foliage and tall grasses make it harder to spot animals and daytime temperatures can rise to a sweltering 40°C; afternoon rains are also common.

The winter months are good for game viewing because the dry weather forces animals to congregate around waterholes and there is less foliage for them to hide in. However, the animals tend not to be in their best condition. The winter months of June, July and August are more comfortable with daytime temperatures of around 30°C, but nights can be surprisingly cold with temperatures at times dropping to 0°C.

Kruger is at its most crowded during the South African school holidays. Accommodation within the park will be completely full and the heavy traffic on the roads can detract from the wilderness experience.

MALARIA

Kruger National Park is regarded as a seasonal low-risk malarial region, especially during and just after the rainy season (roughly May to September) when there is a lot of free-standing water. Advice is available from the very useful Kruger malaria hotline, T082-234 1800. Also visit the Malaria Research Programme of South Africa's website, www.malaria.org.za. Take local advice and precautions if necessary.

→ STAYING IN THE PARK

Kruger has 12 main rest camps, five bushveld camps, two bush lodges and five satellite camps, owned and managed by **South African National Parks** (SANParks), head office in Tshwane (Pretoria). Although there is a choice in the type of accommodation available, all the room rates are very reasonable. There are also a handful of private luxury lodges within Kruger run by concessionaires and not SANParks, such as **Tinga Private Lodge** and **Jock Safari Lodge**. The **SANParks** website, www.sanparks.org, has excellent information on all the lodges within Kruger. If you're looking for luxury, the private game reserves adjoining Kruger offer some of the finest camps in Africa. (For private reserves outside the park, see pages 244-248.)

RESERVATIONS

The direct line for each camp is included with the description of the camp. This number can only be used for making a last-minute booking, up to 48 hours prior to arrival. All other bookings should be made through **SANParks** ① *T012-428 9111, www.sanparks.org*. Once you are in the park it is always worth calling a day ahead or in the early morning to see if there have been any cancellations. The camp receptions will also be able to change your reservations to another camp if there is availability.

As with the conservation fees, children (aged two to 11) pay child rates for accommodation and children under two are free. Price codes listed in the camp descriptions refer to the minimum price per accommodation unit – meaning, for example, a cottage that sleeps six people, can take a minimum of four, so it is these prices that are listed. Expect to pay a little more if you are filling a unit. Disabled travellers should check out the comprehensive Information for People with Disabilities pages on the SANParks website, www.sanparks.org. It has information about which camps have accommodation units equipped for wheelchair users, as well as disabled facilities in every other region of the park such as public toilets and picnic sites.

MAIN REST CAMPS

The majority of overnight visitors to southern and central Kruger stay in one of the 12 main rest camps in the park at **Berg-en-Dal**, **Crocodile Bridge**, **Lower Sabie**, **Pretoriuskop**, **Skukuza**, **Letaba**, **Mopani**, **Olifants**, **Orpen** and **Satara**. Most of the accommodation is in the form of chalets or cottages, which can sleep between two and 12. If you are self-catering, you'll have the choice between a separate fully equipped kitchen, a kitchenette or the use of a communal kitchen. All accommodation comes with a refrigerator, bedding and towels. If in doubt, always check when booking exactly what you will be getting. More precise details of the choices are listed under the separate entry for each of the camps.

Some of the older camps feel a little outdated, but the grounds are universally clean and well kept. The facilities vary from one camp to the next but in most cases they include a shop selling basic self-catering supplies, a petrol pump, a restaurant or cafeteria, launderette, toilets and hot showers, braai areas with seating, public telephones and an office with information on the other camps. During the school holidays, the atmosphere in the larger camps can feel like holiday camps, and you can easily forget you are in the middle of a game reserve.

CAMPSITES

Although most of the main rest camps have a separate area for caravans, tents and camper vans, there are two separate campsites at **Maroela** and **Balule**. The only facilities here are washblocks and communal kitchen facilities – there are no power points. Camping costs R165 (with an electric point), R135 (wiper site for two people, and R54 per extra adult and R27 per extra child, up to a maximum of six people per site.

BUSH LODGES

Bush lodges offer secluded luxury accommodation and are smaller and more remote than public camps, without facilities such as shops, restaurants or petrol stations. These camps are ideal for a large group of friends, since the whole camp has to be taken with each booking. The two bush lodges are **Boulders**, which sleeps 12, and **Roodewal**, sleeping 16. Reservations should be made well in advance, as they offer exceptionally good value if the maximum number of people stay in the camp. The camps are located away from the main rest camps but are close enough for visits to the shops for supplies. Although they are privately owned, all bookings are dealt with by SANParks.

BUSHVELD CAMPS

The five bushveld camps at **Biyamiti**, **Shimuwini**, **Talamati**, **Bateleur** and **Sirheni** are smaller and offer more of a wilderness experience than the main camps, but they also have far fewer facilities. Staying in these camps is one of the best ways to experience Kruger, but it does involve a degree of advanced planning. The chalets are all self-catering with fully equipped kitchens; bedding and towels are provided, and each chalet can sleep up to four people.

EATING

The camp restaurants are open daily for breakfast (0700-0900), lunch (1200-1400) and dinner (1800-2100). Some of the camps also have a bar. At small camps, or when there are fewer guests, you will be asked to order your evening meal in advance.

SHOPPING

Camp shops are open daily April to June 0800-1800; March, September and October 0800-1830; and November to February 0800-1900. The closer you are to Skukuza (the largest camp), the fresher the produce stocked in camp shops. Most shops stock firewood and braai lighters, bread, frozen meat, tinned vegetables, jams, biscuits, beer, wines, spirits, cool drinks, books and a few curio items. If you don't have a cool box in your car and you are self-catering, it is still possible to buy all you need for a meal from the shops each day.

OTHER FACILITIES

Some of the camps have swimming pools for residents, a good option if you choose to base yourself at a camp for several days in summer and want to relax during the midday heat. Camping areas have laundry blocks and hot, clean showers. The communal kitchens have power points, instant boiling water machines, electric rings and a sink. It is your responsibility to clean up after yourself. Always secure rubbish to minimize the risk of baboons raiding the bins. There is a bank with ATM and an internet café at Skukuza.

→ GAME VIEWING, TRAILS AND TOURS

GAME VIEWING

Kruger is, of course, home to the Big Five: lion, elephant, buffalo, black rhino and leopard. The highest concentrations and variety of game are around **Lower Sabie**, **Satara** and **Skukuza**. The best times for game viewing are after dawn and just before dusk, as animals tend to rest during the heat of the day.

There is a network of tarred and dirt roads linking the camps and looping through the best game-viewing areas. They are only open to the public during daylight hours and are subject to speed limits, which are monitored by radar. Game viewing takes time and it is best to drive below 20 kph to maximize your chances of spotting animals. Although there is a temptation to head for the most isolated dirt tracks and to neglect the tarred roads, this can be a mistake as cars are quieter on tarred roads and the animals living near them are more used to traffic. The run-off from tarred roads also makes the vegetation greener and attracts more animals. Driving around Kruger can be very tiring, so it's a good idea to visit one of the get-out points (marked on park maps) and to spend time game viewing at a waterhole.

Kruger shops sell a wide choice of identification guides. Their own publications, including the map, travel guide and the comprehensive *Find it* guide are an excellent introduction to the geology, history, vegetation and wildlife of Kruger.

Because Kruger straddles a variety of ecosystems, birdwatching throughout the entire park is excellent, and is an ideal activity to accompany game viewing, especially during quiet moments of animal activity. Kruger is home to over 500 of South Africa's 800+ bird species, and is a superb place to see woodland and savannah birds. Numbers are greatest in summer, when all the Palaearctic and intra-African migrants are present. The numerous rivers and waterholes, as well as the rest camps and picnic sites, are exceptionally rewarding vantage points. Hornbills, starlings, vultures, rollers, bee-eaters and shrike typify the ubiquitous dry bushveld, and birdwatchers can look forward to pursuing the Big Six: saddle-billed stork, kori bustard, Martial eagle, lappet-faced vulture, Pel's fishing owl and ground hornbill. By and large restricted to the Kruger region, these six species are easily indentified and instantly recognizable (with the exception of the Pel's fishing owl, which is seldom seen, because of its nocturnal habits). Eagles are also common and, as well as the Martial, bateleur, black-chested snake, brown snake, African hawk, African fish and tawny eagles are all regularly seen, and in summer, there are Wahlberg's, steppe and lesser-spotted eagles too. Numerous field guides on South African birds are available, and Kruger bird checklists are available in the park's shops and can be downloaded from SANParks website (www.sanparks.org).

GAME DRIVES
A guided tour with a game ranger can increase your chance of game spotting and provides a deeper understanding of the wilderness. Most camps offer guided day and night drives. Both are very popular and should be booked in advance at camp reception as soon as you arrive. A drive costs from R150-230, children (aged two to 11) half price, depending on the camp and time of day. Night drives are an added attraction as private vehicles are not allowed outside the camps after sundown. These usually depart around 1700. Make sure you have warm clothing as temperatures drop in the evenings. The drives finish in time for guests to have an evening meal at the camp restaurant. Some camps also offer a late drive after dinner, departing at 2030 and lasting for up to three hours.

GAME WALKS
A number of camps offer two- or three-hour walks in the morning or afternoon accompanied by an armed game ranger from around R340 per person, no children under 12. Groups are kept small – up to eight people – and the rangers are trained in field guiding. These provide an excellent way of getting close to smaller animals and are a thrilling way of exploring the bush.

WILDERNESS TRAILS
The wilderness trails offer three-day guided walking safaris. Seeing the park on foot is the most exciting way to experience the wilderness, and places on hiking trails are booked up months in advance. A maximum of eight people go on each trail and they are accompanied by an armed ranger. Hikers spend every night at the same rustic bush camp and go out on day walks. Food, water bottles, sleeping bags, rucksacks and cutlery are all provided.

The wilderness trails last for two days and three nights, and cost R3900 per person, no children under 12. For reservations contact **South African National Parks (SANParks)** offices;

bookings can be made up to a year ahead and places fill up quickly. The best time of year for hiking is March to July when the weather is dry and daytime temperatures are cooler.

Bushman Wilderness Trail This is a good area for seeing white rhino and wild dogs, and the walks also visit nearby San paintings. The camp is in an area of mountain bushveld, southwest of Kruger in an isolated valley surrounded by koppies. Hikers stay in thatched bush huts. Hikers check in at Berg-en-Dal, which is an hour's drive by Land Rover from the camp.

Napi Wilderness Trail Passes through various habitats following the banks of the Biyamiti River through thick riverine bush and crossing mixed woodlands. This is a good area for black and white rhino, duiker, jackal, kudu and giraffe. Hikers check in at Pretoriuskop.

Metsi-Metsi Wilderness Trail The camp is in an area of mountain bushveld near the N'waswitsontso River. The trail also visits areas of marula savannah where many plains animals are seen. Hikers check in at Skukuza.

Olifants Wilderness Trail Crosses through a region of classic African plains. It is excellent for seeing large herds of buffalo, wildebeest and zebra. The hutted camp overlooks the Olifants River and is 1½ hours by Land Rover to Letaba. Hikers check in at Letaba.

Sweni Wilderness Trail Southeast of Satara overlooking the Sweni River and crossing knobthorn and marula savannah where large herds of buffalo, wildebeest and zebra can be seen. Interesting species are cheetah, lion, kudu, sable and steenbok. Hikers check in at Satara.

Wolhuter Wilderness Trail Passes through Lowveld savannah, where it is possible to see lions, cheetah, black and white rhino, roan, sable and wild dog. The trail is named after the park ranger Harry Wolhuter, who killed a lion with his knife in 1903. The bush camp has wooden huts and is near the Mlambane River. Hikers check in at Berg-en-Dal.

THE OLIFANTS RIVER BACKPACK TRAILS

This is run from April to October and is different to the wilderness trails in that hikers cover the 42 km over four days and three nights but camp in a different place each night, and the guide picks out a suitable spot. As such, hikers have to carry packs with tents and sleeping gear, and all their own cooking equipment and food, which they cook themselves. Hikers also take turns carrying a fold-up shelter used as cover for when going to the toilet. Orientation (and pack-checking) is at Olifants, before hikers are transferred by vehicle to the western edge of the park where the Olifants River enters Kruger, and then trace the river back to the rest camp again over four days. This is a tough hike – 10-15 km a day carrying heavy packs – hikers need to be fit and show a medical certificate of good health. Don't be deceived by the short distances, as the Olifant's River Valley features hills, deep gullies and dense thickets. Bookings are made per trail and it costs R16,400 for four days for up to eight people.

TOURS

Organized tours of Kruger are widely available throughout South Africa and can be booked in all major cities. The variety of tours on offer can be baffling, so it is a good idea to shop around. Prices vary according to the quality of accommodation, the length of the tour, additional destinations, and whether you travel by minibus, open-air game vehicle or air-conditioned coach. There are dozens of companies offering tours in Nelspruit and Johannesburg.

→ CAMPS IN SOUTHERN KRUGER

The greatest concentrations of game and most of Kruger's large camps are in the southern section of Kruger and many visitors only ever see this section of the park. The landscape here is far more varied than the rest of the park and therefore supports a wider range of animals.

ARRIVING IN SOUTHERN KRUGER

The entrance gates at **Crocodile Bridge** and **Malalane** are on the southern boundary of the park and are clearly signposted from the N4 running between Nelspruit and Komatipoort. The entrance gates at Numbi, Paul Kruger and **Phabeni** are on the southwestern boundary. **Numbi Gate** is signposted off the R538 between Nelspruit and Hazyview; **Paul Kruger Gate** is on the R536 from Hazyview (see page 256).

BERG-EN-DAL

ⓘ *12 km to Malalane Gate, T013-735 6106 for last-minute reservations (maximum 48 hrs before arrival).*

This large, modern camp has a rather austere, institutional feel to it. It is set in a hilly landscape, wooded with acacia, marula and jackalberry overlooking the Matjulu Dam. Facilities include a swimming pool, in-camp trail, environmental centre showing wildlife films, petrol station, camp shop, restaurant, telephones and launderette. There are 23 cottages (**$$$**) which are slightly larger than at the other camps and sleep six to eight people, 69 three-bed **bungalows** (**$$**) and 70 camping and caravan sites with ablution blocks and kitchen units.

BIYAMITI

ⓘ *26 km to Crocodile Gate, 45 km to Malalane, T013-735 6171 for reservations (maximum 48 hrs before arrival).*

This bushveld camp is in the far south of Kruger on the banks of the Mbiyamiti River set in an area of crocodile thorn thicket. The camp sleeps 70 people in 15 one- or two-bed cottages (**$$$-$$**) with kitchen.

CROCODILE BRIDGE

ⓘ *34 km to Lower Sabie, 175 km to Orpen, 125 km to Pretoriuskop, 127 km to Satara, 77 km to Skukuza, T013-735 6012 for reservations (maximum 48 hrs before arrival).*

This small camp is next to the park's southern gate set in acacia woodland. There is a hippo pool on the dirt road to Malalane where elephant and other animals come to drink. The camp has 20 two- or three-bed self-catering **chalets** (**$$**), eight safari tents (**$**), and 15 camping and caravan sites with ablution block and kitchen unit. Facilities include a petrol station, camp shop, café, telephones and launderette. As with the other camps, day and night drives and game walks can be booked at reception and these are open to people staying outside the park.

LOWER SABIE

ⓘ *113 km to Berg-en-Dal, 141 km to Orpen, 53 km to Paul Kruger Gate, 213 km to Phalaborwa, 90 km to Pretoriuskop, 342 km to Punda Maria, 93 km to Satara, 43 km to Skukuza, T013-735 6056 for last-minute reservations (maximum 48 hrs before arrival).*

The region around Lower Sabie is part of a classic African savannah landscape, with grasslands, umbrella thorn and round-leaf teak stretching off into the distance. This is one of the best regions for seeing game, particularly rhino. Game is attracted here by water at the Mlondosi and Nhlanganzwani dams and the camp overlooks the Sabie River. The accommodation is impersonal but the camp itself is fairly peaceful. Facilities include the **Ingwe Restaurant**, a bar, shop, petrol station, launderette, phones and a swimming pool.

Accommodation is provided in large two or five-bed cottages (**$$$-$$**) with two bathrooms and a kitchen; two- or three-bed **chalets** (**$$**) with bathroom, fridge and hot-plate; two-bed **rondavels** (**$$**) with bathroom and fridge; two-bed **huts** (**$$**), with bathroom and fridge; small, two-bed **cottages** (**$$**) with a/c, fridge, veranda, ablution block; one-bed **safari tents** (**$$**) with ablution block; one-bed **huts** (**$**) with a/c, fridge and ablution block; plus camping and caravan sites, with ablution blocks and kitchen facilities.

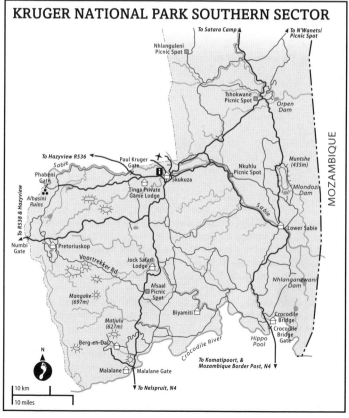

KRUGER NATIONAL PARK SOUTHERN SECTOR

MALALANE

ⓘ Check in at Berg-en-Dal.

Malalane is a satellite camp to Berg-en-Dal, set in a rugged area of mountain bushveld on the banks of the Crocodile River on the southern boundary of the park. It has five three- and four-bed **cottages ($$)**, with bathroom and solar-powered communal kitchen unit, plus camping and caravan sites with ablution block and kitchen unit.

PRETORIUSKOP

ⓘ Near Numbi Gate, 92 km to Berg-en-Dal, 125 km to Crocodile Bridge, 90 km to Lower Sabie, 184 km to Orpen, 140 km to Satara, 49 km to Skukuza, T013-735 5128 for last-minute reservations (maximum 48 hrs before arrival).

This is the oldest camp in Kruger and is also the third largest, with a fairly institutional feel. The game drives around Pretoriuskop pass through marula woodland and tall grassland, with good game-viewing areas to the north along the Sabie River and to the south along the Voortrekker Road, which follows the original wagon route through the veld. Rhino are often seen close to Numbi Gate. More animals congregate in this area in the summer than in the winter but it is always a rewarding area for game. Facilities include a restaurant, cafeteria, swimming pool made out of natural rock, petrol station, shop and launderette. It is also possible to join a night drive at Numbi Gate if you are staying outside the park in the Hazyview Area.

There are 142 sleeping units: six-, eight- and nine-bed guest **cottages ($$$)**, with two bathrooms and a kitchen; four-bed **cottages ($$$-$$)** with one bathroom and a kitchen; two- to four-bed **bungalows ($$)** with bathroom, fridge and hot plate; two-, three-, five- and six-bed **huts ($)** with a/c, fridge and ablution block, plus 45 camping and caravan sites with ablution blocks and kitchen units.

SKUKUZA

ⓘ 72 km to Berg-en-Dal, 77 km to Crocodile Bridge, 43 km to Lower Sabie, 137 km to Orpen, 213 km to Phalaborwa, 49 km to Pretoriuskop, 342 km to Punda Maria, 93 km to Satara, T013-735 4152 for last-minute reservations (maximum 48 hrs before arrival).

Located on the south bank of the Sabie River, Skukuza is Kruger's largest camp and the administrative centre of the park. The camp has grown to such an extent that it resembles a small town and you can forget that you're in a national park. Despite its size, Skukuza is at the centre of Kruger's prime game-viewing area and is a good base for game drives. The road heading northeast towards Satara has high concentrations of game and is said have one of the densest concentrations of lion in Africa – and the densest population of cars in Kruger.

Facilities here cater to almost every need and include a supermarket, petrol station, car wash, two restaurants, bank, post office, telephones, internet café, two swimming pools, a nine-hole golf course, doctor and launderette. There is also an open-air cinema showing wildlife videos in the evenings, a good information centre and library, and a small nursery selling indigenous plants including baobabs. **Kruger Emergency Road Services** is also based here.

Skukuza accommodates over 1000 people in four-, six- and eight-bed **cottages ($$$$)**, with two bathrooms and kitchen; two-, three- and four-bed **cottages ($$$)** with one bathroom and kitchen; two-bed **chalets ($$)** with one bathroom and kitchen; three-bed **chalets ($$)** with bathroom, fridge and hot-plate; three-bed **bungalows ($$)**, with bathroom and fridge; two- and four-bed **safari tents ($)** with ablution block, kitchen units, plus 80 camping and caravan sites, ablution blocks and kitchen units.

Central Kruger is quieter than the south, with large areas of flat mopane woodland inhabited by herds of buffalo, elephant, wildebeest and zebra. Olifants camp is in a spectacular location.

ARRIVING IN CENTRAL KRUGER

Orpen Gate and **Phalaborwa Gate** are on the western boundary. Orpen Gate is on the R531 from Klaserie and Phalaborwa is on the R71 route from Polokwane and Tzaneen.

BALULE

① *11 km from Olifants where visitors must check in, T013-735 6606 for last-minute reservations (maximum 48 hrs before arrival).*

Balule is on the banks of the Olifants River and is one of Kruger's wildest camps. It is little more than a patch of cleared bush surrounded by an electrified chain-link fence; visitors can see animals wandering by only metres away. There are six three-bed **huts ($)**, with an ablution block but no electricity, though there are gas stoves and lanterns are provided, and 15 basic caravan and camping sites, with ablution block and braai sites; firewood is on sale here. The smell of barbecued meat attracts hyenas who patrol the fence all night in search of scraps (but don't under any circumstances feed them).

BOULDERS

① *54 km to Letaba, 31 km to Mopani, 54 km to Phalaborwa Gate; check in at Mopani, the camp must be booked as a single unit, maximum 12.*

This unfenced private camp is in an area of acacia, knobthorn and mopane woodland. The camp blends in beautifully with its environment and is set amongst massive granite boulders. The four thatched **bungalows ($$$$)** are raised on stilts and have a veranda from which to observe the wildlife wandering through the camp. Each sleeps three people and has a communal kitchen and solar power.

LETABA

① *234 km to Berg-en-Dal, 117 km to Orpen, 51 km to Phalaborwa, 69 km to Satara, 162 km to Skukuza, T013-735 6636 for last-minute reservations (maximum 48 hrs before arrival).*

Letaba is one of the larger camps in central Kruger. On the banks of the Letaba River, it is pleasant and neatly laid out. The restaurant is in a magnificent setting for watching game come down to drink. Some interesting species can be seen here, most notably large herds of elephant, but also cheetah, lion, ostrich, roan, sable, steenbok and tsessebe. There is good game viewing to the east of Letaba along the river and at Engelhardt Dam. The two hills rising in the distance to the east of the dam are Longwe, 480 m, and Mhala, 465 m. They are flanked by some beautiful round-leaf teak woodland and baobabs. Middelvlei windmill is 20 km north of Letaba on the H1-6 and provides the only source of water for miles around. Facilities include a mini supermarket, good restaurant, swimming pool, launderette, petrol station, museum with exhibits on Kruger's elephants, TV lounge showing wildlife films and Kruger Emergency Road Services.

Accommodation is available in six-, eight- and nine-bed **cottages ($$$)** with two bath rooms and kitchen; two- and three-bed **chalets ($$)** with bathroom, fridge and hot plate; three- bed **bungalows ($$)** with bathroom and fridge; four-bed **huts ($$)** with a/c, fridge and veranda; four-bed **safari tents ($)** with ablution blocks and kitchen units, plus a large, shadeless campsite, with 35 camping and caravan sites with ablution blocks and kitchen units.

MAROELA AND TAMBOTI SATELLITE CAMPS

① Check in at Orpen Gate, 4 km.

These are both satellite camps to Orpen. Maroela large camp ground is on the south bank of the Timbavati River, and has 20 camping and caravan sites, ablution blocks and

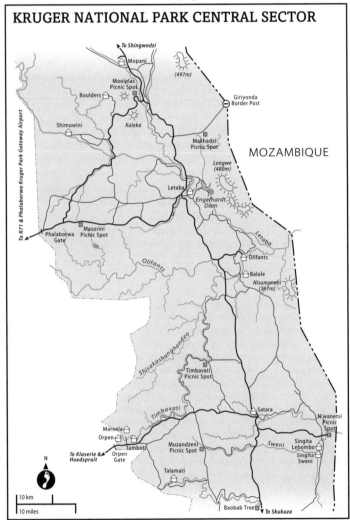

KRUGER NATIONAL PARK CENTRAL SECTOR

To Shingwedzi

Mopani

Mooiplas Picnic Spot

(497m)

Boulders

Giriyonda Border Post

Shimuwini

Kaleka

Makhadzi Picnic Spot

MOZAMBIQUE

Longwe (480m)

Letaba

Engelhardt Dam

To R71 & Phalaborwa Kruger Park Gateway Airport

Phalaborwa Gate

Masorini Picnic Spot

Olifants

Letaba

Olifants

Balule

Nisumaneni (367m)

Shisakashanghondzo

Timbavati Picnic Spot

Satara

N'wanetsi Picnic Spot

Timbavati

Maroela

Orpen

Tamboti

Muzandzeni Picnic Spot

To Klaserie & Hoedspruit

Orpen Gate

Sweni

Singita Lebombo

Singita Sweni

Talamati

N

Baobab Tree

To Skukuza

10 km

10 miles

kitchen units. There are no other facilities here, but there is a shop at Orpen Gate where you check in and where you can also arrange day walks and night drives. Not far from Maroela, **Tamboti ($$)** is a tented camp on the banks of the Timbavati River, offering 35 furnished safari tents for two to four people, either fully equipped or sharing communal kitchen, ablutions and eating boma. This is the ideal spot for people looking for a complete bush experience without having to bring all the equipment. There is no restaurant or shop.

MOPANI

ⓘ *281 km to Berg-en-Dal, 47 km to Letaba, 86 km to Olifants, 74 km to Phalaborwa Gate, 258 km to Punda Maria, 209 km to Skukuza, T013-735 6535 for last-minute reservations (maximum 48 hrs before arrival).*

This is one of Kruger's largest public camps set on a rocky hill overlooking the Pioneer Dam. It is only a few kilometres south of the Tropic of Capricorn, set on a seemingly endless plain of mopane shrub. The accommodation at Mopani has been made from natural materials and is more pleasant and spacious than some of the older camps. Choose from an eight-bed **cottage ($$$$)**; six-bed **cottages ($$$)** with kitchen; or two- and three-bed **bungalows ($$)** with kitchen. Facilities include swimming pool, nature trail, petrol station, shop, restaurant, bar overlooking the dam, cafeteria and launderette.

OLIFANTS

ⓘ *219 km to Berg-en-Dal, 147 km to Lower Sabie, 102 km to Orpen, 158 km to Paul Kruger Gate, 83 km to Phalaborwa Gate, 212 km to Punda Maria, 147 km to Skukuza, T013-735 6606 for last-minute reservations (maximum 48 hrs before arrival).*

This peaceful camp is in a spectacular setting high on a hill overlooking fever trees and wild figs lining the banks of the Olifants River. The game drives in the immediate area pass through flat mopane woodland in the north and a hilly area of rocks and woodland in the south where klipspringer are often seen. Olifants is one of Kruger's most attractive camps, blending into the surrounding woodland. Facilities include a restaurant, shop, information centre, wildlife films, petrol, launderette, open to day visitors. A thatched veranda perched on the edge of the camp looks down into the river valley and is a superb place for game viewing. The thatched accommodation, shaded by large old sycamores and sausage trees, encompasses eight-bed **cottages ($$$$)**; four-bed **cottages ($$$)** with kitchen; two-bed **chalets ($$)** with kitchen or bathroom, fridge and hot plate; and three- or two-bed **bungalows ($$)** with bathroom and fridge.

ORPEN

ⓘ *Just beyond Orpen Gate, T013-735 6355 for last-minute reservations (maximum 48 hrs before arrival).*

Orpen is a small camp past the entrance gate on the western central plains, set amongst acacias, marulas and aloes. The road passing along the Timbavati River offers a chance of seeing game, and the area around the camp is known as a good place to see leopard, lion and cheetah. There are six-bed **cottages ($$$)** with bathroom and kitchen, and three-bed **bungalows ($$)** with bathroom and kitchen. Facilities include a petrol station and camp shop.

SATARA

ⓘ *15 km from Berg-en-Dal, 127 km from Crocodile Bridge, 69 km from Letaba, 93 km from Lower Sabie, 48 km from Orpen, 104 km from Paul Kruger Gate, 140 km from Pretoriuskop,*

245 km from Punda Maria, 93 km from Skukuza, T013-735 6306 for reservations (maximum 48 hrs before arrival).

Satara, Kruger's second-largest camp looks rather like a motorway service station in the middle of the bush, although the institutional atmosphere of the accommodation is softened by its trees and lawns. Satara is set in the flat grasslands of the eastern region, which attract large herds of wildebeest, buffalo, kudu, impala, zebra and elephant. There is good game viewing on the road to Orpen.

Accommodation is available in guest **cottages ($$$$)** sleeping six, eight or nine, with one or two bathrooms and kitchen; two- or three-bed **bungalows ($$)** with bathroom and kitchen; two- or three-bed **bungalows ($$)** with bathroom and communal kitchen; and 87 camping and caravan sites, with ablution blocks, kitchen units. Facilities include petrol station, car wash, Kruger Emergency Road Service, camp shop, cafeteria, restaurant, launderette and swimming pool.

SHIMUWINI

① 66 km to Letaba, 118 km to Olifants, 52 km to Phalaborwa, T013-735 6683 for reservations (maximum 48 hrs before arrival).

This bushveld camp is set in a region of bushwillow and mopane woodland, with less of a concentration of wildlife, compared to the south of Kruger. However, this is still an interesting wilderness area with a good variety of wildlife. The private access road leading to Shimuwini follows the Letaba River where elephant can sometimes be seen bathing and the riverine forest around the camp is good for birdwatching.

The camp overlooks the Shimuwini Dam. Visitors to the camp have private access to the dam, which is surrounded by giant sycamore trees. There is a hide here from which to see crocodiles, hippo, waterbuck and waterbirds. The camp consists of a row of four- and six-bed thatched **cottages ($$$)** with kitchen and veranda, some have additional outside showers, shaded by appleleaf trees and acacias.

TALAMATI

① 30 km to Orpen Gate, T013-735 6343 for reservations (maximum 48 hrs before arrival).

This rustic bushveld camp is set on the banks of the Nwaswitsonto River, which is normally dry. The grassland and acacia woodland along the western boundary attract kudu, giraffe, sable and white rhino. Klipspringer can be seen on the rocky outcrops. There are two hides in the camp for game viewing and birdwatching. The camp has two-, four- and six-bed **cottages ($$$)**, with bathroom and kitchen.

→ PRIVATE GAME RESERVES

The reserves fringing the western border of Kruger offer some of the most exclusive game viewing in the world. Here you have the chance of seeing the Big Five and exploring the natural environment of Kruger from the comfort of a private 4WD, with the promise of luxury accommodation and superb cuisine at the end of your game drive. Each lodge has its own secluded setting, providing an enjoyable 'in the wild' experience. But the biggest advantage of staying in the private reserves are the excellent game guides, who provide a fantastic introduction to the bush – usually with far better game-spotting skills, too, which means you'll see much more than if you were self-driving.

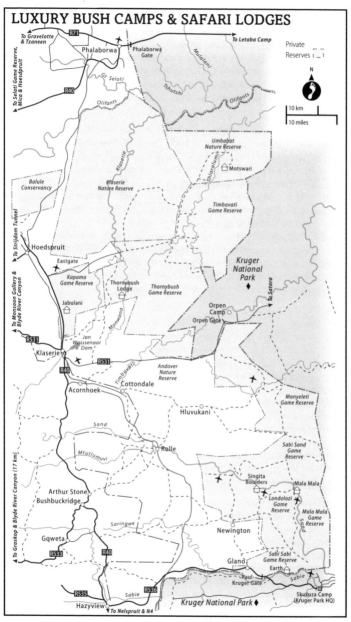

LUXURY BUSH CAMPS & SAFARI LODGES

To Gravelotte & Tzaneen

R71

Phalaborwa

To Selati Game Reserve, Mica & Hoedspruit

R40

To Letaba Camp

Phalaborwa Gate

Gr Selati

Olifants

Mulaluni

Tshutshi

Olifants

Private Reserves

N

10 km

10 miles

Umbabat Nature Reserve

Klaserie

Shlaralumi

Motswari

Balule Conservancy

Klaserie Nature Reserve

Timbavati Game Reserve

To Strijdom Tunnel

Hoedspruit

Eastgate

Kapama Game Reserve

Thornybush Lodge

Thornybush Game Reserve

Kruger National Park

To Satara

To Monsoon Gallery & Blyde River Canyon

Jabulani

Monwana

Orpen Camp

Orpen Gate

R531

Jan Wasssenaar Dam

R531

Klaserie

R40

Timbavati

Andover Nature Reserve

Manyeleti Game Reserve

Acornhoek

Cottondale

Hluvukani

Sand

Sabi Sand Game Reserve

Mtutlumuvi

Rolle

Singita Boulders

Mala Mala

To Graskop & Blyde River Canyon (17 km)

Arthur Stone Bushbuckridge

Londolozi Game Reserve

Mala Mala Game Reserve

Saringwe

Newington

Sand

Gqweta

R533

R40

Sabi Sabi Game Reserve

Glano

Earth

Sabie

R535

R536

Paul Kruger Gate

Skukuza Camp (Kruger Park HQ)

Hazyview

To Nelspruit & N4

Sabie

Kruger National Park

ARRIVING AT THE PRIVATE GAME RESERVES

Access to the lodges is straightforward. Guests are collected from either **Phalaborwa Kruger Park Gateway Airport**, **Eastgate Airport** at Hoedspruit, or **Kruger Mpumalanga International Airport (KMIA)** near Nelspruit (scheduled flights or charter flights are usually included in packages) and driven by safari vehicle to the lodge. Alternatively, a charter by light aircraft will take you directly to those lodges that have a private airstrip, or you can drive yourself – it takes around six hours from Johannesburg.

RESERVES

There are now numerous private reserves, each holding countless game lodges. The best-known private reserves include **Klaserie**, **Timbavati**, **Thornybush**, **Mala Mala** and **Sabi Sabi**, which together form the largest private game area in the world. The first three are in Limpopo, but are included here together with the Mpumalanga reserves. Within these reserves are several smaller reserves, which have been incorporated into a single wilderness area; some still retain their original name which can be a bit confusing. For example, **Idube Game Reserve** and **Londolozi Game Reserve** are now both part of the much larger Sabi Sand Game Reserve.

In the last 20 years, the fences between all these reserves have been removed, including, most significantly, the western Kruger National Park fence. This development has helped, in part, to restore natural east–west migration routes and has created an area that is most often dubbed the **Greater Kruger National Park**. Despite a confusing range of names for reserves and camps, they all now fall into this greater area.

GAME VIEWING

Game viewing is, of course, the main activity in all the lodges. Days normally begin with an early-morning game drive, returning in mid- to late-morning for breakfast. Guests can then either choose to go on a game walk or relax by the pool before lunch. When the worst of the day's heat has passed, the vehicles set off on another game drive, returning for dinner. Optional night drives are usually also available.

Game viewing can vary from lodge to lodge, depending on how many vehicles patrol an area and, of course, how much effort the rangers put into showing visitors around. Nevertheless, game viewing is always dependent on luck, and staying in a five-star private game lodge does not mean that you will be guaranteed better animal sightings than if you were travelling around Kruger in a hire car and staying in a SANParks campsite. The benefits, however, are that you will have a personal and knowledgeable guide, and you're unlikely to come across many other tourists.

LODGES

Most guests spend between two and three days at a lodge to get the most out of game viewing. Prices vary considerably, and can range from fairly expensive, old-fashioned lodges, to full-on luxury living, with extravagant accommodation, sumptuous cuisine and a variety of extras such as butler service. Most lodges are fairly luxurious, however, and in between outings you can appreciate the full extent of your surroundings: most camps have platforms overlooking a waterhole or a river, there are usually comfortable lounge areas, libraries of books and magazines about wildlife, and most lodges have swimming pools. Some camps also have gyms, spas and conference facilities.

Special deals are often available, and it is worth looking out for fly-drive packages and discounts out of peak season. The daily cost of staying at a lodge vary from R5000 to R10,000 for two people sharing, though rates can soar to over R20,000; prices include all meals, game walks and game drives. Reservations should be made well in advance because the most popular lodges get fully booked very quickly.

TIMBAVATI GAME RESERVE

Timbavati extends from Orpen to the region just south of the Olifants River. As well as large herds of elephant, giraffe, blue wildebeest, zebra and impala, this area is known for its white lions, although these have largely become assimilated in to the larger lion population. Open savannah, riverine forest, acacia, marula and mopane woodlands support a tremendous variety of wildlife, including 350 species of bird. The reserve was created in the 1950s from a group of privately owned farms where hunting was banned. Game, such as cheetah, sable and white rhino, was reintroduced to re-establish populations which were originally present in this area. You can get to the lodges in the northern part of the reserve via the turning 7 km south of Hoedspruit off the R40. The nearest airport is **Eastgate**, although many of the lodges have private airstrips. Camps in the southern areas are accessed by the turning 9 km north of Klaserie at Kapama, off the R40. ▸▸ *There are 13 luxury lodges and camps dotted about the reserve, www.timbavati.co.za.*

KAPAMA PRIVATE GAME RESERVE

Kapama Private Game Reserve is one with the easiest to access as it's right next to **Eastgate** airport near Hoedspruit in Limpopo Province. The reserve covers approximately 13,000 ha of prime big game territory, with three luxury lodges within its borders. A highlight here are the elephant-back safaris offered at **Camp Jabulani**, the first of now many operations of its kind in South Africa. Guests are seated on canvas-covered saddles positioned behind an experienced elephant handler. From this vantage point, they are able to view game from a close proximity as the elephants move silently and in a single file through the bush. The reserve also offers game drives, clay pigeon shooting, bush walks, birdwatching from a bird hide on the banks of a large dam, sundowner cruises, traditional dancing, hot-air ballooning and quad-biking. All the activities are exclusively for the guests at the luxury lodges within the reserve. ▸▸ *There are four luxury lodges in the reserve, www.kapama.co.za.*

THORNYBUSH NATURE RESERVE

Thornybush started life as a private farm sharing a border with Timbavati. It was converted into a private game reserve of 11,500 ha and is now part of the Greater Kruger National Park. There are eight game lodges here. The main entrance is 9 km north of Klaserie off the R40; look out for the signs for Kapama and the Hoedspruit Cheetah project. The nearest airport is **Eastgate** at Hoedspruit. ▸▸ *There are eight luxury lodges in the reserve, www.thornybush.co.za.*

MALA MALA GAME RESERVE

Mala Mala was one of the first private reserves to identify and cater for the top end of the luxury market. Guests have exclusive access to over 50 km of riverfront along the Sand River, offering some of the best game viewing in South Africa thanks to the fact that this is a perennial river. Seeing the Big Five is a central part of the Mala Mala experience and guests get a certificate to authenticate their sightings. The camps in the south of the reserve are approached from the R536, the Hazyview to Skukuza road. For the lodges to the north, turn off the R40 about 15 km north of Hazyview. It is at least a further 50 km to the accommodation. ▸▸ *There are three luxury lodges in the reserve, www.malamala.com.*

SABI SABI GAME RESERVE

Sabi Sabi Private Game Reserve is a relatively small area of land in the extreme south of the block of contiguous reserves which stretch all the way from the Olifants River to the Sabie River. To get there, follow the R536 from Hazyview to Skukuza, turn off at Glano. Although it is now part of the Greater Kruger National Park, the collection of private lodges and camps in Sabi Sabi couldn't be more different than the Skukuza camp across the Sabie River. Sabi Sabi has an excellent reputation by virtue of being the only private reserve on the perennial Sabie River. ▸▸ *Sabi Sabi is home to four of the most fashionable lodges, www.sabisabi.com.*

SABI SAND GAME RESERVE

Sabi Sand has the highest density of lodges and game-viewing vehicles and is slightly more crowded than Timbavati or Thornybush. However, the Sand River has water all year round, which does attract large numbers of game. The reserve was established in 1934 by the owners of farms in this area but the first lodge wasn't opened to the public until 1962. Some of the most famous private concessions are within Sabi Sand, including Londolozi and Ulusaba. The game-viewing experience here is intended to give visitors a deeper understanding of the wilderness and don't just concentrate on the Big Five. To reach the reserve, turn off the R40 about 15 km north of Hazyview; this is the same road for Mala Mala Game Reserve. It is at least a further 50 km to the accommodation. ▸▸ *There are no fewer than 19 lodges in the reserve, www.sabisand.co.za.*

KRUGER NATIONAL PARK LISTINGS

WHERE TO STAY

Nelspruit

$$$ Sheppard Boutique Hotel,
23 Sheppard Drive, T013-752 3394,
www.sheppardboutique.co.za. The only
luxury offering in town, with 17 tastefully
decorated suites with large beds, antique
furnishings, stylish prints and low-key
lighting. Elegant, old-fashioned lounge and
dining room serving good South African
cuisine. Swimming pool and tennis courts.
No children under 8.

Kruger Park Concessions

For SANParks accommodation within the
different sections of Kruger, see page 233.
$$$$ Jock Safari Lodge, southeast
of the park, 35 km from Malalane Gate,
reservations T041-407 1000, www.
jocksafarilodge.com. This very expensive
camp is in an area of mixed woodland
between Malalane and Skukuza. 15
thatched suites decorated with prints of
the original illustrations from the novel,
Jock of the Bushveld, each with viewing
deck, plunge pool and outside showers
overlooking the Mitomeni and Biyamiti
rivers. Rock swimming pool and spa.
$$$$ Singita Lebombo, on the banks
of the Sweni River near the Mozambique
border, 64 km from Orpen Gate,
reservations T021-683 3424, www.singita.
com. A modern, stylish and very expensive
lodge with gym and spa built of glass,
steel and stone. Fashionable alternative
to the usual colonial or ethnic themes.
15 suites, linked by walkways, with sleek
decks, designer furniture, infinity pool
with white loungers and bar area.
$$$$ Singita Sweni, near Singita
Lebombo. Smallest of the Singita lodges,
with just 6 very expensive suites built on
stilts tucked away in the trees with views
over the bush, stylish dining room with
floor-to-ceiling windows and views over the
river. Decor is dark wood, ethnic fabrics and
earthenware with splashes of bright lime.

Private game reserves

There are far too many lodges in the private
game reserves to list in full. Be sure to shop
around when choosing where to stay. Most
reserves have excellent websites.
$$$$ Camp Jabulani, Kapama Game
Reserve, reservations T012-460 5605, www.
campjabulani.com. Opulent accommodation
and elephant-back safaris, with 7 stylish
suites, with private decks and splash pools,
butler service, open showers, fireplaces,
fashionable fusion food spread over several
courses. Rates (very expensive) are inclusive
of everything except spa treatments.
$$$$ Earth Lodge, Sabi Sabi Game
Reserve, set on the banks of the Sabie
River. This innovative lodge feels like an
ultra-trendy boutique hotel set deep in
the African bush. The design cuts into
the earth, which means that the lodge is
virtually invisible, with smooth stone and
grass-covered roofs blending into the
surroundings. 13 suites with stylish decor of
muted colours and natural materials, private
plunge pool, glass-fronted bathrooms and
butler. Bar area made up of the roots of
trees, luxury spa, and meals are served
in an open-air boma cut into the ground.
$$$$ Mala Mala Main Camp, Mala Mala
Game Reserve. 18 ochre-coloured thatched
rondavels, extremely spacious, each with his
and hers bathrooms, 1 room for wheelchair
users. Lounge area is decorated with
elephant tusks, hunting rifles, spears and
African memorabilia. The whole camp is set
in a shady wood beside the river, good meals
served, swimming pool.
$$$$ Motswari, Timbavati Game Reserve,
reservations T011-463 1990, www.motswari.
co.za. One of the smaller luxury camps,
located in the northern region of Timbavati

with exclusive access to a large area, 15 luxury and expensive bungalows with magnificent bush and river views from the beds, traditional open-air boma, spacious lounge and bar overlooking a dam, art gallery exhibiting original wildlife art, and pool.

$$$$ Ngala, Timbavati Game Reserve, reservations T011-809 4300, www.ngala. co.za, www.andbeyond.com. This very expensive lodge is on the Timbavati Flood Plain, a region known for its elephant and lion. 20 a/c thatched cottages and tents, filled with antique furnishings, set in an area of mopane woodland overlooking a waterhole. Meals are served on the open decking area overlooking the waterhole, or in a lantern-lit lapa area. The food here is particularly good, and the game rangers very knowledgeable.

$$$$ Singita Boulders, Sabi Sand Game Reserve. Impressive lodge built of curving thatch and stone moulded into the rock set on the banks of the Sand River. 12 luxurious suites, stone theme, natural decor and cool, neutral colours, beautiful views from the beds and plunge pools. Spa, sundeck, swimming pool, attractive lounge, and game viewing deck.

$$$$ Tanda Tula, Timbavati Game Reserve, reservations T015-793 3191, www.tandatula.co.za. Set in an area of thick acacia woodland, 12 expensive thatched East African-style safari tents furnished with wicker furniture and Victorian bathrooms. The bar on the veranda overlooks the pool and a waterhole. In the evenings, weather permitting, dinners are held in the dried-up river bed in front of the camp.

$$$$ Thornybush Game Lodge, Thornybush Nature Reserve, reservations T011-253 6500, www.thornybush.co.za. Although this lodge (very expensive) is the largest in the reserve, you can still enjoy a relaxing and private time in the bush here. 20 suites with outdoor showers, the bar and the boma are a popular feature beside the Monwana River, children's activities, pool and spa.

WHAT TO DO

Tour operators

The tour operators listed below can organize a wide range of day and overnight trips to the local sights including Kruger and Blyde River Canyon, and will pick up from any hotel in Nelspruit. A day tour to Kruger costs in the region of R1200 per person, and longer 3-day, 2-night Kruger tours start from around R3700.

Isivuba Tours & Safaris, T082-887 0666, www.isivuba.co.za.

Kruger Park South Safaris, T082-887 0666, www.krugersouthsafaris.co.za.

Place of Rock, T013-751 5319, www.placeofrock.co.za.

Vula Tours, T031-741 2826, www.vulatours.co.za.

Walking safaris

Transfrontier Walking Safaris, T015-793 3816, www.transfrontiers.com. Offers 4- or 5-day walking safaris in the private reserves accessed from Hoedspruit and is popular with budget travellers. Rates include transfers to and from Johannesburg and Tshwane (Pretoria), though you can arrange to meet them in Hoedspruit. The 5-day safari (R6100) starts on Mon and the 4-day safari (R4575) starts on Fri; there's a maximum of 8 people so early booking is advised. Accommodation is in 2 simple bush camps with pre-erected walk-in tents with twin beds, and communal ablution facilities, and daily walks leave from these. Each camp has an honesty bar and a dining tent, and costs include all meals. No children under 16 and you need to be reasonably fit. Highly recommended for a peaceful, authentic and informative bush experience well away from the crowds.

PANORAMA REGION

The area of the eastern Drakensberg along the southwest boundary of Kruger and to the north of Nelspruit is referred to as the Panorama Region. It is dotted with small towns, popular with local tourists who come for the craft shops and restaurants, but the main reason for a visit is the spectacular Blyde River Canyon, the third largest canyon in the world. The mountains provide blessed relief from the heat on the plains of the Lowveld. A visit to the region is often combined with a safari to the southern and central parts of Kruger, and the Panorama towns give easy access to the park's gates on the southwestern side.

➔ HOEDSPRUIT AND AROUND

Hoedspruit is Afrikaans for 'hat creek', and the place acquired its name when, after a long trek over the mountains into the heat of the Lowveld, one of the Voortrekkers removed his hat, threw it into the cool waters of the Sandspruit River and decided to stay. Today, the town has barely expanded beyond its string of shops, banks and petrol station, and remains a sleepy outpost surrounded by game-rich country, loomed over by the Drakensberg escarpment.

GETTING THERE AND MOVING ON

Hoedspruit is close to Central Kruger's Phalaborwa Gate, the private game reserves (see page 246) and the Panorama Region. There is little of interest to keep you in town itself; the main attractions and accommodation options are along the R531 towards Blyde River Canyon.

MOHOLOHOLO REHABILITATION CENTRE

ⓘ *30 km south of Hoedspruit on the R531, T015-795 5236, www.moholoholo.co.za, 2½-hr tours Mon-Sat 0930 and 1500, Sun during school holidays only 1500, they leave promptly so get to the gate in plenty of time, R100, children (7-12) R50, under 7s free.*

Moholoholo is a rehabilitation centre for abandoned, injured and poisoned wildlife. Animals are brought here from all over South Africa and, once healthy enough, are reintroduced into their natural environment. Some of the big cats however, cannot be rereleased into the wild, so the centre is now home to them. There are a number of big birds such as raptors and vultures, many of which have been injured from flying into power lines. Another important function of the centre is breeding and they have successfully bred and released into the wild the endangered crowned eagle, serval and many other species.

KHAMAI REPTILE PARK

ⓘ *15 km west of Hoedspruit on the R531, T015-795 5203, www.khamai.co.za, 0800-1700, R50, children (4-14) R25, under 4s free.*

This impressive reptile park was established in 1984 by Donald Strydom, one of Africa's leading snake specialists, as a refuge and platform for understanding reptiles. There are numerous enclosures holding a wide variety of snakes, lizards, tortoises and crocodiles, and Donald's staff provide a good understanding of how many snakes are needlessly killed by farmers in South Africa. For an extra fee you can have a photo taken with a python wrapped over your shoulders. The park also offers a free service to cure people of their phobias of snakes and spiders.

The Blyde River Canyon is the third largest in the world after the Grand Canyon in the USA and Fish River Canyon in Namibia. It is the product of the Blyde River, which tumbles down from the Drakensberg escarpment to the Lowveld over a series of waterfalls and cascades that spill into the **Blydespoort Dam** at the bottom. Blyde means 'river of joy', and the river was so named after Hendrik Potgieter and his party returned safely from Delagoa Bay

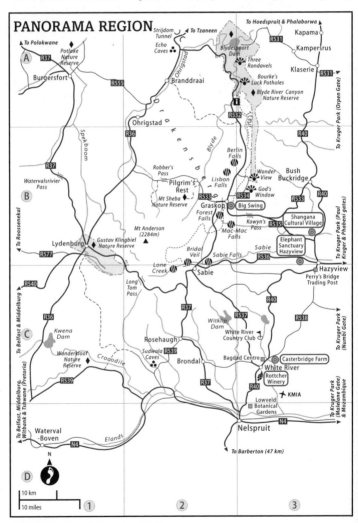

PANORAMA REGION

(Mozambique) in 1844. Voortrekkers, who had stayed behind at their camp, first named it Treur River ('river of mourning'), under the mistaken impression that the party had been killed, so when Pogieter returned, they had to rename it.

The winding canyon is 26 km in length and is joined by the similarly spectacular 11 km **Ohrigstad Canyon** near Swadini. The 27,000-ha **Blyde River Canyon Nature Reserve** extends from God's Window down to the far side of the Blyde River dam. The canyon drops down 750 m, and for most of its length it is inaccessible. There are no roads crossing the reserve or linking the top and bottom of the canyon, but there are some short walking trails, and a number of viewpoints snake off the along the R532 and overlook the Canyon and Lowveld beyond. Do take the time to drive down to the viewpoints, as you can't see much of the spectacular canyon if you stick to the R532.

VIEWPOINTS

The most famous of the viewpoints is **God's Window**, right on the edge of the escarpment overlooking an almost sheer 300-m drop into the tangle of forest below. The views through the heat haze stretch over the Lowveld as far as Kruger. At the top of the hill there is a tiny patch of rainforest, which survives in the microclimate on the very tip of the ridge. At 1730 m, **Wonder View** is the highest viewpoint accessible from the road and **Pinnacle Rock** is a 30-m-high quartzite 'needle' that rises dramatically out of the fern-clad ravine. From here it is possible to see the tops of the eight waterfalls that take the Blyde River down 450 m in a series of cascades to the dam.

The most developed viewpoint is at **Bourke's Luck Potholes**, an unusual series of rock formation resembling Swiss cheese. The smooth rock has been moulded and formed by the swirling action of whirlpools where the Treur and the Blyde rivers meet, creating spectacular dips, hollows and holes. The name 'Bourke's Luck' comes from Tom Bourke, a prospector who worked a claim here in the vain belief that he would find gold. There is a **visitor centre and kiosk** ① *0700-1700, R25, children (under 12) R15, serving snacks and light meals.* The visitor centre includes an exhibition outlining the geological history of the area. From here, a wood walkway winds around and over the potholes. A short drive further north, the viewpoint at the **Three Rondavels** is by far the most dramatic. At the car park by the walkway is a small craft market and some toilets. From here, a walkway leads out onto the lip of the canyon, with the vast cleft in the rock opening out in front of you, and **Blydespoort Dam** shimmering intensely blue at the bottom. The Three Rondavels easily recognized as the three circular rocky peaks opposite, capped with grass and vegetation and looking distinctly like thatched African rondavel huts.

South of the Blyde River Canyon on the R532 towards Graskop, you'll pass Berlin Falls and Lisbon Falls. Berlin Falls are 45 m high, and the water cascades into a circular pool surrounded by forest. At 92 m, Lisbon Falls are the highest in the area, and the river is separated into three streams as it plunges into the pool below.

→ GRASKOP

This small town lies just south of the Blyde River Canyon but, despite having a large selection of holiday accommodation, restaurants and craft shops, it remains surprisingly quiet and makes a peaceful base from which to explore the region. Miners arrived here during the 1880s and established a camp, but modern Graskop is surrounded by forestry plantations and is an important centre of the timber industry. Today Graskop attracts fame as being home of the South African stuffed pancake – the famous **Harrie's** restaurant started it all, and the stuffed sweet and savoury pancakes are renowned throughout the country. Local residents have capitalized on this reputation, and there is now a line of pancake houses along the main street.

Information is available in the private **information office** ① *Louis Trichardt St, T013-767 1866, www.graskop.co.za, open 0800-1700.*

Graskop is 1000 m higher than the Lowveld at the bottom of the escarpment and temperatures here are normally up to 8°C cooler; night-time temperatures in winter often go below 0°C and even in summer a sweater can be useful. This is also one of the wettest regions in South Africa but most of the rain falls during torrential thunderstorms in the summer months. This is the best time of year to see the waterfalls; the force of the water crashing into the pools below is spectacular.

Heading east out of Graskop towards Hazyview, the road goes over **Kowyn's Pass** a few kilometres from Graskop. Before descending towards the Lowveld it passes **Graskop Gorge**, where adrenalin junkies try out the **Big Swing** ① *T013-767 1621, www.bigswing. co.za, 0900-1700 weather permitting,* and there are views looking up to **God's Window** (see page 253). This is a fruit-growing area of mangoes and lychees, which are sold at stalls on the side of the road in season.

→ PILGRIM'S REST

Northwest of Graskop on the R533, Pilgrim's Rest is a tiny mining town dating from the late 19th century that has been totally reconstructed as a living museum to preserve a fascinating part of South Africa's cultural heritage. It's a pretty spot: lining the main street, a row of miners' cottages with their corrugated-iron roofs and wooden walls nestles in a lush, leafy and utterly quiet valley. It's easy to imagine how it must have once looked, with a magistrate's court, church, local newspaper and schoolhouse. Although most of the buildings are strung out along one long street, the settlement has a very clear division between Uptown and Downtown, and today many of the reconstructed cottages house gift shops and cafés, and there's a large craft market at the entrance to the village.

BACKGROUND

The history of Pilgrim's Rest is a fascinating tale of gold fever in southern Africa during the late 19th century, as prospectors opened up new areas in search of a fortune. The town was named by one of the first prospectors, William Trafford, because he believed that his wandering days in search of gold had finally ended and yelled out "the pilgrim is at rest!". The first gold was found by Alec 'Wheelbarrow' Patterson, in a fertile valley then known as Lone Peach Tree Creek, in September 1873. Once Trafford announced that he had also found gold, the newspapers quickly spread the word and by the end of the year more than 1500 prospectors had pitched their tents along the creek. Life was far from easy for these fortune seekers, who slept on grass mattresses in makeshift tents, often sick with malaria and exposure, in a place where lawlessness and violence was rife.

Although some of the best finds were made in 1875, the region continued to produce gold until 1972, when the last mine was closed. In 1881, a financier, David Benjamin, formed the Transvaal Gold Exploration and Land Company, which effectively ran the gold fields until they were closed. Although there were poor years there were also some bountiful periods: in the 1890s a particularly rich reef – the Theta Reef – was discovered, which yielded more than five million ounces of gold over a period of 50 years. In 1986 Pilgrim's Rest was declared a National Monument and restoration of the old mining buildings began.

PLACES IN PILGRIM'S REST

Historical displays and exhibits on gold-panning techniques can be found at the **Pilgrim's Rest Information Centre and Museum** ① *Main St, T013-768 1060, www.pilgrims-rest. co.za, 0900-1600*. There are several other small village museums, housed in old miners' cottages, within walking distance. They are open 0900-1245, 1345-1600, and entry fee for each one is R10, children (under 16) R5, tickets from the tourist office.

Both in Uptown, the **House Museum** is a wooden and corrugated-iron structure typical of Pilgrim's Rest and displays Victorian furniture, while the **Printing Museum** has some old printing presses from the 1900s when news of the expanding goldfields was distributed to interested stockbrokers, prospectors and the Boer government in the *Gold News* newspaper which was established 1874. In Downtown, the **Dredzen Shop & House Museum**, has been fitted out as it would have been when it was built as a general dealers in the 1930s, with bicycles and brooms hanging from the ceiling, and the house of the proprietor has furnishings typical of a middle-class family of the period.

The **Diggings Site Museum** ① *daily tours 1000, 1100, 1200, 1400 and 1500 with gold-panning demonstration, R10, children (under 16) R5, tickets from the tourist office*, is at the top of Uptown where the tour coaches park. A visit here helps visitors gain an insight into the lives of the diggers and prospectors during the gold rush at the end of the 19th century, before the first gold mining company took control of the town. Gold panning is demonstrated and visitors can have a go themselves.

The **Alanglade Period House Museum** ① *guided tours only and at least 30 mins' notice needed, daily 1100 and 1400, R20 per person, tickets from the tourist office*, is north of the village on the Mpumalanga escarpment. Built in 1915, the house is typically early 20th century and was the official mine manager's residence for Pilgrim's Rest up until 1972. Today it is furnished with Edwardian, art nouveau and art deco pieces.

→ SOUTH OF GRASKOP

South of Graskop, 11 km before reaching Sabie, Mac Mac Falls and Mac Mac Pools ① *R5 per person*, are 65 m high. Over 1000 miners rushed to the falls in 1873 after gold was discovered above them. Originally there was a single fall, but in their eagerness to get to gold, some miners tried to divert the waterfall's flow and an over-enthusiastic application of dynamite created the second fall. The name of Mac Mac Falls originates from the large numbers of Scottish miners who came here. The tourist office has leaflets on day hikes which visit these and other local waterfalls: Bonnet Falls, Maria Shires Falls and Forest Falls. These are signposted off the road from Graskop.

→ SABIE

Once a gold-mining town, Sabie has little left to show of its glistening age and is now a prosaic timber-processing centre. Nevertheless, it has a pretty setting, ringed by mountains, pine and eucalyptus plantations, and it attracts a fair number of visitors who flock to its main road, lined with pleasant craft and coffee shops.

Prospectors first found gold in the region during the 1870s, but it wasn't until 1895 that gold was discovered at Sabie. The land here belonged to a big game hunter named Glynn who found the gold while on a picnic at Lower Sabie Falls. Glynn and his friends began shooting at a row of empty bottles on an outcrop of rock – the bullets chipped away at the rock revealing flecks of sparkling gold. This led to an influx of fortune hunters who came and camped on the banks of the Sabie River. In the process, many indigenous forests were chopped down to meet the demand for mine props and firewood. Fortunately, the far-sighted mine manager, Joseph Brook Shires, realized that man-made forests were necessary and planted the first trees in 1876. Planting continued into the next century, creating forestry jobs during the 1930s depression.

Today, Sabie lies in one of the largest man-made forests in the world. Driving around this region, the roads pass through endless tracts of neat rows of trees – impressive, but only a very few patches of indigenous forest remain. Tourist information is available from **Sabie Information** ① *Sabie Market Sq, T013-764 3599, www.sabie.co.za, Mon-Fri 0800-1630, Sat 0900-1300.*

The **Forestry Museum** ① *Ford St, T013-764 1058, www.komatiecotourism.co.za, Mon-Fri 0800-1630, Sat 0800-1200, R5, children (under 14) R2,* has displays on the development of South Africa's plantations and the timber industry, including an interesting cross-section of a 250-year-old yellowwood tree, which highlights aspects of South African history on its rings. The museum is also home to a satellite office of **Komatiland Forestry**, T013-764 1392, which has information on hiking and mountain-bike trails in the region, and you can download information and maps for several trails in the forests around Sabie from the website.

→ HAZYVIEW

Hazyview, 58 km from Nelspruit, lies on the banks of the Sabie River in the hot Lowveld country on the southwestern border of Kruger, surrounded by banana plantations. There is a wide range of accommodation from caravan parks to luxury private game reserves, useful if you'd rather not stay in the park itself. Information is available from **Big 5 Reservations** ① *Rendezvous Tourism Centre, Main Rd/R40, T013-737 7414, www.big5country.co.za, Mon-Fri 0800-1700, Sat 0800-1400,* which acts as an agent for a range of tour operators and safari lodges in the region and can organize adventure activities.

Elephant Sanctuary Hazyview ① *on the R536, 5 km before Hazyview on the road from Sabie, T013-737 6609, www.elephantsanctuary.co.za, 0800-1700, elephant walks R450, children (4-14) R225, walks and elephant riding R750, children (8-14) R375,* is run by the same outfit that established the elephant sanctuaries on the Garden Route (see page 90) and Hartbeespoort Dam (see page 226). There are two elephants here and pre-booking is advised as activities start at specific times. The Trunk-in-Hand experience is a 1½-hour interaction with the elephants, including a walk through the bush holding on to their trunks, an informative talk on African elephants and an optional 20-minute elephant ride. Visitors can also brush down the elephants and accompany them to their stables at the end of the day. Check out the website for the programmes and times.

The Shangana family that lives in the **Shangana Cultural Village** ① *on the R535, 5 km from Hazyview on the road from Graskop, T013-737 5805, www.shangana.co.za, 0900-*

1600, tea garden, 1-hr tour R90, tour and lunch R195, evening festival R310, children (under 12) ½-price, are descendents of Chief Shoshangana, an important tribal leader in the early 19th century. This is not a typical 'tribal village' experience as the family are keen to preserve their traditional lifestyles. One-hour tours take place throughout the day and follow a path from the **Marula Market** (a cut-above-the-rest curio market) to the village, and a guide explains traditional practices such as farming, food preparation, hut building and clothing, and there is ample opportunity to interact with the family members. On the midday tour a traditional lunch is included, and in the evening a festival dinner is served and the history of the Shanganas is presented by singers and dancers, which begins with drumming and a procession of flaming torches. The food is quite delicious; crocodile in groundnut sauce, baked vegetables, salads, venison and oxtail stews and fresh fruit.

→ WHITE RIVER

This small country town is at the centre of a citrus fruit-growing area; fresh local produce includes macadamia nuts, pecans, cashews, avocados, lychees and mangoes. The first settlers here were Boer cattle ranchers who arrived in the 1880s; at the end of the Anglo-Boer War a settlement was created to accommodate a new farming community made up of newly demobilized soldiers. There's little in the town itself, although the Motor Museum and Orange Winery attract a fair share of South Africa tourists. **Lowveld Tourist Information** ① *T013-750 1073, www.lowveldtourism.com, Mon-Fri 0900-1700, Sat 0900-1500,* has a small helpful office on the Hazyview road, at Casterbridge Farm (see below), which can give local advice and make reservations for lodges in Kruger.

The **Casterbridge Farm** ① *2 km from town on the Hazyview road/R40, T013-750 1540, www.casterbridge.co.za, Mon-Fri 0900-1630, Sat-Sun 0900-1600, restaurant hours vary*, is a very attractive old farmstead that has been converted into a shopping centre for arts and crafts, and there's a good bookshop selling new and second-hand books. One of the shops is an outlet for **Rottcher Wineries**, a macadamia nut farm and orange winery in the nearby valley that produces a range of orange liquors. There are also a number of restaurants, a little cinema, the Barnyard Theatre for local productions, a farmer's market every Saturday morning, and the **Casterbridge Hollow Boutique Hotel**. Children will enjoy the **Farmyard Petting Zoo** ① *Tue-Sun, 0900-1730, adults free, children (under 12) R15*, which has the likes of bunnies, ponies and goats, as well as a bouncy castle and baby quad-bikes. There's also a plant nursery and a pleasant garden café.

Also here is the **White River Local History and Motor Museum** ① *T013-750 2196, open 0900-1630, R20, children (under 12) R10*, which has small displays on local history, but more impressive is the collection of over 60 vintage cars on three floors of exhibition space.

MOVING ON
From White River it's a 25-km/30-minute drive back to Nelspruit on the R538 and from there it is another 355 km along the N4 toll road back to Johannesburg for your flight home (see page 201).

PANORAMA REGION LISTINGS

WHERE TO STAY

$$$ Hulala Lakeside Lodge, 22 km from White River on the R40 towards Hazyview, T013-764 1893, www.hulala.co.za. Situated on a peninsula in a lake that gives the feeling of being on an island, with 28 tastefully decorated rooms, with fireplace, DSTV, secluded patios overlooking the garden or lake, fine dining in the restaurant, a pool and 2 bars. Choice of canoes, rowing boats, or the nightly sundowner cruise.

$$$-$$ Hippo Hollow Country Estate, 3 km north of Hazyview off the R40, T013-737 6628, www.hippohollow.co.za. 37 thatched cottages set in lush grounds with kitchenettes and balconies overlooking the Sabie River, which is populated with hippos. There are also 54 hotel rooms with stylish, understated decor overlooking the 2 swimming pools. Good restaurant, bar and curio shop. Watch the hippos on the lawn at night, Kruger game drives can be arranged for those without a car.

$$ Graskop Hotel, Hoof St, Graskop, T013-767 1244, www.graskophotel.co.za. An excellent renovated hotel in the centre of town, decorated with a mixture of modern and African furniture (from the shop next door), with 15 garden rooms with patios, and 19 individually themed 'artist's' rooms which have funky splashes of colour and modern art by contemporary South African artists. Restaurant, bar with large fireplace, swimming pool in the gardens.

$$ The Royal, Main St, Uppertown, Pilgrim's Rest, T013-768 1100, www.royal-hotel.co.za. Dating from the time of the gold rush, this historical hotel with corrugated-iron roof and wooden walls, has 50 charming rooms set around courtyards, featuring period-style antique furniture, floral fabrics, claw-foot baths, wash-stands, and very rickety brass beds. Also has rooms in cottages spread around the village. Great restaurant and bar.

RESTAURANTS

$$$ Magnolia, Casterbridge Farm, White River, T013-751 1947, www.mag-nolia.co.za. Open 0700-2200. Contemporary decor and mixed menu with a take on French bistro-style, such as quail, lamb shank or rib-eye steak. Less formal café menu during the day when the garden tables with kids' play area are a good option.

$ Harrie's Pancakes, Louis Trichardt St, Graskop, T013-767 1273, www.harriespancakes.com. Open 0800-1730. Graskop's original pancake house enjoys a countrywide reputation. A wide selection of pancakes; try the chicken, mushroom and cashew nut, spicy butternut, and mouth-watering banana and caramel or chocolate mousse and milk tart ice-cream.

SHOPPING

Monsoon Gallery, on the R527 next to the **Mad Dogz Café**, Hoedspruit. Tasteful gallery selling fine African art, jewellery, cloth and antiques, plus some contemporary pieces. International shipping can be arranged. There is also a shop here selling items produced at the **Bombyx Mori Silk Farm**.

Perry's Bridge Trading Post, corner Main St and Sabie Rd (R40), Hazyview, T013-737 6929, www.perrysbridge.co.za. Open 0900-1630. Set in colonial buildings on a former citrus estate this includes the curio shop with good-value African crafts maps, books and gifts, an internet café, a deli and restaurants; the **Perry's Bridge Hollow Boutique Hotel** is here too.

GOING FURTHER
Swaziland

With an area of just over 17,000 sq km (less than the Kruger National Park), Swaziland may be the smallest country in the southern hemisphere but it has myriad African landscapes, and a full complement of southern African wildlife in the parks and reserves. Swaziland was plundered by European gold prospectors in the 19th century but, unlike South Africa, huge fortunes were never really made here and even during the colonial period, the government was more or less left in the hands of the royal family. Following independence in 1968, Swaziland has remained one of only three monarchies left in Africa, and is the only absolute monarchy on the continent.

On the whole, Swaziland is an accessible country to visit; it has moderate temperatures all year round, you can travel between the Highveld and the Lowveld in a day, and none of the major sights are more than a two-hour drive away. Additionally, given that the tiny country is hemmed in by KwaZulu Natal to the south and west, Mpumalanga to the north, and Mozambique to the east, a visit here can easily be combined with numerous other attractions in the region. Thanks to a handful of pioneering conservationists, effective anti-poaching initiatives and substantial animal restocking, Swaziland's game parks have improved dramatically in recent years. It's also a good destination for adventurers, with an effective backpackers' set-up and a number of adventure activities on offer. The Swazi people are friendly and expert craftmakers, producing a wealth of high-quality African curios. Compared to South Africa, Swaziland is a country where tribal values, craftsmanship and royal loyalty have withstood the test of encroaching modernization.

MBABANE AND AROUND

Swaziland's capital Mbabane (pronounced 'M-buh-ban') is a small modern town built on the site of a trading station on the busy route between Mozambique and the Transvaal. After the Boer War the British established their administrative headquarters here and the town grew up around them. The first government building was erected on Allister Miller (now Gwamile) Street, which today is the site of the Mbabane Branch of the Swaziland Building Society. The town derives its name from Chief Mbabane Kunene, who was ruler over the area when the British arrived. Mbabane was proclaimed the capital of Swaziland in 1903, although records show that it was declared an urban area only in 1912. It was declared a city by King Mswati III in 1992, but with a population of just under 100,000, it remains small.

ARRIVING IN MBABANE

Getting there and around Swaziland's Matsapha International Airport is 8 km outside of Manzini. The most popular route by road into Swaziland is through the Oshoek/Ngwenya border post, which is only 20 km west of Mbabane on the N17/MR3 from Ermelo in South Africa to Mbabane. This border is about 350 km from Johannesburg along the N17. There are long-distance buses from Johannesburg. From Mbabane there are buses to all major centres in Swaziland. Minibus taxis also run on regular short routes, but the vehicles are generally overcrowded, of a poor standard and can be driven recklessly. Nevertheless they are cheap and frequent. Mbabane's bus rank is centrally located opposite the Swazi Plaza.

Tourist information The **Swaziland Information Office** ⓘ *Swazi Plaza, T2404 2531, www.welcometoswaziland.com, Mon-Fri 0800-1700, Sat 0830-1230*, is an extremely helpful office with a wide range of information on hotels, nature reserves and tour operators. It also produces a useful map and annual brochure, covering the whole country.

PLACES IN MBABANE

Mbabane is a cluster of concrete shopping malls at the bottom of a hill, surrounded by ring roads and the highway that leads to the nearby Ezulwini Valley. There isn't much to do here and it's the valley itself that holds the best of the Swazi attractions, but the **Swazi market** near the central roundabout is worth a quick look for its excellent display of fresh produce.

EZULWINI VALLEY

Clearly signposted from Mbabane, the Ezulwini Valley (the Valley of Heaven) is the centre of Swaziland's tourist industry. The tourist route follows the old main road through Ezulwini. Take the fly-off at the bottom of Malagwane Hill. In the daytime there are superb views as you leave the Highveld and drop into the Middleveld. The valley itself has no real centre, but every few hundred metres you will pass a smart hotel, craft shop or restaurant. The 30-km-long valley ends at Lobamba, the Royal Village of the King.

LOBAMBA

At the eastern end of the Ezulwini Valley before the airport is the royal village of Lobamba, set amongst typical open bush countryside. This is where the present monarch, King Mswati III, lives and from where he rules Swaziland with his Queen Mother or Ndlovukazi, meaning 'she-elephant'. Every year at the end of August or beginning of September (depending on the harvest) the king gets to add to his growing stable of wives at the **Umhlanga** (**Reed**) **Dance** when virgins perform in front of the 'she-elephant' and present her with tall reeds which are used to act as windbreakers around her house. It is also the time that the King may pick out his next wife (which doesn't happen every year – but is an honour she cannot refuse). The custom has attracted increasing criticism over the years, notably in 2003 when the king's choice was not supported by the bride's family. Nevertheless, it is an astounding event, where thousands of young women from across the country congregate and dance bare-breasted in front of a congregation of royalty, subjects and curious tourists. The king currently has 14 wives and 24 children.

All of the royal buildings are closed to the public, but the **Somhlolo National Stadium** is the venue for major celebrations, including sports events, musical shows and royal events such as the annual independence celebrations and the Reed Dance. On no account try to take any photographs of the Lozitha Palace or the Embo State Palace. The parliament buildings are open to visitors but the effort to gain admittance is not worth the tour.

Of much greater interest is the **National Museum** and the **King Sobhuza II Memorial Park** ① *T2416 1516, Mon-Fri 0800-1300, 1400-1545, Sat-Sun 1000-1300, 1400-1545, E20, children (under 16) E10, memorial park E10, children (under 16) E3, combination entry E25, children (under 16) E15,* which has some excellent displays relating to Swazi life throughout history, with old photographs, traditional dress and Stone Age implements. If you wish to find out more ask for a guided tour, well worth it for an insight into local life and customs. Opposite the museum is the King Sobhuza II Memorial Park, which has a small museum depicting his life. The showroom houses his three rather splendid royal black limousines. His statue stands under a domed cover with open arches and an immaculate white tiled floor.

MLILWANE WILDLIFE SANCTUARY

Mlilwane is the most popular of Swaziland's nature reserves and covers 4560 ha of varied landscape of Highveld and Lowveld along a section of the Ezulwini Valley. It is a peaceful and beautiful reserve, allowing a wide range of activities, from self-guided walking to mountain biking, with a good chance of getting very close to wildlife. It is possible to see a wide variety of bird and animal species, including hippo, giraffe, crocodile, eland, zebra, blue wildebeest, kudu, nyala, klipspringer, waterbuck, impala, steenbuck, duiker, warthog, suni antelope, oribi, many species of bird, especially waterfowl, and if you are lucky, possibly the purple-crested lourie, the brilliantly coloured national bird of Swaziland.

BACKGROUND

James Weighton Reilly (nicknamed Mickey), Ted Reilly's father, settled at Mlilwane in 1906 and built the main homestead, which today is part of the accommodation in the reserve. He mined tin on the farm and for many years was the largest employer of industrial labour in Swaziland. He married Billie Wallis in 1920, who was for a long time the only white woman between Mbabane and Manzini, and Ted Reilly was born in 1938. The Reilly family witnessed the rapid disappearance of Swaziland's game and the last wild animal was seen at Mlilwane in 1959. This had a profound impact on young Ted Reilly. Coupled with this, his father's (now defunct) tin mining operation, meant that the hydraulic sluicing used to mine the tin with high pressure water jets had caused massive damage to the landscape leaving it scarred with ravines. Ted Reilly decided to regenerate the land back to its natural state, and turn over the Mlilwane farm to provide a wildlife sanctuary. In 1963 the rest camp opened and in 1969 Mlilwane was gazetted as a wildlife sanctuary.

ARRIVING IN MLILWANE WILDLIFE SANCTUARY

Getting there The reserve is signposted just past the Caltex service station at Lobamba. Turn right and travel 4 km to Sangweni Gate at eSitjeni. Gates are open 24 hours allowing guests staying in the reserve to visit the restaurants in the Ezulwini Valley. The **Interpretorium** in the rest camp and the Sangweni Gate complex has interesting information on nature conservation in Swaziland, including anti-poaching efforts.

Tourist information ① *T2528 3992, www.biggameparks.org, gate hours 24-hr, reception 0830-1900, E35 per person, which covers the whole length of your stay within the sanctuary.*

PLACES IN MLILWANE WILDLIFE SANCTUARY

There are over 100 km of dirt roads, with some marked for 4WD vehicles only. As there are no predators in the park, the wildlife is quite relaxed, enabling close viewing. Alternatives for exploring the sanctuary include guided horse rides, open 4WD game drives, guided mountain-bike rides, and an extensive system of self-guided walking trails, including the Macobane, Sondzela, Hippo and Mhlambanyatsi trails. The 8-km **Macobane Trail** offers an easy gradient and particularly good views of the Ezulwini Valley as it winds its way along the contours of an old aqueduct on the Nyonyane Mountain (1136 m). All activities can be booked through the activity centre at the main camp. A minimum of two people is usually necessary and children under 13 pay half price. Rates vary, but start from R150 per person for a guided bird walk, R110 per hour for guided mountain biking, R135 per hour for horse riding, and R230 per person for a sunset game drive.

MANTENGA NATURE RESERVE AND CULTURAL VILLAGE

① *1 km south of the Ezulwini Valley road, clearly signposted, T2416 1151, www.sntc.org.sz, day visits between 0800-1700, E150 per person, dance shows 1115 and 1515.*
Close to the Mantenga Lodge is an area of outstanding beauty and mature patches of forest between the main road and the Mantenga Falls. The Little Usutu River flows through

the 725-ha reserve and the well-known waterfalls are about a 2-km walk away. Despite Mantenga's small size, it is home to a number of medium-sized mammals, including vervet monkey, baboon, bushpig, porcupine, rock dassie, bushbaby, kudu, nyala, klipspringer and grey and red duiker. Birdlife abounds, including the endangered bald ibis. Picnic spots and walking trails have been marked out and you can drive as far as the waterfall. The **Cultural Village** is just beyond the gate of the reserve and every aspect of this 'show' village is based upon traditional methods and materials. This is exactly how a medium-sized Swazi homestead would have looked in the 1850s. There are 16 beehive-shaped huts built from local materials such as reeds and cow dung, laid out in a plan that can be seen throughout rural Swaziland. The huts form a semicircle partly surrounded by a cattle kraal. The focal point is a larger hut, the 'great hut', and the kraal. This is a polygamous homestead – each wife has her own circle of huts for cooking, making beer and sleeping in. Slightly separate are the huts for unmarried mature boys and girls and for married sons.

The whole complex is brought to life by traditional dance performances and songs as the guides show visitors around. You will also see food being prepared, clothes and household objects being made. Meals are served at the **Swazi River Café**.

MANTENGA CRAFT CENTRE

ⓘ *At the entrance of the Mantenga Nature Reserve and Cultural Village, you don't need to pay entry fee into the reserve to visit, T2416 1136, daily 0830-1700.*
Swaziland is an excellent place to buy curios, with a wider selection and lower prices than in South Africa. The **Mantenga Foundation** was formed in 1974 to retail the finished works of local artists in the Mantenga Craft Centre. From the outset, the project has been managed on the basis of long-term self-sufficiency. The centre stocks an excellent range of jewellery, crafts, clothes, gold and silver, screen prints, leather goods, ceramics, rugs and carvings. There is also a coffee shop and snack bar and a small tourist information desk with a selection of brochures. **Swazi Trails** are also based here, see page 272.

HLANE ROYAL NATIONAL PARK

ⓘ *T2383 8100, www.biggameparks.org. Park gates close at sunset, notify in advance if you think your arrival will be after dark. E35 per person, which covers the whole length of your stay.*
Formerly a royal hunting ground, Hlane was declared a protected area in 1967 by King Sobhuza II. Covering 30,000 ha, this is the kingdom's largest protected area. Following heavy poaching in the 1960s, the park has been restocked by **Big Game Parks**, with wildlife from neighbouring countries as well as species propagated at Mkhaya Game Reserve. A number of predators have been reintroduced and the park now has healthy numbers of lion, cheetah and leopard. Other game includes elephant, white rhino, herds of wildebeest, and zebra, kudu, steenbuck, bushbuck, giraffe, impala, hyena and jackal. In the past, poaching was such a serious problem that the rhino had to have their horns removed for their own protection. Hlane supports the densest population of raptors in the kingdom, with vultures in particular being very visible at kills and waterholes. The nesting density for the white-backed vulture is the highest in the whole of Africa, and the most southerly nesting colony of marabou stork is found here. Birdlife in and around the two camps is prolific.

ARRIVING IN HLANE ROYAL NATIONAL PARK

Getting there The park is 67 km from Manzini towards Simunye, where the main road bisects the park. Turn left into the Ngongoni Gate, where all arrivals must report.

PLACES IN HLANE ROYAL NATIONAL PARK

The western area of the park is linked with a network of roads which the visitor can use for game viewing. The area around the **Black Mbuluzi River** attracts animals during the dry winter season. Close to Ndlovu camp is an **Endangered Species** area, where elephant and rhino have been concentrated for security reasons. The **Mahlindza** waterhole, with its hippo, crocodile and waterbird population, is one of the most peaceful picnic sites in the country. There are two camps in the park and a wide range of activities are offered, including guided walks (2½ hours; E150), guided mountain biking (2½ hours; E170), and two-hour game drives (day or night; E255). There is also the option to pick up a guide to accompany you in your own car to a nearby Swazi village (E65 per person; minimum four), 20 km from the park gates, where you will meet the people, take a tour of the village, watch dancing and possibly sample some home-made beer. These can all be booked at the park office, or through Big Game Parks, and are available between 1000 and 1600 to day visitors, who can park their cars at the gate and buy lunch at the Ndlovu Camp.

Maputaland and Zululand

Named after the Maputa River, which flows through southern Mozambique, Maputaland covers an area of 9000 sq km stretching north from Lake St Lucia to the Mozambique border and east from the Indian Ocean to the Lebombo Mountains. One of South Africa's least developed regions, Maputaland has preserved a traditional African atmosphere. The land is unsuitable for intensive modern agriculture, and small farmsteads and fishing communities dot the landscape.

Zululand extends from the northern bank of the Tugela River up to Mkhuze and Maputaland. The homeland of Shaka, this region will forever be associated with the classic movie starring Michael Caine as the redoubtable British officer fighting Zulu warriors. Today, despite being one of the more traditional areas of South Africa, it has thriving industrial cities and vast areas of sugarcane and eucalyptus plantations. However, it also offers long, unspoilt beaches, a chance to experience traditional Zulu culture, and the excellent game reserves like Hluhluwe-Imfolozi are a natural magnets for tourists.

MKHUZE GAME RESERVE

This 40,000-ha reserve was proclaimed a protected area in 1912, and constitutes the northwestern spur of the iSimangaliso Wetland Park (see page 266), and conserves a representative cross-section of the Maputaland ecosystem. The reserve has an astonishing diversity of natural habitats, from the eastern slopes of the Lebombo Mountains along its eastern boundary, to broad stretches of acacia savannah, swamps and a variety of woodlands and riverine forest. The Mkhuze River curves along the reserve's northern and eastern borders with a fine stretch of fig forest along its banks. The area to the north is tropical whereas the southern part of the reserve is more temperate. Mkhuze is not visited as often as Hluhluwe-Imfolozi (see page 264) as there are not as many rhino, but it offers opportunities to go on guided bush walks and see some of Maputaland's more unusual animals.

ARRIVING IN MKHUZE GAME RESERVE

Getting around A 100-km network of roads crosses the reserve, but some pass through areas of thick bush, which are not ideal for game viewing; the grasslands, however, are more open and animals are easier to see. The best game-viewing areas are the **Loop Road**, the **Nsumo Pan** and the **airstrip**. There are four game-viewing hides next to the Kubube, Kumasinga, Kwamalibala and Kumahlala pans. The viewing here is excellent and you can watch the game coming down to drink. There are car parks nearby where you can leave your car and walk to the hides. Day and night drives, R200, children (under 12) R100, which last about two hours, and two- to three-hour game walks, R110 children (under 12) R55, can be booked through the camp offices.

Tourist information ⓘ *Clearly signposted off the N2, turn off at the village of Mkhuze, which is 35 km north of Hluhluwe, follow the gravel road for 18 km to the eMshophi Gate, T035-573 9004, www.kznwildlife.com, gates open Oct-Mar 0500-1900, Apr-Sep 0600-1800, office 0800-1600, R25, children (under 12) R15, plus R35 per vehicle.* There is some frozen food for sale in the curio shop and a selection of books on natural history and postcards. It's also a good place to pick up some informative leaflets on birds, trees, walks and drives. There's petrol for sale at the entrance gate. Reservations for camping should be made here.

WILDLIFE

Mkhuze is an excellent place to see some of Maputaland's big game. Elephant, hippo, crocodile, giraffe, blue wildebeest, eland, kudu, black and white rhino, cheetah, leopard and hyena are all present in the reserve. It is also one of the best places to see the shy nyala antelope – nearly 8000 live here. Over 450 bird species have been recorded here, and as part of the Mozambique coastal plain, Mkhuze attracts many tropical birds often only seen further north. Look out for Neergard's sunbird, the yellow-spotted nicator and the African broadbill. Many aquatic birds visit the pans here during the summer when you can see woolly-necked storks, herons, flamingos, pink-backed and white pelicans, ibises, spoonbills and jacanas from the hides overlooking the pans. Bird checklists are available from the curio shop.

HLUHLUWE-IMFOLOZI GAME RESERVE

This is one of Africa's oldest game reserves and one of the few parks in KwaZulu Natal where you can see the Big Five. What were traditionally two reserves have been joined into one. Hluhluwe is named after the umHluhluwe or 'thorny rope', a climber which is found in the forests of this area. Their aerial roots hanging from the sycamore figs where the Black Imfolozi and the White Imfolozi rivers meet give the area its name. Imfolozi is named after *uMfula walosi* or the 'river of fibres'. The reserve has a variety of landscapes – thick forests, dry bushveld and open savannah – that are home to a number of species of game, including healthy populations of rhino and the rare nyala. What is unusual about the park is the hilly terrain, which provides a great vantage point for game viewing.

ARRIVING IN HLUHLUWE-IMFOLOZI GAME RESERVE

Getting there and around Hluhluwe-Imfolozi is 280 km north of Durban just off the N2. There is a turning at Mtubatuba leading west on the R618 (50 km) to the **Imfolozi sector** ⓘ *Oct-Mar 0500-1900, Apr-Sep 0600-1800, office 0800-1230, 1400-1630, conservation levy (per day) R110, children (3-12) R55, under 3s free,* and a turning opposite the exit to Hluhluwe village, which leads (14 km) to the northern Memorial Gate entrance to the **Hluhluwe sector** ⓘ *same hours and levies as above, camp reception at Hilltop daily 0700-1930.* This is an easy park to visit on a day trip if you are staying in the Maputaland or St Lucia regions.

A network of over 300 km of dirt roads crosses the reserve which can easily be negotiated in a saloon car. There are hides at Mphafa waterhole and Thiyeni waterhole but much of the best game viewing can be done from a car. Good areas for viewing are the Sontuli Loop, the corridor linking Imfolozi to Hluhluwe and the areas around the Hluhluwe River.

Tourist information Day and night drives, R270, children (under 12) R135, which last about two hours, and two- to three-hour game walks, R215 (no children under 13), can be booked through the camp offices. Remember if you're staying at the private lodges, you'll have your own game guard for wildlife activities.

Best time to visit The best time to see the park is March to November. The park's vegetation is lush during the summer months, when the weather is hot and humid, but this makes it more difficult to see the game. During the winter months the climate is cool and dry and you might even need a sweater in the evenings. Animals congregate at the waterholes and rivers at this time of year and the lack of vegetation makes viewing easier.

BACKGROUND
The confluence of the Black and White Imfolozi rivers is where Zulu King Shaka dug his hunting pits. Once a year game was driven into the area and would fall into the pits, where it was speared by young warriors eager to prove their courage. Consequently, Hluhluwe-Imfolozi was established as a protected area as long ago as 1895. Since then the park has suffered a number of setbacks, such as temporary de-proclamation and the massive slaughter of thousands of game animals in a campaign to eliminate tsetse fly. Aerial spraying of the chemical DDT eventually eliminated the tsetse fly but at great cost to the environment. In 1947 the newly formed **Natal Parks, Game and Fish Preservation Board** took control of the park and reintroduced locally extinct species such as lion, elephant, rhino and giraffe. Since then it has been instrumental in a number of conservation initiatives, especially with rhino, and now has the world's largest populations of white rhino (around 1600). It was renamed Hluhluwe-Imfolozi Game Reserve using a more accurate local spelling.

WILDLIFE
The varied landscapes of Hluhluwe-Imfolozi provide a wide range of habitats which support large numbers of big game and this is one of the best reserves in KwaZulu Natal for seeing wildlife. The Big Five are present and there are large populations of three rarely seen animals: the white rhino, the black rhino and the nyala. Despite the thriving hippo populations in nearby St Lucia, there are few hippo in this park because the rivers flow too fast. Over 300 species of bird have been recorded in Hluhluwe-Imfolozi and bird lists are available from the camp offices.

Hluhluwe is the northern sector of the reserve and has a hilly and wooded landscape; elephant are often seen in the area around the Hluhluwe Dam, where the thick forests are inhabited by the rare samango monkey. There are some areas of savannah in this sector where white rhino and giraffe can be seen feeding.

Imfolozi, in the south, is characterized by thornveld and semi-desert; the grasslands here support large populations of impala, kudu, waterbuck, giraffe, blue wildebeest and zebra. Predators are rarely seen but cheetah, lion, leopard and wild dog are all present.

WILDERNESS TRAILS
One of the most exciting ways to see wildlife here is on foot. Although this experience is not always as spectacular as viewing from a car, it tends to be more intense; there is little that can compare with the excitement of tracking wildlife through areas which are totally

undisturbed by man – there are no roads and access is only allowed on foot. Several guided wilderness trails cross the reserve and run from mid-March to December. They are limited to a maximum of eight people and are extremely popular, so should be booked well in advance. Food, drinks, water bottles, cutlery and cooking equipment, bedding, towels, day packs, backpacks and donkey bags are all provided by KZN Wildlife. The trails cover about 15 km per day and cost from R220015 to R3200 per person for up to three nights (accommodation is in tented camps in the wilderness area). Reservations can be made up to six months in advance through **KZN Wildlife** ① *T033-845 1000, www.kznwildlife.com.*

HLUHLUWE VILLAGE

Hluhluwe is a small village in an area surrounded by large luxury game farms. It is a good base to explore the region as it is within easy reach of many of the local game parks and is only 15 km from St Lucia's False Bay. **Dumazulu Traditional Village**, a short drive from Hluhluwe, is one of the better local craft villages, with displays of Zulu dancing, spear making and basket weaving.

The **Hluhluwe Tourism Association** ① *next to the Engen garage, Main St, T035-562 0353, www.elephantcoasttourism.com, Mon-Fri 0800-1700, Sat 0900-1300*, acts as a booking agent for the area.

ISIMANGALISO WETLAND PARK

The **Greater St Lucia Wetland Park** was declared a World Heritage Site in 1999, the first place in South Africa to be awarded this status. In 2008 it went under a name change to iSimangaliso Wetland Park – iSimangaliso is isiZulu for 'miracle'. The protected area is the largest estuarine lake system in Africa, with a variety of flora and fauna which compares favourably with the Okavango Delta or Kruger National Park. The birdlife is outstanding, with a staggering 420 species recorded here.

ARRIVING IN ISIMANGALISO WETLAND PARK

Getting there and around The area now known as the iSimangaliso Wetland Park consists of a number of formerly separate nature reserves and state forests. These are still referred to locally under a bewildering array of old and new names, but the greater area is considered to be South Africa's third largest park. The entire 328,000-ha reserve starts south of the St Lucia Estuary, stretches north to the border with Mozambique and is about 280 km in length. The terrestrial section of the park varies from 1 km to 24 km wide, and the marine section extends 5 km out to sea, protecting 155 km of coastline.

In the southern region, accessible from the town of St Lucia, the park falls into three main areas: **St Lucia Public Resort and Estuary National Park**, which is a good area to see crocodile and hippo, and provides access to the public beaches around the town of St Lucia; the **coastline up to Cape Vidal**, 32 km north of St Lucia, with the beautiful Cape beach; and the **western shore of the lake**, which is much quieter than the other two and has a good choice of private accommodation.

Tourist information For information about the iSimangaliso Wetland Park, visit the St Lucia office of **KZN Wildlife** ① *Pelikan Rd, near Eden Park campsite, T035-590 1340, 0800-1630*. It has a small selection of brochures and can help with accommodation and trail information. Advance reservations for accommodation and wilderness trails should be made through **KZN Wildlife** ① *T033-845 1000, www.kznwildlife.com*. For more information on the park also visit www.isimangaliso.com.

Best time to visit Each season in the wetlands has its own attraction. From November to February there tends to be more rain, making the vegetation greener. June to August is the best time for birdwatching, as this is the breeding season. The best months for walking are March to November when it is less hot and humid.

BACKGROUND
The land now occupied by the park has had human inhabitants since the Early Iron Age. Archaeological excavations have uncovered the remains of settlements and middens, and large areas of forest and dunes are thought to have been cleared to provide charcoal for iron smelting. St Lucia was named by the Portuguese explorer Manuel Perestrello in 1575, although European influence in the area was minimal until the 1850s. Up to that time the area was inhabited by a relatively large population of Thongas and Zulus who herded cattle and cultivated the land.

Professional hunters began visiting the lake in the 1850s in search of ivory, hides and horns, which were at one point the Colony of Natal's main source of income. So successful were these hunters that within 50 years the last elephant in this region had been shot. Amongst the big game hunters here were William Baldwin, Robert Briggs Struthers, 'Elephant' White and John Dunn who recorded having shot 23 seacows in one morning and a total of 203 seacows in the following three months. Hunting parties would kill hundreds of elephants, crocodiles and hippos on each expedition.

During the 1880s the British government annexed St Lucia in a move that would foil the Boers from the New Republic in their search for access to the sea. It was after this that land was distributed to settlers and that missions were founded at Mount Tabor, Cape Vidal and Ozabeni.

St Lucia Lake, along with Hluhluwe-Imfolozi, was one of the first game reserves to be established in Africa in 1895. Further moves to protect wildlife also took place in 1944 with the addition of False Bay Park to the protected areas, and in 1975 South Africa signed the international RAMSAR Convention to protect wetlands. It was then that the Greater St Lucia Wetland region was declared. Many more conservation initiatives were introduced when St Lucia won World Heritage status in 1999. Species have also been reintroduced, including cheetah and elephant.

In spite of these measures to protect St Lucia, the survival of the lake system has been under constant threat since the turn of the 20th century. One of the most intractable problems has been the effect of agriculture on the lake's water supply: land reclamation, drainage canals, the diversion of the Imfolozi River and the damming of the Hluhluwe River for irrigation have all contributed to the silting up of the lake. In the 1960s salinity levels increased to such an extent during a series of droughts that the water in the lake system was twice as salty as sea water, killing numerous plants, fish and crocodiles. Today, a continuing drought has dramatically reduced the level of water in some areas, notably Charter's Creek, False Bay and Fanies Island, where two of the three KZN Wildlife camps in these places are no longer open to the public and boat trips cannot be operated on the low water. Recently the drought has become so severe, that since 2007 the St Lucia rivermouth has become completely silted up, closing off access to the sea.

WILDLIFE
The Mkhuze, Mzinene, Hluhluwe and Nyalazi rivers flow into the northern end of the lake system. The lakes are shallow and interspersed with islands and reedbeds and are bounded by papyrus, mangrove and forest swamps. The other inland areas in the park

are grasslands with zones of thornveld, coastal and dune forest. The animals that are most often seen in these environments are large populations of common reedbuck, hippopotamus and Nile crocodile (there are an estimated 2000 crocs in the entire lake system). Depending on where you are in the park, there is also the chance of seeing impala, waterbuck, kudu, wildebeest, zebra, elephant and buffalo.

From November to March, giant leatherback and loggerhead turtles nest on the park's beaches up to 10 times each season. They are protected by KZN Wildlife who monitor them and protect them from predators such as honey badgers and jackals.

The birdlife is the main attraction, and the fish eagle, easily spotted, has become the unofficial symbol of the area. Other species often seen around the water include kingfishers and weaverbirds, and large numbers of unusual migrant birds can also be spotted. Southern African waterbirds migrate depending on regional droughts between Bangweulu and Kafue in Zambia, the Okavango Delta in Botswana, the Zambezi Delta in Mozambique and the wetlands of Maputaland and St Lucia. The St Lucia waters are high in nutrients and support large populations of pink-backed and white pelicans, greater and lesser flamingos, ducks, spoonbills and ibises.

ST LUCIA

The holiday resort of St Lucia lies to the south of the lake and is surrounded by the iSimangaliso Wetland Park. St Lucia is the largest seaside holiday destination on this part of the coast and is particularly popular during the South African school holidays. Although it can get very busy around Christmas, it remains a sleepy provincial town off season, making a pleasant base from which to explore both the wetlands and the nearby wildlife parks.

Many visitors come for a day trip, to explore the narrow reaches of the estuary leading up to the lake. Boats leave regularly from the jetty at the far end of McKenzie Street, usually seating around 20 people and taking a two-hour tour upriver. These provide an excellent introduction to the wetlands, with chances of seeing large pods of hippo and crocodile, and prolific birdlife.

Arriving in St Lucia The end of the R618 leads directly into the centre of the resort on McKenzie Street, which is lined with supermarkets, banks, restaurants, curio shops and boat charter companies. Continuing down past the end of McKenzie Street, the road leads to the large KZN Wildlife office to the left, and the jetty from which river cruises leave to the right.

The best source of tourist information is **Advantage Cruises and Charters** ① *McKenzie St, close to the Spar, T035-590 1259, www.advantagetours.co.za, daily 0700-1900*, who act as a booking agent for all local activities and accommodation, and run their own boat excursions. For information on the iSimangaliso Wetland Park, see page 266.

Beaches The beaches lying to the east of St Lucia are large swathes of pristine white sand backed by dune forest, which stretch all the way to Cape Vidal. The vegetated sand dunes here can exceed 180 m in height and, estimated to be over 30,000 years old, they are considered to be some of the highest vegetated coastal dunes in the world. Visitors can swim here but do so at their own risk as there are dangerous currents, no shark nets and no lifeguards.

St Lucia Public Resort and Estuary national parks These areas directly surround St Lucia village. There is a 12-km network of self-guided trails, which start in the area near the Crocodile Centre (see below). They cross several different habitats such as dune forest, grasslands, mangroves and swamps, and close to the estuary take you to some good hippo-viewing spots. However, avoid the water's edge – hippos kill more people than any other mammal in Africa. If you come across one on land, retreat slowly and quietly. Swimming in the lake is prohibited due the presence of crocodiles. The grasslands to the north of the village are a source of *ncema* grass, traditionally used by Zulus to make sleeping and sitting mats. The cutting season starts on 1 May when thousands of people come for the annual harvest.

The **Crocodile Centre** ① *T035-590 1386, Mon-Fri 0800-1600, Sat 0830-1700, Sun 0900-1600, R30, children (under 12) R20, crocodile feeding Sat 1500*, is next to the entrance gate to Cape Vidal, where a small display highlights the important role crocodiles play in the ecosystem of the park. The Nile, long-snouted and dwarf crocodiles that are kept here in pens, are all endangered in the wild and are part of an international breeding programme to protect them. KZN Wildlife routinely releases Nile crocodiles back into Lake St Lucia. The curio shop here is one of the best in St Lucia with a good selection of books and leaflets.

CAPE VIDAL
① *32 km north of St Lucia, T035-590 9012, gates Oct-Mar 0500-1900, Apr-Sep 0600-1800, office 0800-1230, 1400-1630, R25, children (under 12) R15, R35 per vehicle.*
Cape Vidal makes an easy and pleasant day trip from St Lucia. A road heads north from the park gates (near the crocodile centre), passing through an area that was until recently pine forest but is now returning to indigenous wilderness. The area is home to reedbuck, waterbuck, kudu and buffalo, and in the lake to the west of the road, crocodile and hippo.

Mission Rocks is 16 km from St Lucia, signposted off the dirt road. Snorkelling and scuba-diving are allowed here and tours can be arranged from St Lucia. The rock pools here are full of life and are best seen at low tide.

Cape Vidal is an area of vegetated dunes along what must be one of the most spectacular beaches in KwaZulu Natal. The sand is pure white and the Indian Ocean is warm and inviting; the rocks just off the beach are teeming with tropical fish and the shallow water is safe to swim and snorkel in. The beach is never crowded even at the busiest of times. The camp has facilities for launching powerboats and is popular for game fishing, but as Cape Vidal marks the beginning of a marine reserve that stretches north to the Mozambique border, anglers require permits and many fish are on a tag-and-release system.

WESTERN SHORES
There are three reserves on the western shores of Lake St Lucia, and access is via the N2 north of St Lucia. However, a continuing drought has dramatically reduced the level of water in this area, and two of them, **Charter's Creek** and **Fanies Island**, have been closed to visitors for some time. The KZN Wildlife camps are no longer open to the public and boat trips cannot be operated on the low water. **False Bay** ① *T035-562 0425, gates Oct-Mar 0500-2000, Apr-Sep 0600-2000, office 0800-1230, 1400-1630, R20, children (under 12) R10*, is still accessible. To get there from the N2 take the turning to Hluhluwe village (see page 266); the road continues 15 km to the park. It is a good place to see flamingos and pink-backed pelicans during the breeding season from December to April. The accommodation here is more basic than at the other camps but this is offset by the splendid landscape. The surrounding sand forests are similar to Mkhuze Game Reserve and are inhabited by the rare suni antelope and nyala. The banks and marshlands along the Hluhluwe River are rich in birdlife. There are two self-guided walks and a viewing platform near the camp looks over the lake, but swimming is prohibited because of crocs.

SWAZILAND, MAPUTALAND AND ZULULAND LISTINGS

WHERE TO STAY

Mbabane

$$ Mountain Inn, 4 km out of town on the road to Ezulwini Valley, T2404 2781, www.mountaininn.sz. 52 smart, comfortable rooms with en suite bathrooms, telephone and TV. Swimming pool, neat lawns, **Friar Tuck** à la carte restaurant, balconies have commanding views over the mountains and valley. Excursions and mountain bike hire can be arranged.

Ezulwini Valley

$$$$ Royal Swazi Spa, T2416 5000. The most luxurious hotel in Swaziland, with 149 a/c rooms with DSTV, all with magnificent views of the valley and mountains. Swimming pool, gym, and several bars and restaurants including **Planter's** a colonial-themed restaurant specializing in grills, curries and seafood. The extensive spa features a number of indoor and outdoor pools fed by a natural hot spring and is also open to day visitors.

Mlilwane

$$$-$$ Forester's Arms, near Mhlambanyatsi on the MR19, 27 km southwest of Mbabane and 12 km north of Bhunya, T2467 4177, www.forestersarms.co.za. Delightful hotel set in the cool Usuthu highlands surrounded by forest in its own colourful garden. 30 en suite rooms, restaurant and occasional Swazi dancing performed in the evenings. Swimming pool, sauna, trout and bass fishing in the local dams, tennis and squash courts, hiking, horse riding from their own stables, mountain bikes for hire. A fine country retreat.
$$-$ Reilly's Main Camp. A mixture of stone cottages, thatched rondavels and traditional domed Swazi thatched huts known as the Beehive Village, camping ground under the shade of eucalyptus trees with neat ablution block and self-catering facilities. The **Hippo Haunt** restaurant has a lovely deck overlooking a hippo pool. Warthogs, ostriches and impalas frequently wander through the grounds. Swimming pool. Traditional dancing team, made up of park staff, performs on a nightly basis.
$ Sondzela Backpackers, 15 mins' walk from the main camp. Excellent backpackers in a stunning setting overlooking the Nyonyane Mountains, in the centre of the reserve. Spotless dorms, twins and doubles in the large main house, plus very comfortable and spacious thatched rondavels sleeping up to 4, with shared ablutions. Camping, tents and bedding can be hired, pool, volleyball court, bar with pool table.

Mkhuze Game Reserve

$$$ Ghost Mountain Inn, T035-573 1025/7, www.ghostmountaininn.co.za. Next to the northern entrance to Mkhuze, with 50 a/c rooms with DSTV, stylish decor and patios leading to indigenous gardens and rolling lawns, restaurant serving excellent food, spa and 2 swimming pools. Good-value safari packages and Zulu cultural experiences with knowledgeable guides and this is a good option if you don't want to self-cater. Look out for specials on the website that include activities and spa treatments.

Hluhluwe-Imfolozi Game Reserve

$$$-$$ Hilltop Camp, Hluhluwe sector. This, the largest and most accessible of the camps, has a fabulous hilltop location, with sweeping views over much of the park and parts of Swaziland. Although it doesn't have the exclusivity of the smaller bush camps, the central lounge, restaurant, bar, pool and veranda are welcome at the end of the day. There's a shop selling souvenirs and some food. Game drives and guided walks can be arranged here. The main camp was refurbished a few years ago and offers 4 types of accommodation. At the top end are 22 **4-bed chalets** (**$$$**) with 2 bedrooms, 2 bathrooms and fully equipped kitchen; slightly cheaper are the 7 **2-bed chalets** (**$$**), with fully equipped kitchen, and the 20 2-bed rest huts (not self-catering) with fridge and kettle. The cheapest options are the 20, **2-bed rest huts** (**$$**), with communal kitchen and ablution block.

$$$-$$ Mpila Camp, Imfolozi sector. Commands magnificent views over the wilderness area to the east and the Msasaneni Hills to the west. The shop stocks curios and cold drinks but no food, there's a petrol station. Accommodation is in 2 self-contained 3-bed cottages (**$$$**) sleeping 7 (cook on hand to prepare food supplied by guests); 6 self-catering 2-bed chalets (**$$$**), sleeping up to 5, with fully equipped kitchen; tented camp with 9 walk-in en suite tents (**$$**), self-catering with a communal kitchen and dining area; and 12 1-bed self-catering thatched cottages (**$$**), sleeping 4 with a communal kitchen and ablutions.

Hluhluwe
$$$$ Phinda Private Game Reserve, 23 km northeast of Hluhluwe off the R22 towards Sodwana Bay, the gate to the reserve is 6 km to the west of the road, reservations T011-809 4314, www.phinda.com. One of KwaZulu Natal's most renowned private Big Five reserves covering 23,000 ha and sandwiched between the iSimangaliso Wetland Park and Mkhuze Game Reserve, with 6 luxury 5-star lodges, each with its own unique atmosphere and bush or wetland views. The very expensive rates are all-inclusive of game drives and fine cuisine, and other activities include rhino tracking on foot, canoeing on the Mzinene River, horse riding or beach excursions.

$$$$ Thanda Private Game Reserve, 23 km north of Hluhluwe, 6 km to the left of the N2, T035-573 1899, www.thanda.com. A very expensive 7800-ha Big Five reserve, with 9 villas with private plunge pool and deck, 4 spacious colonial-style tents, and a super luxury suite sleeping 10. Main lodge has a Zulu theme with dining and lounge areas, decks overlooking a waterhole, library, wine cellar and spa. Other than game drives, there are visits to Zulu villages and the beach at Sodwana Bay.

St Lucia
$ Bibs Backpackers, 310 McKenzie St, T035-590 1056, www.bibs.co.za. Dorms, doubles with DSTV and a/c, and chalets with kitchenette sleeping 2-4. Kitchen, evening meals on request, relaxing gardens with hammocks, rock swimming pool, and braai and bar area, Zulu dancing on Sat nights, internet access. Well-organized day trips to Hluhluwe-Imfolozi and other local sights.

RESTAURANTS

$$-$ Swazi River Café, Mantenga Nature Reserve and Cultural Village, T2602 2183. Tue-Sun 0730-late. Specializing in dishes such as stroganoff made from game meat and peri-peri chicken livers, there's a late bar with live music on Fri and Sat evenings, and it's a great place for a sundowner on the wooden deck. Also has specials such as fresh fish, crab and prawns delivered direct from Maputo in Mozambique, and weekly braais on a Sun starting at 1000 at the waterfalls.

$$ Farmhouse Restaurant & Pub, Malandela's, T2528 3115, www.malandelas.com. 1100-1500, 1800-late. Excellent restaurant in a stylish setting, surrounded by gardens, pleasant shady deck, great menu using organic home-grown vegetables and fresh milk, fusion food mixing African and European dishes. Also has a popular pub with draft beer and DSTV for sports. It's attached to the **House on Fire** live music venue.

WHAT TO DO

Swaziland

Swazi Trails, Mantenga Craft Centre, T2416 2180, www.swazitrails.co.sz. A leading countrywide tour operator specializing in Swaziland culture, wildlife and adventure tours, and ideal if you don't have your own transport. Guided 4- to 5-hr adventure caving excursions (R595-695) go to the largely unexplored Gobholo cave system. This is the only known major cave system in granite rock in southern Africa, and the total distance travelled underground is about 800 m. Whitewater rafting is offered year-round on the Great Usutu River with a couple of Grade II and IV rapids (R750-850). 2-man rafts are used, shepherded by guides in kayaks, and the average full-day trip is 13 km. Additionally there are 1- to 2-hr quad-bike trails (from R350) and 4- to 8-hr mountain-bike trails (from R275), as well as guided hikes and visits to the wildlife parks. Of the several cultural tours, which last from 4 hrs, the full-day Swaziland Highlights Tour does a big figure of 8, taking in Mantenga, Lobamba, Manzini, the Malkerns Valley and Mbabane, among other stops, and includes lunch for R1375. All guides are local Swazis with excellent local knowledge. **Swazi Trails** also manages an excellent community tourism initiative and part of the fee you pay goes to the local Mphaphati community. Pickups for activities and tours are from the office or hotels in the Ezulwini Valley.

St Lucia

Advantage Cruise and Charters, McKenzie St, close to the Spar, T035-590 1259, www.advantagetours.co.za. Open 0700-1900. A wide choice of boat rides, including 2-hr estuary trips, 0900, 1200, 1500 and 1600, R170, children (under 12) R85. Whale-watching trips run Jun-Nov when humpback, mink and occasional southern right whales travel along the coast heading for the warmer breeding waters of Mozambique. Trips cost R850 per person, 40% of which is refundable if no whales are spotted after 2 hrs at sea. This, the only licensed whale-watching operator in St Lucia, is permitted to get within 50 m of the whales. If you don't have a car, this is a good-value tour operator for day trips to Cape Vidal, which include a guided drive up the coast, snorkelling at Mission Rocks and lunch on the beach for R600, children (under 12) R480. Can also arrange deep-sea fishing from R700 per person.

Santa Lucia, T035-590 1340, www.kzn wildlife.com. 80-seater double-storey launch with a bar departs from the jetty next to the bridge at 0830, 1030 and 1430, R140, children (under 12) R70. The tour lasts for 1½ hrs and travels up the estuary past thick banks of vegetation as far as the Narrows. There is a good chance of seeing hippo and waterfowl.

Shaka Barker Tours, 4 Hornbill St, T035-590 1162, www.shakabarker.co.za, run night time trips to see the turtles laying at Leven Point, which is normally a restricted area, between Nov and Feb. It's not uncommon to see crocodiles and snakes, as well as turtles, on the beach. This is a very special wildlife experience conducted in an eco-friendly way and highly recommended. The tour departs at 1830 and returns at 0300 the following morning. A minimum of 2 people are required and advance booking is essential. The cost is R1950, which includes supper and night drives in search of genets, leopard, bush babies, chameleons and hippos.

PRACTICALITIES

INS AND OUTS

→ BEST TIME TO VISIT SOUTH AFRICA

South Africa has a moderate climate and long sunny days for most of the year. You will only come across truly tropical conditions in the northeast corner of KwaZulu Natal around Kosi Bay and the border with Mozambique. During summer it rarely gets hotter than 30°C, though Gauteng and KwaZulu Natal get very humid. The coast around Cape Town and the Garden Route is at its best during the spring and summer months, though the best time for whale watching is in winter. During July and August, in the middle of winter, it can get cold at night in Cape Town and the interior mountains in the Drakensberg and Eastern Cape, with frosts and snowfalls. Most of the rain falls in the summer months and, when it does rain, there are often very heavy storms. If driving in these conditions, slow down and pull over. Also be on the lookout for flash floods, especially if you're camping.

The best time of year for game viewing is during the winter months, when vegetation cover is at a minimum and a lack of water forces animals to congregate around rivers and waterholes. Winter is also the best time for hiking, avoiding the high temperatures and frequent thunderstorms of the summer months. Despite being cooler, July and August are a popular time for visitors as they coincide with the European school holidays. December and January are by far the busiest months for South African tourism. Be sure to book your car hire and accommodation well in advance during these periods. One major disadvantage of visiting during the summer is that much of the accommodation is fully booked months in advance, and the coastal towns become horribly overcrowded. For further advice on when to go to South Africa, visit www.weathersa.co.za.

→ GETTING TO SOUTH AFRICA

AIR

The three main international airports in **South Africa** are: OR Tambo International Airport in Johannesburg, page 201, **Cape Town International Airport** in Cape Town, page 35, and **King Shaka International Airport** in Durban, page 131. Johannesburg is the regional hub with numerous daily flights to and from Europe, North America, Asia and Australia. Although most flights arrive in Johannesburg, a fair number of carriers fly directly to Cape Town, and a couple directly to Durban. There is a huge choice of routes and flights, but for the best fares you need to book well in advance, especially over the Christmas and New Year period which is the peak summer holiday season in South Africa.

For live flight information visit the Airport Company of South Africa's website, www.acsa.co.za, T0867-277888, or send an SMS to T38648 with the flight number, in reply to which you'll receive up-to-date flight details.

Jet lag is not an issue if flying from Europe to South Africa as there is only a minimal time difference.

→ TRANSPORT IN SOUTH AFRICA

South Africa has an efficient transport network linking its towns and cities, making travelling the considerable distances a straightforward experience. Affordable domestic flights link the cities, a sophisticated army of private coaches criss-crosses the country, and the train system, although painfully slow, offers another way of getting from A to B. City transport is limited, though, and South Africa's cities generally lack safe and reliable urban public transport. This is improving all the time, however, and new transport systems are being developed at a rapid pace, while existing ones are being upgraded. Nevertheless, having your own transport on a visit to South Africa remains the most flexible option.

AIR

South Africa There is a far-reaching and efficient domestic service and regular daily flights connect the major cities; all of which are within a couple of hours' flying time of each other. On popular routes where there is some competition, such as Johannesburg–Cape Town or Johannesburg–Durban, a single flight can sometimes be only a little more expensive than a bus ticket.

RAIL

Most of the major cities are linked by rail and, while this is a comfortable and relaxing way to travel, it is very slow. The trains are run by **Shosholoza Meyl**, part of the national network **Spoornet**, T0860-008 888 (in South Africa), T011-774 4555 (from overseas), www.shosholozameyl.co.za. Timetables and fares can be found on the website. All the trains travel overnight, so they arrive at some stations en route at inconvenient times. There are sleeping carriages, with coupés that sleep two or four people, with a wash basin, fold-away table and bunk beds. Bedding can be hired for an extra fee on the train (an attendant makes up the bed), though taking your own sleeping bag is also an option. Always book well in advance for sleeping compartments, especially during local holidays. The 'sitter' carriages are not recommended for long journeys as there is only open coach seating. Refreshments are available from trolleys or dining cars, but don't expect brilliant food and it's a good idea to take extra snacks.

The routes are: **Johannesburg–Cape Town** (daily in both directions, 27 hours); **Johannesburg–Durban** (daily except Saturday in both directions, 13 hours); and **Johannesburg–Port Elizabeth** (Sunday, Monday and Friday in both directions, 20½ hours).

Spoornet also operate a more upmarket service, the **Premier Classe**, T011-774 5247, www.premierclasse.co.za, between Johannesburg and Cape Town (25 hours), Johannesburg and Durban (14 hours), both twice a week. This is a pleasant alternative to flying if you have the time, and the carriages are a lot nicer than the regular train, with two-bed coupés and extras like dressing gowns, toiletries and 'room service', and there's a good restaurant car serving breakfast, high tea and dinner; fares include all meals. The train between Johannesburg and Cape Town has an additional 'spa-car' for pampering, and, vehicles can be taken on the trains, which gives the option of taking the train in one direction and driving in the other.

Luxury trains If the journey is more important than the destination, then old-fashioned luxury trains operate much like five-star hotels on wheels. The **Blue Train**, T021-334 8459, www.bluetrain.co.za, is considered to be southern Africa's premier luxury train. The wood-panelled coaches feature luxury coupés with en suite bathrooms, elegant lounge cars and fine dining in the restaurant car. The company runs scheduled services between Tshwane (Pretoria) and Cape Town and takes one day and one night. There are also occasional trips to Durban and Pilanesberg Game Reserve. A similar luxury train experience is the **Pride of Africa**, operated by **Rovos Rail**, T012-315 8242, www.

rovos.co.za, which also runs between Tshwane (Pretoria) and Cape Town with occasional trips to Victoria Falls. Check out the websites for routes and prices.

Metro commuter trains and high-speed rail links Tshwane (Pretoria), Johannesburg and Cape Town have a network of metro commuter services linking the suburbs to the business districts. These should generally be avoided as there have been many cases of robbery. Avoid the metro around Johannesburg and Tshwane (Pretoria) at all costs. If you do use it, stick to first class and travel only during rush hour (0600-0800, 1600-1800). Nevertheless, there are exceptions, in particular the route run by **Metrorail** (www.metrorail.co.za) in Cape Town from the city to Simon's Town on the Cape Peninsula. This is frequently used by tourists who experience few problems, and is one of the most scenic and enjoyable train rides in South Africa (see page 66).

The **Gautrain** (call centre T0800-428 87246, www.gautrain.co.za) is a high-speed rail link between Johannesburg, Tshwane (Pretoria) and OR Tambo International Airport in Gauteng (see box, page 203).

ROAD
Bus and coach Baz Bus: The Baz Bus, T021-439 2323, www.bazbus.com, is a hop-on, hop-off bus and remains one of the most popular ways of seeing the country on a budget. One of the best aspects of the service is that the bus collects and drops off passengers at their chosen backpacker hostel. There are a few exceptions such as Hermanus, Coffee Bay and Sani Pass, where the bus will drop you off at the closest point on the main road, and the hostels will then meet you for an extra charge, though you must arrange this in advance. The Baz Bus route is **Cape Town–Durban** along the coast, and **Durban–Tshwane (Pretoria)** via the Drakensberg. Visit the website for the full timetable.

Intercity coaches: Greyhound, T083-915 9000 (in South Africa), T011-276 8550 (from overseas), www.greyhound.co.za; Intercape, T0861-287 287 (in South Africa), T012-380 4400 (from overseas), www.intercape.co.za; and **Translux**, T0861-589 282 (in South Africa), T011-774 3333 (from overseas), www.translux.co.za, are the three major long-distance bus companies that run between towns and popular destinations. All bus tickets can be booked directly with the companies or through the national booking agency, **Computicket**; online at www.computicket.com, or at any of their kiosks in the shopping malls or any branch of Checkers and Shoprite supermarkets in South Africa. The coaches are air conditioned and have a toilet; some sell refreshments and show videos. They will stop at least every three to four hours to change drivers and give the passengers a chance to stretch their legs. Note that long-distance buses are more than twice as fast as the trains.

Car Hiring a car for part, or all, of your journey is undoubtedly the best way to see South Africa; you get to travel at your own leisurely pace and explore more out-of-the-way regions without being tied to a tour or a timetable. Driving isn't challenging; the roads are generally in excellent condition and, away from the major urban centres, there is little traffic. Petrol, not a major expense, is available 24 hours a day at the fuel stations in the cities and along the national highways. Driving is on the left side of the road and speed limits are 60 kph in built-up areas, 80 kph on minor roads and 120 kph on highways.

The minimum age to rent a car is usually 23. A driver's licence (with a translation if it's not in English) and a credit card are essential. Tourist offices usually recommend large international organizations such as **Avis** or **Budget**, but there are a number of reliable local companies, usually with a good fleet of cars and follow-up service. It is worth asking at hotels for recommended local car hire companies, and be sure to shop around. There is a range of vehicles to choose from, from basic hatchbacks and saloon cars, to camper vans and fully equipped 4WD vehicles.

Costs for car hire vary considerably and depend on days of the week, season, type of vehicle and terms (insurance, excess, mileage, etc). A compact car starts from as little as R150-200 per day; a fully equipped 4WD or camper van with tents and equipment from R800-1300 per day.

In the event of an accident, call your car hire company's emergency number. For emergency breakdown and traffic update information contact the **Automobile Association of South Africa**, T083-84322, www.aa.co.za.

If you wish to take the car into one of the neighbouring countries, make sure you have the registration document, insurance and a driving licence printed in English with a photograph.

Hitchhiking This is not common in South Africa and is not recommended as it can be very dangerous. Women should never hitch, under any circumstances, even in a group. If you have to hitch, say if your vehicle has broken down, be very wary of who you are accepting a lift from, and a car with a family or couple is usually the best option.

Taxi Except in the major cities there are few taxi ranks in South African towns so it's generally a better idea to order a taxi in advance. Any hotel or restaurant will make a booking for you. Taxis are metered and charge around R9-11 per kilometre. Groups should request a larger vehicle if available as these can carry up to seven people. Some can also accommodate wheelchairs.

Minibus taxi: The majority of South Africa's population travel by minibus taxis and, in many areas, including inner cities, they are the only way of getting around. However, the accident rate of such vehicles is notoriously high, with speeding, overcrowding and lack of maintenance being the main causes. There is also the problem of possible robbery, especially at the taxi ranks, so many visitors and locals are wary of using them.

Nevertheless, minibus taxis remain the cheapest and most extensive form of transport in the country. Many routes have experienced little or no crime, but you should exercise extreme caution and always ask people in the know before using them. In central Cape Town minibus taxis provide an efficient (and relatively safe) means of transport into the city centre from places such as Observatory, Camps Bay, Sea Point, Rondebosch and Claremont.

→ WHERE TO STAY IN SOUTH AFRICA

South Africa offers a wide variety of accommodation from top-of-the-range five-star hotels, game lodges and tented camps that charge R3000-8000 or more per couple per day, to mid-range safari lodges and hotels with air-conditioned double rooms for R1500-3000, to guesthouse or B&Bs that charge R500-1500 and dormitory beds or camping for under R200 a day. Generally, there are reasonable discounts for children and most places offer family accommodation. Comprehensive accommodation information can be found on the regional tourism websites listed in each area. All accommodation in South Africa is graded a star value by the **Tourism Grading Council of South Africa**, www.tourismgrading.co.za, and the website has comprehensive lists in all categories. There are numerous resources for independently booking accommodation in South Africa;

PRICE CODES

WHERE TO STAY

$$$$	over US$365	**$$$**	US$180-365
$$	US$75-180	**$**	under US$75

Prices refer to the cost of a double room with breakfast, not including service charge or other meals unless otherwise stated. See page 282 for exchange rates.

Prices for all private game reserves fall into the **$$$$** category, but are based on two people sharing and are inclusive of all meals and game drives. In these cases we indicate in the text whether they are very expensive (over US$1150), expensive (US$725-1150), mid-range (US$500-725) or cheap (under US$500).

RESTAURANTS

$$$	over US$40	**$$**	US$20-40	**$**	under US$20

Prices refer to the cost of a two-course meal for one person including a soft drink, beer or glass of wine.

exploring the websites of **AA Travel Guides**, www.aatravel.co.za, **SA-Venues**, www.sa-venues.com, and **Sleeping Out**, www.sleeping-out.co.za, is a good start.

Hotels There are some delightful family-run and country hotels, boutique hotels with stylish interiors in the cities and towns and, for those who enjoy the anonymity of a large hotel, chains like **Sun International**, **Protea** and **City Lodge**. Many of the more upmarket hotels offer additional facilities like spas, golf courses and fine restaurants, which are almost always open to non-guests. Every small town has at least one hotel of two- or three-star standard, and although some tend to be aimed at local business travellers and may be characterless buildings with restaurants serving bland food, they nevertheless represent good value.

Guesthouses Guesthouses can offer some of the most characterful accommodation in South Africa, with interesting places springing up in both cities and small towns. Standards obviously vary enormously; much of what you'll get has to do with the character of the owners and the location of the homes. Some are simple practical overnight rooms, while at the more luxurious end, rooms may be in historic homes filled with antiques. For further information contact the **Guest House Association of Southern Africa**, T021-762 0880, www. ghasa.co.za, or the **Portfolio Collection**, T021-689 4020, www.portfoliocollection.com.

Backpacker hostels Apart from camping, backpacker hostels are the cheapest form of accommodation, and a bed in a dormitory will cost as little as R100 a night. Some also have budget double rooms with or without bathrooms, while others have space to pitch a tent in the garden.

You can usually expect a self-catering kitchen, hot showers, a TV/DVD room and internet access. Many hostels also have bars and offer meals or nightly braais, plus a garden and a swimming pool. Most hostels are a good source of travel information and many act as booking agents for bus companies, budget safari tours and car hire. The **Baz Bus** (see page 276) caters for backpackers and links most hostels along the coast between

Cape Town and Durban, and some on its route between Durban and Johannesburg via the Drakensberg. For information, visit **Backpacking South Africa**, www.btsa.co.za, or **Coast to Coast**, www.coastingafrica.com, which publishes a free annual backpackers' accommodation guide and is available in all the hostels.

Camping and caravan parks Every town has a municipal campsite, many of which also have simple self-catering chalets.

As camping is very popular with South Africans, sites tend to have very good facilities, although they may be fully booked months in advance, especially during the school holidays. Even the most basic site will have a clean washblock with hot water, electric points, lighting and braai facilities. Some sites also have kitchen blocks. At the most popular tourist spots, campsites are more like holiday resorts with shops, swimming pools and a restaurant – these can get very busy and are best avoided in peak season.

Camping equipment is widely available in South Africa and usually at lower prices than in the UK. If your time is limited, you should bring your own tent and sleeping bag, but if you're not on a tight schedule you may want to shop around once you've arrived. Lightweight tents, sleeping bags, ground mats, gas lights, stoves and cooking equipment can be bought at good prices in all the major cities and some car hire companies rent out equipment.

Self-catering Self-catering chalets, cottages or apartments are particularly popular with South African holidaymakers and the choice is enormous, especially along the coast. The quality and facilities vary, from basic rondavels with bunks, to chalets with a couple of bedrooms and fully equipped kitchens. They can be excellent value and are often the only budget accommodation available in a town. If you are travelling in a group, the cost could be as little as R100-200 per person per day and these are ideal for families on a budget.

National park accommodation While the larger rest camps in Kruger have supermarkets, launderettes, post offices and banks, most camps are rather more basic. All have at least a small shop selling maps, basic food provisions and firewood. Most accommodation is self-catering, but larger camps may have restaurants. Reception can arrange guided walks and game drives. Some parks also offer night drives where visitors have the chance of seeing unusual nocturnal animals.

National parks across South Africa are under the jurisdiction of **South African National Parks (SANParks)**, central reservations T012-428 9111, www.sanparks.org, which also has drop-in offices in Tshwane (Pretoria), T012-428 9111; tourist office on the corner of Burg and Castle streets, T021-487 6800; and at the Tourist Junction in Durban, T031-304 4934. In the Western Cape, the smaller nature and game reserves are managed by **Cape Nature**, T021-659 3500, www.capenature.org.za, and in KwaZulu Natal, **KZN Wildlife**, T033-845 1000, www.kznwildlife.com. In Swaziland, the parks and reserves are administered by **Big Game Parks**, T2528 3944/3, www.biggameparks.org.

Luxury game lodges The most famous luxury game lodges are on private game farms adjoining Kruger National Park, although there are many others around the country. Their attraction is the chance to combine exclusive game viewing in prime wilderness areas, with top-class accommodation, fine dining, vintage wines and a spectacular natural setting.

The cost of staying in a luxury game lodge varies from R2500 to over R8000 per person per night. This includes all meals, most drinks and game-viewing activities. In order to get the most from the experience, guests tend to stay for at least two nights. The lodges are often isolated and not easily accessible by road so many reserves offer shuttle transfers from the nearest city, and some have their own airstrips where charter aircraft can land.

→ FOOD AND DRINK IN SOUTH AFRICA

FOOD

South African food tends to be fairly regional, although a ubiquitous love of meat unites the country. In and around Cape Town visitors will find many restaurants offering Cape Malay cuisine, a blend of sweet and spicy curries and meat dishes cooked with dried fruit. Seafood along the coast is excellent and usually very good value. KwaZulu Natal is famous for its Indian curries, especially the delicious bunny chow, served in a hollowed-out loaf of bread. Portuguese influences, thanks to neighbouring Mozambique, are strong – spicy peri-peri chicken or Mozambiquan prawns are widespread. Meat, however, is universal and South Africa offers plenty of opportunities to try an assortment of game, from popular ostrich or springbok to more acquired tastes such as crocodile or warthog. A local meat product which travellers invariably come across is biltong – a heavily salted and spiced sun-dried meat, usually made from beef but sometimes from game.

Supermarkets have a similar selection of groceries to that found in Europe. There are several large supermarket chains and plenty of farmers' markets and roadside *padstalls*, for tasty home-made goodies, organic vegetables, wine and olives.

DRINK

South Africa is a major player in the international market and produces a wide range of excellent wines. The Winelands in the Western Cape have the best-known labels (see pages 113-127) but there are a number of other wine regions dotted around the country. South Africa also produces a range of good beer. Major names include Black Label, Castle and Amstel. Bitter is harder to come by, although a good local variety is brewed at Mitchell's Brewery in Knysna and Cape Town and can be found at outlets along the Garden Route.

No liquor may be sold on Sundays (and public holidays) except in licensed bars and restaurants. The standard shop selling alcohol is known as a bottle store, usually open Monday-Friday 0800-1800, Saturday 0830-1400 (some may stay open until 1600). Supermarkets do not sell beer or spirits, stop selling wine at 2000, and don't sell alcohol on Sundays.

Soft drinks Tap water in South Africa is safe to drink. Bottled mineral water and a good range of fruit juices are available at most outlets – the Ceres and Liquifruit brands are the best. Another popular drink is Rooibos (or red bush) tea.

RESTAURANTS

A great starting point for choosing a restaurant is the *Eat Out* website, www.eatout.co.za, which features South Africa's best choice of restaurants, or you can buy the latest edition of their magazine, available at CNA and Exclusive Books. *Dining Out*, www.dining-out. co.za, is another excellent resource and provides hundreds of reviews and contact details for restaurants throughout the country.

ESSENTIALS A-Z

Accident and emergency
Police, T10111; Medical, T10177;
Fire, T10111. All emergencies from
a cell phone, T112.

Electricity
Voltage 220/230 volts AC at 50 Hz
(Swaziland 220-240v). Most plugs and
appliances are 3-point round-pin (1 10-mm
and 2 8-mm prongs). Hotels usually have
2-pin sockets for razors.

Embassies and consulates
For embassies and consulates of South
Africa, see www.embassiesabroad.com.

Health
See your GP or travel clinic at least 6 weeks
before departure for general advice on
travel risks and vaccinations. Make sure you
have sufficient medical travel insurance, get
a dental check, know your own blood group
and if you suffer a long-term condition such
as diabetes, epilepsy or a serious allergy,
obtain a Medic Alert bracelet/necklace
(www.medicalert.co.uk). If you wear glasses,
take a copy of your prescription.

Vaccinations
Confirm your primary courses and boosters
are up to date. Courses or boosters usually
advised: diphtheria; tetanus; poliomyelitis;
hepatitis A. Vaccines sometimes advised:
tuberculosis; hepatitis B; rabies; cholera;
typhoid. The final decision, however,
should be based on a consultation with
your doctor or travel clinic. A yellow fever
certificate is required if over 1 year old and
entering from an infected area. If you don't
have one, you'll be required to get one
at the airport. Specialist advice should be
taken on the best anti-malarials to use.

Health risks
Diarrhoea Symptoms should be relatively
short lived but if they persist beyond
2 weeks specialist medical attention should
be sought. Also seek medical help if there is
blood in the stools and/or fever. Adults can
use an antidiarrhoeal medication to control
the symptoms but only for up to 24 hrs. In
addition keep well hydrated by drinking
plenty of fluids and eat bland foods. Oral
rehydration sachets taken after each loose
stool are a useful way to keep well hydrated.
These should always be used when treating
children and the elderly.

The standard advice to prevent problems
is to be careful with water and ice for
drinking. If you have any doubts then boil
the water or filter and treat it. Food can
also transmit disease. Be wary of salads, re-
heated foods or food that has been left out
in the sun having been cooked earlier in the
day. There is a simple adage that says 'wash
it, peel it, boil it or forget it'. Also be wary of
unpasteurized dairy products as these can
transmit a range of diseases. On the positive
side, very few people experience stomach
problems in South Africa.

HIV/AIDS Southern Africa has the highest
rates of HIV and AIDS in the world. Visitors
should be aware of the dangers of infection
and take the necessary precautions with
sex, needles, medical treatment and in the
case of a blood tranfusion.

Malaria There is a low seasonal (Oct-May)
risk of malaria in the extreme east of the
country along the Mozambique border.

To prevent mosquito bites wear clothes
that cover arms and legs, use effective insect
repellents in areas with known risks of insect-
spread disease and use a mosquito net
treated with an insecticide. If your doctor or
travel clinic advises you to take anti-malarials,
ensure you finish the recommended course.

Sun Protect yourself adequately against the sun. Apply a high-factor sunscreen (greater than SPF15) and also make sure it screens against UVB. Prevent heat exhaustion and heatstroke by drinking enough fluids throughout the day. Use rehydration salts mixed with water to replenish fluids and salts and find somewhere cool and shady to recover. If you suspect heatstroke rather than heat exhaustion, you need to cool the body down quickly (cold showers are particularly effective).

If you get sick
There are plenty of private hospitals in South Africa, which have 24-hr emergency departments and pharmacies, run by **Medi-Clinic** (www.mediclinic.co.za) or **Netcare** (www.netcare.co.za). It is essential to have travel insurance as hospital bills need to be paid at the time of admittance, so keep all paperwork to make a claim.

Language
There are 11 official languages in South Africa. Afrikaans is spoken by 60% of white South Africans and the majority of the Cape coloured population. In addition to this, there are 6 Asian languages spoken, mostly in KwaZulu Natal. English is widely spoken and understood and is the language used in education and business, but it is always a good idea to learn at least a couple of basic phrases in the predominant language of the area that you're travelling in – a simple 'hello' in isiXhosa (*molo*) or 'thank you' in Afrikaans (*dankie*) can go a long way. *Lekker* is a widely used Afrikaans word for 'very good' or 'things are going well'.

Money
➔ *US$1 = R8.5.; £1 = R13.7; 1 € = R11.5 (Jan 2013).*

Currency
The South African currency is the **rand** (R) which is divided into 100 **cents** (c). Notes are in 200, 100, 50, 20 and 10 rand, and coins are in 5, 2, 1 rand and 50, 20 and 10 cents. You can carry your funds in traveller's cheques (TCs), credit cards, rand, US dollars, euros or pounds sterling.

Changing money
South Africa's main banks are ABSA, **First National**, **Nedbank** and **Standard Bank**. All have foreign exchange services. You can also change money at **Master Currency**, www.mastercurrency.co.za, which has branches at the main airports and large shopping malls in the cities. **American Express Foreign Exchange Service**, www.americanexpress.co.za, has offices in the larger cities and offers a poste restante service to card holders. Larger hotels offer exchange facilities, but these often charge exorbitant fees.

Credit and debit cards
Lost or stolen cards American Express, T0800-110929; Diners Club, T0800-112017; **MasterCard**, T0800-990418; **Visa**, T0800-990475.

You can get all the way around South Africa with a credit or debit card. Not only are they a convenient method of covering major expenses but they offer some of the most competitive exchange rates when withdrawing cash from ATMs, and you can only hire a car with a credit (not debit) card. The chip and pin system is common, though not yet universal in South Africa. ATMs are everywhere; Plus, Cirrus Visa, MasterCard, American Express and Diners Club are all accepted. The amount you can withdraw varies between systems and cards, but you should be able to take out at least R1000 a day. Note that theft during or immediately after a withdrawal can be a problem, so never accept a stranger's help at an ATM and avoid using street-side ATMs. Instead, go into a bank or shopping mall, where guards are often on duty.

Cost of travelling
South Africa is fairly good value for money for tourists spending US dollars, pounds

sterling or euro. If you are travelling independently and propose to hire a car, you will need to budget R200-400 per day, depending on the season and type of vehicle. If this is shared among a group of 4 it's the most affordable way to get around. The cost of fuel is about two-thirds of what Europeans are used to, but distances travelled can be considerable so longer holidays will run up a hefty fuel bill.

Accommodation will represent your other principal daily expense. In first-rate 5-star hotels, luxury lodges or tented camps expect to pay in excess of R2000-3000 per night for a double, rising to R6000-8000 in the most exclusive establishments. If staying in mid-range hotels and lodges, expect to pay in the region of R1500-3000, and in B&Bs and guesthouses, budget R500-1500 per couple per night. By staying in self-catering accommodation, camping or staying in backpacker dorms, you can bring this down to R100-200 on average per person per night. See also page 278.

Food and drink is still good value in southern Africa and a 2-course evening meal with wine in a reasonable restaurant will cost under R300 for 2 people, and you can be pretty assured of good food and large portions. For the budget traveller there are plenty of fast-food outlets, and almost every supermarket has a superb deli counter serving hot and cold meals. Food in supermarkets is considerably cheaper than, say, in Europe, especially meat and fresh fruit and vegetables, and a bottle of wine and beer are an affordable R30 and R10 respectively. See also Restaurants, page 280.

Safety

Dangers facing tourists are on the whole limited to mugging or, on occasion, carjacking. You should be aware that your assailant may well be armed and any form of resistance could be fatal. South Africa has had more than its fair share of well-publicized crime problems. In the 1980s and 1990s Johannesburg was frequently dubbed the most dangerous city in the world, although crime rates there have declined considerably. Despite the statistics, much of the serious, violent crime is gang-based and occurs in areas that tourists are unlikely to visit, such as the inner-city ghettos like Hillbrow or Yeoville. The crime rate in Johannesburg's suburbs, where most of the hotels, hostels, nightlife and shops are located, has dropped significantly in recent years, due mainly to an increase in security measures; you should experience few problems in these areas.

Apart from Johannesburg, city centres are generally safe during daylight hours, although listen to advice from locals about which areas to avoid. Closed-circuit cameras (CCTV) and private security guards have made Cape Town and Durban city centres as safe as European cities, but the likelihood of being mugged increases sharply after dark. The safest way to travel around cities at night is to take a taxi directly to and from your destination.

While by no means out of bounds to tourists, it would not be wise to wander into a township by yourself. On the other hand, if you know a local or have friends living and working in South Africa who know their way around, a trip to a township market or nightclub can be an interesting and rewarding experience. Alternatively, go on a township tour, which will undoubtedly give you a different picture of the way a very large number of urban South Africans live.

Avoid driving after dark. If you are going to be travelling alone in a car, it's a good idea to bring (or hire) a mobile phone; useful in any case if you break down.

Tax

Tourists can reclaim the 14% VAT on purchases bought in South Africa whose total value exceeds R250. You can do this when departing, at the VAT reclaim desks at airports in Johannesburg, Cape Town and Durban or at border posts. For more information visit www.taxrefunds.co.za.

Telephone → *Country code: +27; international direct dialling code 00; directory enquires T1023; international enquires T1025.*

You must dial the full 3-digit regional code for every number in South Africa, even when you are calling from within that region.

The telephone service is very efficient. Card and coin phones are widespread and work well. Cards are available in supermarkets, some pharmacies and Telkom vending machines. Even in remote national parks there are usually card phones from which one can dial direct to anywhere in the world. Note that hotels usually double rates.

Mobile phones

Overseas visitors should be able to use their mobiles on international roaming. Alternatively, you can buy a local SIM card and start-up pack from any of the phone shops and at the 3 international airports, which also offer phone and SIM hire.

Time

South Africa has only 1 time zone: GMT +2 hrs (+1 during UK Summer Time Mar-Oct).

Tipping

Waiters, hotel porters, chambermaids and tour guides should be tipped 10-15%. When leaving tips make sure it goes to the intended person. It is common practice to tip petrol pump attendants, depending on their service – up to R5 for a fill up, oil and water check and comprehensive windscreen clean. It is also customary to tip car guards R2-5 if parking on the street. They are usually identified by a work vest or badge. On safari you are expected to tip guides. If in any doubt, ask the company that you booked with for advice on how much to tip.

Tourist information
South African Tourism (SATOUR),

T011-895 3000, www.southafrica.net, has a very useful website with information on special interest travel, maps, latest travel news, airlines, accommodation and national parks. The website is published in 15 languages and each version provides specific information for people coming from specific countries. SATOUR also has offices around the world. Regional and local tourism authorities are some of the best sources of information once in the country; even the smallest town will have a tourist office with details of local sights and accommodation. Local tourist offices are listed under individual towns.

Visas and immigration

Most nationalities including EU nationals and citizens from the USA, Canada, Australia and New Zealand don't need visas to enter South Africa. On arrival, visitors from these countries are granted a 90-day **visitors' permit**. You must have a valid return ticket or voucher for onward travel and at least 2 empty pages in your passport to get a permit.

It is possible to apply for an extension to the permit at one of the offices of the **Department of Home Affairs: Cape Town** T021-462 4970; **Durban** T031-308 7930; **Johannesburg** T011-836 3228; **Tshwane (Pretoria)** T012-314 8109; **Nelson Mandela Bay (Port Elizabeth)** T041-487 1026; www.home-affairs.gov.za. This can take up to 10 days and costs R425. You will need to produce documentation to show when you are leaving the country, as well as proof of funds such as a credit card. Citizens of countries other than those listed above should consult the South African embassy or consulate in their country for information on visa requirements.

See www.home-affairs.gov.za, to find the nearest office.

Weights and measures
The metric system is used in South Africa.

INDEX

CREDITS

Footprint credits

Managing Editor: Felicity Laughton
Production and layout: Emma Bryers
Cover: Pepi Bluck
Colour section: Angus Dawson
Maps: Kevin Feeney

Publisher: Patrick Dawson
Advertising: Elizabeth Taylor
Sales and marketing: Kirsty Holmes

Photography credits
Front cover: Richard Du Toit/Minden Pictures/FLPA
Back cover: sculpies/shutterstock.com; InnaFelker/shutterstock.com; Johan Swanepoel/shutterstock.com
Inside front flap: Gustav/shutterstock.com; Mogens Trolle/shutterstock.com; Stacy Funderburke/shutterstock.com; michaeljung/shutterstock.com
Colour pages: title page: Hongqi Zhang/Dreamstime.com. p2: Dominique de La Croix/shutterstock; Peter Wollinga/Dreamstime.com. p3: Instinia Photography/Dreamstime.com; michaeljung/shutterstock. p4: Steffen Foerster/shutterstock. p6: Mari Swanepoel/shutterstock. p7: Soft Focus Photography/shutterstock; Holger Karius/Dreamstime.com; Dennis Donohue/Dreamstime.com; EcoPrint/shutterstock. p8: michaeljung/shutterstock; Richard Cavalleri/shutterstock; bjogroet/shutterstock. p9: Squareplum/Dreamstime.com; Alexandre Fagundes De Fagundes/Dreamstime.com; Sean Nel/shutterstock. p10: Holger Karius/Dreamstime.com; Ken Moore/Dreamstime.com. p11: Pieter Stander/shutterstock; Zambezishark/Dreamstime.com; Louie Schoeman/shutterstock; Anna Omelchenko/Dreamstime.com. p12: Sean Nel/shutterstock. p13: Xvaldes/Dreamstime.com; Riaanvdb/Dreamstime.com. p14: Hongqi Zhang/Dreamstime.com; Viktoriya Field/shutterstock. p15: Andre Klopper/shutterstock; Petr Vostrovsky/shutterstock; BasPhoto/shutterstock. p16: Francois Loubser/shutterstock; Mark Dumbleton/shutterstock; Fultonsphoto/Dreamstime.com; JONATHAN PLEDGER/shutterstock. p17: Kevin Brown/Dreamstime.com; michaeljung/shutterstock; Stuartapsey/shutterstock. p19: PhotoSky/shutterstock. p20: Luke Schmidt/shutterstock; Ecoimages/shutterstock. p21: Daleen Loest/shutterstock; Macker54321/Dreamstime.com. p22: Riaanvdb/Dreamstime.com; Meadowhawk/Dreamstime.com; Dave Pusey/shutterstock. p23: Holger Karius/Dreamstime.com; Johannes Gerhardus Swanepoel/Dreamstime.com; Fatomousso/Dreamstime.com. p24: Coplandj/Dreamstime.com. p25: Hein Welman/shutterstock. p26: Felix Lipov/shutterstock. p27: Patrick Allen/Dreamstime.com. p28: Annemario/Dreamstime.com; Pal Teravagimov/shutterstock; Chris Van Lennep/Dreamstime.com; Riaanvdb/Dreamstime.com. p29: Leon Marais/shutterstock; Ericsch/Dreamstime.com; michaeljung/shutterstock. p30: Chuckaitch/Dreamstime.com. p31: Dietmar Temps/Dreamstime.com. p32: EcoPrint/shutterstock.

Publishing information
Footprint DREAM TRIP South Africa
1st edition
© Footprint Handbooks Ltd
February 2013

ISBN: 978 1 907263 69 9
CIP DATA: A catalogue record for this book is available from the British Library

® Footprint Handbooks and the Footprint mark are a registered trademark of Footprint Handbooks Ltd

Published by Footprint
6 Riverside Court
Lower Bristol Road
Bath BA2 3DZ, UK
T +44 (0)1225 469141
F +44 (0)1225 469461
footprinttravelguides.com

Printed in Spain by GraphyCems

Every effort has been made to ensure that the facts in this guidebook are accurate. However, travellers should still obtain advice from consulates, airlines etc about travel and visa requirements before travelling. The authors and publishers cannot accept responsibility for any loss, injury or inconvenience however caused.

Distributed in the USA by Globe Pequot Press, Guilford, Connecticut